Smashing Review
for a Terrific B
About a Fabu

"This is an excellent biography, worth every penny. Like the lady herself, it's full of facts, controversy, and straightforward information. She was never one to skirt an issue, and Bette Davis' biography comes across in the same manner as the actress on screen . . . to say she is outspoken would be an understatement . . . a totally rewarding book, not only for film buffs and Bette Davis fans but for people interested in people."

Los Angeles Free Press

"This is a unique semi-autobiography in which the subject has been allowed to interject her own comments . . . some are warm, some are humble, some are gracious, others caustic, witty, hurt, or inevitably bitchy. But together they reveal the basic mortar of a long and gallant career." *Chicago Tribune*

"It is a treat. It is as if you were reading about Bette Davis with her reading over your shoulder and kibbitzing and that's a nice thing to have."

Gene Shalit, NBC-TV

"An extremely likeable book."

Rex Reed, *New York Sunday News*

"The woman is a national treasure; she is what movies are all about." *The Philadelphia Inquirer*

Bette Davis in her first photographic session at Universal Studios, September, 1930. (*Photograph by Ray Jones, Universal Pictures Corp.*)

Mother Goddam

The Story Of The Career Of Bette Davis
by Whitney Stine
with a running commentary
by Bette Davis

A BERKLEY MEDALLION BOOK
published by
BERKLEY PUBLISHING CORPORATION

Tonight my comic spirit runs fast
along—the last G string.

> Mother Goddam
> in *The Shanghai Gesture*

PROLOGUE

English critic E. Arnot Robertson in 1935: "I think that Bette Davis would probably be burned as a witch if she had lived two or three hundred years ago. She gives the curious feeling of being charged with power which can find no ordinary outlet."

Actor George C. Scott, 1972: "I don't think any actress has given as many multifaceted performances." Director John Cromwell, 1934: "Your career could have been ten years shorter if you hadn't been born in Boston." Studio head Jack L. Warner, 1964: "The magic quality that transformed this sometimes bland and not beautiful little girl into a great artist when she was playing bitchy roles first showed up [in 1934] in *Cabin in the Cotton.*" Singer Tommy Smothers, 1969: "She loves to mess around!" *[In actual fact he asked if I'd like to mess around with him? This asked of me on the "Johnny Carson Show."]* Director Frank Capra, 1961: "I wanted to remake the picture *[Pocketful of Miracles]* with harder people. Well, she's about as hard as you can get." *[It takes one to know one.]*

Actress-singer Judy Garland, 1939: "She's my idol." *Time* magazine, 1938: "Popeye the Magnificent." Director Joseph L. Mankiewicz, 1951: "On your tombstone should be written *She did it the hard way.*" Actress Olivia De Havilland, 1971: "I love her dearly." Actor Errol Flynn, 1946: "She thought that she was the greatest actress who ever lived." *[As to this quote from Errol: It is as untrue as all his other comments in his book—about working with me. He had no respect for me as an actress because I was a worker at my profession and he wasn't.]* Twelve-year-old Roddy McDowall, 1942: "If you get tired of playing opposite Errol Flynn or any of those other old men on your lot, I would be proud to be your leading man.''

Actress Tallulah Bankhead, 1954: "I'd seen Bette Davis play Regina Giddens on the screen. Thus, I knew I had nothing to worry about. Speaking of imitations . . ." *[Miss Bankhead gave a great performance of Regina Giddens. I begged Samuel Goldwyn to ask her to play it on the screen, as Tallulah played it the way the playwright Lillian Hellman wrote it—there was no new way to be Regina—and we have always resembled each other facially, hair, etc. So what could poor little me do? As a matter of fact, William Wyler wanted me to play it differently, but I could only see it Tallulah's way.]* Actor James Mason, 1946: "Still may be the greatest actress of our time." Columnist Dorothy Manners, 1971: "I heard a wasp stung her. Knowing Bette Davis, I'm surprised she didn't sting back." *[Here we go again, boys. I have always had this kind of reputation—due partly to the belief of many people that I personally am as difficult as many of the parts I've played. T'aint true!]* *Time* magazine, 1939: "Wide-eyed Bernhardt." Actress Mary Astor, 1959: "She handed *The Great Lie* to me on a silver platter." Actress Joan Crawford, 1971: "I'm the quiet one, and Bette's explosive. I have discipline, she doesn't. I don't know who suffers the most." *[I have never felt satisfied with my performances, but my head is high as to my discipline as an actress. I can provide witnesses, Joan.]* Actress Katharine Hepburn, 1973: "She's awfully good."

Singer Alex Kanner, 1969: "Bette Davis is a great swinging chick." Actor Edward Everett Horton, 1961: "There's a lot of electricity when she's around." *Time* magazine, 1964: "Duse of the depression era." Actor Humphrey Bogart, 1939: "She's a scrapper!" Critic Rex Reed, 1968: "At her best, she is devastating . . . at her worst, she is merely the best Bette Davis caricature out of all the other stars who've built careers doing Bette Davis caricatures." Actor Claude Rains, 1947: "She's an absolute joy to work with!" *Time* magazine, 1961: "Mother Goddam." *[I have often called myself this to my children.]*

That's awfully sweet of you, Wade—the really swell one around here is Mary Ann. You're in love with her, aren't you?

BETTE DAVIS AS LAURA MADISON
IN *Bad Sister*

The test was going badly. *[My first test was for Sam Goldwyn, made in New York for a Ronald Colman film. When Mr. Goldwyn saw it, he said, "Who did this to me?" I was not tested for a Universal contract. I was signed in New York after David Werner saw me on the stage in* Solid South *with Richard Bennett.]*

The nervous little girl with the soft ash-blonde hair drawn back in a bun at the nape of her neck stood in the middle of the set and very carefully raised her dress slowly upward to her knees and beyond. "What have *legs* got to do with acting?" crimson-faced twenty-two-year-old Bette Davis shyly asked.

"You don't know Hollywood," the test director laughed.

"When I saw the test," she wrote in the *Ladies Home Journal* in July, 1941, "I let out a blood-curdling scream and ran from the projection room . . . I was not aware that the camera had turned continuously while I was in front of it, and I had mugged horribly between the shots of my sample emotions. After I had finished registering rage, I would make a terrible face and then register joy. There is no use trying to describe it. Words are inadequate."

Bette Davis was rushed into the portrait gallery; the "new kid" on the lot was scheduled for her first fashion layout.

Still photographer Ray Jones surveyed her critically, hiding uncertainty with a smile. She wore a bit of powder, a trace of lipstick, and her natural eyebrows were a full shade darker than her hair. This was the stage actress they had brought out all the way from New York for the role of glamorous Isabelle Parry in *Strictly Dishonorable* opposite Paul Lukas? Eastern talent scout David Werner must be losing his touch!

Jones quickly posed her in a succession of bromidic attitudes, arranged in a blue brocade evening gown (with and without furs), a set of Oriental pajamas, and a coat with a fox collar and a cloche hat. In an unusual way, she was rather pretty. Because she was scared and had little confidence, he tried to place her at ease with a couple of light comments. She needed a professional manicure, he noticed, and, when he pulled the prints out of the "soup," he wrote a note to the retoucher on the back: *add fingernails.*

The Universal lot (telephone HEmpstead 3131) in North Hollywood featured a line of small, white, pseudo-Spanish offices facing Lankershim Boulevard and an unimposing front gate. The studio, a 230-acre property, including the new sound stages, lay between the boulevard and the hills and roughly followed the course of the empty Los Angeles River.

Founder "Uncle Carl" Laemmle was a benign dictator who always wore a carnation in his buttonhole, showed all of his teeth when he laughed, and posed for pictures with his hands in his pockets. Uncle Carl was the finest exponent of nepotism in town. Relatives and friends on payroll were located from the green department to accounting and numbered about seventy. Son Junior, a slender edition of his father, was fond of popping in and out of doors at inopportune moments.

Publicity director John LeRoy Johnston was fond of the glitter and gold of old-fashioned press agentry hoopla and truthfully found the little girl from New York an enigma. The stills piled on his desk showed her looking soulfully at the camera; she was no beauty and apparently had problems looking provocative in lounging pajamas or a bathing suit.

His assistant had come back from Union Station with the usual bouquet of red roses in a wilted condition, complaining that the new girl from New York had not arrived.

At that moment the phone rang, and the whispery voice of Bette Davis informed them she was at the Hollywood Plaza Hotel. Why had no one met her at the depot? He replied somewhat testily that his assistant had said that no one got off the train who looked like an actress. She replied equally testily, "I may not have been wearing a mink coat, but I was traveling with a dog. That should have made you think I was an actress!'' It was December 13, 1930.

After the first few days on the lot it was the consensus of opinion that Davis definitely did not look like the charmer called for in *Strictly Dishonorable*. Instead of a glamorous plumed bird they were stuck with a "little brown wren.'' *[Ash-blonde hair was considered brown by Hollywood in those days. It was the era of very bleached blonde hair—thus the title "little brown wren."]*

After Sidney Fox was cast as Isabelle Parry in *Strictly Dishonorable*, William Wyler, a distant cousin of Uncle Carl's who worked on the lot, tested Davis for *A House Divided*, which would star Walter Huston. *[The Universal wardrobe department did not have a dress that fit me. The neckline was too low—much cleavage was in sight, to my utter embarrassment.]* Wyler assumed that she was just another Hollywood actress trying to get a part by being sexy. *[In actual fact, Mr. Wyler said in a loud voice, "What do you think of these dames who show their chests and think they can get jobs?'' It was truly one of the most heartbreaking moments of my career.]*

Helen Chandler got the part. Eventually Wyler was responsible for a trio of Academy Award-nominated Davis pictures *(Jezebel, The Letter, The Little Foxes)* but years later, when told of his remark, never even remembered the incident. *[Mr. Wyler did not remember the incident but believed me and said, "I am a much nicer person now.'' This was at our first meeting before starting* Jezebel.*]*

Since she was drawing a salary of $300 per week and no pictures were on her schedule, the talent head asked her to appear in some tests. Davis amiably agreed and arrived to meet James Hall, a sensation because of his role in *Hell's Angels*. She was promptly seated on a low divan, and the cameras started to roll. Hall spoke a few lines, then took her in his arms and kissed her. The director yelled "cut.''

In 1971, on the "Dick Cavett Show,'' Davis told of the incident: "They didn't know what to do with something that looked like me. At that age, I want to tell you, in 1930, I was the *Yankee-est,* most modest virgin who ever walked the earth! They laid me on a couch, and I tested fifteen men.''

The audience burst into laughter, and both Cavett and Davis joined in the merriment. When quiet had been restored, Cavett asked slyly, "Do you want to reword that?"

"I am not kidding you!" Davis laughed. "They all had to lie on top of me and give me a passionate kiss. Oh, I thought I would die; just thought I would die!"

Cavett grinned, "Are you *sure* there was film in the camera?"

"Oh yes, there was film in the camera, there certainly was . . ."

"Do you ever see any of those men," Cavett asked, "or do you remember?"

"Yes, interestingly enough, one was Gilbert Roland."

"Oh?"

"I must say that, after he kissed me, I said to myself, 'This is not so bad.' " Davis giggled, "And years later I worked with him in *Juarez*. He is a smashingly beautiful guy."

Davis was scheduled for several fan magazine interviews and established an immediate rapport with the press. Most of the reporters had heard about her stage work in *Broken Dishes* and *Solid South* and were delighted to find her wholesome and "un-actressy." She often spoke about the lean days in New York, shared with her mother, whom she called Ruthie, and her sister Barbara, known as Bobby.

Ruthie was an extraordinary woman, who had often worked as a professional photographer to help support the family after divorcing Harlow Morrell Davis in 1915. She was not the typical stage mother. She did not push her daughter's career forward by calling producers or setting up appointments with casting directors. Rather, she worked hard to provide the initial wherewithal so that Bette Davis could fully concentrate on stage work. Once the money began to roll in, as Hollywood began to recognize the talents of her infanta, she could relax the vigil and vicariously enjoy the growth of fame.

A studio photographer traveled up to her little house on Alta Loma Terrace behind the French Village across from Hollywood Bowl and took shots of her inside the door and outside among the greenery.

THE WIDE-EYED INGENUE

After being rejected by Wyler, press releases announced Davis would appear in a remake of Booth Tarkington's *The Flirt,* which had been filmed by Bluebird in 1916 and again by Universal in

1922. The current version was first called *What a Flirt,* then *Gambling Daughters* and finally *Bad Sister.* Davis assumed she would get the title role opposite Conrad Nagel. She was assigned the small part of the good sister, Laura Madison. The role of the vivacious sibling went to Sidney Fox.

Junior Laemmle produced and Hobart Henley, who had worked on the 1922 version, directed. The script, by Raymond L. Schrock and Tom Reed, featured additional dialogue by Edwin Knopf—who would soon carve a niche for himself as a director of important women's pictures at Metro-Goldwyn-Mayer.

Davis, nervous about her appearance, went to studio makeup chief Jack Pierce. "My first makeup man surveyed me critically, almost resentfully," she wrote in an April 1938 article, *"You Don't Have to Be Beautiful,"* for *Good Housekeeping.* "Your eyelashes are too short," he drawled, "hair's a nondescript color, and mouth's too small. A fat little Dutch girl's face, and a neck that's too long." He did little to help her dilemma, except suggest a different shade of lipstick and advise use of eye shadow.

Universal, one of the last major plants to get on the talkie bandwagon, was far behind other studios until Lewis Milestone used sound successfully in 1930 in *All Quiet on the Western Front.* After that, each film employed dialogue more adroitly, but shooting schedules could not be followed exactly because technicians never knew when the camera would have to be stopped in order to iron out an unforeseen emergency. Cameras, powered by electricity, made a whirring noise that was picked up by the microphone and so were enclosed in a large soundproof box with a tempered plate-glass "window" through which scenes were shot. Movement was curtailed; for a time, pictures were filmed almost like stage plays—straight on—because the camera could not *pan* or *tilt* or *dolly up* for close shots. Microphones were concealed in various areas about the set, and the players' movements and dialogue were "choreographed" from one mike to another.

But, by the time Davis reached Universal, the cameras had been liberated from the "sweat box" and were muffled in heavy blankets. Recording equipment had been perfected, microphones were suspended overhead, and a sound man followed the actors with the mike. Even so, countless rehearsals were necessary because dialogue was often lost by the shuffling of feet, the creaking of a rocking chair, or the contact of hand props on furniture.

Hobart Henley called his cast together on the first day of shooting

Bad Sister and for the benefit of the "stage people" emphasized that the microphone picked up every nuance of speech. "Talk in a normal tone," he advised.

Rotund, expressionistic cameraman Karl Freund, who had photographed a brace of famous German silents, including *Variety, Metropolis,* and *The Last Laugh,* was assigned to the film. But Freund was not working for UFA, a German studio, or under the direction of E. A. Dupont, Fritz Lang, or F. W. Murnau; he was toiling for Uncle Carl at Universal, with Hobart Henley at the helm. The direction was so uninspired that both the cast and the crew lost interest. Occasionally Freund would set up an interesting camera angle, like placing the camera in the middle of a dinner table and swinging into a daring 360-degree angle to photograph each player in turn, but usually he followed basic camera angles.

The players were either on their way up the Hollywood ladder or on their way down. Sidney Fox, Davis's nemesis, would eventually finish her career by committing suicide. Zasu Pitts, whose ultradramatic role in Erich von Stroheim's *Greed* in 1922 was laughed off the screen because audiences could only identify with her comic ability, would be forever cast as a limpwristed comedienne. Slim Summerville, the epitome of the awkward homespun cornball, would hone this hayseed characterization to perfection. Charles Winninger's next film, *Sin of Madelon Claudet,* would bring an Academy Award to Helen Hayes, and newcomer Humphrey Bogart would spend a lifetime humanizing cinematic mobsters. Freund would bring forth a Merlinesque genius for the atmospheric *Dracula* and *The Mummy* and eventually a more popular image in his old age as the cameraman for dozens of the "I Love Lucy" television shows.

Davis and Ruthie drove to San Bernardino for the sneak preview of *Bad Sister.* One wit remarked later that she looked like she was "whipped by the rain" in the film. In the scene where she changed a baby's diaper (the fact that the infant was male was hidden from her until the take) her slow, all-encompassing blush was recorded on film as a deep gray color. Davis and her mother were out of the theater before the ending title was flashed on the screen. She cried all the way back to Alta Loma Terrace.

Robert Florey, directing *Murders in the Rue Morgue,* thought Davis might do as the frightened ingenue, but Laemmle cast Sidney Fox, again! *[Pretty obvious, the relationship between studio head and actress . . . real reason I did not get* Strictly Dishonorable. *Miss Fox was not right for the part.]* As it turned out, this was one of the wisest decisions ever made. Otherwise Davis might have gone on at Universal as the Egyptian girl friend of *The Mummy* and ended up as the assembled *Bride of Frankenstein*.

2

If you'd give the kid a chance, Kelly, he might amount to something, instead of always thinking about yourself.

BETTE DAVIS AS PEGGY
IN *Hell's House*

Uncle Carl shook his head after seeing *Bad Sister* and cracked, "Can you picture some poor guy going through hell and high water in a picture and ending up with *her* at the fade-out?" Although Davis at five feet, two inches, was the same height as her boss, they still didn't see eye-to-eye.

John M. Stahl was set to produce the screen adaptation of the controversial Charles G. Norris novel *Seed,* which advocated birth control. Gladys Lehman was assigned the thorny job of converting the "hot" material into a workable screenplay. At one point even the title was thought to be too suggestive.

None of the contract actresses on the lot were quite right for the role of Margaret Carter, the sweet young thing, so Stahl sent scouts to various high schools in Los Angeles, but to no avail. He then ran a second contest in a local paper. One day, in the commissary, he spotted Davis, who he felt had the right appearance for the role—*she looked so fragile.*

Stahl specialized in women's pictures, dealing with unrequited love and the pursuit of happiness along the milk route, but he was out of his element with *Seed.* Davis, in an unbecoming wardrobe that looked off the racks of Sears & Roebuck, could not understand why Stahl had gone to such pains to cast the part, which was insipid and unrewarding.

Seed opened at the Rivoli Theatre in Manhattan on May 14, 1931. Most reviewers did not even mention Davis's name. *[If you blinked for a second, Margaret had disappeared.]*

DECISION AT WATERLOO

The studio picked up Davis's option for another three months after *Seed*, only because Freund remarked that she "has nice eyes" and Ted Kent, who had also edited *Bad Sister*, said that he felt she "had something."

The studio had purchased *Waterloo Bridge*, Robert E. Sherwood's moving tale of the love-torn life of a flier during World War I. The watered-down script was the work of Benn W. Levy. Tom Reed contributed the "continuity and additional dialogue" and in the process managed to truncate most of the bright lines. Arthur Edeson, who had photographed Douglas Fairbanks, Sr., so brilliantly in *Robin Hood*, made the trek from Sherwood Forest to Sherwood, Robert E., without distinction. James Whale, more at home directing various members of the Frankenstein family, turned out to be little more than a "traffic cop" who planned entrances and exits.

Mae Clarke was assigned the role of the unemployed chorus girl, Myra, forced into the life of a whore. Flier Kent Douglas (who later changed his name to Douglass Montgomery), playing Roy Wetherby, marries her, but while he is at the front, she backslides into her old occupation. Davis played the role of Douglas's sister in such a shy manner that she was again ignored by the press.

Mordaunt Hall wrote in the September 5, 1931, issue of *The New York Times,*

> Considering the scarcity of opportunities, Mr. Whale has done excellent work on this film, which is his second attempt at motion picture direction. To impress one with the idea that Roy and Myra are in the country, this British director gives familiar farm yard noises, such as the crowing of a rooster and the mooing of a cow. When the soldier and the girl are in her dismal abode, one hears the vaguest suggestion of a regimental band passing in a distant thoroughfare. After the bombing raid is over, the "all clear" signal is heard, but it is rather surprising to

observe that Mr. Whale causes the blinds to be pulled up, which was not permitted . . .

[In light of what is allowed on the screen today, this is hysterical. Who says the film industry hasn't forged ahead?]

Mae Clarke's acting of Myra is capital.

[Yearned all during shooting of film to play Myra. I could have!]
Davis was listed next to last on the screen credits. *[Perfectly logical. I had about four lines and was a "new kid."]*

NEXT WEEK, EAST LYNN

Uncle Carl looked at the print of *Waterloo Bridge* and, turning to Junior, said, "Whale can't do any better with her than Stahl. *Her sex appeal simply ain't! No man could ever be interested in her!*" *[Actually, Junior Laemmle himself, after seeing* Bad Sister, *said, "She has about as much sex appeal as Slim Summerville." I was in Mr. Laemmle's outer office at the time and overheard this remark. Having been considered attractive and definitely a success with the opposite sex—prior to my Hollywood arrival—this was a desperate moment for me. I didn't recover for a long time.]*

A few days later he received a call from RKO producer Pandro S. Berman, who asked to borrow Davis for the role of Mary Lucy in *Other People's Business*. The crafty Laemmle was delighted. If it became known that she was available for loan-outs, he might make a little money, even at $300 a week.

Other People's Business was to star Mr. and Mrs. Phillips Lord, who had achieved wide popularity via a radio show called "Seth Parker."

The production, budgeted at a high $400,000, was filmed at Santa Cruz, a California hamlet with a New England town atmosphere. William A. Seiter, an expert at dispensing light comedy and homespun wit, directed from a script by Jane Murfin, who, along with Gladys Lehman and Frances Marion, was one of the few women writers to survive the talkies.

Besides the Lords, the film featured "Down East" types Bennett Kilpack and Raymond Hunter, along with Frank Albertson as Mary Lucy's vis-à-vis. Cinematographer J. Roy Hunt took the time to photograph Davis well. *[This was the first encouragement I had had, as to my face on the screen. I was truly overjoyed. Plus the part I played was an important one—and a charming one. It gave me some confidence in myself for the first time since leaving the theater in New York.]*

Although yet unbilled, Max Steiner, the little German composer, invested the film with an interesting and thoroughly American score. *[This man was one of the great contributors to countless films with his musical scores. Many a so-so film was made better through his talents.]* He found a certain empathy with Davis and in later years would be credited with musically assisting her characterizations in certain weak films and adding dramatic structure to many of her good ones. Steiner, whose godfather was Richard Strauss, had studied in Europe with Gustav Mahler, Robert Fuchs, and Herman Groedner, and had orchestrated and conducted Broadway shows for George Gershwin and Florenz Ziegfield. When the composer arrived in New York from Vienna in 1925 and was without work, an acquaintance asked what he did for a living. Steiner replied that he was a conductor, whereupon the man, who worked for the transit system, broke into smiles and handed him a card of introduction to a subway foreman!

The reviews were disappointing, especially to the Lords, who had envisioned Hollywood as the pot of gold at the end of the microphone. Thankfully they went back to radio, and the name of the picture was changed to *Way Back Home,* but the original title was used in Great Britain. *Weekly Variety* was especially caustic: "As entertainment the film is unbelievably bad. The story is strictly an old-style proposed tearjerker. It runs 81 minutes which seems like 181." But Andre Sennwald in *The New York Times* of January 16, 1932, liked the film:

> The twangy speech, the homely wit, the barn dances, taffy-pulling gatherings, singing bees—all the real and mellow phases of Yankee Village life—are shown humanly and without the elephantine burlesque that might have killed the illusion. . . . Bette Davis and Frank Albertson are the lovers.

[It must be remembered there was great skepticism and snobbery about films in those days, in the critique area. Way Back Home was a charming film; the Lords and their radio company, I thought,

*were enchanting. I'm glad Sennwald felt about it as I did. He
obviously accepted it for what it was meant to be—not a
masterpiece, just a slice of Yankee village life.]*

Although not singled out for praise, at least the name of Bette
Davis was *mentioned*.

PEGGY & PEGGY & CO.

Ray Jones was pleased with the change in Davis's appearance. The
fan books, which had "discovered" her, were clamoring for new
photos.

Laemmle loaned her to Columbia for *The Feathered Serpent*,
based on the book by Edgar Wallace, who was working at RKO—
but the small budget would not allow recompense in terms of his
current salary, so Dorothy Howell and Charles Logue wrote the
script. Roy Chanslor created extra dialogue.

The picture, directed by Roy William Neill, was made in eight
days—including the inserts. Davis was not on the lot long enough to
meet Frank Capra, Jean Harlow, Loretta Young, or Barbara
Stanwyck. Strangely enough she would have a date with Capra
thirty years later for *Pocketful of Miracles*, when she would portray
Apple Annie in the remake of the same story he was preparing then,
Lady for a Day, with May Robson as the hag with airs. In 1956 she
would also have a rendezvous with Columbia for the controversial
film *Storm Center*.

The Feathered Serpent, produced by Sam Nelson, no relation to
Harmon O. Nelson, the young musician whom Davis was dating,
had a remarkable cast for such a small undertaking: H. B. Warner,
Walter Byron, Natalie Moorhead, William B. Davidson, and a man
who would change the course of her career—that impeccable
character actor Murray Kinnell.

The slight plot concerned an escaped convict who uses plastic
surgery, a new gimmick at the time, to elude the police. Davis is
Peggy, his former girl friend, who fails to recognize him after his
surgery—although the scalpel made only minor changes
(mentioned in all the reviews). She fainted, fell out of closets, and
was consequently seldom mentioned in the notices.

After viewing the finished product, Columbia, concerned the
public would think the picture an adventure film instead of a murder

mystery, changed the title first to *The Squeaker* and then to *The Menace*.

To finish the contract at Universal Uncle Carl loaned Davis to Capital Films for *Juvenile Court,* later released as *Hell's House.* This thirteen-day reform school quickie, produced by Benjamin F. Zeidman and directed by Howard Higgin from his own story, featured a topical screenplay by Paul Gangelin and B. Harrison Orkow. Ex-Huckleberry Finn juvenile actor James (''Junior'') Durkin, whose career would end as soon as his fans discovered he shaved, headed the cast.

Pat O'Brien, the heavy, played a bootlegger named Kelly, who allows Durkin to take the rap when the police raid the still. Davis, assaying a similar part as in *The Menace,* even with the same name, Peggy, convinces O'Brien to give himself up so the boy can be released from a three-year prison sentence.

Higgin, known for fast-paced vehicles, kept the story and the players moving. *Hell's House* had a message and thirty years later was still playing in passion-pit theaters on various Main Streets in the United States.

Davis had been in Hollywood for nine months and had made six pictures—all flops. It was the middle of September, 1931, when Uncle Carl allowed her option to drop. Disconsolate, Davis and Ruthie made preparations for the long trek back to New York.

The phone rang as Ruthie was in the midst of packing. Davis answered, and a professional matter-of-fact male voice said, ''This is George Arliss. Would it be possible for you to come to Warner Bros. immediately for an interview with me for my next film, *The Man Who Played God*?''

[I replied in an imitative English accent, thinking it was a joke played on me by a friend, ''Of course, Mr. Arliss. How jolly decent of you.'' After about three sallies back and forth, Mr. Arliss said, ''Miss Davis, this is George Arliss!'' After a long pause—and a gasp—I said, ''I'll be right there!'' My excitement and joy were indescribable. If I was accepted by Mr. Arliss, I would not have to return to the New York theater a failure in Hollywood! An Arliss film was a prestige film—a far cry from The Menace, *and, yet, Murray Kinnell of* The Menace *cast had suggested me for the part in the Arliss film. Out of all bad comes some good. I have always believed this.]*

Betty Davis as Laura Madison and Conrad Nagel as Dr. Dick Lindley in Davis' first film, *Bad Sister*, 1931. (*Photograph by Universal Studios, from the collection of Eddie Brandt.*)

Bette Davis as Peggy and Walter Byron as Ronald in the thriller *The Menace*, 1932, based upon Edgar Wallace's novel *The Feathered Serpent*. (*Photograph by Columbia Pictures Corp.*)

Pat O'Brien and Bette Davis in *Hell's House*, filmed as *Juvenile Court*, on a thirteen-day shooting schedule in 1931. (*Photograph by Capital Films.*)

Bette Davis as Janet Wetherby in *Waterloo Bridge,* 1931, with Doris Lloyd, Kent Douglas, Mae Clarke, and Frederick Kerr. (*Photograph by Universal Pictures.*)

Rube Turner (Stanley Fields) seeks out Mary Lucy (Bette Davis) and David Clark (Frank Albertson) in *Way Back Home,* 1932, originally released as *Other People's Business.* (*Photograph by RKO Radio Pictures, from the collection of Gunnard Nelson.*)

3

*I feel mean at going, Monty. But, you see, I promised
Alice Chitterdom way back in Paris, and she's giving a
house party on my account . . . I don't think I ought to
leave you.*

BETTE DAVIS AS GRACE
IN *The Man Who Played God*

Although Olive Avenue in Burbank separated Universal's back lot
in North Hollywood from Warner Bros. First National Pictures on
one side and the dry bed of the Los Angeles River divided it on the
other, the lines of demarcation could not have been more
pronounced if one were the Champs-Elysées and the other the River
Styx. Universal was run as a kind of family business, while Warner
Bros. was more of a conglomerate.

When Bette Davis made the seven-mile trip from Alta Loma
Terrace to Warner Bros. for the Arliss interview, the lot looked like
the huge factory out of *Modern Times*. The twenty-three-acre
property included a back lot the size of Fort Dix and seven commodious sound stages. She could not dream that in ten years money
from her films alone would build four more stages, two of which
would replace the double parking lot that parted Olive Avenue from
the front gate. She was scared stiff.

Warner Bros. was ruled in California with an iron fist by forty-
year-old Jack L. Warner ("J.L.") and his older brother Harry while
Albert ran the New York office. Tough businessmen with alligator

hides, they could stretch one dollar into four without drawing undue attention to the sleight-of-hand.

Essentially, however, they were fair men. Expensive productions and temperamental actors were their special bane. Self-made men, who had known poverty, neglect, failure, and ridicule, they had survived one of the most quixotic professions in the world through tenacity and perseverance. *[I am often asked what the difference is between the Hollywood of yesterday, my Hollywood, and the Hollywood of today. In many ways there are not enough changes—too technical a discussion to go into here. As to kinds of films, an enormous difference. Theater and, of course, films reflect the times we live in, and the tastes of the public often reflect the world of the present. There is, however, one fatal change. Gone are the gamblers: Zukor, Goldwyn, Mayer, Warner, Cohn, Thalberg, Zanuck, and countless others. They gave us our careers—sometimes they won, sometimes they lost millions in promotion of a script and a star. People of my era—the 1930s, 1940s, 1950s—owe these men our careers. They were our fathers. This is the big change in the Hollywood of yesterday and today.]*

Bette Davis was to meet a man who in any other profession would be retired. Arliss had come to Hollywood in 1929 after forty brilliant years on the stage. He had complete control over his pictures and at sixty-four was a gentle martinet who worked assiduously to promote his image. No matter what role he played, and they were varied, from the Oriental potentate in *The Green Goddess* to the British prime minister in *Disraeli*, he was the universal father figure. *[He certainly was my first professional father. I owe him the career that finally emerged.]*

The plot for *The Man Who Played God* (based on the play *The Silent Voice*, by Jules Eckert Goodman, under which title the film was later released in the United Kingdom) concerned Montgomery Royale, a brilliant concert pianist who loses his hearing when a bomb meant for a king is detonated in his presence. Unable to play, he becomes bitter but gains his self-respect by distributing gifts to unfortunates whom he watches through binoculars in the park below his penthouse. By monitoring conversations through lipreading, he becomes conversant with their problems. Among the supporting parts was the role of Grace, a young girl with whom he falls in love and who stands by him when he loses his hearing.

Having played in the silent version in 1922, Arliss knew from experience that Grace must be handled with great tenderness and

finesse because of the great differences in their ages. The older man
-younger woman business had been a problem ten years before,
when he was fifty-four, and it would be a greater problem now. The
girl must indicate not only love for him as a person but hero worship
as well. Arliss had no intention of giving the impression in the film
that they were having a physical affair. Grace had to be expertly
played or he would appear ridiculous.

Davis came into the "presence" with her heart in her mouth.
"My friend Murray Kinnell believes you would be an excellent
choice for my leading lady," he said, beaming in that special way
that lit up his face like a beacon. "Tell me, my dear, how long have
you been on the stage?"

"Three years."

"Just enough to rub the edges off."

*[Arliss told me to go to the wardrobe department to choose the
clothes for the part of Grace. I raced to the wardrobe department—
called mother, who also was flabbergasted—started jumping up
and down, to the consternation of all concerned. Am sure they
thought a lunatic had been let loose. They weren't far from wrong. I
was hysterical with joy.]*

In his autobiography, *My First 100 Years in Hollywood,* J. L.
Warner tells it differently:

> What really happened is this:
> Rufus LeMaire . . . said: "Jack, there's a very
> talented little girl over at Universal named Bette Davis. I
> first saw her in some New York shows, and I caught her in
> a bit in *Bad Sister. . . .*"
> "Okay. Bring her over."
> Bette came to our lot, and when we were casting *The
> Man Who Played God,* we gave her name to the director,
> and he liked her at once.

*[Dear J.L.: I hate to contradict your version of my arrival at
Warner Bros. for* The Man Who Played God. *Arliss had interviewed countless young actresses for this part. Murray Kinnell
did suggest me to Arliss. They were good friends from the theater
days. Plus I didn't have a bit part in* Bad Sister; *I had one of the
leads. As to Mr. Arliss's examining my soul instead of my legs, he
was far too reserved for any such nonsense. As was the custom of
the day, in order to receive a part like Grace, one had to give the*

studio an option on one's services. If they chose, they could put you under contract. My contract with you lasted eighteen years. I will be forever grateful to you and all concerned that you picked up my option. These were the greatest eighteen years of my life.]

From wardrobe Davis was sent to makeup. Perc Westmore—pronounced "Perse," he told a contract player, not "Perc," that's something a coffee pot does!—studied her face carefully, designed a slick hairdo, and told her to bleach her hair. *[According to the standards of the world I came from, I was a blonde—technically, an ash blonde. According to the Hollywood standards of the 1930s, when bright bleached hair reigned supreme, my hair was nondescript. He was wise enough to know my photographic appearance would be heightened by the blonder hair. He was right. In* The Man Who Played God—*for the first time—I really looked like myself. It was for me a new lease on life. As a matter of fact, I was compared to Constance Bennett. I was very flattered. I had always liked so much the way she looked on the screen.]* Perc became a close friend, and together they would create history-making makeups.

Westmore, twenty-eight, the son of an English wigmaker, had begun his Hollywood career in 1921 after fashioning part of a phony mustache for Adolphe Menjou, whose razor had slipped one morning. Warner Bros. "inherited" him after he had established the makeup department at First National the year before. During the silent era screen makeup had been a hit-and-miss affair, with many of the performers simply applying their own, with the result that a succession of close-ups, shot on different days, often revealed totally different skin tones.

Great emphasis, then, was placed upon the ability of the cinematographer to light his subjects. Hal Mohr and Ed DuPar had gained awesome reputations for being able to enhance the appearance of a star simply by light placement. But spots, juniors, broads, could not be maneuvered with the dexterity of old because talkies had to be shot in long scenes. Extremely short scenes, which silent cameramen had previously set up carefully and explained with a short title, took too much time for the recording of one or two words.

Few stars had photogenically perfect features; makeup often obliterated the best facial bone structure. Westmore yearned to develop cosmetics that would look the same under diverse lighting conditions and with different types of film. Willing to look into any area that would save money, J.L. gave carte blanche in materials for experimentation. Eventually Westmore came up with a complete line of natural-looking cosmetics to be used only for the camera.

At Warner Bros. Bette Davis joined Al Jolson, Paul Muni, Edward G. Robinson, Leslie Howard, James Cagney, Joe E. Brown, Warren William, Richard Barthelmess, Frank McHugh, Lyle Talbot, Ann Dvorak, Ruby Keeler, Dick Powell, Joan Blondell, Glenda Farrell, Humphrey Bogart, Alan Hale, Guy Kibbee, Eugene Pallette, Loretta Young, Mae Clarke, Margaret Lindsay, Patricia Ellis, Allen Jenkins and Grant Mitchell.

THE FIRST YEAR ON OLIVE AVENUE

The script for *The Man Who Played God* was written by Julien Josephson and Maude T. Howell, the latter the first and only woman on the Warner lot whose every wish was a command. She had been with Arliss on all of his pictures, either as a scenarist, coordinator, or supervisor, and was invaluable to the old man.

The cast was made up of many Arliss regulars, including Violet Heming, Ivan Simpson, Louise Closser Hale, Hedda Hopper, newcomers Donald Cook and Ray Milland, and, of course, Murray Kinnell.

The director was John Adolfi. [*In actual fact Arliss directed his own films. He was also the first star to rehearse for ten days before actually filming.*] Cinematographer James Van Trees had a particularly difficult assignment because he had to make Arliss look as young as possible in makeup that harked back to the silents. Paying no attention whatsoever to Westmore, Arliss used the same light base and dark lip rouge as on the stage!

Darryl F. Zanuck had been instrumental in bringing Arliss to the studio in 1929 for *Disraeli,* and, after that film was in the can, Harry Warner thought no one would know the identity of the British prime minister and suggested the title be changed to something with marquee value. Arliss slyly suggested *Wild Nights with Queen Victoria.* The subject was never brought up again!

Sandy-haired and buck-toothed, Zanuck was twenty-nine years old and had been with the studio for eight years, during which time he had risen from a hack writer for wonder dog Rin Tin Tin to chief of production. He was ambitious, demanding, irascible, and drove himself relentlessly day and night. Besides his various other duties he had already personally written or supervised thirty-seven pictures and had a hand in assembling many others. As a writer he used three noms de plume: Melville Crossman, Gregory Rogers, and Mark Canfield.

Arliss painstakingly practiced the piano. He did not wish to be accused of displaying "spaghetti arms," although the actual solos were recorded by Salvatore Santaella. Zanuck realized that the old man was twenty years too old for the part, but his acting ability enabled him to be convincing. Davis was more than adequate, she was *good*. He did not think that she was very beautiful, but she had good timing and diction and could deliver a line with conviction. She would do very well as the clever secretary, Kay Russell, in a story he was writing called *The Dark Horse,* which dealt satirically with political corruption. But before this big part he would cast her in a couple of supporting roles in big-star vehicles to give her stature.

Because the plot of *The Man Who Played God* concerned the loss of hearing, more than normal attention was given to the use of sound. In sequences where the deaf Arliss is reading lips and the player sharing the scene turns away while speaking, the sound men erased the dialogue from the sound track, so the audience also lost the dialogue.

Experts at performing audio tricks, Colonel N. S. Slaughter and Ben Levinson, under Sam Warner's direction, had brought talkies to the screen eight years before—*sound,* that elusive gold-plated factor that added the touch of magic to the flickering shadows on the silver screen.

When no other studio would touch synchronized pictures with a three-foot painted wooden sword, the little studio had grabbed the bait. A sure gambling instinct guided the brothers in the right direction, but faulty judgment lured them down the primrose path. When offered *two* methods of transferring sound to the silver screen, they chose what turned out to be the wrong one: sound-on-disc instead of sound-on-film! The process was called *Vitaphone.*

THE WHEAT AND THE CHAFF

The still gallery at Warner Bros. was a busy place. Publicity had to keep the fan books supplied with an abundance of photographs to herald each new picture. It was up to Elmer Fryer, Bert Longworth,

Scottie Melbourne, et al., to photograph the players from the best possible angle. Full-time retouchers were employed to blot out circles under the eyes, firm crepey chins, remove beards, paint out freckles, gloss over pimples, and repair runny makeup. The slogan appeared to be, When in doubt, retouch everything except the eyes, nose, lips, and brows; and the result was a blob of glamorous jelly. These artists, often women, could do more for a hangover than pills.

Davis, who had shown affection and understanding for the press at Universal, was Miss Cooperation. Having opinions about everything from the way to cook corned beef hash to performing the backstroke, she delighted in giving unconventional interviews. She helped the underpaid members of the press out of their sugary doldrums with salty comments. These friends did not forget early kindnesses, and, when her career lost momentum in the late 1940s, she was nonetheless championed in the fan books. When her personal life was in shambles and would have been the crux of juicy confession-type stories, not one bitchy article ever appeared about her.

Tired of the demure image portrayed in early portrait sittings, she now turned on sophistication for the still camera. Gone were such photo captions as "Little Bette Davis of the drooping eyelids and sullen mouth" or "In spite of Bette's slimness she once worked as a life guard," and, instead, "Gone is the crestfallen Bette Davis, who was beginning to rival Zasu Pitts for mournful poses. In her place is a sparkling young person who bears a striking resemblance to Connie Bennett and wears clothes like a Parisienne mannequin."

James ("Marion") Fidler did a piece for the *Saturday Evening Post* in 1932, "The Best Bette in Pictures," where he wrote,

> Older than she looks, but younger than she talks, she is
> a curious combination of child and woman. She is not
> only beautiful, but she bubbles with charm and good
> fellowship. She bears a striking resemblance to two other
> famous stars. Her eyes and nose and forehead are
> astonishingly like Constance Bennett. Her mannerisms
> and way of talking are remindful of Olive Borden . . . An
> inferiority complex is her one weakness . . . It was
> because of this complex that she became discouraged
> when she saw herself on the screen in *Bad Sister,* that first
> picture in which she played an ugly duckling. It is for the

same reason that she never sees daily rushes of pictures she works in.

[The real reason for not seeing rushes is that I never liked my face on the screen—or off! I still spend my life wishing I looked like Katharine Hepburn!]

After J.L. looked at the rough cut of *The Man Who Played God*, Davis was called into the front office and handed a five-year contract with yearly options. She signed her name on all the copies and walked out of the building in a daze. This was the epitome of her life so far: the year in Hollywood of nothing but flop movies, the year of nothing but disappointments. She did not know it then, but these same huge sound stages on the Warner lot would become an inescapable prison, and J.L. an uncompromising warden. *[The stages became later a prison because I had scripts and a contract that gave me no choice in the parts I played. That was the difficult side of the contract system. The great side of the contract system was the constant work and the investment by the studio to further your career. Publicity departments in those days made your name known all over the world. They were as important to a career as the work on the screen. One supplemented the other. Through them and the films, the public discovered you. The public has always made the star. I thank God I was brought up in films under this system. Newcomers today, I feel, are at a disadvantage, because there are few contracts given to actors anymore.]*

THE CLIMB BEGINS

The warden looked over the properties on tap for a role that would showcase his new contract player. The studio had successfully launched the gangster cycle with *Doorway to Hell* and *Little Caesar*. Now, with the masculine audience surfeited with blood and the rat-a-tat-tat of machine gun fire, a series of handkerchief films made especially with women in mind might start a new trend.

In January, 1932, when Zanuck heard through the grapevine that Jesse Lasky at Paramount had inadvertently failed to pick up options on Ruth Chatterton, Kay Francis, and William Powell, he started negotiations. Press releases were prepared to the effect that the trio of stars would make the trek from Marathon Street in Hollywood to Olive Avenue in Burbank. Barbara Stanwyck, who had been having contract difficulties at Columbia, signed a new contract whereby

Grace (Bette Davis) and Montgomery Royale (George Arliss) have a May–December romance in *The Man Who Played God*, 1932. (*Photograph by Warner Bros.*)

Bette Davis as Norma Frank Morrell and Charles Farrell as husband Jimmy in *The Big Shakedown*, 1934. (*Photograph by Scotty Welbourne, Warner Bros.*)

Caroline Van Dyne (Ruth Chatterton, "the First Lady of the Screen") greets Malbro (Bette Davis), Julian (George Brent), Greg (John Miljan), and Allison (Adrienne Dore) in *The Rich Are Always with Us*, 1932. (*Photograph by Warner Bros., from the collection of Gunnard Nelson.*)

both Warner Bros. and the Gower Street studio would share her services. A remake of Colleen Moore's 1925 silent hit *So Big*, based on Edna Ferber's best seller, was placed on her schedule, and Davis was assigned the small part of artist Dallas O'Mara. Stanwyck was only a year older, twenty-five, than Davis, but Selina Peake was her first "character" part, calling for her to age from a lovely young girl to a woman of mid-fifty.

Director William ("Wild Bill") Wellman soon learned what Frank Capra already knew: Stanwyck gave her best performance on the first take. Also cast was twenty-eight-year-old George Brent, an alumnus of the Abbey Players of Dublin. Prematurely gray, he dyed his hair blue-black. Possessing a certain docility, mixed with a strong masculine personality, Brent complemented Davis's charisma. They were destined to appear in eleven films together, as well as a radio serial based on the Broadway play *Woman of the Year* twenty years later.

With a week to go on the film Davis was cast in the new Chatterton film *The Rich Are Always with Us*, upon which she would work in the daytime while finishing her scenes in *So Big* at night. *[My part in* So Big *was one of my all-time favorites. During all the years I found few roles that had the naturalness in the character, a naturalness similar to my own personality. This I often regretted. Another role with the same attributes was Kit in* Old Acquaintance. *Even though my career was dedicated to character parts from the beginning, every now and then I selfishly wanted an audience to know what kind of a person I really was—anyway, the kind of person I felt I was.]*

THE REIGN OF MISS PEACHES

Caroline, while we're all taking our hair down, what is a girl to do when she's terribly in love with a man and he won't take her seriously?

BETTE DAVIS AS MALBRO BARCLAY
IN *The Rich Are Always with Us*

At thirty-nine Ruth Chatterton, "the First Lady of the Screen," was the synthesis of what a motion picture star could become in an industry that had been pulled to its knees through sound. In 1929 her career had been saved by her "vocal instrument," which

"Vitaphoned" well despite crude recording techniques. She quickly became the epitome of the suffering wife, the wronged woman, the ennobled lover, the aristocratic mistress. She was touching and beautiful, sanguine and vulnerable, and she ruled her sets, if not with the urbane charm of Arliss, at least with the command of a deity. But she was entering that dangerous age, when the backlog of experience tips the scales, when the queenly manner begins to pall on crew and public alike.

Chatterton had been through the mill, from the chorus line of a Washington, D.C. musical at fourteen to a score of stage plays through mentor-actor-producer Henry Miller, who called her Miss Peaches. She had made fifteen films in the five years she had been in Hollywood. Because of an awesome reputation, she was to receive the singular distinction of being billed as *Miss* Ruth Chatterton in *The Rich Are Always with Us,* an honor not given out lightly by Hollywood and particularly by the Warner *frères.* Paul Muni would wait for six years to be billed *Mr.* in *The Life of Emile Zola,* but Davis would not achieve the distinction until *The Empty Canvas* in 1964. *[This distinction I could have had many years before. I never wanted it. I felt it would make audiences feel less friendly toward me.]*

Zanuck and Ray Griffith, the associate producer, sought the creamy gloss of class, assigning the wizard of gauze, cinematographer Ernie Haller, to make the picture worthy of its title. Haller's main problem was to make Queen Chatterton look both svelte *and* young. He shuddered at the thought of the wardrobe that she would bring from New York for the role of the sophisticated Caroline Grannard. He knew she was given to girlish organza for evening and tweed suits for daytime, but there was very little he could do with a gown with an unflattering line or a suit with a bulky silhouette. He was astounded when she displayed an array of photogenic costumes during wardrobe tests. *Not one piece of clothing had to be redone.* He inquired where she had purchased the clothing. "Why, Mr. Haller," she said in her best Henry Miller voice, "Mr. Kelly, the new designer in wardrobe, made them especially for me."

Jack Kelly had been given a contract based on his superior work for Stanwyck and Chatterton. With the Queen's costumes designed on the lot, not even Kay Francis could take umbrage. Within a year every studio in town placed fashion designers on the payroll, thereby saving thousands of dollars.

Jack Kelly's real first name was Orry, from the Australian carnation; publicity added a hyphen, and Orry-Kelly was born.

Haller took a good look at ingenue Davis, who was to play the role of Malbro, a Park Avenue debutante. She looked somewhat like the Tenniel drawings of Alice in Wonderland, with wide forehead, incredibly long neck, tiny mouth, and huge eyes. She also had an inclination to wiggle her body under stress and would squint in close-ups if not watched. Her assets were a good complexion, blue eyes that photographed steel gray, and an engaging profile. With expert makeup and given time to light her properly she could be made to look beautiful. *[This he did, plus Orry-Kelly's clothes. For the very first time I had a certain chic.]*

He was destined to photograph fourteen of her pictures and have the distinction of being her favorite cameraman. *[I presented an Academy Award to the winning cinematographer some years ago. I said, "It gives me extreme pleasure to present this award. Without our cameramen, where would we be today? They have made us what we are. True, they are miracle men, to whom we owe so much." Ernest Haller was my miracle man during all the glory years. I wish he were alive today to read this, although I told him so many times.]* Thirty years later on *What Ever Happened to Baby Jane?,* he would have the opposite problem. For the first time he would not lie awake nights thinking up tricks to show her to advantage. For in that picture Davis was playing her own age and wanted to look as unattractive as possible.

Film on prospective leading men was run off in the projection room for the Queen, including the test of George Brent. She was captivated at once. Later, upon meeting him, she uttered the most famous of all clichés, "Where have you been all my life?" Although she was *supposed* to be in love with him on the screen, her growing attachment became obvious on the set. *[I watched this romance with a saddened heart. I had an all-time crush on George myself—had had for a year or so—to no avail. Had to wait quite a few years before he felt the same way—when we made* Dark Victory, *in fact.]* The director, Alfred E. Green, was delighted because their love scenes were charged with static electricity. But there was so much talk about the romance that she explained in an interview in *The New York Times* that she and her husband, actor Ralph Forbes, had not been getting along. It surprised no one when

Forbes established a six-week stopover residence in Las Vegas, leaving her to marry Brent, which she did seven months later, in August, 1932.

Davis, who had not been frightened of either Arliss or Stanwyck, was in such awe of the Queen that she was speechless in their first scene together. Chatterton, realizing the cause of her discomfiture, was very helpful and placed her at ease. She admired this energetic youngster whom she remembered from the stage. Thus, in her first two pictures at Warner Bros. Davis benefited immeasurably from the assistance of two superstars secure enough in the Hollywood firmament to give good advice and not be disturbed because of the presence of an electric newcomer. *[Miss Chatterton and I were friends from then on. I will always consider her one of the great actresses of her day.]*

Davis's height in a key scene posed a problem. She was supposed to knock down and then kick Adrienne Dore, a tall statuesque blonde who outweighed her by twenty pounds. For close-up and medium shots Dore wore sneakers. Because of logistics the scene was shot seven times. Each time the camera turned, Davis repeated each action and voice inflection *exactly* as before, and Green was impressed with her concentration and craftsmanship.

During production *The Man Who Played God* was released to universally good reviews. *Weekly Variety* thought that "Bette Davis, the ingenue, is a vision of wide-eyed blonde beauty." But Arliss gave her the most flattering compliment of all, in his autobiography:

> I think that only two or three times in my experience have I ever got from an actor at rehearsal something beyond what I realized was in the part. Bette Davis proved to be one of those exceptions. I knew she had a "nice little part," important to me—so I hoped for the best. I did not expect anything except a nice little performance. But when we rehearsed, she startled me; the nice little part became a deep and vivid creation, and I felt rather humbled that this young girl had been able to discover and portray something that my imagination had failed to conceive. She startled me, because, quite un-expectedly, I got from her a flash that illuminated mere words and inspired them with passion and emotion. That

is a kind of light that cannot be hidden under a bushel, and I am not the least surprised that Bette Davis is now the most important star on the screen.

[Thank you, dear, kind George Arliss.]

Mordaunt Hall, in his review of *The Man Who Played God* in the February 11, 1932, edition of *The New York Times,* said,

> Besides Mr. Arliss's masterful acting, there is an excellent performance by Violet Heming, who appears as Royale's sincere and sympathetic friend. Bette Davis, who plays Grace, often speaks too rapidly for the microphone.

[Mr. Hall, I agree. It was always difficult for me to speak slowly on or off the screen, always difficult for me to do anything slowly. William Wyler, when he directed me in Jezebel, *was constantly making me slow down—to say nothing of wiggling less. He forced me to get over these two very bad habits.]*

Hall's May 16 report, in part, on *The Rich Are Always with Us* in *The New York Times* read,

> Miss Chatterton, according to all reports, now has the choice of her stories, and it is therefore surprising that she should have picked this one . . . George Brent, who impersonates Julian, does capitally. He handles his lines as well as possible. Bette Davis, as a devoted admirer of Julian, also serves this film well.

[I didn't agree with Mr. Hall as regards the choice by Chatterton of this film. I loved the story and, of course, the part—my best to date under my Warner contract.]

The review in the June, 1932, issue of *Photoplay* was somewhat more arch:

> Here the characters have so much money that they just have to find something else to worry about. So, Ruth Chatterton, always the aristocrat, becomes torn between her love for a young author, George Brent, and the husband she's had for twelve years. Adrienne Dore and

Bette Davis are perfect "Park Avenue pests." It's all very leisurely, but you'll go crazy about Chatterton's gowns.

[Typical catty review of the day. Probably Chatterton had snubbed someone on the Photoplay *staff. All of us were subject often to revenge by the press for some action of ours. We still are.]*

4

Many a good brain has been found behind bars. After all,
Bunyan wrote Pilgrim's Progress *in prison, and Oscar*
Wilde wrote The Ballad of Reading Gaol *in a cell.*

BETTE DAVIS AS KAY RUSSELL
IN *The Dark Horse*

''B'' films, turned out with great alacrity in two or three weeks on
the Warner lot, consumed more time in preproduction and post-
production than in shooting. With sets being assembled and struck
daily, Bill Koenig, the studio manager, required tight coordination
between directors and supervisors (producers were not given screen
credit until the late 1930s) to assure that each picture had the proper
sets in working order and the right crews available when needed.

Since location work was frowned upon because of the enormous
expense of transporting cast and crew to distant points, the back lot
was used extensively for all scenes requiring massive exterior sets.
Interiors were constantly switched from picture to picture. The
observant movie fan would often look for—and spot—the same
wallpaper, fireplaces, furniture, and props from feature to feature.
With sixty-one pictures filmed in 1931 alone, all phases of production were kept busy. Yet a sense of family was in evidence from grip
to supervisor, from crew to supporting player. *[In retrospect, over a*
period of forty-odd years—1930-1974—I have been fond of more
members of my crews and counted them my best friends than I have
ever been fond of in my personal life. They will do anything for you,
given an even break. They are the greatest of human beings.] The
personnel working together often achieved a kind of repertoire
intimacy that particularly sheared below-the-line costs, contributing to fast shooting schedules.

The stars were kept so busy learning lines and working on

characterizations that few complaints were registered. When a player became difficult and rushed to the front office to see J.L., a good portion of sentiment or wit—depending upon the gravity of the beef—was administered, and great plans were cunningly alluded to *if* the errant actor would return to the set. This tactic almost always worked. The star, momentarily placated, resumed the current production, and work on the next picture followed immediately. Davis appeared in nine films in 1932, James Cagney in six in 1931, Edward G. Robinson in four in 1932, Joan Blondell in eleven in 1931, Kay Francis in seven in 1932, Frank McHugh in fifteen in 1933, and Warren William in seven in 1934. Directors were equally busy; Michael Curtiz and William Dieterle each guided six films in 1932.

"B" films, economically shot, were trimmed down to a fast hour or hour and five minutes by Warren Low, Owen Marks, George Amy, or William Holmes, fitting neatly into the lower half of a double bill. *[In my opinion Warren Low was the greatest editor at Warner Bros. I owe him a lot. He used to fight for me when something of mine was going to be cut that would hurt my performance. When Hal Wallis left Warner Bros. and formed his own company, he took Warren with him. They are still together. I'm sure Hal Wallis feels the same way about Warren Low.]*Even a screen buff could not always differentiate between an "A" or "B" film strictly by the players but could make the distinction within the first five minutes by counting the close-ups! Pictures shot on a lean budget featured few camera setups. Most scenes were established in medium long shots, and the camera would cut to a medium shot as the scene progressed. Close-ups, especially of women, took too much time and money to light and shoot for a quickie budget.

Pictures, ground out like sausages, were created for the moment—usually from topical subjects—for that special niche in the year's production lineup of "block booking." Today many of these "B" films turned out en masse during the 1930s are regarded as minor classics on the not-so-late-show yet were fashioned for movie-going consumption at a time when 90 million persons per week were stricken with the movie-going habit.

Zanuck and his supervisors always kept an eye on the newspapers and an ear to the radio for possible story material—a holdover from the old days when the studio was located on Sunset Boulevard and the wolf was at the door. With a sidelong glance at the depression and a possible change in the White House, Zanuck brought his comedy outline for *The Dark Horse* out of the trunk. Detailing political shenanigans, Joseph Jackson, Courtenay Terrett, and Wilson Mizner wrote the screenplay, which was assigned to director Alfred E. Green. Ray Griffith was the supervisor, and Warren William, Guy Kibbee, Frank McHugh, and Vivienne Osborne were the players. Bette Davis had already been set for the female lead, Kay Russell.

The feature, photographed by Sol Polito, was edited down to a furious seventy-five minutes by George Marks. Zanuck declined to take credit for the plot, and "story by anonymous" was listed in the credits.

Davis told *Screen Book* magazine in December, 1932, that she really did not want to go on the personal appearance tour in the East with Warren William after *The Dark Horse* finished filming. "I was afraid people would say, 'Who is she?' Personal appearances always give me the fear that the audience is going to be terrifically disappointed in me when compared with what they see on the screen."

She and William did a sketch at the Capitol Theatre, *The Burglar and the Lady,* a witty piece about two people who plan a robbery. The denouement comes when the stage manager calls "Cut" and the audience discovers it is a scene for a movie.

There was good press coverage, and Davis discovered that she was not only known but admired. She also garnered extra news space when William failed to show up for a press conference; she handled herself quite professionally, to the delight of the harried press agent.

A NEW KIND OF TEMPTRESS

Ah'd love t'kiss yo, but ah jes washed mah hayuh.
                    BETTE DAVIS AS MADGE NORWOOD
                    IN *Cabin in the Cotton*

[The above quote is my favorite line of all time in any film—with the exception of Margo Channing's "Fasten your seat belts—it's going to be a bumpy night."]

Michael Curtiz, the fiery Hungarian director, was engaged in the preproduction planning of *Cabin in the Cotton* while still shooting the thriller *Doctor X. Cabin in the Cotton* featured a Paul Green script based on the book by Harry Harrison Kroll. Richard Barthelmess, near the end of a distinguished career going back to the silents when he made $8,750 a week, was set to play Marvin Blake, an impoverished sharecropper's son. The thirty-seven-year-old actor, held over on an original First National contract, was increasingly difficult to cast because of his age bracket. For ten years he had tackled boyish roles. Several films, particularly *The Patent Leather Kid,* showed his age, but he had a decent fan following.

Zanuck visited Lionel Atwill and Fay Wray on the *Doctor X* set and casually mentioned to Curtiz that he felt Davis would be great as the seductive siren in *Cabin in the Cotton.* The director turned crimson and sputtered, "Are you kidding? Who would want to go to bed with her?"

Zanuck stood his ground. "She may surprise you."

Without a word Curtiz furiously turned back to the scene and left Zanuck chomping angrily on his cigar.

The head of production was used to the director's short-lived rages; they had worked together on some twenty-two films since 1927, and both turned out salable products that adhered to budget and shooting schedules.

It was true that Curtiz was the most versatile director on the lot. He could milk as many laughs out of comedy as he could tears from romance. A grim realist, his specialty was blood and guts. He was the terror of sissified actors who faked difficult scenes with stunt men. One of the favorite stories making the rounds concerned John Barrymore, who was watching that popular grind-a-foot, a marathon dance. His female companion remarked she didn't know how those "poor people could go on dancing for days on end." The Great Profile laughed, "That's nothing! Have you ever worked for Michael Curtiz?"

Zanuck surrounded Barthelmess with experienced players: Dorothy Jordan as the heroine, Henry B. Walthall (the famous little colonel in *Birth of a Nation),* Berton Churchill, Walter Percival, and Hardie Albright of *So Big,* again cast as Davis's juvenile love interest.

The story begins on the old Peckerwood plantation (possibly more fully realized than Patrick Dennis's grotesque estate of the same name in *Auntie Mame* twenty-six years later on the same sound stage) where owner-planter Norwood has been cheating the tenant farmers at the company store. Barthelmess, the bookkeeper, is taken under the commodious wing of the planter, whose daughter Madge fancies she is in love with the poor accountant. Norwood forms a posse, which searches out and lynches a cotton thief, and, in return, the sharecroppers burn the store—containing records of indebtedness. The climax of the picture is reached when Barthelmess arranges a truce between the two factions.

Davis's big scene occurs when she sings,

Did you ever hear the story 'bout Willy the Weeper?
Made his livin' as a chimney sweeper.
He had the dope habit and he had it bad.
Sister while I tell ya 'bout the dreams he had the

Teet tee dee dee—tont too doo doo doo-doo
Yah dee dah dah, dee dee dee dah dah!

[Cab Calloway made "Willy the Weeper," an old folk song, into "Minnie the Moocher" later.]

The sequence was shot in a hammock, Davis on top of Barthelmess. She has since revealed that, although she liked her leading man personally, his method of acting was foreign to her. He did absolutely nothing in the long shots, followed basic stage directions for medium shots, and reserved his talent for the close-ups. *[In that way it was necessary to use his close-ups almost entirely.]*

Curtiz lurked about the set like a man bent on revenge and made nasty remarks that could be heard all over the sound stage; sample: "God-damned lousy actress!"

[Curtiz put me through a "trial by fire." But, because of Mr. Zanuck's belief that I could play this part, I was determined not to let Mr. Curtiz ruin it for me. I knew I could play it also. Actually this part was the first indication of my niche on the screen. Had Zanuck stayed at Warner Bros., I think he would have found other parts in this same vein. Those who remained in charge didn't seem to realize a quality I displayed in this role. Guess they didn't think I was sexy. I thought I was!!]

When the film opened at the Strand Theatre in New York on September 29, 1932, the critics liked the way Davis tackled the role. *The New York American* noted, "that flashy, luminous newcomer, Bette Davis, romps off with the first honors, for hers is the most dashing and colorful role . . . The girl is superb"; while

The New York Herald Tribune found, "Miss Davis shows a surprising vivacity as the seductive rich girl."

After *Cabin in the Cotton,* Davis looked forward to an even better part in her next film. Instead, she was billed fourth in a seedy melodrama.

A MATCHLESS TRIO

It must be a grand feeling to get everything you want.
BETTE DAVIS AS RUTH WESCOTT
IN *Three on a Match*

[As to the dialogue quote above—Ha! I certainly wasn't getting anything I wanted by being cast in Three on a Match.*]*

Griffith had a screenplay by Lucien Hubbard on his desk called *Three on a Match,* based on an original story by Kubec Glasmon and John Bright, which detailed in a leisurely fashion the lives of three girls over a twelve-year period.

But the saying around which the story was framed (that three on a match means one will die soon) was actually the inspiration of Swedish Match King Ivar Kreuger, who conceived the idea solely to boost sales. Supposedly the "superstition" originated in the trenches during World War I, when the last soldier to light a cigarette from the same match was killed because the flame burned long enough to attract enemy fire. An insert of a newspaper debunking the legend was used prominently in the script. Further interest was heightened while the picture was being shot when Kreuger, rather than face bankruptcy, committed suicide on March 12, 1932.

Since all directors on the lot were filming except Mervyn LeRoy, who was preparing *I Am a Fugitive from a Chain Gang* to star vacationing Paul Muni, J.L. ordered him to shoot *Three on a Match* before Muni returned. *[Mr. LeRoy, while being interviewed after he'd finished* Three on a Match, *told the reporter that Bette Davis would never have any kind of a career at all. I'm glad you were wrong, Mervyn.]* LeRoy, married to Harry Warner's daughter Doris, was a former song-and-dance man who had been "inherited" along with the First National regime. While he had no personal filming style, he was adaptable and had worked well with Edward G. Robinson in *Little Caesar.*

The cast was composed from the usual Warner stock company: Joan Blondell, Warren William, Ann Dvorak, Grant Mitchell, Lyle Talbot, Glenda Farrell, Humphrey Bogart, Allen Jenkins, Jack LaRue, and Edward Arnold.

Davis had a few sexually oriented scenes: she put on her hose attired in a chemise, and later at Zuma Beach—where she happened to be living at the time—dressed in a provocative swim suit, she posed for fan book photos. *[One of the few times I permitted myself to pose for "cheese cake"—can't think why I allowed this set of pictures to be taken. Must have been in a much too willing mood.]*

The device of beginning a story in childhood, then picking up the main action with the principals later in life, was much in vogue. Used cleverly, a slight story could be instilled with more than warranted importance. With *Three on a Match* nothing was gained by starting with three little orphans on a playground or later showing them in reform school. Their adventures after graduation made up the major section of the film. An expert montage (making use of headlines and the current music of the day) leisurely brought the story from 1919 to 1931.

A memorable moment occurs in the reform school sequence when Sheila Terry, accompanying herself on the piano, sings "My Diane" in a clear, bell-like soprano. The trio meet as adults and light up cigarettes. Dvorak is the bored, unhappy wife of millionaire Warren William; Blondell is an entertainer (the budget was too low to allow a musical number); and Davis is a stenographer who later becomes a nursemaid-tutoress to Dvorak's child when she leaves her husband for a cheap hood (Lyle Talbot, in a vigorous performance) who kidnaps her son.

Sol Polito used a kind of *film noir* feeling in photographing the story, filming Dvorak's décline realistically; her spectacular fall is brilliantly recorded for the camera. *[Was always impressed with Ann Dvorak's performances. She also was a smashingly nice person.]*

Reviews were lukewarm; in fact, *The New York Times* felt it was "distasteful." *[Have often disagreed with reviews in* The New York Times, *particularly when they disapproved of me, naturally, but this time they were right!]* Honorable mentions deservedly went to Dvorak.

Zanuck thought Davis and David Manners might create an interesting twosome in *They Call It Sin,* which detailed the adventures of a midwestern girl who falls for callous sophisticate Louis Calhern. The parts were eventually taken by Loretta Young and George Brent.

THE VIRGIN MARRIES

Harmon O. Nelson finally persuaded Davis to marry him. It was a spur-of-the-moment decision on her part, and they started out for Yuma, Arizona, after midnight on August 18, 1932. The wedding party, in two cars, consisted of Ruthie, Bobby, an aunt, a cousin, and two poodles.

Davis told interviewer Gladys Hall for *Modern Screen:* "Came dawn and we were still a hundred miles from Yuma, which was hundreds of miles more than we had thought. The thermometer registered 107 in the shade! Ham and I had not spoken one word the whole way. It was on the tip of my tongue to say, 'This is horrible, I won't go on.' Ruthie stopped me. She sensed the furies boiling and said, 'Let's not go on,' which was, of course, the one divinely inspired thing to say, for the mule in me immediately gave a back kick of the heels and told Ham to step on the gas.

"We arrived in Yuma. Everyone was soaked to the skin. We managed to get three hotel rooms. We all took baths and sat around draped in the counterpanes while our wet rags dried. Ham had to go out and get a new shirt and a wedding ring. I kept muttering, 'This is so awful, it's funny!'

"When asked whether this was my first marriage, I said, 'My third.' That got back to the studio!

"We were married in the house of a Methodist minister. The two poodles washed themselves all through the ceremony. I wore a two-piece beige street dress that resembled the sands of the Arizona desert after the rain it never gets, brown accessories, and two limp gardenias. I kept thinking of the picture I'd always had of myself as a bride—dewy and divine in white satin and orange blossoms, coming up a white-ribboned aisle to the strains of Mendelssohn."

THE CASTLE ON THE HUDSON

Oh, don't do it, Tom, don't do it. . . . You promised you wouldn't leave me—you've gotta stay with me . . . Don't

> *do it, please. Please give me the gun, for my sake—I
> won't let you go back up there . . . Now you're free.*
>
> BETTE DAVIS AS FAY
> IN *20,000 Years in Sing Sing*

In fall, 1932, Curtiz showed a print of *Cabin in the Cotton* to RKO
director John Cromwell, who was interested in using Barthelmess
for a picture. But it was not the hero of the piece who caught his eye.
Davis's exciting bitch caused his imagination to rise; her screen
presence and sincerity illuminated the screen.

Cromwell discovered that Pandro Berman of RKO had purchased
W. Somerset Maugham's best seller *Of Human Bondage* for Leslie
Howard. Cromwell felt that Davis was right for the part of the
unpleasant waitress-slattern-tramp, Mildred Rogers. Berman
agreed. The part was such a departure in terms of screen heroines
that it would be difficult to sell to an established star.

Wilson Mizner, who always had his ear affixed to the Hollywood
underground, brought the novel to Davis who was playing her first
gun moll, Fay, in *20,000 Years in Sing Sing* (which he coscripted
with Brown Holmes from the best seller by Warden Lewis E.
Lawes). She read the book with growing fascination, overcome
with the same compulsion to get her teeth into the part of Mildred as
she had years before when Blanche Yurka cast her in the dream part
of Hedvig in the Ibsen stage drama *The Wild Duck*. J.L. refused to
loan her to RKO for *Of Human Bondage*.

Originally James Cagney had been set for the hard-nosed mobster
Tom Connors, who believes his political friends will get him a
parole on a felony conviction in *20,000 Years in Sing Sing*. But the
fiery little Irishman was having one of his periodic battles with the
studio. Having made eleven hit pictures in his two years under
contract, he was a valuable property. By the time his $1,250 per
week was raised to the demanded $3,000, the picture was already in
production with Spencer Tracy, who was borrowed from MGM.
Cagney went into *Hard to Handle,* which, ironically, was shot on an
adjoining sound stage.

Curtiz used a harsh semidocumentary style, which perfectly
captured the doomed half-world of the prison. Davis was thrilled to
work with Tracy, whom she had admired since her stage days in
New York. Their chemistry lent conviction to the strange romance.
[That is the only time I ever worked with Spencer Tracy. One of my

great dreams in later years was that we could find a really great script to do together. Spencer and I were both born on April 5. What a marvelous actor he was. How we all miss him.]

Curtiz, possibly because of the excellent Davis notices in *Cabin in the Cotton,* found less wrong with her acting style. Besides, he had violence galore to stage, and he was never better than when pulling out all the stops in a rough-and-tumble fight. Since this was essentially a man's picture, he actually paid scant attention to Davis and in fact did not reshoot when her head lolled to one side in a key bed scene. For several moments the audience gazes up her nostrils, while Tracy is enjoying a flattering profile view. Cinematographer Barney McGill, however, lit a couple of marvelous close-ups framed artistically by the pillow.

Davis was unusually attractive in Orry-Kelly's fur-tipped cape, cloche, and gloves flared at the wrist in her first scene, where she visits Tracy in prison. When he wants to know how she can afford obviously expensive attire, she shows up the second time in a mannish black suit, with a black necktie and dark felt hat!

The irony of the ending is that Fay, who killed the hood who betrayed her boyfriend, is let off scot-free, while felon Tracy goes to the electric chair. This tactic would not have been permitted a couple of years later, when the new code was in force, but it added a realistic touch to the plot.

Davis's most difficult sequence was not the hysterical bed scene but involved her handling a gun. Terrified of firearms, it took all of her courage to fire the pistol. She never conquered this fear, and in later films, when the action required maneuvering a gun, she always broke out in a cold sweat.

THE SECRETARY WITH A PAST

One of those "high-in-the-sky-airplane-hijinks-and-the-women-who-wait-below" epics was programmed as Davis's next picture, called, appropriately enough, *Parachute Jumper.* Based on a Rian James story, *Some Call It Love,* the screenplay was written by John Francis Larkin, who made clever use of aerial "stock" footage and leftover newsreel "out-takes." A sixty-five-minute program, action was substituted for plot, and Alfred E. Green directed in hurried, slapdash manner.

Mordaunt Hall in the January 26, 1933, edition of *The New York Times* reported that Davis was the secretary, Alabama, "who speaks with a most decided Southern drawl." Claire Dodd is the rich-bitch mistress of racketeer Weber, played by Leo Carrillo, who employs Douglas Fairbanks, Jr., as her chauffeur. He is later hired by the hood in "perhaps one of the most unique positions on record in real life or on the screen. He is paid to sit behind a screen with two pistols ready to fire on any of Weber's threatening callers."

There is dope smuggling by air, hijackers, and the sort of breathless action that would attract the Tailspin Tommy adolescent. (In 1961, selecting footage for the prologue to *What Ever Happened to Baby Jane?* producer-director Robert Aldrich chose a scene from *Parachute Jumper* and *Ex-Lady* to document the fact that the young Jane was a flop as a movie star.)

Davis hated *Parachute Jumper* and refused to do *The Mind Reader,* with Warren William, in which director Roy Del Ruth wanted her to play the girl friend of the clairvoyant; Constance Cummings took the part.

This was a low point in her career, and once again George Arliss came to the rescue, asking her to be his leading lady in *The Working Man. [It was wonderful to work with Mr. Arliss again. This time, with lots of work behind me, I was far more secure and not as frightened of this great man as I was in* The Man Who Played God. *Sitting on the set one day between takes, Mr. Arliss said to me, "My little bird has flown, hasn't she?" He was right. Again I say, I owe my first big chance on the screen to him.]*

Based on a novel by Edgar Franklin, *The Adopted Father,* the plot was a perfect example of depression-day entertainment. A shoe manufacturer (Arliss), bored with his own company, turns the management over to a nephew and goes on a fishing trip to Maine. While landing flounder and bass, he meets a reckless brother-and-sister team—Jenny (Davis) and Tommy (Theodore Newton)—devoted to jazz and cocktails, who turn out to be the children of his biggest rival in the shoe business. Incognito, he is given a job in the factory and reorganizes the routine until he becomes a sharp rival of his nephew! He also reorganizes the lives of the shiftless youngsters, who get jobs and become "proper citizens."

Davis, as the madcap debutante, was photographed beautifully by Sol Polito. John Adolfi directed the screenplay by Maude T. Howell and Charles Kenyon with a sure flair for gentle comedy. Arliss again had a hand in selecting her wardrobe and told Orry-

Kelly to discard a low-cut negligee for a more sedate high-at-the-neck nightgown. The old man did not believe in cleavage.

Three days after *The Working Man* was press previewed, a hurricane hit the studio. Zanuck walked out on his $5,000-a-week contract on twenty-four-hour notice.

5

What do you mean you think I have a good figure?
BETTE DAVIS AS HELEN BAUER
IN *Ex-Lady*

On March 4, 1933, the Great Depression came to a head when Franklin D. Roosevelt enforced a three-day "bank holiday." Pushing the panic button, the studios collectively asked the Academy of Motion Picture Arts and Sciences to intervene in industry relations. With pressure on all sides, the Academy appointed an emergency committee, which, after meeting with the employers' committee, came up with an interim solution: *graduated pay cuts for all industry personnel.*

Besides the highly paid hierarchy at Warner Bros. the stars in the upper brackets would receive as much as 50 percent salary cuts: Ruth Chatterton and William Powell at $6,000 a week; Kay Francis, Douglas Fairbanks, Jr., and Edward G. Robinson at $4,000; and James Cagney at $3,000, as well as sundry executives in the $1,000 and $2,000 bracket. Other personnel were given a 20 percent cut.

The lot was especially quiet. Most of the contract players were on a long publicity whistle-stop junket to Washington for the inauguration. The Forty-Second Street Special, a glittering train of stars, was scheduled to stop in thirty-two cities in thirty-two days as the picture of the same name was opening. The trip served as a makeshift honeymoon for the Nelsons. The moratorium caught the train in Boston, where scrip was issued to players witout cash. Warner Bros. permitted box office money collected in their theaters to be dispensed to executives in charge of the train.

42nd Street, which would make screen history and start a new trend of musical pictures at every studio in town, had been personally supervised by Zanuck, but Warner Bros. was still in great financial trouble and would lose $3,761,224 during the year. The studio, looking at improved grosses, the new films in the can awaiting release, and the national outlook toward business with Roosevelt and his New Deal, jubilantly announced that, as of April 1, salary cuts would be restored. Many technicians had been laid off—notably Colonel N. S. Slaughter, Arthur Haddock, and Walter Wolf—all sound men.

April 1 passed, and no cuts were restored. Zanuck was furious, feeling that the employees would hold him responsible. He could not understand the do-nothing attitude of the front office and regarded the silence as a slap in the face. When April 15 brought no change in the pay checks, he went to see J.L. and Harry, and a tremendous fight ensued. Zanuck handed in his resignation on twenty-four-hour notice. The word spread around the studio like wildfire, with Zanuck's prestige running high—even among associates who had often enough felt the sting of his temper or the stigma of his decisions. It was the first time in Warner Bros. history that a high-ranking executive had dramatically championed a cause for the employees.

Zanuck was now thirty years old, and his ability was well appreciated around town. Although he had many offers from rival studios, he wanted to carve a bigger niche for himself in the industry. The boy wonder took himself over to United Artists, where he formed Twentieth Century Pictures with William Goetz and Joseph Schenck. In order to complete the financial obligations connected with the new company, Louis B. Mayer of MGM advanced $750,000 to Goetz (his son-in-law), and Nicholas Schenck loaned a like amount to his brother. Zanuck, at $5,000 per week (presumably having shared some profits with Warner Bros. since 1927), had saved a similar cache.

At the producers' level the most logical executive to take over head of production was Hal Blum Wallis, whose creative ability had been in evidence since he had been promoted from head of publicity to full producer.

As careful a man as Zanuck had been, there still remained tremendous work on pictures currently before the cameras, as well as the selection of new story material. Wallis's job was by no means an eight-hour-day affair. He immediately placed "escapist" material into production, in the form of light frothy comedies, love stories with smart sets and elaborate costumes, and musicals with fantastic dance routines choreographed by Busby Berkeley, as well as continuing the gangster cycle.

Forty years later Bette Davis was to say that Hal Wallis was responsible for her career. *[It was Hal Wallis, as head of production at Warner Bros., who raised my status as regards scripts and directors.* Jezebel *was the* real *beginning of my box office years as a prestige star. He hired William Wyler as the director; he gave me a superb cast. For the next five or six years he brought me one great property after the other. Without material there can be no progress in an acting career; next, no progress without a truly talented director. William Wyler is my all-time choice for the greatest films—directorially. Certainly he sped my career onward and upward.]*

Several months before Zanuck left to form Twentieth Century Pictures, he decided to bow to the demands of exhibitors, reviewers, and fans by officially billing Davis's name over the title of a picture. He selected the remake of a Barbara Stanwyck picture made the year before, called *Illicit,* and assigned David Boehm to rewrite the original story by Edith Fitzgerald and Robert Riskin. The finished script—renamed *Ex-Lady*—read well, the dialogue appeared witty, and there were a number of rather daring scenes. This was a year before the production code was inaugurated, and actresses regularly appeared in chemises and teddies; chorines were often shown seminaked, covered with strings of beads or other decorative paraphernalia.

Lucien Hubbard was appointed production supervisor, and Robert Florey, late of Universal, was signed as director. J.L. met Florey, far afield from the *Rue Morgue,* while having dinner one night at the Musso Frank Grill on Hollywood Boulevard, and a contract developed.

Zanuck advised cinematographer Tony Gaudio to make Davis as beautiful as possible, and he spent a great deal of time in lighting her correctly. Orry-Kelly designed the costumes, 60 percent of which were sheer negligees and underwear!

Gene Raymond, free of his contract at Fox, was signed as leading man; others in the small cast were Frank McHugh, Monroe Owsley, Claire Dodd, Kay Strozzi, Ferdinand Gottschalk, Alphonse Ethier, and Bodil Rosing.

Harold McLernon edited the final product down to two minutes over an hour, and the result was still repugnant. Davis was embarrassed over the half-naked billboards, the risqué dialogue, and the titular part. Andre Sennwald's review in *The New York Times* on May 15, 1933, was typical of how most critics viewed the finished product:

> Bette Davis, a young actress who has shown intelligence in the roles assigned to her in the films, has had the misfortune to be cast in the principal role of *Ex-Lady* now on view at the Strand. What that somewhat sinister event meant to her employers was that Miss Davis, having shown herself to be possessed of the proper talent and pictorial allure, now became a star in her own right. What it meant to her embarrassed admirers at the Strand on Thursday night was that Miss Davis had to spend an uncomfortable amount of her time en deshabille in boudoir scenes engaged in repartee and in behavior which were sometimes timidly suggestive, then depressingly naive and mostly downright foolish.

[I could not have said it better. Mr. Zanuck was unwise to force stardom upon me—I wasn't box office enough as yet to carry a film, and a more unsuitable part in a cheaper type film I don't think could have been found to launch me into stardom. It was a disaster. The Hollywood Reporter *review I have never forgotten. It said, "Why didn't Warners shoot the entire script of* Ex-Lady *in one bedroom on one bed."]*

But *Ex-Lady* was an example of the Davis pattern. Given a good part with sensitive direction, she could be delightfully serene, reading lines with assurance and tenderness. Her study of the character she was playing always brought out unusual traits to give the part punch, but, if the other players walked through their roles, as was often the case, her performance would stand out in bas-relief. Her hard work would seem too intense.

Her next film was a potboiler that was more than usually un-believable.

CRIME, INC.

> Curiosity got the better of me. I wanted to see what I'd
> look like in a coffin.
>
> BETTE DAVIS AS NORMA PHILLIPS
> IN *Bureau of Missing Persons*

[I found out!!!]

Bureau of Missing Persons was of the "calling all cars, follow
that cab" type of fast-paced police story, shot on a tight budget in a
series of crowded interior sets of dark offices, cramped diners, and
sleazy hotel rooms. The few exteriors featured murky background
projection. The production was supervised by Henry Blanke and
directed by Roy Del Ruth from a screenplay by Robert Presnell
(based on the book *Missing Men* by Police Captain John H. Ayers
and Carol Bird). It was the sort of cheapie that Warner Bros. turned
out at the rate of forty a year. Although top billed, followed by
Lewis Stone and Pat O'Brien, Davis did not appear until the third
reel and then in only six scenes.

The meager plot dealt with several cases, cast with stereotyped
actors, handled by the bureau. One running gag involved comic
Hugh Herbert (playing straight), one of the bureau's boys who is
constantly seeking a woman named Gwendolyn Harris, who
eventually turns out to be clerk Ruth Donnelly, working under his
very nose!

Davis's vignette saw her applying to the bureau for aid in finding
her husband, murdered ten days before in Chicago. In the usual
switch, she is actually wanted for the murder of Therme Roberts,
her employer, whom she claims has an insane twin brother who was
the real murder victim. She then disappears, and her clothing is
found by the East River. Believing she is not really dead, the bureau
publishes her picture in the paper, saying the body has been found
and a $200 funeral is held using the body of a "hop head." When
Davis shows up to view the body, Roberts also appears and is
nabbed for the murder of his idiot brother.

The only thing imaginative about the film was the main titles,
which (to save lab costs) were composed of a type-set title and a
stack of photographs of the stars. A hand simply reached into the
frame and removed the cards.

There were bits of unintentional hilarity. For instance, when a
ransom note arrives demanding that money be attached to a carrier

pigeon, Stone seriously tells the boys to hire a plane and follow the bird to the kidnapers!

The reviews were of the "ho-hum" variety.

THE WORLD OF HAUTE COUTURE

In fall, 1933, with Davis raising hell about her last few pictures and begging to be loaned to RKO for *Of Human Bondage,* J.L. and Wallis looked over the properties on tap. They selected a musical-of-a-sort, *The Fashion Plate,* by Harry Collins and Warren Duff, about New York dress pirates who copy Paris *haut monde* fashions. The story was slight but timely, and a brace of contract writers were assigned to the script: F. Hugh Herbert, Gene Markey, Kathryn Scola, and Carl Erickson. The star was to be the expensive William Powell, assisted by the reliable Frank McHugh, the sophisticated Verree Teasdale, and many of the Warner stock company.

Since Davis was cast as Powell's glamorous assistant, Perc Westmore was *ordered* to give her "the business." He fashioned a sleek Garbo-like platinum wig, made up her face heavily, and added long, false eyelashes—the full Hollywood glamour treatment.

Orry-Kelly had a field day in designing "Paris" creations. His mentor, Paul Periot, who had influenced his early work, was the inspiration for what Hollywood thought Paris would be wearing the next year. He made Davis into a clotheshorse, delighted to at last get away from little dressmaker suits: furs and furbelows replaced Peter Pan collars and straight buttoned tunics. The film's title was changed to *Fashions of 1934.*

Busby Berkeley did the choreography, which featured chorus girls disguised as harps, but the trusty William Dieterle directed the "straight" scenes.

[Never again did I allow anyone to go against my type with makeup, hair, etc. There was nothing left of Bette Davis in this film. I had hit the bottom of the barrel. What I individually had to contribute as an actress was possibly not going to make it, but there was only one way to go. No makeup in the world was going to turn me into a glamour star such as Harlow. It just wasn't my type.]

When she went once more to J.L. and pleaded for the role of Mildred in *Of Human Bondage* at RKO, he put her into a crime melodrama, the title of which told the plot—*The Big Shakedown.*

DEBUT OF A STAND-IN—SALLY SAGE

Robert Florey, back on the lot after filming backgrounds in the Orient for *Oil for the Lamps of China,* and author Emil Ludwig began negotiations with J.L. for a film about Napoleon to star Edward G. Robinson in the title role and Davis as Empress Josephine, with Reginald Owen as Talleyrand. The project failed, only because Robinson turned down the part.

The role of Norma Frank in *The Big Shakedown* was little more than a bit, and the exploitation boys went light on publicity. A new stand-in was employed for Davis. Her name was Sally Sage, an aspiring actress, and she would pose under the lights for the star in thirty-seven films. Charles Farrell, who had made eleven memorable pictures with Janet Gaynor, was deemed a proper leading man, while Ricardo Cortez played the heavy. Glenda Farrell (no relation to Charles) had the best female role—that of Lil, a bawdy, shady lady.

The trite screenplay by Niven Busch and Rian James, from an original story by Samuel Engel, *Cut Rate,* dealt with the counterfeit drug racket. The film was supervised by Samuel Bischoff, who told a newshen, "If you want anything out of Davis—say overtime—let someone without executive authority ask her, and she'll always say, 'Sure, for you I'll do it!' "

John Francis Dillon, who had directed such feminists as Mary Pickford and Clara Bow, was not at his best with the flimsy story but devised an exciting opening sequence detailing the life-style of postprohibition racketeers. For a bedroom sequence Dillon wanted to add a suggestive footnote to Davis's performance. He "back lit" the scene strongly, but his leading lady, knowing what he was striving for, showed up with her filmy nightgown *fully lined.* He did not get his sexy body profile through the material after all.

Early in the year Davis was handed the script of *The Case of the Howling Dog,* the first Perry Mason film, which she refused to do; Mary Astor was assigned the role of Bessie Foley, with Warren William as Mason and newcomer Helen Trenholme as Della Street. As it turned out, the picture got fair reviews and was intelligently directed by Alan Crosland.

James Cagney, who had momentarily settled a new beef with the studio, was given the title role in *Always a Gent,* released as *Jimmy the Gent.* Based on an original story by Laird Doyle and Ray Nazarro, *The Heir Chaser,* who took the theme of missing heirs

Madge Norwood (Bette Davis), rich plantation owner's daughter, plans to seduce share-cropper Marvin Blake (Richard Barthelmess) in *Cabin in the Cotton*, in 1932. (*Photograph by Warner Bros., from the collection of Gunnard Nelson.*)

Helen Bauer (Bette Davis) and Don Peterson (Gene Raymond) are in a "lights out" mood in Davis's first starring picture, *Ex-Lady*, in 1933. Filmed before the production code, it led one reviewer to remark that it could have been shot in one bed. (*Photograph by Warner Bros.*)

Sitting between Frank McHugh and William Powell in *Fashions of 1934*, 1934. Davis was almost unrecognizable as a platinum blonde. The salon saleslady was Verree Teasdale. (*Photograph by Warner Bros.*)

Silver Slipper entrepreneur Johnny Ramirez (Paul Muni) humors hi
drunken employer Charlie Roark (Eugene Pallette), while young wife
Marie (Bette Davis) regards the proceedings with disgust, in *Bordertown*, 1935. (*Photograph by Warner Bros., from the collection of Gunnard Nelson.*)

Davis and sister
Bobby on the set of
Bordertown in 1934.
(*Photograph by
Warner Bros., from
the collection of
Robert F. Silvia.*)

from the tabloids, and screenplayed by Bertram Milhauser, the film was directed with such a hectic pace by Michael Curtiz that even nonsense seemed logical.

Curtiz, who could direct action melodramas with his eyes closed, was a bit gentler than usual with his cast—probably out of exhaustion. Davis was cast as a secretary again and had little to do, although she was given billing directly under Cagney. These two stars, constantly at odds at this time with the studio, were disconsolate because they were never cast in an important film together. Seven years later when they made the unrewarding comedy *The Bride Came C.O.D.*, it was only because the studio wanted stars to have a change of pace, but both went back to drama.

Hal Wallis told Joyce Haber in January, 1971, "In the old days, you might have Bogart in a picture and use an unknown; it gave us a chance to build a girl. Or you might have Bette Davis and use a man." The point was not to use two expensive top stars together if one could carry a film alone. The exceptions were historical pictures or a book or play that demanded two stars of the first water. Thus, for her next feature, *Fog over Frisco,* Davis was given top billing over Donald Woods and Margaret Lindsay by supervisor Henry Blanke. *[This was the second time I was directed by William Dieterle and almost the beginning of my professional relationship with Henry Blanke, a producer of infinite taste, an understanding man, whatever our problems. He was a great contributor to the Warner product during the great Hal Wallis years at Warner Bros. He was an enormous contributor to my personal career. The part in* Fog over Frisco *was one I adored. It also was a very good script, directed superbly by Dieterle.]*

THE FEMME FATALE

Housewife, next on the agenda, cast her as sexpot Patricia Berkerley, opposite George Brent and Ann Dvorak, a happily married couple that she tries to break up. The advertising business gets a workout in this one as copywriter Davis turns out a hit radio commercial for Dupree cosmetics (with actual music and lyrics courtesy of Mort Dixon and Allie Wrubel). When Brent is about to fall for the charms of the seductress, he realizes he still loves his wife, and they are reconciled. *[Dear God! What a horror!]*

A DATE WITH DR. FREUD

You're nothing but a barroom bouncer . . . You'll al-
ways be one. If it wasn't for me, you'd still be rolling
drunks at the Silver Slipper. I made you rich, I put those
swell clothes on your back. Now, just because you got
your neck washed, you think you're a gentleman. No one
can make you that—you're riffraff, and so am I. You
belong to me, and you're going to stay with me because
I'm holding on to you. I committed murder to get you!
                                    BETTE DAVIS AS MARIE ROARK
                                    IN *Bordertown*

Paul Muni, after finishing *Hi, Nellie!* (playing the managing editor
of a newspaper reduced to writing a sob-sister column), came back
to the lot to star as an unsuccessful Mexican lawyer-turned-
gambling-casino-entrepreneur, Johnny Ramirez, in *Bordertown*.
Archie Mayo directed the screenplay by Laird Doyle and Wallace
Smith from an adaptation by Robert Lord, who, in turn, culled *his*
material from the novel by Carroll Graham. J.L. and Wallis cast
Davis in the meaty role of Marie Roark, a nympho married to a fat,
impotent old man, Eugene Pallette, who owns a casino located in a
town on the Mexican border—probably Tijuana.

The first scenes of the film included establishing shots of Olvera
Street in downtown Los Angeles, and there was reality depicted in
unraveling scenes of racial discrimination. Muni becomes disbarred
when he fails to prepare a case properly and in humiliation becomes
a bouncer at Pallette's toilet. Turning the joint into a first-class
gambling emporium that attracts a society crowd, he becomes
infatuated with debutante Margaret Lindsay, who playfully calls
him "savage."

Davis appears in the third reel, playing the sexually un-
dernourished Marie in a fast and passionate style in Orry-Kelly's
bias-cut, beaded, and sequined evening gowns and fur-trimmed
suits. Tony Gaudio brought a drab, documentary flavor to the
cinematography, capturing exactly the hopelessness of the Mexican
ghetto as contrasted to the brightly lighted, garish atmosphere of the
Silver Slipper.

One beautifully realized scene occurs where Davis, looking
lovely in a chiffon negligee, tries to compromise Muni, who refuses

to be seduced. She becomes maudlin: "The only fun I get is feeding the gold fish—and they eat only once a day!" and "You've an adding machine where your heart ought to be!" (Fifteen years later, in *All about Eve,* she has an almost identical line when she tells Anne Baxter, "You can always put that award where your heart ought to be!")

Pallette had a moment that would become famous: He proudly displayed his new "painless Parker" store-bought teeth to the denizens in his dive.

Davis asphyxiates her drunken husband in the garage, and his death preys on her mind. She paces through the empty mansion. To her houseboy she cries, "Stop creeping around!" to which he replies, "I no cleep, walky same alla time!" Each successive scene shows more mental deterioration. In the courtroom scene, when she is being tried for murdering her husband, Marie finally goes insane while on the stand.

Davis told an interviewer, "When I firmly and sincerely believed I should play my role in a certain way, I wasn't afraid to argue about it with my director. I put up a terrific fight to play Marie in *Bordertown* the way I finally did. They wanted me to be a raving lunatic in the courtroom scene, pull my hair, and scream. That is the only way insanity had been played on the screen up to that time. Insanity is a mental illness—you can see it in the eyes, most of all in the speech."

[At the end of shooting of Bordertown *I was called to the front office and told that no one in the audience would know I was insane in the courtroom scene. I said, if this should be so at the preview, I would willingly retake the scene and play it in the usual hair-pulling way. I was never asked to do a retake. The part of Marie was a marvelous acting part—a step in the direction of where I wanted my career to go. I wanted to be known as an actress, not necessarily a star, although that would be the frosting on the cake if it should ever come about. I sincerely doubted at this point that it would ever happen.]*

Davis took up her vigil once more, still determined to play Mildred in *Of Human Bondage.* Worn down by her constant begging to play this part, J.L. finally said yes. *[If my memory is correct, he said, "Go and hang yourself." An evil heroine such as Mildred was really unheard of in that day. J.L. could not possibly understand any actress who would want to play such a part.]* With

Bordertown in the cutting room, *Jimmy the Gent, Fog over Frisco,* and *Housewife* in the can, plenty of Davis product awaited distributors.

Mervyn LeRoy, preparing *Sweet Adeline,* the Jerome Kern musical with Donald Woods, still had not cast the title role. It was arranged that RKO would loan Irene Dunne to Warner Bros. in exchange for Davis. It was thought at the time that RKO got the short end of the stick.

Frank Capra, preparing *It Happened One Night* at Columbia, was having great difficulty casting the role of the wacky spoiled heiress and had been turned down by a number of comediennes. Thinking Davis had the right chemistry, he tentatively asked J.L. if she was available for loan-out. Having put up with her demands for so long concerning Mildred, he refused. Two loan-out pictures in a row for a Warner star? Never! Claudette Colbert was finally persuaded to do the part. Davis lost her one chance to appear with Clark Gable on the screen, and Colbert won an Academy Award for a role she did not really want to play.

[I was heartbroken to miss It Happened One Night. *As for working with Gable—what a thrill it would have been, to say nothing of working with Capra, one of the all-time directors for years! However, of the two, at that time, I'm sure Mildred furthered my career more than* It Happened One Night *would have. Why couldn't I have had the good fortune to be in both? Warner Bros. loaned me out only one more time in all the eighteen years—to Sam Goldwyn in 1941 for* The Little Foxes *directed by William Wyler.]*

6

Yew cad, yew dirty swine. I never cared for yew—not once. I was always making a fool of yuh. Yuh bored me stiff. I hated yuh. It made me sick when I had to let yuh kiss me. I only did it because yuh begged me. Yuh hounded me, yuh drove me crazy, and, after yuh kissed me, I always used to wipe my mouth. Wipe my mouth. But I made up for it—for every kiss I had to laugh. We laughed at yuh, Miller and me and Griffith and me. We laughed at yuh because yuh were such a mug, a mug, a monster. You're a cripple, a cripple, a cripple!

BETTE DAVIS AS MILDRED ROGERS
IN *Of Human Bondage*

The most difficult aspect in portraying Mildred realistically was the learning of the Cockney accent. Leslie Howard, who was to play Philip Carey, the clubfooted antihero, was aghast at Davis, an American, playing Mildred with a British cast.

Davis asked an Englishwoman familiar with the way girls like Mildred spoke to live in her house for eight weeks prior to the start of the picture. Morning, noon, and night she listened to the strange mode of speech and worked tirelessly on the accent.

"I even answered the telephone with it," she told an interviewer, "and naturally I nearly drove my family mad. Poor Ham walked out of the house more than once and swore he'd never come back until I stopped talking like a Cockney. But Mildred meant everything to me. I was to sink or swim with Mildred. It was worth it when I found that I had mastered the accent well enough to win the praise of the British cast."

With John Cromwell directing the Pandro S. Berman production, the supporting players were exceptionally well cast: Frances Dee, Kay Johnson, Alan Hale, Desmond Roberts, and three Reginalds—Denny, Owen, and Sheffield. Cinematographer Henry W. Gerrard brilliantly captured the shabby realism of stark middle-class London—cheap restaurants, bleak hospital rooms, apartments filled with clutter and bric-a-brac—all carefully researched by art directors Van Nest Polglase and Carroll Clark.

Walter Plunkett (who should have won an Oscar for his lush period gowns in *Gone with the Wind*) masterfully designed the wardrobe—print and polka-dot frocks, a silk dress with acres of ruffles worn with a wide, floppy horsehair hat, a stark black waitress uniform with white apron and bibbed hat, and a whorey plumed ostrich negligee for the renunciation scene.

During the first week of filming the cast was icily polite to Davis; Howard fed her lines in a bored manner during her close-ups. However, after viewing rushes, when it became apparent that she was walking off with the picture, he ceased to be bored. He was wise enough to know that the effectiveness of his own portrayal depended upon the reaction of the public to Mildred.

For the sequence near the end, when Mildred is consumed with the last stages of consumption, brought on by illness and neglect, Davis put on her own makeup. In the scene where she is found in her cheap hotel room and taken to the hospital, she had the look of a corpse.

After the strenuous shooting schedule Davis came back to her home lot exhausted and fearful of her performance. Her career hung in the balance.

When the audience at a "sneak" of the picture laughed in the wrong places, RKO executives panicked. They ran the picture over and over again and finally decided the musical accompaniment was at fault. Max Steiner wrote a new score, complete with motifs for the principal players, including a highly effective, poignant "musical limp" for the crippled Philip.

Ruthie Davis and Nelson arrived home one evening to learn that *Of Human Bondage* was to be previewed in Santa Barbara that same night. Ruthie told an interviewer,

> Without a morsel of dinner we took our seats just as the first close-up of Bette flashed on the screen. For one hour and a half of horrible realism, we sat riveted without

speaking a word, with only a fleeting glance now and then at each other. We left the theater in absolute silence. Neither of us knew what to think, for we felt the picture would make or break her, but would the public like the unpleasant story as well as the people at the preview seemed to?

Davis told Gladys Hall in *Modern Screen,*.

Mother and Ham drove home from the preview. I didn't go. I was afraid to go because the reaction to that picture meant so much to me . . . I didn't sleep, naturally. I lay awake, every nerve tense. I worked myself into a lather.

I kept imagining what they would say. Perhaps Ham would come in shouting hosannas, hailing me as a second Sarah Bernhardt. Perhaps he would shudder away from me. The hours crawled. At last the front door opened, and they came in quietly. I hadn't expected that. I crept down the stairs and looked at them. They looked at me. Their faces were blank. They didn't say one word.

. . . At last I managed to say, out of a throat so dry the words scraped like cinders, "Well? Can't you *say* something?"

Then Ham told me that I had given, he thought, a sincere, a painfully sincere, performance, but that it *was* painful, and he doubted that it would do me much good. It might do me harm. It was so powerful that he feared for its popularity. He wasn't sure. Time would tell. I knew that he was telling the truth.

Later I realized that he had spoken as he had for my own good, for my protection. He said, if the picture did go over with any enormous success, that would be my reward. But, if it didn't, he didn't want me to feel too let down.

Fog over Frisco was released on June 6, 1934, to fair reviews. Twenty-two days later *Of Human Bondage* was booked into the new Radio City Music Hall, causing a furor that would go down in the pages of film history. Mordaunt Hall's review in *The New York Times* on June 29 gives an indication of what the talk was all about:

Another enormously effective portrayal is that of Bette Davis as Mildred Rogers, the waitress who continually accepts Carey's generosity and hospitality and reveals herself as a heartless little ingrate. In a climactic episode, which recalls an incident in Kipling's *The Light That Failed,* this sorry specimen of humanity slashes Carey's efforts at art, destroys his medical books and furniture and, in the film, even burns his bonds and private papers, leaving the apartment as though it had been struck by a tornado.

At the first showing yesterday of this picture, the audience was so wrought up over the conduct of this vixen that when Carey finally expressed his contempt for Mildred's behavior applause was heard from all sides. There was further outburst of applause when the film came to an end.

Of Human Bondage suffered two remakes. Warner Bros. cast Eleanor Parker as Mildred and Paul Henreid as Philip in 1946, and MGM cast Kim Novak and Laurence Harvey in the 1964 version. Reviewers were caustic in both cases and compared the performances in a derogatory way to the original. Novak wanted to see the first version, but it was discovered that in the turmoil of several different RKO managements the negative had been destroyed; no prints were left. Davis possessed one of the only existing prints. So, the film was lost for many years. The Bijou Theatre in Hollywood discovered a 16-mm print and gave the first public showing in thirty-seven years on October 13, 1971. A packed house applauded wildly at the end.

As *Of Human Bondage* continued to garner rave reviews everywhere, there was mention of an Academy Award nomination, which befuddled Warner Bros. It was embarrassing that a player should receive such acclaim in a film made at another studio! The controversy raged, while Davis was contacted by the press for interviews in the newspapers and fan books. How could the studio take advantage of all the publicity and not mention *Of Human Bondage*? No advertisements had been prepared for the magazines by RKO, so it was hoped that the fan in the street would simply not know—or care—who made the film. The public was primarily interested in stars, and Davis had a growing multitude of admirers.

Bordertown, long in the can, was viewed again by the

executives, who decided upon a January, 1935, release, leaving six months to create a campaign. Exploitation was prepared and ads set for the fan books, which would mention *Of Human Bondage.*

Andre Sennwald, in *The New York Times,* on January 24, 1935, hit a sensitive chord in his review of *Bordertown:*

> Although some of the irreverent members of yesterday's audience seemed to feel that Miss Davis was being uproariously comic during her conscience-writhings, it seemed to this reporter that she was effective and touching in pathological mazes which the cinema rarely dares to ex.. ...

If there were those in the audience who laughed, it was not an expression of genuine mirth, but rather the uneasy expression of identification. She was a new kind of actress, playing a new kind of woman. Critics, surfeited with the goody-two-shoes style of acting, so prevalent among Hollywood females of the period, were caught up short by her power.

Occasionally a magazine would do a photo lay-out about the star, such as a charadelike game called "Handies"—with hand clues by Mr. and Mrs. Harmon O. Nelson, indicating such simple phrases as "Indian riding in a Ford V-8," "Quints under a shower," "Three men on a horse," or "Worm turning a corner."

In "Not That Kind of a Girl" in *Modern Screen,* by Carlisle Jones, the interview began,

> Bette Davis believes she has had one of the narrowest escapes on record in Hollywood. She missed being an ingenue by such slim margins that she still shudders when the word is mentioned.
>
> No screen fate could have been worse in Bette's considered opinion. The role of Mildred in *Of Human Bondage* removed her once and for all from the list of actresses who are best at playing sweet young things in ruffles.

When the Academy Award ballots were mailed, the most outstanding female performances for 1934 included: Grace Moore in *One Night of Love,* Norma Shearer in *The Barretts of Wimpole Street,* and Claudette Colbert in *It Happened One Night.* When

Davis's name was not mentioned for *Of Human Bondage,* hundreds of angry actors wrote in her name on the ballot. *[I cannot let this page go by without shamefacedly admitting that I was heartbroken not to win my first Academy Award for* Of Human Bondage, *not that I honestly ever have approved of my performance as Mildred, as I have upon only a very few occasions approved of other performances. But due to the reviews and the acclaim given me by friends in my profession I just took it for granted I would win. One must never take anything for granted—especially Academy Awards. I made the same mistake three more times. Shame on me—never will again.]*

THREE LITTLE STINKERS IN A ROW

The story is briefly this: Stone was about to kill Coul' ⌐. so Inez stabbed Stone in order to save her sweethe(life. . . . The minute that Inez stabbed Stone, Coulter grabbed the knife out of her hand. Then they heard the fire engines.

BETTE DAVIS AS ELLEN GARFIELD
IN *Front Page Woman*

If Davis expected her scripts to improve, she was in for a rude awakening. Henry Blanke was preparing a property called *The Girl from Tenth Avenue,* which almost tells the story in one line. She was billed before the title for the first time since *Ex-Lady.* Alfred E. Green was again at the helm. The screenplay by Charles Kenyon was based upon a play by Hubert Henry Davies.

Reviewers were kinder than either the picture or her performance as Miriam Brady deserved. Said Frank Nugent in the May 27 edition of *The New York Times,* "Miss Davis, as a growing number of film-goers are coming to know, is one of the most competent of our younger screen actresses. Aided by a scenarist who seems to have a good working knowledge of the female brain, she gives a performance which is both truthful and amusing."

For the next screenplay for Davis and George Brent a story by Richard Macaulay, *Women Are Bum Newspapermen,* was assigned to Roy Chanslor, Lillie Hayward, and Laird Doyle. Sam Bischoff was the supervisor, and Michael Curtiz was the director.

The Picture of the Month

The title was changed to *Front Page Woman* before production began.

Frank Nugent reported in the July 12, 1935, issue of *The New York Times,*

> The nicest thing about these Hollywood reflections on the newspaper business is that you meet such interesting reporters. *Front Page Woman,* at the Strand, has two. There is Ellen Garfield who is *The Star's* only bulwark against the beats of Curt Devlin of *The Express.* And Mr. Devlin—ah, there's a reporter! His nose for news is so keen that a sniff of perfume on a dead man's coat collar is all he needs to track down a murderer. And when he walks up to a police lieutenant, hands him two photographs, and says, "Mac, arrest these people for the murder of Marvin Stone"—and the lieutenant does!—then, my friends, you have newspaper work at its best.

Davis was next assigned the role of private secretary Julie Gardner in *Special Agent.* Based upon an idea by New York newspaperman Martin Mooney, who also acted as associate supervisor under Bischoff, the material detailing the nefarious activities of a racketeer who is finally nailed because of failure to file an income tax return, was transformed into a rough-and-tumble screenplay by Laird Doyle and Abem Finkel. William Keighley directed in a fast-paced, hard-hitting style. Davis's big moment came when she turned in her boss to undercover agent Bill Bradford, portrayed in a breezy fashion by George Brent.

When the Hays office, in charge of censorship in films, looked at the completed film, several cuts were ordered. Since certain scenes could not be eliminated without confusing the story line, a bit of dialogue was deleted from the sound track—leaving Ricardo Cortez with silently moving lips. Also cut was an important "reaction" shot, where innocent bystanders were gunned down. With a budget so low, retakes were impossible after the preview.

The studio allotted no advertising money for the fan books for *The Girl from Tenth Avenue, Front Page Woman,* or *Special Agent.*

There was still great dissension in Academy circles, but the write-in campaign brought on by *Of Human Bondage* was disclaimed because it established a precedent; no leeway existed in

Colin Clive, Davis, and Ian Hunter on the set of *The Girl from Tenth Avenue*, 1935. (*Photograph by Warner Bros.*)

Bette Davis as Julie Gardner and George Brent as Bill Bradford in *Special Agent*, 1935. (*Photograph by Bert Longworth, Warner Bros.*)

Ian Hunter as Geoffrey
Sherwood and Bette Davis
as Miriam Brady in
Girl from Tenth Avenue,
1935. (*Photograph by
Warner Bros., from the collection of Whitney Stine.*)

George Brent and
Davis pose "in charac-
ter" for newsmen on a
San Francisco trip to
publicize *Front Page
Woman,* July, 1935.
(*Photo by Interna-
tional News.*)

Academy bylaws. A new, more organized method of tabulating votes was ordered, and Price Waterhouse was commissioned to do the accounting, a procedure that has remained to this day.

Always a dog lover, Davis acquired a female Scottie that she named Tibby—who, along with President Roosevelt's dog Fala, was to be the most photographed dog of her time. She was half dog, half ham, and knew her mistress was a famous and admired film star. She would be Davis's companion and "confidante" for twelve years.

With fire in her eyes Davis was determined not to play another gun moll-reporter-bookkeeper and was entertaining the idea of going on suspension. Downhearted and weary, she could not know that she was on her way toward her first Academy Award.

Bette Davis in 1936—photographed by Elmer Fryer. (*Photograph by Warner Bros.*)

A rare cheesecake photo of Davis taken at Zuma Beach on a day off from *Special Agent*, 1935. "Duse of the Dunes" was the title of a fan book story that featured the picture. (*Photograph by Warner Bros.*)

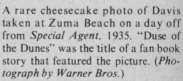

Davis and husband, Harmon "Oscar" Nelson, at the Del Monte Lodge, Pebble Beach, Calif., August 28, 1935. (*Photograph by Acme News-pictures, Inc.*)

7

It's going to be your life or mine! If you're killed, I'll be free. . . . If I'm killed, it won't matter any longer . . . and, if we both die—good riddance.

BETTE DAVIS AS JOYCE HEATH
IN *Dangerous*

For the fifth Davis picture to be shot in 1935 the brilliant young writer Laird Doyle fashioned a romantic melodrama called *Hard Luck Dame,* said to be based on the life of famous stage star Jeanne Eagels, who had died at thirty-five from drugs in 1929.

Production reins were given to Harry Joe Brown and the directorial assignment to Alfred E. Green. Davis outlined what she wanted to do with the character of Joyce Heath. First of all, she told them bluntly, if she was supposed to play a "jinxed lady of the theater"—a drunk who had seen better days—she wanted to *look* like a Broadway castoff. During her stage days in New York she had often enough seen young women driven to prostitution and depravity stumbling up Forty-second Street, lost in an alcoholic haze, concerned only about the price of the next drink.

Orry-Kelly read the script with misgivings. Davis appeared in the first half of the film in a man's bathrobe, pajamas, and trousers. For her introductory scene, where she is discovered staggering down the street, he designed (and aged) a tweed suit with a printed blouse that was just respectable enough to be associated with a better era in her stage career. He made two smart frocks, one to be worn in the "play within a play" and another for the ending. Perc Westmore combed her hair into a short pageboy—a style peculiarly suited to the Davis personality—which she would wear on and off the screen for the next thirty-five years. When Joyce Heath became "respectable," he provided a longer "fall" with bangs for her rehabilitation scenes.

During the first sequences Ernie Haller photographed Davis harshly, without benefit of glamorous lighting. Later, as she kicks the habit and becomes more wholesome looking, he photographed her attractively.

The key part of the architect was the most difficult to cast. None of the male members of the Warner stock company quite exhibited the polish necessary for the role. Franchot Tone, who had just finished *Mutiny on the Bounty*, was borrowed from MGM; *Hard Luck Dame* was also *his* fifth picture for 1935. The chemistry between the two stars was electric, and they worked smoothly together. *[If the truth be known, I fell in love with Franchot professionally and personally—alas—Joan Crawford had him!]*

The supporting players were unusually capable—Alison Skipworth, Tone's pithy housekeeper, and Margaret Lindsay, the "other woman," which she was so often in Davis's pictures. John Eldredge was the weak, effeminate husband whom she purposefully injures in a car accident after he refuses to give her a divorce.

In an ending harkening back to *Stella Dallas,* and necessary because of the production code, Davis watches Tone and Lindsay emerge from the church where they have just been married and then takes an armload of roses to her invalided husband in the hospital.

Davis brought an uncanny, desperate power to her no-makeup-hair-awry drunk scenes, and, when overtaken by "the Mahoney Boys," the 1930s expression for delirium tremens, her reactions are very real. Whether spouting Shakespeare in a disreputable bar or laughing gaily at her big toe poked through a hole in her stocking, she is glowing and believable.

After stills from the film and the narrative plot line had been handed to the press and *Hard Luck Dame* was typeset in fan books, the title was changed to *Dangerous.* Warner Bros., not content to let a good title fall by the wayside, initially used *Hard Luck Dame* again as the working title for a remake of *The Maltese Falcon* the next year—under which that film was first reviewed by some of the press.

The reviews were mixed. *The New York Times* on December 27, 1935, said, "That Bette Davis has been unable to match the grim standard she set as Mildred in *Of Human Bondage* is not to her discredit. In *Dangerous,* the new film at the Rivoli, she tries again.

Except for a few sequences where the tension is convincing as well as deadly, she fails.'' *[With all due modesty, I don't feel it was a question of failure. There could hardly be any comparison between the script of* Dangerous *and that of* Of Human Bondage, *nor any comparison at all between the opportunities offered in playing Joyce Heath to playing Mildred.]* ''The audience Christmas night was fidgety and given to tittering at the wrong time. . . . Say this for Miss Davis: she seldom lets down.'' *[What a picture to see Christmas night—usually a holiday audience, having imbibed a few.]*

Dangerous was remade in 1941 as a ''C'' picture called *Singapore Woman* starring Brenda Marshall. Set in the South Seas and, ironically, using some of the sets from *The Letter,* little was left of the plot line except the ''jinx.''

Fifty-three films were placed in production in 1936, mostly ''B'' programmers. One of the big productions of the year was *Anthony Adverse,* starring Fredric March. Davis ached to play the role of the fresh country girl, Angela, who becomes a famous opera singer and ends up as the mistress of Napoleon. The role went to Olivia De Havilland.

FIRST STAB AT PORTRAYING A PAINTER

Immediately after finishing *Dangerous,* Davis was pleased to be cast as Gabrielle Maple, the artist-waitress opposite Leslie Howard's Alan Squier in Robert E. Sherwood's psychological melodrama *The Petrified Forest. This* time her name would be placed directly under Howard's, above the title of the picture. The British actor, who had won praise in the stage play, insisted that Humphrey Bogart be assigned the screen role of the gangster, Duke Mantee, which had brought him great success in 187 Broadway performances.

Henry Blanke gave the film careful production. The single exterior set of Black Mesa, Arizona, took up all of Stage Twenty-two and featured a complete gas station set against a painted cyclorama of the desert. Wind machines created the loneliness of tumbling tumbleweeds and a howling sand storm.

Archie Mayo resisted the impulse to film the play in *film noir* fashion and imbued the picture with a slow but poetic style. Davis's performance as Gabby had a wholesome, innocent, little-girl quality. She had only two costume changes. In the opening sequences she wore a striped dress, and later a simple blouse and dirndl. *[Up to this time my hair was still bleached. I knew I couldn't portray Gabby with bleached blonde hair. It would lose all reality. Up to now no parts had been hampered by my lighter hair. I knew that, if I tried to get permission from the studio to dye it back to my own ash-blonde color, I would not be allowed to! So, like the conspirators we were, Perc Westmore and I hid away for a day and returned my hair to its natural color. A year and a half later Mr.* *Wallis casually asked me if my hair weren't darker? That proves a point—don't ask permission from your boss, do it! I'm afraid my bosses will tell you I often did.]*

The success of the screenplay by Charles Kenyon and Delmer Daves depended upon the electricity engendered between vagabond Howard, the waitress-artist who dreams of going to France to study painting, and the hoodlum who, surrounded by police, runs out into the night, commandeering the rich couple's car and using them as hostages. Bogart's last line to Howard—"Be seein' ya!"—lets the audience know that he believes he is going to his death.

Also of interest are the two black men in the cast. The chauffeur is a man with the same upper-class pretensions as his employers, and the other, a convict who escaped with Mantee, has been kicked and scuffed about but still retains a sardonic sense of humor.

The studio insisted that a new ending be shot for the picture showing Howard recovering from the gunshot wound inflicted upon him by Bogart. Howard pulled rank and the picture ended with his death.

OSCAR, FOURTEEN POUNDS OF ADMIRATION

There was great excitement among coworkers at the studio when the Academy Award nominations were released. Davis's name was prominently included in the best-actress category for *Dangerous*.

The Academy was going through "labor" pains. Frank Capra, the new president, faced a great challenge. Besides a reduced membership and virtually no money, the possibility loomed that the organization, which had been formed in 1927 to help pull the film industry together, might be disbanded out of pure Hollywood dissension. There was an all-out war between management, labor, and the artistic endeavors of stars and technicians.

The studios had fought long and hard to prevent contract

personnel from forming unions. In retaliation the existing guilds decided to boycott management and do away with the Academy so that the studios could not use the award to exploit award-winning films. All Hollywood was engaged in a poker game in which the stakes would be the industry itself—and the winner would emerge the loser!

Capra fought with all of his famous Sicilian energy. With both the Actors Guild and the Writers Guild threatening to boycott the award dinner in March, 1936, Capra looked around for a star that would bring together all the dissatisfied multitudes. The answer was old-time director David Wark Griffith.

Griffith was the "name" he needed for two superlative reasons. A pioneer whom everyone respected, his hallowed place in the industry could not be disputed. The second reason he was exactly right for the part was that Hollywood had turned its back on the old genius, and he had not made a major film in years. Hollywood, sentimental to the core and realizing that even an honorary award was long overdue, showed up in huge numbers.

But even in strife and chaos Hollywood protects its own, and none of the inner bickering between studios, personnel, and the Academy was publicized—although even third-rate fan book writers knew the complicated strategy blow by blow. In the old days James Quirk, editor of *Photoplay,* would have written editorial after editorial, chastising the studios, but he was gone from the ranks.

The Academy dinner was glossy and somewhat pretentious, but Bette Davis won her award for *Dangerous.* She was ecstatic, although she knew the award was actually for *Of Human Bondage.* Her winning consort was Victor McLaglen for *The Informer.*

At this time the statuette was given a nickname, Oscar. Noting that the rear end of the statuette resembled the behind of Nelson, whose middle name was Oscar, Davis gave that epithet to the little man. Margaret Herrick, former executive director of the Academy, believed she named him after her uncle, and columnist Sidney Skolsky swore he was responsible for the sobriquet. The controversy has yet to be settled. *[A sillier controversy never existed. I don't feel my fame and fortune came from naming Oscar "Oscar." I relinquish once and for all any claim that I was the one—so, Academy of Motion Picture Arts and Sciences, the honor is all yours.]*

Warner Bros. rushed *The Golden Arrow* to the Strand Theatre, New York, for a May 3, 1936, opening after a dismal sneak preview in Long Beach, California, in April. *The New York World Tele-gram* gave the plotline:

> Based on the play *Dream Princess* by Michael Arlen.
> "It is all about a young and beautiful heiress who
> persuades a handsome reporter to marry her to save her
> from a lot of foreign fortune hunters. The reporter agrees
> to do so in order to get the time and means to finish a
> novel. After the marriage ceremony the audience, if not
> the reporter, is let in on the secret that the girl isn't really
> an heiress at all, but a former waitress who has been
> turned into the wealthiest girl in the world by a high-
> pressure publicity man to exploit a beauty cream."

Stage magazine had a point in its June 1, 1936, review: "Miss
Bette Davis . . . was whisked into a routine comedy for obvious
reasons of timeliness. There is not a true note in the entire production. It is safe to say that Miss Davis will not win the Academy's
1936 honors with this performance." *[This film was the beginning
of the end, temporarily, of my contract with Warner Bros. I was
actually insulted to have to appear in such a cheap, nothing story as*
The Golden Arrow *after* Of Human Bondage, The Petrified Forest,
and Bordertown. *The end did come after the next film*—The Man in
the Black Hat. *My career was obviously going downhill at a rapid
rate. What to do? I was desperate.]* The advertisements for *The
Golden Arrow,* to Davis's horror, mentioned her hard-won Oscar.

Warner Bros., perhaps more than any other studio in Hollywood,
firmly believed in remaking successful films. The advantages were
manifold. Having purchased a well-known book or play, it was
economical, after a period, to assign a contract writer to turn out
another version—sometimes with a title change and sometimes not.

Bryan Foy, head supervisor on the lot and known as the Keeper of
the "B's," was one of the studio's unsung heroes, and he was as
technically proficient as he was a good arbiter of story material.
Although supervising hundreds of films, he received screen credit
as director on only three pictures and as original author on one. His
contribution to the solvency of the studio was immeasurable.

For Davis's thirty-first picture Dashiell Hammett's *The Maltese
Falcon,* filmed five years previously, was handed to writer Brown
Holmes to redo; he retitled the new version *The Man in the Black
Hat,* then *Men on Her Mind.* (Five years later the property would be

filmed again under its original title and bring a host of awards to
writer-turned-director John Huston.)

The Davis version contained only the bare bones of the original
plot. The characters underwent all sorts of metamorphoses, name
changes, personality changes, and in one case a sex change!

But Holmes fiddled with the story even more; the gem-encrusted
falcon became a ram's horn filled with jewels; the serious-minded
Sam Spade secretary, Effie, became a flighty, harebrained creature,
Miss Murgatroyd; and villain Gutman became "Madame"
Barabas! A strange relationship is built up between the madame,
portrayed by Alison Skipworth, and her son, excellently played in
petulant little-boy style by Maynard Holmes. A sample line of
dialogue is, "He's more than a son to me"—a line that remains
intact in the Huston version and builds all sorts of images as
delivered by Sydney Greenstreet concerning Elisha Cook, Jr.!

The last scene shows Davis and Warren William on a train with
the police closing in. Davis runs to the washroom and persuades the
black lady attendant to "turn her in" so that she, instead of William,
will get the $10,000 reward for finding the murderer! The title of the
picture was changed to *Satan Met a Lady.*

After Max Parker edited the picture, Warner Bros. executives
looked at the result and were mystified at the numerous twists of the
plot. Warren Low was asked to re-edit the material.

"Projections—Bette Davis" in *Silver Screen* in September,
1936, recorded, "She would like to play the Helen Mencken role in
Congai some day, and the Miriam Hopkins role in *Jezebel* and the
Florence Reed role of Mother Goddam in *The Shanghai Gesture*—
although she is quite certain that, if, by any fluke, this stage play
ever reached the screen, she would be called Mother Goodness
Gracious. In other words, our little Bette craves something with
guts, and wishes to leave the sweets to the sweet."

As it turned out, when Emeric Pressburger and Josef Von
Sternberg *did* film *The Shanghai Gesture* in 1941, the part of
Mother Goddam was taken by Ona Munson, who had made a hit as
Belle Watling in *Gone with the Wind*, but her name was changed to
Mother Gin-Sling!

When Davis pleaded for a good property, J.L. personally sent her
the script of *God's Country and the Woman*, in which she would
portray a lumberjack. Davis was incredulous. "But it's to be in
Technicolor," J.L. told her. "You'll have George Brent as a

costar, and it's going to be shot at Longview, Washington, up in the big pine country.''

"I *won't* do it!" she cried. *"Satan Met a Lady* was bad enough, but this is *absolute tripe.''*

"If you'll be reasonable and do the picture, I promise you a great role when you return. I have just optioned a wonderful novel that isn't out yet called *Gone with the Wind*. You were born to play the heroine.''

"I bet it's a pip!" she replied angrily and went on suspension.

8

I know all the angles and I'm smart enough to keep one step ahead of them, until I get enough to pack it all in and live on easy street the rest of my life.

BETTE DAVIS AS MARY DWIGHT
IN *Marked Woman*

The man who had produced *Henry the VIII* with Charles Laughton and *Catherine the Great* with Elisabeth Bergner, a Signor Ludovic Toeplitz, offered Davis $50,000 to star in two films. *I'll Take the Low Road,* with Douglass Montgomery and Nigel Bruce, was to be shot in Italy, and an untitled film with Maurice Chevalier was to be made in France. *[I had accepted this deal with Toeplitz before leaving for England. Toeplitz was well aware of the fact that under my contract with Warner Bros. I could be prevented from making these films. We both faced the fact that we might end up in a court of law in England to settle the matter.]* J.L. in his autobiography says, "Now, Bette knew she couldn't do that, according to our contract. I think she might have hesitated except for the prodding of a new villain in the case, who turned out to be my old pal, the almost bankrupt agent Mike Levee. Mike convinced Bette that she could wallop evil old Jack Warner by going to England and filing suit there to break her contract." *[Dear J.L.: There never was or will be an agent who urges a client to break a contract in the manner I tried to—all agents were afraid of being barred from any motion picture lot where this occurred, thus endangering the deals pending for other clients. This was an independent revolt of my own—I could no longer bear the scripts I was being given under my Warner contract. I was forced into some very definite action for the future of my career.]*

Davis knew that she must get out of the country before the studio could serve her with papers. Knowing that injunctions could not be presented on Sunday, Nelson and she took a plane for Vancouver at 12:01 A.M. on Saturday, then trained across Canada to Montreal, where they boarded the *Duchess of Bedford* for England. On a second honeymoon, they spent several weeks sightseeing and being interviewed by the press, which regarded Davis as a cause célèbre. As it happened, J.L. and his wife Ann were also celebrating *their* second honeymoon, in Austria, having left Los Angeles at about the same time as Davis.

Warner Bros. served an injunction through the law firm of Denton, Hall, and Burgin, on September 9, 1936, to prevent her from filming. Although *I'll Take the Low Road* was postponed, she had just returned from wardrobe fittings in Paris.

J.L. says in his autobiography, "Ann and I moved into a London hotel, and she suggested in her own diplomatic way that it might be wise to settle the case. She was very fond of Bette—so was I—and she could foresee a great flood of perhaps unpleasant publicity. But there was a principle at stake—whether a highly paid star could dictate to a studio, and make only those pictures that pleased him or her. If Bette were to win, all the studio owners and executives in Hollywood would get trampled in the stampede."

Justice Lewis renewed the writ until the case was brought before the court. J.L. employed the famous Sir Patrick Hastings to represent the studio. *[Never will I forget Sir Patrick Hastings's opening remark as the trial began. "I can't help but think, M'Lord, this is the action of a very naughty young lady."Not naughty, desperate. I was like a lioness fighting for her cub. My cub was my future in my profession and a dearly cherished cub it was.]* Davis engaged Sir William Jowitt (recommended by Toeplitz), who was willing to wait for the £250 fee traditionally given to solicitors before appearing in court. Davis, not having worked for some months, was short on cash. Nelson decided to return to New York to find a job, leaving Davis to fight the battle alone.

She told a London reporter, "I am only a contract player and do not possess the power or the weapons a star can employ to combat unfavorable conditions. I was assigned to pictures, and I objected. The studio officials at first tried to placate me, and then they decided to ignore me. I would do what I was told or else! I felt the end had been reached. I knew that, if I continued to appear in any more mediocre pictures, I would have no career left worth fighting for."

Meanwhile, back in the States *Satan Met a Lady* was released to blistering reviews. *The New York Times* on July 23 said, "So disconnected and lunatic are the picture's ingredients, so irrelevant and monstrous its people that one lives through it in a constant expectation of seeing a group of uniformed individuals appear suddenly from behind the furniture and take the entire cast into protective custody. There is no story, merely a farrago of nonsense representing a series of practical studio compromises with an unworkable script."

Davis was in awe of the ritualistic machinery by which a case is brought to court in England, with the somber courtroom, the "dock" instead of the witness stand, and the bewigged judge and solicitors. It was a solemn and frightening atmosphere; plus, after her husband returned to America, she was a foreigner alone in a strange country. She was petrified.

Sir Patrick Hastings's opening got the expected response. He read a letter that Davis had written to J.L. where she had mentioned the word "money" and had called her contract a form of slavery. The barrister intoned, "This slavery has a silver lining because the slave was, to say the least, well remunerated." *[This was not a fight for more money. Warner knew this. It was a fight against slavery from the standpoint that, according to the standard motion picture contracts of the day, I could be forced to do anything the studio told me to do. They could even ask a contract player to appear in a burlesque house. The only recourse was to refuse, and then you were suspended without pay. These original documents were so one-sided in favor of the studio that, as Sir William Jowitt, my counselor, believed, it was restraint of trade—as, when under suspension from your contract, with no salary, you could not even work in a five-and-dime store. You could only starve, which of necessity often made you give in to the demands of the studio.]*

"I think it right," Hastings continued, "that I make it plain to your Lordship that this really is a case of great importance to the whole industry, because, although the contracts vary, no doubt in some minor points, from other contracts that are the standard form in the industry in substance, it is the common form. . . . What this young lady is seeking to do, in effect, is to tear up the contract and say, whether she is right or wrong, the court will not grant an injunction against her. That is tantamount to saying that these ladies and gentlemen can come over to this country, and the courts will say that they cannot be stopped from doing this sort of thing."

He then spoke of Davis's graduating pay scale as included in the contract, which by the expiration date in 1942 would be paying her the sum of $2,400 per week. "If anybody wants to put me into perpetual servitude on that basis of remuneration, I shall prepare to consider it. And what is more, I shall not ask Sir William Jowitt, K.C., to stand up for me and argue that it would be slavery." *[I believe at the time of the trial I was making about $500 a week. I had a lousy contract monetarily, which had nothing to do with the case, and Hastings knew it. He also knew any motion picture salary seemed a fortune to the outside world and knew this was the easiest way to make a fool of me in the press—and he succeeded—and the easiest possibility of winning the case.]*

He called J.L. to the stand, who nervously explained that the studio had, at great expense, built Miss Davis into the star that she was. *[I was not a full-fledged star as yet, and at this point my career had become a serious acting potential career—due to Of Human Bondage made by RKO Studios, not Warner Bros.!]* He admitted she was a serious performer and could be upset by inferior scripts.

Sir William Jowitt then cross-examined J.L., whom he induced into admitting that the standard contract required an actress to "assist in commercial advertising, such as the use of a face cream or eating a particular kind of oatmeal for breakfast." (As a matter of fact, Warner Bros. *had* endorsed Quaker Puffed Rice for her, and the advertisement read, "Breakfast fit for a queen of the screen" and mentioned the fact that she was the winner of the 1935 Academy Award and was currently starring in *The Golden Arrow.)* *[This advertisement was running in America at the time of the trial—in other words, behind my back—hardly suitable publicity for an Academy Award winner.]* He also brought out that she could be forced to make personal appearances at a Republican National Convention, even though she was a Democrat, and that the studio could insist that she not divorce her husband for three years. Sir William produced a poster showing Davis almost nude and asked, "Would you like to see any woman that you were fond of portrayed to the public like that?"

"If she is a professional artist," J.L. replied, "it would be part of her duty." *[What an answer. My duty as an actress was to give the best performances I could—not have my body reproduced by an artist, in the nude. If I remember correctly, I had a far better figure nude than the artist reproduced!]*

When she wore the same sports suit to court each day, there was a decided coolness in the air and much eyebrow-raising. One evening the phone rang. "Miss Davis," said a voice, "this is so-and-so of the Evening-something-or-other. Would you mind wearing something different into court tomorrow?" She slammed down the phone. *[I wore the same tailored suit on purpose each day. I did not intend to make the trial a fashion show. The prejudice in England against Hollywood film stars was rampant. The English press only talked about how much money we made and how many clothes we owned. They still do! An amusing outcome of the one outfit every day in court was told to me by an Englishman: When his wife asked if she could buy a new dress, he said, "If Bette Davis wears the same outfit day after day, why can't you?"]*

The next day Sir William made his summation. "She is chattel in the hands of the producer. I suggest that the real essence of slavery is no less slavery because the bars are gilded. Even if she decides to wait until 1942 and not work for anyone else, there is a clause whereby the period will never have to come to an end. It is, therefore, a life sentence. . . . As the contract stands, she cannot become a waitress, an assistant in a hairdresser's shop in the wilds of Africa—if they have hairdressing establishments there—and cannot engage in any other occupation whether for love or money.

"She cannot allow her husband to take a snapshot of her in the back garden, because that is 'an appearance' of a kind. There are penalties for absence. If she becomes a mother, the employers have the option of terminating her contract or adding to the end of the contract the period in which she is unable to act. . . .

". . . I do not know much about art or artists . . . I do not suppose that any artist can turn on his inspiration as one turns on a tap. His mood and inspiration have to suit. It is a contract that can be rendered tolerable and bearable by a human being only if the persons for whom the artist is working show tact, good temper, and consideration."

Sir William Jowitt refused to call witnesses, thereby thwarting Sir Patrick's thrill of cross-examining Davis. Sir Patrick was so angry that he took off his wig and threw it across the courtroom.

Davis checked out of her small, inexpensive room at the Park Lane and fled to the Tudor Close Inn at Rottingdean on the English coast some sixty miles from London to await the court's decision.

At the beginning of the week the news arrived. The verdict: the studio had won a three-year injunction, or the duration of the contract—whichever was shorter. She decided to appeal. She was broke. Besides Sir William's £250 she was saddled with the Warner Bros. court costs, as well as her own—over $30,000 for a mean total of $103,000.

A few days later she received a letter:

I should like to come down to see you on Thursday.
George Arliss

He had hardly changed at all. He was the same kindly, slightly aloof man she remembered. They had tea and discussed the case. "There are two things that you can do, Bette; continue your rebellion or take your medicine. In the first case you can go off and hide. That's a child's trick. You're grown up, my dear."

"You don't mean go back and give up? Oh, I couldn't do that!"

"What's to prevent? All it requires is courage, and you've plenty of that."

"Not enough, I'm afraid. They could put me through purgatory."

"I don't think they will. But, whatever they put you through, you must accept it. Because either you work in California or you never work in this industry again. One road or the other—you've got to choose."

She knew that he made sense. Even if she made the appeal and could make pictures in France or Italy, no American company would release the films.

"You've carried the fight to the last gasp and lost," Arliss continued. "Maybe the fighting was important, but the outcome isn't. All your thinking has been poisoned by the notion that there's something shameful about defeat. . . . Rise above it, and you'll be a bigger person than if you were going back at the head of the parade."

She knew that Arliss was right. "This is Thanksgiving Day in my country," she said. "You'll never know how much I have to thank you for." *[This was the last time I ever saw Mr. Arliss. In the years that followed I so often would have given most anything for his advice. He was a wise and beautiful man. I think he loved me as a father hopefully would. I have a signed photograph of him. The inscription reads: "with adopted fatherly affection."]*

She had asked Ruthie to come over to be with her during the appeal; now she cabled her to cancel the trip and boarded the *Aquitania* for home. The studio had made it clear to publicity that no one was to meet her at the three-mile limit, and she had to brave the onslaught of reporters alone. It was a trying ordeal. Taking the Super Chief to California, she was again smothered by the eager press, but in Chicago Warner publicity man Ted Todd came secretly to the railroad station to give assistance. "They had to give dishes away wherever *Satan Met a Lady* was shown," he told her jubilantly. "It can't be any worse than that ever again." *[This beautiful friend of mine took a chance of losing his job with Warner Bros. by coming to the train to see me. He really saved my life. I was ̴ετrified to return and have to face J.L.]*

Once again she drove over Barham Boulevard to the studio, prepared for the worst. All fight gone, she met with J.L., who held out his hand. "Let's forget all about it, Bette. We've got work to do." Wallis was equally cordial. Wherever she went, there was an attitude of new respect.

The studio picked up the court costs. She walked out of the front office onto the lot and looked up at the enormous sound stages. Although she had lost her case, she had won an important victory. She could sense in everyone's manner that her fight had proved that she was serious about her work, that she only wanted parts commensurate with her growing stature.

Bosley Crowther in *The New York Times* on July 23, 1936, expounded,

> Without taking sides in a controversy of such titanic proportions, it is no more than gallantry to observe that, if Bette Davis had not effectually espoused her own cause against the Warners recently by quitting her job, the federal government eventually would have had to step in and do something about her. After viewing *Satan Met a Lady* . . . all thinking people must acknowledge that a "Bette Davis reclamation project" (BDRP) to prevent the waste of this gifted lady's talents would not be a too-drastic addition to our various programs for the conservation of natural resources.

[I never saw the above remarks of Mr. Crowther until I was reading this screen biography by Mr. Stine. I wish I had. I would have sent him dozens of long-stemmed roses. Now that I think of it, I guess at that time I couldn't have afforded it!]

THE GIRL WITH THE SCAR ON HER CHEEK

To be away from pictures for even a few months (in an era where four or five pictures a year was considered normal output for a star) was considered damaging to a career. Davis did not return to Warner Bros. until December. J.L. and Wallis knew that it was imperative to put her to work immediately.

While she was in England, Robert Rosson and Abem Finkel wrote an original screenplay scripted out of current headlines—*Marked Woman*. Socially conscious *Life* magazine on April 19, 1937, revealed the source:

> *Marked Woman* is based on the spectacular trial of the New York "Vice Tsar" Charles Luciano. Racketeer Luciano was sent to prison last spring largely on the testimony of prostitutes. In *Marked Woman* the five girls . . . are "clip joint" hostesses, an overlapping but slightly less tawdry profession. They are nonetheless counterparts of Cokey Flo, Dixie, and Jenny the Factory. . . .
>
> . . . Lucky Luciano was the heir of Dutch Schultz to some of the most lucrative rackets in New York. His own development was vice, which he put on an organized, chain store basis, collecting $10.00 a week from each of 1,000 prostitutes. A shadowy character, known to most of his subordinates only as "The Boss," Luciano was uncovered by Thomas E. Dewey, New York's shrewd and energetic young rackets investigator. It was Dewey who persuaded the prostitutes and their madames to testify, at the risk of their lives.

Before shooting began, Seton I. Miller created additional dialogue for the girls under the direction of Lou Edelman, producer, and Lloyd Bacon, director. Cinematographer George Barnes brought a smoky, but somewhat harsh documentary flavor to the story, creating stark contrast between the high, flossy living style of gangster boss Johnny Vanning, played with malevolent flair by Eduardo Ciannelli, the bleak courtroom atmosphere of special prosecutor David Graham, played by Humphrey Bogart, and the violent half-world of the girls—Mary (Bette Davis), Emmy Lou (Isabel Jewell), Florrie (Rosalind Marquis), Estelle (Mayo Methot), and Gabby (Lola Lane), with newcomer Jane Bryan as Mary's innocent kid sister Betty, who becomes involved with, and killed by, underworld characters.

Davis read the script and was thrilled. Such a good part in the first film after her defeat was an encouraging sign. The title *Marked Woman* was derived from the fact that, when Mary threatens to expose the gang, Vanning has her severely beaten up and has a double cross carved on her right cheek.

The morning the branding scene was to be shot, Davis appeared as usual for a makeup call at 7:00 A.M. The doctor on the set added an attractive "motion picture" bandage. Davis looked in the mirror and without permission left the set to see her personal doctor. She asked him to bandage her face as if she had been severely beaten up. The doctor complied, and, as she drove back through the front gate, the studio policeman phoned Wallis that she had been in a terrible accident.

Wallis met her back on the set and was horrified. *[In my usual "convinced that I was right" voice I said, "We film this makeup or we don't film me today!" We continued filming that day. Another fight for integrity had been won.]*

Marked Woman opened at the Strand Theatre, New York, on April 11, 1937, to powerful reviews. Eileen Creelman in *The New York Sun* said,

> [It] is one of those stories culled right from front-page headlines, a tabloid story come true, a glimpse of the underworld that is exciting, unsavory, and probably pretty close to the truth. *Marked Woman* gives Bette Davis the type of role she handles so well, a theatrical, showy part in which she goes in for fireworks now and then. She is constantly believable throughout.

[Warner Bros. was the only studio during many years that

attempted to expose existing evils in our country, for which they should be commended—gangs, Nazis, politicians—I could go on and on. They had a group of very talented young writers—Laird Doyle, Casey Robinson, Robert Rosson, who so brilliantly wrote Marked Woman—*for a period of at least ten years, with Wallis as production head. There has never been another studio to equal the Warners' product. They were the first studio to film a Shakespearean play,* Midsummer Night's Dream. *They filmed short subjects with the dancers from the Russian Ballet, all innovations for the screen at that time.]*

In 1968, Pauline Kael would write, "As the smart, lively young 'clip joint hostess' who turns informer, Bette Davis in *Marked Woman* is the embodiment of the sensational side of the thirties movies. (The closest modern equivalent is Jeanne Moreau in *Bay of Angels,* but Moreau is different, more purely conceptional; she's never as vibrantly, coarsely *there* as Davis swinging in her beaded fringe dress.) . . . And when Davis tells Luciano-Ciannelli, 'I'll get you if I have to come back from the grave to do it,' you believe it. . . ."

The Hays office okayed the film without a quibble, realizing that turning the prostitutes into "hostesses" was the biggest concession the studio could make. The Legion of Decency gave the picture an "Adult" rating.

Marked Woman, in a more permissive age, had strange some twenty-eight years later when CBS pulled the film from a scheduled showing with the following announcement: "Due to circumstances beyond our control, we cannot bring you *Marked Woman* tonight." The "circumstances" were explained to the press by spokesman Wes Elliott: "The central characters play prostitutes. Of course, there are classics in which central characters are prostitutes, or play illicit roles, but this type of thing shouldn't be fed into the home. Where it is euphemized to the point that adults know—but you don't spell it out—it may be okay. But in this picture it is too graphically spelled out to be acceptable according to CBS and NARTB standards." *[This kind of censorship I so thoroughly disagree with. It is* important *for the public to know about the evil of a Lucky Luciano. Films have the opportunity to delve realistically into life itself. The more knowledge one has, the sooner the cure—at least an awareness. Too often, film-makers ignore their responsibilities and do not often enough use the fantas-*

tic medium of motion pictures for the advancement of the thinking of the general public.]

The realistic ending—where the girls, after the court battle, go out into the street and disappear in the fog—was a symbol of Davis films in the future, which would find her walking down a street for the ending shot. In commemoration *The New Yorker* eventually tabbed her ''The Alley Duse.''

Joyce Heath (Bette Davis) and Don Bellows (Franchot Tone) share a tender moment in *Dangerous*, 1935, which won Davis her first Academy Award. (*Photograph by Warner Bros.*)

Gabrielle Maple (Bette Davis) and Alan Squier (Leslie Howard) in Robert E. Sherwood's *The Petrified Forest*, 1936, are held at bay by Duke Mantee (Humphrey Bogart). (*Photograph by Warner Bros.*)

Radio's "Seth Parker," Phillips Lord, and Davis meet for the first time since *Way Back Home* at a dinner party at the Hotel Ambassador, N.Y., while Davis is in Manhattan for the opening of *The Golden Arrow*, 1936. (*Photograph by Acme Newspictures, Inc.*)

Bette Davis as Valorie Purvis and Warren William as Ted Shayne in *Satan Met a Lady*, 1936, the second version of *The Maltese Falcon*. Film was variously titled *The Man in the Black Hat* and *Men on Her Mind*. (*Photograph by Warner Bros.*)

Davis poses for photographers in London during Warner Bros. trial, 1936. (*Photograph by Associated Press.*)

Douglass Montgomery and Davis meet for the first time since *Waterloo Bridge* to discuss *I'll Take the Low Road*, to be filmed abroad, 1936. Picture was never made because Warner Bros. brought an injunction to restrain her from working in England and subsequently won the case. (*Photograph by International News.*)

9

*Do you want to be champion? . . . Even I wanted to be
one once. I was going to panic New York with dance and
song. So, I end up with featured billing in a Bronx
cabaret.*

BETTE DAVIS AS LOUISE ("FLUFF") PHILLIPS
IN *Kid Galahad*

After Davis wearily walked off into the night in *Marked Woman*,
she was given another script where she also disappeared down a
lonely street in the ending sequence—this time grieving her heart
out for "her man." The picture was *Kid Galahad*, a brutal, tough,
exciting Edward G. Robinson exercise. *[I still think this is one of the
best pictures about prizefighting that was ever made. I was
delighted with my role in it—the second film after my disastrous
court battle. I remember writing Mr. Arliss at this time and thank-
ing him again for his advice, which was proving to be so right!]* In
the British publication *Film Weekly,* on June 19, 1937, she said,
"*Kid Galahad,* while not giving me much of a role in the artistic
sense, had such a lot of good robust fight stuff in it that it was bound
to appeal to a totally different cinema audience, an audience with
which I nevertheless need to be kept in touch. It has always been my
object to avoid too strict typing for the reason that one can only
enjoy the maximum following as an actress when one is seen in
varied roles with the widest range of public appeal."

The picture could have been subtitled *The Prizefighter and the
Lady,* for the plot concerned a bellhop, Ward Guisenberry (Wayne
Morris), who is turned into a prizefighter by promoter Nick Donati
(Robinson), and his torchsinger mistress Fluff (Davis). Tying her

handkerchief around his arm, Fluff christens him Kid Galahad after he defends her "honor" when Chuck McGraw (William Haade)—a fighter managed by Turkey Morgan (Humphrey Bogart)— insults her at a freewheeling Runyanesque party. Donati decides to double-cross Guisenberry and bets money on McGraw for the championship fight, then changes his mind, and advises the Kid to change tactics in the eighth round, which turns the fight in his favor.

Seton I. Miller wrote the action-packed screenplay from a *Saturday Evening Post* novel by Francis Wallace. Tony Gaudio photographed the plush backgrounds of the nouveau riche fighters in brilliant high key as contrasted to the smoky atmosphere of the ring and the grimy confines of the gym.

Michael Curtiz staged the fight scenes with great attention to detail and with no holds barred. During a take in which Morris flattened Haade, Curtiz screamed, "Retake! Retake! Fake fight!" When Haade did not respond, it became evident that Morris had actually knocked him cold. The studio doctor was sent for immediately, and another scene, involving other cast members, was quickly set up while the actor recovered.

Davis expertly lip-synced the song "The Moon Is in Tears Tonight" by M. K. Jerome and Jack Scholl for her nightclub number and imparted a good-natured, woman-of-the-world aura to her characterization. Her moll had grown in age and stature, no longer brittle and hardboiled but taking the rackets with a grain of salt. Furthermore, she was helped considerably by Curtiz, who secretly admired her guts in taking her case to the English courts; he did not hound her as he had in *Cabin in the Cotton*.

"The standard ending of three out of four Edward G. Robinson pictures is death by gunfire," *Life* magazine commented on May 24, 1937, "Actor Robinson, who first died in *Little Caesar*, repeated in *Silver Dollar, Bullets or Ballots, I Loved a Woman*, and *Barbary Coast*. No exception is *Kid Galahad*. Even though his fighter wins the world championship, Robinson dies. He is shot after the fight by a rival promoter, helped to a rubbing table by Kid Galahad and a trainer (Harry Carey), mourned by Bette Davis and the kid sister whom Galahad loves (Jane Bryan)."

During the death scene with Davis and Bryan in tears, Robinson, milking his death scene to the utmost, turned to Curtiz and complained, "Don't you think the girls are crying a little *too* much?"

The film went through two remakes. The first was *The Wagons Roll at Night* in 1941, which transported the story to a circus background and featured Bogart in the Donati role, Sylvia Sidney in the Davis part, and Eddie Albert as the "fighter." In 1962 Paramount purchased the story as a background for an Elvis Presley musical. Subsequently the Robinson version was retitled *The Battling Bellhop* on television in order not to conflict with the new picture, which reverted back to the original title, *Kid Galahad.*

In "I Tell Little White Lies" Davis told Gladys Hall in the February, 1937, issue of *Modern Screen,* "Acting is, really, an art form of ingenious lying. The more skillfully you lie, the better the acting. I certainly do not feel the emotion of love for the men I play love scenes with on the screen, for heaven's sake! I certainly do not suffer every ache and pain, every murderous impulse, every passionate emotion I act as though I am feeling . . . And if I succeed in making my audiences believe that I am feeling the emotions I portray, then I am an actress."

AT LAST, THE "STAR" TREATMENT

Delicacy is your long suit, isn't it, Mr. Merrick? You hold all the cards, all the trumps. You're the winner . . . except for once I have something you can never take away . . . that's Jack's love for me. You want to take my son away from me? All right, I'll take your son away from you!

BETTE DAVIS AS MARY DONNELL
IN *That Certain Woman*

Wallis looked around for a director and a story for Davis's first woman's picture. Director Edmund Goulding suggested a remake of his *The Trespasser,* which had garnered an Academy Award nomination for Gloria Swanson in 1929. Ernie Haller was the photographer.

The plot of *That Certain Woman,* reduced to one paragraph, sounds like a story from one of the grimmer works of the Brothers Grimm: one-time gun moll Mary Donnell works as a secretary to Lloyd Rogers (Ian Hunter), who secretly loves her. Mary is in love with playboy Jack Merrick (Henry Fonda), whom she marries, only to have the ceremony annulled by his cruel father (Donald Crisp). When the inevitable baby (Dwane Day) is born, she beseeches

Rogers to keep secret the fact that the child belongs to Merrick, who in the meantime has married society girl Flip (Anita Louise), confined to a wheelchair because of a car accident that occurred on their honeymoon. Rogers, dangerously ill, visits Mary, who comforts him until his wife arrives. As he lays dying, Davis exchanges places with his wife, as a conveniently hidden newspaperman, Virgil Whitaker (Hugh O'Connell), takes a photo of both women holding Rogers's hand. Davis gives up the boy to Merrick and Flip after the senior Merrick threatens to prove her an unfit mother. She tours European spas with the fortune left to her by Rogers. At Monte Carlo she is called to the phone by Whitaker and discovers that Flip is dead. Merrick proposes, and they live happily ever after.

The ending revealed a new facet of Davis's talent. As the sophisticated woman of the world, she gave evidence of the same sort of beauty and vulnerability she would exhibit five years later in *Now, Voyager.*

Goulding's manner of direction was at first foreign to Davis, because he acted out the big scenes, taking the place of each actor in turn.

In "The Screen's Best Bette" Arthur Janisch reported,

> In *That Certain Woman* . . . it was decided that Bette was to wear her hair in a page-boy bob, smooth and sleek with the ends turned under—until Bette heard about it.
>
> "Nothing doing," she said. "If I came to work with my hair fixed like that in those dignified offices, I'd be fired so quickly my head would swim."
>
> Director Edmund Goulding saw the wisdom of Bette's reasoning and she wore a hairdress in keeping with the character.
>
> A studio worker dropped into the wardrobe at the moment the head was giving some instructions to an assistant.
>
> "She wants those mules and sandals dyed to match her robe," said the wardrobe head. "In those scenes she is going to wear the mules when she gets up and the sandals later on where she is lounging—."
>
> "Don't tell me," said the studio worker, striking an exaggerated pose. "You're talking about Bette Davis."
>
> It would have been equally obvious to anyone else who knew Bette Davis intimately—for only Bette Davis pays

such close attention to what, to others, might seem inconsequential detail in the delineation of a character.

It was true; she constantly battled to preserve the integrity of the character she was playing. She objected to looking glamorous when awakened in the middle of the night or appearing without a hair-out-of-place in a rainstorm. She always insisted that she *look* as the character would have looked in a given situation.

Dolores Gilbert in Britain's *Film Weekly* said, "How disappointed I was with *That Certain Woman.* Old time melodrama, complete with baby—what a waste of Bette Davis's wonderful talents. That was hardly the stuff for brilliant actors. Bette must have better parts, or else!"

Liberty, in its October 2, 1937, review, was not encouraging, "Our condolences to the interesting, highly promising Bette Davis. She is having bad luck with her films since she returned contrite to the Warners' studio after her rebellion. This completely false and theatric effort will not help her."

[I had not had bad luck since my return from England. Marked Woman and Kid Galahad were fine films with good casts. That Certain Woman was certainly not one of my favorite scripts. I agree with the press; there was a falseness to the whole project. But I did meet and work with Edmund Goulding, the director, for the first time. He became a very important part of my career in the years that followed: Dark Victory, The Old Maid. *He was one of Hollywood's greatest directors. He made films at Metro for years. He was what we called a "woman's director" and a "star-maker." There was a certain amount of progress toward stardom for me in this film. He concentrated on attractive shots of me—in other words, gave me the "star" treatment. It was the first time I had had this. I was always a member of the cast—a leading member—but not made special in the way Goulding made me special in this film. And in the last scene in chiffon, a large beautiful picture hat, and a glamorous hairdo, I looked really like a "movie star."]*

IT'S BOX OFFICE I'M AFTER

Since Davis's return from England she had played a prostitute, a moll-mistress, and the wife of a rackets chief turned respectable; now Wallis sought a property that would offer more challenge—

perhaps a new facet to the Davis image. Casey Robinson had adapted an original story by Maurice Hanline called *Gentleman after Midnight,* which dealt with a famous Shakespearean acting couple, similar to the Lunts, who battle incessantly, only to end up in each other's arms at the fade-out. Robinson, thirty-four, was coming into his own as a screenwriter. His dialogue had punch, rhythm, and wit, and, when he was writing comedy, his work depended as much upon sight gags as upon dialogue.

The leading role of Basil Underwood was tailored to the talents of Leslie Howard, who had played Romeo ''straight'' with Norma Shearer the year before at MGM. Joyce Arden, his vis-à-vis, had been thought perfect for either Gertrude Lawrence or Ina Claire—both expert at turning an arch line in conjunction with an adroit, sophisticated characterization. However, these ladies had only appeared in films sporadically and did not have large fan followings. It was decided to give Davis the change-of-pace role and Olivia De Havilland the part of the star-struck society girl.

Directed by Archie Mayo, the story crackled with innuendo and comic undertone. The leads were aided considerably by the supporting cast of character people, each of whom slightly burlesques his usual type of role. Eric Blore embroidered his manservant role with hilarious bits of business. Patric Knowles as the stuffed-shirt boyfriend, Bonita Granville as the meddling youngster, George Barbier as De Havilland's blustering father, Spring Byington as the fluttery Aunt Ella, and E. E. Clive as the perfect butler, were all fine in support. The title was changed to *It's Love I'm After* before release.

The opening sequence, where the acting couple is performing the tomb scene from *Romeo and Juliet* before an audience, sets the mood for the picture. While rendering Shakespeare's lines in proper dramatic fashion, they are also having a violent *sotto voce* quarrel. He nips her ear. She covers his face with her hand; when he kisses her, she has been eating garlic. He pinches her. He trips her as she takes her curtain call. It is all highly mannered, funny, and very successful.

GONE WITH THE WIND, AGAIN

David O. Selznick was finally casting *Gone with the Wind,* and polls were conducted in the fan books. *[As you may remember, when Warner told me he had optioned a great new book for me to play the leading role, Scarlett O'Hara, my reply was, as I angrily left his office, "I bet it's a pip." This was our last meeting before the trial in England. I returned many months later to find I had walked out on one of the greatest woman's roles of all time!]* People from all walks of life wrote in their choices for Scarlett O'Hara and Rhett Butler. Clark Gable was the 90 percent choice for Butler. "Of the write-ins," Gavin Lambert reported in the February, 1973, issue of *Atlantic Monthly*, "Bette Davis was easily the most popular candidate, with 40 percent of the vote, but her refusal to play opposite Flynn had taken her out of the running." *[In the meantime, David Selznick had bought the book from Warner. He wanted Errol Flynn and me on a loan-out from Warner Bros. Thrilled as I was, I knew Flynn was* not *good casting as Rhett Butler, and therefore my performance would be hampered. Oh, if only I could have played it with Gable!]*

Not long afterward one of Davis's dreams came true. For a year or so she had begged Warner Bros. to buy a play called *Jezebel*. *[J.L. asked me why? He insisted no one would want to see a film about a girl who wore a red dress to the New Orleans Comos Ball. The custom was to wear a white dress. I told Warner only 10 million women would want to see this film. As it turned out, I was right.* Jezebel *was released a year before* Gone with the Wind. *Selznick accused J.L. of deliberately attempting to sabotage his film. The roles of Scarlett and Julie were very similar in type—and the setting of both films was in the South. Plus I won my second Oscar for* Jezebel.]*

THE GIRL IN THE RED DRESS

> *Amy, of course it's your right to go, you're his wife. But are you fit to go? Lovin' him isn't enough. If you gave him all your strength, would it be enough? . . . Do you know the Creole word for fever powder—for food and water? . . . His life and yours will hang on just things like that —and you'll both surely die.*
>
> BETTE DAVIS AS JULIE MARSDEN
> IN *Jezebel*

When Miriam Hopkins opened the senior Owen Davis's *Jezebel*, produced by Katharine Cornell and Guthrie McClintic, at the Ethel Barrymore Theatre on Broadway, December 19, 1933, the reviews were scathing, and the play lasted only thirty-two performances. Owen Davis, Sr., had been in a contractual dispute with the studio over one of his plays, and to solve the dilemma *Jezebel* was purchased for Davis.

A high $1.25 million budget was set for *Jezebel,* and the job of turning the play into a workable script was assigned to Clements Ripley, Abem Finkel, and John Huston. Robert Buckner was brought in later to do polish work. Wallis borrowed William Wyler, who had just finished *Dead End,* to direct. Davis, wishing to clear the air and remembering his rejection of her seven years before at Universal, told him about the "incident" when they first met! *[I very seldom planned any revenge on anybody. But, from the day Mr. Wyler humiliated me while making a test for him at Universal a few years before, I prayed for the day when I would be in the position of not only telling him about what he said but also being in a position to either accept or reject him as a director. I was in this position when Wallis engaged Mr. Wyler as the director of Jezebel. In a state of elation I went to his office at Warner Bros. for my first interview with him about playing the part of Julie in Jezebel. I sat down and immediately told him that he had tested me at Universal many years ago. He did not remember. I told him he had said, "What do you think of these dames who show their chests and think they can get jobs?" There was a long pause, and Mr. Wyler said, "I am a much nicer person now!" They say revenge is sweet. I found it to be futile that day.]*

Davis discovered to her delight that Wyler was a perfectionist. For the first time she discovered what it was like to be directed by a man who knew exactly what he wanted; it was true collaboration. He was demanding, temperamental, and often rude. He would retake a scene forty times to get what he wanted, then be very noncommittal. *[For the first two weeks Wyler never, after the printed take of a scene, would tell you whether it was good, bad, or indifferent. I am the type of actress who desperately needs the approval of my director. I told him so. He smiled graciously, said nothing, but for the rest of the day, after a scene was completed, would say, "Marvelous, Miss Davis, just marvelous!" This was worse. I laughed and told him to go back to being noncommittal!]*

Time magazine, in a cover story on Davis, on March 28, 1938, described the plot:

Jezebel . . . [is] as like to *Gone with the Wind* as chicory is to coffee. After some badly drawled atmosphere-setting about the propriety of mentioning a lady's name in a barroom, audiences knew that the girl to be reckoned with would be high-stepping Julie Marsden (Bette Davis) who had turned down a horse-and-hounds aristocrat named Buck Cantrell (George Brent) for one Preston Dillard (Henry Fonda.)

That Pres Dillard is in trade (banking) is bad enough, but that he neglects his lady for business is worse. To chastise Pres Julie wears red to the Mardi Gras Comos Ball, where unmarried girls traditionally wear white. To chastise Julie Pres dances her feet off while proper and white-frocked New Orleans belles primly withdraw to the sidelines. That night Julie's goodnight to Pres is a slap fully as resounding as that which Scarlett O'Hara deals to Ashley Wilkes to give *Gone with the Wind* its real start. When Pres goes, Julie is confident he will come back. A year later he does return with a Northern bride (Margaret Lindsay). With every vixenish wile she can think of, Julie tries to satisfy her longing and her hate. When a duel, born of her scheming, results in Buck Cantrell's death, even her motherly aunt (Fay Bainter) calls Julie a Jezebel.

But yellow fever sweeps out of the bayous, and the people of New Orleans, among them Pres Dillard, begin to drop. When it comes time to remove Pres to the leper and fever colony on Lazarette Island, from whence few return, Julie, strong in apparent regeneration, goes to nurse him, while his trustful Northern bride stays behind to pray for their return.

[Pooh! Time magazine! Wyler had so brilliantly directed this film—the triteness of the plot was not evident in the way Time described it. In the hands of a less-talented director, I think this would have been true. Anyway, nothing but the people went to see it!]

There was a great problem while shooting the film; Henry Fonda's scenes had to be finished by the first week in December because his wife was pregnant, and he wanted to be with her in the East when the baby was born. *[The baby was Jane Fonda.]* Davis was left to film many close-ups without her leading man to read the lines off camera, an almost impossible feat. Wyler, being a perfectionist, was behind schedule from the beginning. *[After a few weeks Mr. Warner threatened to fire Wyler unless he finished on time. He ignored the threats, only caring whether we made a good film or not. Came the day when J.L. said he was replacing Wyler. I knew by then my performance of Julie had a chance of making me an "honest to goodness" box office star because of the great direction I was receiving from Wyler. If he was fired, I would be lost. I went to see Mr. Warner and said, "If you don't fire Mr. Wyler, I will work every night until nine or ten o'clock and start shooting every morning at the usual time, nine o'clock." Warner agreed, and Wyler finished the picture.]*

Art director Robert Haas designed the enormous exterior plantation set of Halcyon, complete with huge pillars, moss-hung trees, and a dusty road that ran along the frontage—from which pickaninnys heralded the arrival of guests for the climactic party scene, "Carriage comin'! Carriage comin'!"

Besides George Brent and Henry Fonda, the cast included Fay Bainter, who had the most telling line in the screenplay: "I'm thinking about a woman called Jezebel, who did wrong in the sight of God." *[Miss Bainter, a truly great star of the American theater, played Auntie Belle. Her performance in* Jezebel *was an enormous contributing factor to the believability of the picture as a whole and to my performance in particular. Julie would never have been as great a success for me without her. She also won an Academy Award for* Jezebel *as the best supporting actress of the year. Also my favorite cameraman, Ernie Haller, won an award for his photography of* Jezebel.] Donald Crisp, Margaret Lindsay, Henry O'Neill, John Litel, Gordon Oliver, Spring Byington, and Richard Cromwell completed the supporting cast.

Orry-Kelly designed the costumes, the most controversial of which was the daring strapless red dress that Davis wore to the Comos Ball. He chose a deep rust-colored satin, which *looked* red, even in black and white. For the *Time* magazine cover Davis posed in the great hall at Halcyon in a gray damask gown trimmed at the neckline and bodice with pale olive velvet, her blonde hair drawn smoothly back from her face, with loose sausage curls at the nape. *[Interestingly enough, the gown was from a photograph taken at the time we tested the clothes for* Jezebel. *It was a gown that never appeared in the film!!!]*

The picture opened at Radio City Music Hall to crowds waiting

DARLING OF DIXIE! . . . "Meanest when she's lovin' most!"

Half angel, half siren, all woman! The screen's greatest actress comes to you in the hit picture of her career . . . as the most exciting heroine who ever lived and loved in Dixie!

WARNER BROS.
PRESENT

BETTE DAVIS in
"*Jezebel*"

THE GREATEST ROMANCE
OF THE SOUTH

HENRY FONDA • GEORGE BRENT • Margaret Lindsay • Donald Crisp • Fay Bainter

RICHARD CROMWELL • HENRY O'NEILL • SPRING BYINGTON • JOHN LITEL

Screen Play by Clements Ripley,
Abem Finkel and John Huston

A WILLIAM WYLER PRODUCTION

From the Play by Owen Davis, Sr.
Music by Max Steiner

in line, and throngs gathered wherever the picture was shown. The reviews, while praising Davis's performance, carped on various aspects of the plot.

THREE LITTLE MAIDS ALL IN A ROW, THREE LITTLE MAIDS FROM SILVER BOW

> *I want you to go in there and write the best fight story you've ever written in your life. Something people will talk about. We can't take chances now . . . I'm going to have a baby.*
>
> BETTE DAVIS AS LOUISE ELLIOTT MEDLIN
> IN *The Sisters*

All Warner contract players were shocked at the treatment of Kay Francis, who had been brought from Paramount with such fanfare six years before. She was on the last year of her contract and still the highest-paid star on the lot, at $4,000 per week. *The Sisters,* which had been purchased for her, was shelved, and she was given the remake (with a sex change in the Muni part) of *Dr. Socrates.* The studio *announced* to the trade press that she would work out the remaining months in "B" pictures. Francis made light of the edict by telling reporters that she looked forward to retiring but later told British critic W. H. Mooring that Warner Bros. almost broke her heart.

Davis was told her next picture would be *Comet over Broadway* from a story by Faith Baldwin with a screenplay by Mark Hellinger and Robert Buckner. Davis was to portray actress Eve Appleton, who gives up her career to tend her unwanted husband when he leaves state prison on a murder charge. Davis asserted that the part, the lines, and, above all, the story were old-fashioned dribble and told J.L. that she wouldn't do it. *[This was the first nothing script I was given since my court battle in England. It was heartbreaking to me. After winning a second Academy Award, working with a truly great director, Willie Wyler, in a beautifully produced film, I was asked to appear again in junk. One would think that after winning an Oscar a studio would work even harder to find a picture even better than* Jezebel*!]*

After a few weeks Davis was sent the script for a musical, *Garden of the Moon,* by Jerry Wald and Richard Macaulay, to be directed by Busby Berkeley. Costarring with Dick Powell and Pat O'Brien, she was to play the part of Toni Blake, the girl friend of the manager of a nightclub in Los Angeles called Garden of the Moon. Feeling the script was of little consequence, she preferred to stay on suspension. Powell also took a powder and was supplanted by John Payne. Margaret Lindsay played Toni Blake. *[I was on suspension for a good part of the year following* Jezebel. *So much wasted time at a time when I felt my career could from then on become a truly successful one. Plus one does have to eat. It took a lot of courage to go on suspension. One received no salary. This is what the studios counted on. We would work because we couldn't afford not to be paid every week. I couldn't afford it; nor could I afford, career-wise, to make films such as* Comet over Broadway *and* Garden of the Moon *!]*

Davis came off suspension when assigned to *The Sisters,* an adaptation of the best seller by Myron Brinig. The literate screenplay by Milton Krims was to be produced by Wallis in association with David Lewis, with Anatole Litvak as director.

The thirty-six-year-old director, born Mikhail Anatol Litvak in Kiev, emigrated to Berlin in 1925 to make a number of important German films, the most important of which was *Mayerling,* shot in 1936, with Charles Boyer and Danielle Darrieux, after which he came to the U.S. He had made two films at Warner Bros., *Tovarich* with Charles Boyer and Claudette Colbert and *The Amazing Dr. Clitterhouse* with Edward G. Robinson. He was a perfectionist, requiring many rehearsals and many takes from a script already worked out in complete detail before shooting. He was fond of moody, atmospheric photography, making use of long tracking shots, visually complicated setups, and luminous low-key lighting.

Her role of Louise Elliott Medlin in *The Sisters* provided a new, docile, and very different Bette Davis. *[I was delighted with this part because it was a change of pace. My ambition always has been—and still is—for variety in the kinds of parts I play. My career has proved this. I was always challenged by a new type of person to play.]* Besides the principals a great cast was assembled: Ian Hunter, Donald Crisp, Beulah Bondi, Alan Hale, Dick Foran, Patric Knowles, Henry Travers, Lee Patrick, Laura Hope Crews, Harry Davenport, Mayo Methot, and Irving Bacon. Her costar was Errol Flynn. *[I was extremely happy to be costarred for the first time with Errol Flynn. He was a big box office star at the time, and it could only be beneficial to me to work with him. At that time I had no billing clause in my contract. I felt after Jezebel that my name should always appear above the title. That is star billing. Warner Bros. decided to bill Errol Flynn as the sole star— Errol Flynn in* The Sisters, *with Bette Davis—my name below the title. Not only did I feel that Errol Flynn in* The Sisters *had its humorous, even "far-out" connotation, I also felt that* The Sisters *was a female star's title. After taking a very definite stand with the studio, the billing read, Errol Flynn, Bette Davis, in* The Sisters.*]*

The plot of *The Sisters* incorporated the four-year period from the inauguration of Theodore Roosevelt to the election of William Howard Taft. "This history of an era still within memory," commented *Life* magazine's October 31, 1939, review, "yet curiously closed and sealed, is reflected in Warner Bros. *The Sisters*. In it the three Elliott girls, daughters of a Montana druggist, find, each in her own fashion, a modicum of grief and happiness. Stolid Grace (Jane Bryan) married the banker's son. Frivolous Helen (Anita Louise) goes to Europe with an aging millionaire. Serious Louise (Bette Davis) shares the life of a sports writer, who fails as a novelist, takes to drink, deserts her for the sea, [and] return humbled and chastened. As the wife who works for her husband, survives the San Francisco earthquake, and remains loyal as the stars, Bette Davis acts with [such] extraordinary grace, sensitivity, and distinction that hers is already being acclaimed the movie performance of the year."

The climax takes place during the San Francisco earthquake, which lasted two and one-half minutes screen time, a considerably more economical holocaust than the same event staged for Metro's *San Francisco,* with Clark Gable and Jeanette MacDonald, two years previously.

The first indication of the disaster of April 18, 1906, occurs when the pendulum of the grandfather clock in Davis's living room begins to swing violently, preceded by a low, ominous rumble. The ceiling crumbles, and the walls disintegrate. Next-door neighbor Flora (Lee Patrick) runs through the ruins to Davis screaming, "It's the end of the world!"

Thirty-four years later Lee Patrick commented that John Hollowell, in an article in *The Los Angeles Times's West* magazine, appeared surprised that Davis had called her autobiography *The Lonely Life,* but went on with the opinion that those featured players who worked with Davis during those early years thought that she never knew they existed. Patrick further stated that although she appeared in the earthquake sequence in *The Sisters* with her, Davis gave the impression in her book that she had appeared in the scene by herself.

[Not until I read this book of Mr. Stine's did I ever know of Lee Patrick's feeling about me. Dear Lee: You and I worked together many times. I always felt you were one of our very best actresses and therefore felt very fortunate when you were in a film of mine. Quite the contrary, the record shows how very many times I fought for featured players not only to be cast with me because they were good actors but stood up for them when difficulties arose during shooting. If I failed to mention your name in connection with the earthquake scene in my book The Lonely Life, *it was an unintentional oversight. I offer my apology. You certainly suffered through it with me!]*

Krims surmounted a major problem in censorship involving Flora (played by Miss Patrick), a "fancy lady," without ever alluding to her character. After the earthquake Patrick tells Davis to go to her mother's house in Oakland if she is unable to locate Flynn, who, unbeknown to them, has taken a slow boat to China. Shaken and disheveled, Davis seeks out the address, only to find that "mother" (Laura Hope Crews) is actually the madam of a bordello and Flora her "daughter." The whorehouse scenes are staged with great cunning with the girls in various poses—temporarily out of work because of the conflagration. Davis, ensconced in an upstairs room, has a miscarriage. When her employer (Ian Hunter) and newspaper friend (Donald Crisp) come to take her home, Miss Crews simply explains the disarray with "We had a party here last night!"—and not a peep was heard from Joseph I. Breen, the censorship czar!

The Sisters ended with the girls reunited at the Taft election ball in Silver Bow. But the studio was displeased at what was an essentially downbeat ending. *[Oh dear, how many films I have been in that have suffered from the change by the studio of the ending. There is always the honest ending to any story. I fought for many honest endings—sometimes was able to prove my point, often was defeated. Certainly the original ending of* The Sisters *was the right one. Those in charge of studios changed endings after a film was finished as often as they changed titles—both detrimental to our work in the film.]* A new scene was written in which Flynn, contrite, returns to his wife. There is the usual ending clinch, staged this time on the balcony of the hall, with the returns coming in as the new president is elected. The stylish score by Max Steiner made use of the folk ballad ''My Darling Clementine,'' used intermittently throughout as the theme for Silver Bow.

The reviews were mixed, but the film made money.

VICTORY OVER THE DARK

Marry? Oh, wouldn't it be marvelous if we could . . . have a real wedding and be given away. . . . church bells, and champagne, and a white frock and orange blossoms, and a wedding cake. That's one thing I won't have missed, and you're giving it to me. I can never love you enough.

BETTE DAVIS AS JUDITH TRAHERNE
IN *Dark Victory*

It can be said with accuracy that 1939 was undoubtedly the high point in the career of Bette Davis. Four money-making films were released and favorably reviewed in the span of twelve months. *Dark Victory* was shown to the press in March, *Juarez* in April, *The Old Maid* in August, and *The Private Lives of Elizabeth and Essex* in September. In some parts of the country all four were playing simultaneously. The fan books devoted more space to Davis than to any other star in 1939.

There would be other years when a smash Davis picture would bowl over public and critic alike; when Academy Award nominations spoke of Hollywood's regard for her—*Dark Victory* (1939), *The Letter* (1940), *The Little Foxes* (1941), *Now, Voyager* (1942), *Mr. Skeffington* (1944), *All about Eve* (1950), *The Star* (1953), *What Ever Happened to Baby Jane?* (1962)—but her truly herculean efforts in 1939 would make these successes possible.

In 1934 Tallulah Bankhead appeared on Broadway as Judith Traherne in a play by George Emerson Brewer, Jr., and Bertram Block entitled *Dark Victory*—which dealt with an heiress who developed terminal glaucoma. Although the play ran for only fifty-one performances, David O. Selznick thought the property would make a good vehicle for Janet Gaynor or Carole Lombard and paid $50,000 for the screen rights.

Four years later Davis discovered *Dark Victory*. She touted the story to every producer on the Warner lot, but only David Lewis showed enthusiasm; together they approached Edmund Goulding, who also recognized the potential of the story. Hopefully, the trio went to Wallis.

With Harry and Albert Warner tabulating the enormous grosses of *Jezebel* and enthusiastic over the reviews of *The Sisters,* J.L. told Wallis, "To keep peace in the family, I'll buy it for her. She's pestered me for six months. Just get her off my back!" He purchased *Dark Victory* from Selznick for $50,000.

An "A" above-the-line budget was set up for the amount of $800,000. Casey Robinson wrote the script, and Ernie Haller was her cameraman again. Max Steiner composed the score, and George Brent was her costar.

No female contract player on the lot was quite right for the part of Ann, Judith's best friend and companion. Geraldine Fitzgerald, a new British actress, was signed to make her American debut. *[Mr. Goulding, this true genius of film-making, whom I had worked with on* That Certain Woman, *worked also on the script. He added the character of the best friend, Ann, played so beautifully by Fitsie, so that Judith would not have to ever complain about her tragedy. Without Ann it was necessary for Judith to do so, in order that the audience would know her problems. This, I feel, is what the play lacked. This addition made* Dark Victory *a much finer film than it would have been otherwise.]* Bogart was assigned the role of an Irish stable hand, while Ronald Reagan, Henry Travers, and Cora Witherspoon supported. *[Bogart, at the time of* Dark Victory, *had not hit the great career he finally had. I thought his performance in this was just perfect. We had some very difficult scenes to play together. I thanked God for the help his performance gave me in playing mine.]*

Fighting for each worthwhile picture at the studio and battling with Nelson at home finally took its toll. They separated, and it was a painful experience for them both.

Prior to starting *Dark Victory* Davis became involved in a personal situation that could have adversely affected her career if made public. Her excellent relations with the press paid off—not one word was ever printed. She was still emotionally upset when the picture started shooting. The sequence in the doctor's office, where Judith first learns of her illness, was shot first. There is no doubt that her personal feelings at this time infused these scenes with a vulnerability caught by the camera. After a week she told Wallis, "Hal, I've wanted to play this part for years, but I don't think I'm up

Davis and Sally Sage, Davis's stand-
in for twenty-seven pictures, on the
set of *That Certain Woman*, 1937.
(*Photograph by Warner Bros.*)

Joyce Arden (Bette Davis) and
Basil Underwood (Leslie How-
ard) rehearse a scene from
Romeo and Juliet in *It's Love
I'm After*, 1937. (*Photograph by
Bert Longworth, Warner Bros.*)

Bette Davis as Louise Elliott Medlin in *The Sisters*, 1938. (*Photograph by Elmer Fryer, Warner Bros.*)

Judith Traherne (Bette Davis) in *Dark Victory*, 1939, heroically sends her husband (George Brent) to a medical convention, knowing that she is blind and will soon die. (*Photograph by Warner Bros.*)

Center, Bette Davis as Louise in *The Sisters; in auto, left to right,*
Dick Foran, Davis; *back row,* Jane Bryan, Beulah Bondi, Henry
Travers, and Anita Louise. (*Photograph by Warner Bros., from
the collection of Whitney Stine.*)

Bette Davis as Empress Carlota of Mexico in *Juarez*, 1939. (*Photograph by George Hurrell, Warner Bros., from the collection of Bill Roy.*)

Bette Davis posed for George Hurrell's still camera in 1939 for the advertisement for *Dark Victory*. (*Photograph by Warner Bros.*)

Optical printing gives the impression that Bette Davis is going insane in *Juarez*. (*Photograph by Warner Bros., from the collection of Gunnard Nelson.*)

to it at this time. I think you should replace me. I'm sick!''

"Bette," he replied, "I've seen the first week's rushes. Stay sick!''

When she came into the portrait gallery, photographer George Hurrell saw something different in her face. "You're beautiful, Bette," he told her and proceeded to take a series of pictures that would be the most outstanding of her entire career. He captured a delicate, extremely appealing quality.

J.L. told Davis on the first day of shooting, "I don't know who is going to want to see a picture about a girl who dies, but it's a great part, and I'm happy to give you the chance to play her."

The "biggest acting problem for the big-eyed Miss Davis," reported the April 24, 1939, issue of *Life* magazine, "was to simulate loss of sight. Her method: 'Driving home at dusk, I'd pretend it was really daylight and I was going blind and I'd try to look just as far as I could into the darkness.' "

Goulding acted out various difficult scenes to show the effect he wanted. The script was always fluid; he could improvise. Mindful of Davis's tendency to squint and her habit of clenching and un-clenching her fists, he did not scream at her as Wyler had done—"Stop moving your head. Do you want me to put a chain around your neck?"—but used gentle tactics. He got from her a controlled performance that still looked effortless.

During a nightclub scene early in the picture, when Judith is on a binge after inadvertently learning of her malignancy and before she has reconciled with the doctor, Goulding underscored the scene with an effective device. With Elsie Janis he wrote a song, "Oh, Give Me Time for Tenderness,''* which was performed in the nightclub. Davis sits at the bar, staring into a cocktail, and sings along with the band singer:

> Oh, give me time for tenderness,
> One little hour from each big day,
> Oh, give me time to stop and bless the golden sunset of a
> summer day.
> Let my heart be still and listen to one song of love,
> Let me feel the thrill of quiet we know nothing of,

Oh, give me time for tenderness,
To hold your hand and understand,
Oh, give me time.

But the most emotionally difficult transition for her was the scene near the end where Ann and she are planting hyacinth bulbs in the garden. It is a bright, sunny, Vermont day. Judith remarks that the sun has gone under a cloud, yet feels the hot sunlight on her face and hands. She knows the end is near. It is the climax of the picture. With sight fading, she asks Ann to dig the holes for the bulbs while she plants them by touch.

As the scene progressed, Davis's empathy with the character was so great that she couldn't help crying. "I don't know what's wrong with me," she told Goulding. "Dammit, I *can't* cry in this scene; it's all wrong!" He did not hound her but quietly ran the scene over and over. Finally, dry-eyed, Davis gave the result they both wanted.

The ads for *Dark Victory* were the most truthful and dignified ever planned for a Davis film. *[I always felt that for the most part the ads for films were misleading, too often intentionally planned this way by the studio. If they were frightened about the success of a film, they made the ads for the purpose of getting the public in. They often portrayed your character in the ad very sexily, or they would draw another body onto your head—particularly if a costume picture, which usually terrified the studios after they had finished them. This, in my opinion, was a cheat. It only took the movie-goer, after buying his ticket, a few minutes of viewing the film to know that the ads were false. For instance, Miss Moffat in* The Corn Is Green *was a middle-aged schoolteacher. The ads showed me in a sexy black satin modern dress. This I put up a battle about. I felt people, not understanding, would subconsciously blame me. Some changes were eventually made in* The Corn Is Green *ad. Thus, my happiness when I saw the ads for* Dark Victory.*]* Featuring Hurrell's superb photographs, the ads proclaimed,

Deep in the heart of every actress lives the ideal role she longs to play—a role that embodies every talent she possesses. Now such a role has come to Bette Davis in *Dark Victory*. Not a "character" part, but a natural, normal woman who faces all that fate can offer—all the sweet and bitter of life—all the joy and pain of love—and comes through the dark with colors gloriously flying. Eight years she has waited to play this role. We sincerely believe it's her greatest screen performance.

Davis had to smile. Eight years indeed! Only a scant half dozen of the thirty-seven films that she had made were worthwhile. *Dark Victory* opened at Radio City Music Hall in March, 1939, to the greatest reviews yet of a Davis picture.

Frank Nugent exclaimed on April 21, 1939, in *The New York Times,* "Miss Davis is superb. More than that, she is enchanted and enchanting. Admittedly, it is a great role—rangy, full bodied, designed for a virtuoso, almost sure to invite the faint damning of 'tour de force.' But that must not detract from the eloquence, the tenderness, the heart-breaking sincerity with which she has played it."

The New Yorker on April 22, 1939, said, "Miss Davis is never so assured in the display of her talent as when she must portray a lady about to die, eaten by dread maladies, consumed by mortal fevers. Such is her part in *Dark Victory,* and the bravado of her agonies will touch the nation's heart. . . . The tumor affects the heroine's sight, and Miss Davis uses all of her very real skill in the wavering gestures of incipient blindness."

Time magazine's reviewer wrote, on May 6, 1939, *"Dark Victory,* if it were an automobile, would be a Rolls Royce with a Brewster body and the very best trimmings. . . . it gives [Bette Davis] a chance to do a good job and puts her well up in line for her third Academy Award."

On the David Frost program devoted to Davis on May 8, 1971, the ending clip from the thirty-two-year-old *Dark Victory* was shown. When the live camera switched back to Davis, she appeared somewhat strained, then smiled, "I always have to laugh a little . . . because there was really no need for Judith to die, because my beautiful Max Steiner did it for me. Even before I got on the bed, the angels were singing!"

THE IMPOSSIBLE DREAM

Can you explain the reason for the intolerable humiliation to which I have been subjected? Although I notified the Emperor Napoleon of my arrival from the Port of St.

PORTRAIT OF A FREE SOUL

NOW SEE THIS FACE ON THE SCREEN!

Out of the blazing fires of her genius, the screen's most gifted actress has created a gallery of unforgettable women. Now Bette Davis, the winner of two Academy Awards, comes to you in the climax of all her dramatic triumphs. In the role she has waited eight years to play. In the greatest picture of a woman's love that the world has yet seen. See "Dark Victory," a Warner Bros. picture, at your theatre Easter Week!

Nazaire, upon reaching Paris there was no one to receive
me—not an equerry—not so much as a carriage waiting!
And I was compelled to proceed . . . to a public hostelry!

BETTE DAVIS AS EMPRESS CARLOTA
IN *Juarez*

In fall, 1937, Paul Muni returned to Warner Bros. after filming *The Good Earth* for MGM and *The Woman I Love* for RKO to prepare *The Life of Emile Zola.* Bette Davis begged for the small role of Nana, knowing Wallis might say yes if Muni wanted her; Muni said no.

Writer Wolfgang Reinhardt suggested the studio turn to the story of *Juarez* for Muni. On September 30, 1937, Aeneas MacKenzie started the first-draft screenplay, under Henry Blanke's supervision. John Huston and Reinhardt did additional work on the screenplay (and Abem Finkel contributed dialogue polishing without screen credit).

The most intriguing aspect about the story was the fact that antagonist Benito Juarez never met protagonist Maximilian von Hapsburg, who had been sent by Napoleon III to rule Mexico. The story actually amounted to *two* screenplays. Contrapuntal editing embraced hundreds of difficult scene transitions to keep both stories going at the same time.

To prevent another version of the movie being made and possible plagiarism lawsuits Warner Bros. bought the screen rights to Bertita Harding's book *The Phantom Crown* and Franz Werfel's play *Juarez and Maximilian,* and with 357 other sources (some in French and Spanish) the difficult screenplay was finally fashioned.

Head of research Herman Lissauer rented 300 volumes on the subject from scholars. All during that year Blanke, William Dieterle, and two historians helped writers with changes.

"Our problem from the outset in preparing this story for the screen," Blanke told Harold Turney, chairman of the drama department at Los Angeles City College for his thesis in *Film Guide,* "was by no means one of glossing over facts, but rather one of cleaving to the exact line. . . . France, England, Austria, Switzerland, and the United States, Spain, Cuba, as well as unfortunate Mexico, were all involved in these events of history between July, 1863, and June, 1868, the period of our story."

In August Wallis, Blanke, Dieterle, and Muni left for a tour of Mexico to obtain local color, stopping at fifteen towns en route to

Mexico City, where the private memoirs of Benito Juarez were found in the National Museum. A 116-year-old soldier was found who had fought with Juarez under Porfirio Diaz. Muni wanted to know how Juarez looked, walked, talked, and if he had mannerisms.

Perc Westmore had a tough assignment in turning the actor into Juarez. "We started by taking photographs of Muni, then painting the likeness of the Indian Juarez over them," the makeup artist reported to Turney. "We took plaster casts of his face. We had to accentuate his bone structure, make his jaws appear wider, square his forehead, and give him an Indian nose. He had to be darker than anyone else in the picture, so we used a dark reddish-brown makeup, highlighted with yellow. We wrote down every step of the process so it could be repeated."

When J.L. saw the makeup tests, he said, *"You mean we're paying Muni all this dough and we can't even recognize him?"*

For Davis, who was playing Carlota to Brian Aherne's Maximilian, Westmore ordered a black wig from his talented wigmaker Sophie. Thirty-two years later, in 1971, Davis wore a copy of the same black wig for *Madame Sin,* a television movie that was released abroad as a feature film. The same Sophie made the copy of the original wig.

To point up Carlota's growing insanity Orry-Kelly used visual psychology in designing her clothes. He created a white dress for her first scene, and, as the picture progressed, the color of the gowns changed from white to gray. Finally, when she was completely mad, she was seen in black.

Among the 1,186 supporting players were Claude Rains as Napoleon III, John Garfield as Diaz, Gale Sondergaard as Empress Eugenie, and Joseph Calleia as Alejandro Uradi.

Art director Anton Grot and assistant Leo Kuter drew a total of 3,643 sketches from which 7,360 blueprints were drawn before the fifty-four sets were constructed—the largest being a recreation of a miniature eleven-acre Mexico on a ranch at Calabasas.

The throne room and living quarters of Maximilian were built on Stage Seven—with a 250-foot-long-by-50-foot-high backdrop of Mexico City and Popocatepetl Peak in the background. Head of the property department James Gibbens invented a ruby-colored stained glass that, when inserted in frames of windows, enabled the many night shots to be filmed in broad daylight.

Two weeks before the October 29, 1938, actual shooting date

Dieterle put a call in for Tony Gaudio and the principals to be at the studio at 8:00 one morning. The superstitious director wanted to film the first scene to correspond with his good astrological aspects! *[This Dieterle always did and became famous for.]*

After seeing the completed scenes, Bella Muni remarked to her husband that it was a complete picture *without* Juarez. Muni added fifty pages to the script, consequently many Davis-Aherne scenes had to be cut.

A new ending was tacked on. After Juarez has Maximilian shot via a firing squad and the archduke is lying in state in the cathedral, Juarez pays him a visit. Looking down at the "blonde god," the Mexican says, "Forgive me." Although this episode had no basis in fact, the studio felt that it made the ending more palatable—and softened Muni's characterization. Although insane, Carlota survived her husband for six decades, dying in a chateau in Brussels in January, 1927.

Erich Wolfgang Korngold composed 3,000 bars of music. "In writing the score," he related in *Film Guide,* "I discovered that the music composed in Mexico during the period from 1864 to 1870 was not Mexican music at all! But unmistakably Viennese. Some of the castanets also tapped out the rhythms of Chopin and Schubert. The European influence was so strong at the time that the composers abandoned their native music. Fandangos and native polkas of the period are actually Strauss waltzes and marches. Only the instrumentation was changed. Instead of violins and cellos the Mexican players undoubtedly used their native guitars and mandolins; thus, the people of the country failed to note the really subtle change. But imagine what would have happened had I not recognized Strauss and used instead the music of those historic years?"

Charles Einfeld, head of publicity, was afraid that the public would mispronounce the title of the picture and suggested to the art department that *Juarez* (war-ezz) be spelled phonetically in the ads.

Juarez opened at the Hollywood Theatre, New York, on April 25, 1939.

The press was enthusiastic, but, even so, the picture was not the moneymaker that Warner Bros. had hoped; yet studio prestige was made by films like *Juarez.*

THE QUEEN BECOMES A LANDOWNER

Look magazine went into some detail when Davis bought a house in 1939:

> It was not until this year that the nervous, glamour-hating Yankee decided to settle down in a home of her own. Previously, in her ten-year Hollywood residence, she had lived in some twenty-five houses—which meant that she moved faster than some of her earlier, now happily forgotten, pictures. When Hollywood's best actress finally went house shopping, she avoided swank Brentwood, where once she had paid $750 per month for a former Garbo retreat, and passed by Beverly Hills and Bel Air. She found a small, but delightful, English farmhouse in the Los Angeles River valley at Glendale, where two years ago a flood washed the neighbors away. . . .
>
> . . . often seeing herself on the screen, she shrieks: "I have the homeliest face I've ever seen." In reality she's attractive, perhaps Hollywood's most vibrant, natural star. Once, lunching at Warners, she shouted over to director Frank Capra: "When are you going to have something for me?" He yelled back: "There isn't anything you haven't got."
>
> . . . Two scotties and a poodle help enliven the Davis household . . . She dislikes formal pictures almost as much as she dislikes being called "Bett." "Dammit," she will remonstrate, "my name is pronounced Betty."

Living five minutes away from the studio at Riverbottom enabled Davis to sleep an hour longer in the morning. Even so, when making a costume film, she had to report at 5:00 A.M. The next picture, a period piece, called for her to age drastically on the screen—her first "older" character part. Davis, at thirty-one, was to play a woman of sixty in *The Old Maid*.

10

Tonight she belongs to me. Tonight I want her to call me mother.

BETTE DAVIS AS CHARLOTTE LOVELL
IN *The Old Maid*

"*The Old Maid,*" said *Time* magazine on August 21, 1939, in a review of the next Davis film, "is a drama of anonymous mother love, circa 1860-80, outwardly as dated and dusty as a Daguerreotype." The review continued,

> To bring Edith Wharton's old-fashioned story to life on Broadway four years ago required the highly finished services of actresses Judith Anderson and Helen Menken, and old-time playwright Zoe Atkins. To make it live on the screen, Warner Brothers teamed their pop-eyed Bernhardt, Bette Davis, with an equally fiery filly from off the home lot, honey-haired Miriam Hopkins. The result flounces its skirts a little more boldly than the stage show, but like it, is hardly more than the sum total of two good, sometimes brilliant, performances . . . Though the musty setting of *The Old Maid* is enough to make anyone susceptible to historical hay fever squirm, few will be unimpressed with the skill with which director Edmund Goulding manages his spirited costars. Instead of trying to divide the fat bits between them, he so deals out their histrionic diet that they banquet as did Jack Spratt and his wife, cooperatively.

This "histrionic diet" was made memorable by the temperament of the two women, who had known each other casually since the George Cukor Stock Company days in Rochester, New York, when Miriam Hopkins was the star and Davis the ingenue. Davis had never costarred with a female before and looked forward to an opportunity of establishing a particularly meaningful chemistry. Hopkins had given some fine performances, notably as *Becky Sharp* in the first feature-length Technicolor feature made three years before.

But Hopkins made life on the set almost unendurable. A fine actress in a fine part, she was not above engaging in such unnecessary amateur shenanigans as upstaging. If Davis had a difficult scene with involved "business," she would spoil the take with "I'm so sorry, one of my buttons came unbuttoned!" or some other ruse. A couch scene took twenty takes because Hopkins kept moving backward into a more favorable angle, which continually spoiled the shot.

Tony Gaudio complained to Goulding that, in a sequence where she was supposed to be elderly, Hopkins's long false eyelashes gave her the look of a starlet, despite character lighting. But her big scene, filmed on the first day of shooting and designed to show who was boss on the set, was fortunately cut before release. Hopkins appeared in a complete replica of the first costume Davis had worn in *Jezebel. [To Miriam's utter disappointment I gave no indication I had any idea that her costume was a copy of mine in* Jezebel.*]* In its August 21, 1939, issue, *Life* magazine hit the nail on the head:

> The fact that Davis and Hopkins dislike each other intensely not only added to their pleasure in making the picture, but also proved so mutually stimulating that Hal Wallis, Warner Bros. production chief, plans to team them again in *Devotion.* Part of the jealousy between Misses Hopkins and Davis may be due to the fact that the stage version of *Jezebel,* starring Hopkins, lasted only four weeks, while the movie version got Bette Davis her second Academy Award.

[Life magazine did not hit the nail on the head, Mr. Stine. The jealousy was completely one-sided. I have never been jealous of an actor I was working with in my life. Any performance of mine has usually been as good as the cast I was surrounded by—plus, if I

*couldn't be good against competition, then I deserved to fail. I
certainly would never be jealous of the actor who proved himself
better than I.]*

In the first part of the film Davis and Hopkins were young
women, and, as the film progressed, they aged gradually, a makeup
feat for Perc Westmore. Instead of marking lines on Davis's face he
used a pale, ashen base, with no eye makeup and lipstick, so she
would look as faded and frail as a withered nosegay. It was a
memorable portrait.

Orry-Kelly was again in charge of costumes. The clothes included everything from an elaborate white satin wedding dress to a
prim moiré and taffeta gown especially befitting the 1880s conception of an old maid.

George Brent assayed the part of the paramour who fathers
Davis's illegitimate child in the Casey Robinson script. Jane Bryan
played the grown-up daughter. Louise Fazenda, Hal Wallis's wife,
known affectionately in Hollywood as "Aunt Kate," and DeWolf
Hopper, who would still recite "Casey at the Bat" at the drop of a
hat, were also in the cast. Fazenda retired from the screen upon
completion of the picture.

*[Jane Bryan in her short career gave some very fine
performances. I worked with her in* Marked Woman, Kid Galahad,
The Sisters, *and now* The Old Maid. *She was also in many other
films while under contract to Warner Bros. I was always interested
in her career. We also became very good friends. When she
confided that she was in love and was going to give up her career, as
the man she loved did not want her to continue if she married him, I
was sorry, as I thought she had a great future in films. She has,
however, never regretted her decision in all these many years. She
has had a happy and rewarding life as Mrs. Justin Dart.]*

The world premiere of the film was held at the Carthay Circle
Theatre in Los Angeles, and all the Warner contract players
attended the opening, but Davis and Hopkins were in the East doing
publicity.

THE LADY AND THE KNIGHT

[The above was the title Warner Bros. gave to the play Elizabeth the
Queen *after purchasing it. The pun, of course, was implied—The
Lady and the (K)Night! To call a queen of England a lady was*

horrific—a more undignified title could not have been found. It was cheap, hoping to disguise the fact it was to be a film of historical importance. Before we started filming, I went to J.L. about the title. At the end of the interview he promised to change it to Elizabeth and Essex. *After a month of shooting the title had not been changed. I left the set one day and confronted J.L. with his promise. The title was changed. Because of title rights it was changed to* The Private Lives of Elizabeth and Essex.*]*

> *I could be young with you, but now I'm old.*
> *I know now how it will be without you. The sun*
> *Will be empty and circle around an empty earth—*
> *And I will be queen of emptiness and death—*
> *Why could you not have loved me enough to give me*
> *Your love and let me keep as I was?*
>
> BETTE DAVIS AS ELIZABETH I
> IN *The Private Lives of Elizabeth and Essex*

Several studios had been interested in the Maxwell Anderson verse-play *Elizabeth the Queen*—the hit of the 1930 Broadway season—which starred Lynn Fontanne as Elizabeth I and Alfred Lunt as Lord Essex. But period dramas, especially after the coming of sound, spiraled expensive, historical productions into the stratosphere.

Actresses of the Irene Rich, Ruth Chatterton, type, old enough to tackle the role, either were no longer box office or would not subject themselves to character roles. MGM had a hit in *Queen Christina* (Greta Garbo) in 1933 and *Marie Antoinette* (Norma Shearer) in 1938, RKO struck pay dirt with *Mary of Scotland* (Katharine Hepburn) in 1936, and Paramount released *The Scarlet Empress* (Marlene Dietrich), the story of Catherine the Great, in 1934.

As far back as the Hepburn film Davis had had her eye on *Mary of Scotland*, in which Elizabeth appeared in a small role. At her request she was interviewed by director John Ford, who told her she talked too much and ended the appointment.

In 1938 Warner Bros. bought the Maxwell Anderson play for Davis for her first Technicolor film. She asked Westmore to shave her head back a few inches, as the queen was bald and at sixty wore a wig. Wallis, long used to her demands, was horrified; no actress had ever appeared bald in a movie before, and Warner Bros.'s top star would not be the first! Elizabeth's age was also troublesome. If she was in her middle thirties, L'affair Essex might appear more plausible to her fans. Davis hotly reminded them that the Queen was sixty-five when she fell in love with Essex. Wallis finally agreed to let Westmore shave her hairline so the various red wigs would give the illusion of baldness.

Davis's old nemesis Michael Curtiz was assigned to direct the Norman Reilly Raine-Aeneas MacKenzie screenplay. But it was not Curtiz who bothered her—it was the casting of Errol Flynn as Essex. *[In all our scenes together I used to dream that Laurence Olivier was Essex.]*

Orry-Kelly researched the Elizabethan period thoroughly, but, when Curtiz saw the costumes for her first tests, he said, *"Too beeg,"* and pointed to the hoop skirts and the ruff around her neck. Orry-Kelly and Davis had been around long enough to win their way. Two sets of costumes were made. Davis tested in the scaled-down gowns and wore the larger historically correct clothes in the film!

Orry-Kelly had every available studio seamstress busy on Elizabeth's wardrobe, because many of the costumes were gem encrusted, quilted, or embroidered. For the hawking-party scene she wore a bottle-green brocade riding habit with a long green velvet cloak. A white quilted satin gown embroidered in pearls served for an important council scene, while a changeable green and bronze taffeta costume with a high delicate ruff was placed aside for a love scene. A subdued black brocade was reserved for the ending, when Essex is sent off to be beheaded. British film critics objected to her going to the tower to visit Essex; queens never did. Instead of the usual canvas "director's chair," the carpentry department built Davis an especially designed long wooden bench to accommodate the huge hoop skirts.

The cast was unusually competent. Olivia De Havilland played the fictional Lady Penelope Gray, a character actually based on Lady Mary Howard. Vincent Price, who had played Albert to Helen Hayes's Victoria on Broadway, was Sir Walter Raleigh. Donald Crisp portrayed Sir Francis Bacon; Henry Stephenson, Lord Burghley; Henry Daniell, Sir Robert Cecil; and Alan Hale, Earl of Tyrone. The bit part of Lady Margaret was assigned to Nanette Fabares (Fabray), who later became a renowned television comedienne.

Because there were a great many tense dramatic scenes, there was more horseplay than on the usual Davis set. Flynn was very fond of De Havilland, who was determined throughout their long association in films to keep the relationship platonic, but he loved to play jokes. While filming *Dodge City* he put a garter snake in her pantaloons. He gave her a magnifying glass that spouted water at the touch of a spring.

It had long been established from stage tradition that the star of a film never appeared in the first scene. The opening sequence was always preparatory to the "grand entrance"—which must be made as interesting and as dramatic as possible. Writers often lie awake nights composing a particularly meaningful introduction.

Curtiz, along with cinematographers Sol Polito and H. Howard Greene, devised a particularly effective introduction for Elizabeth: under urgency Donald Crisp is summoned to the royal chambers. The queen, dressing behind a screen, is thoroughly established by voice and then by a shadow on the wall.

Douglas W. Churchill in the December, 1939, issue of *Redbook* best described the scene where Davis is seen on the throne.

> Startling is the effect then, when the lens finally rests on her bejeweled slippers, and slowly and deliberately rises across her regal robes until it comes to rest on her aged face, white as alabaster with thin, crimson lips, the high forehead crowned with a flaming red wig. Yet within a few feet she becomes genuine; her vitality leaps from the screen; her romance with Essex reveals a passion not at all incongruous. So vivid is her personality, that though she bears no beauty, true glamour envelops her, and Essex's love at once becomes understandable.

It was the time of the lush, full-blown, orchestrated musical score. Erich Wolfgang Korngold incorporated medieval melodies in the music for the picture.

Charles Laughton, who had played Henry VIII some years before, visited the set one day. Davis said, "Hello, Daddy. I have a nerve trying to play Elizabeth at my age!"

Laughton replied, "Never stop daring to hang yourself, Bette!" *[This became a credo of mine—in other words, attempt the impossible in order to improve your work. I was always sad I was not privileged to be in a film of Charles Laughton's—one of the true greats in our profession.]*

Lady Penelope Gray was actually a supporting part for Olivia De Havilland, but she had several good scenes with both Davis and

Flynn. She completed her assignment without complaint knowing that David O. Selznick wanted her for Melanie in *Gone with the Wind*. Using ultrafeminine psychology, she went to Ann Warner who, in turn, went to her husband: "Can you possibly think of anyone else in that role, Jack? And think of the prestige for Warners. After all, you discovered her and made her into a star."

J.L. was adamant and explained that, if he let her out on loan to do the picture, she would be difficult to handle. Ann insisted, and he allowed De Havilland, along with Leslie Howard, to make the trek to Culver City. As a matter of record, J.L. was right, because three years later De Havilland went to court over suspension time being added to the length of her seven-year contract and won the case—establishing for all time that an actor had only to serve the length of calendar years. *[Olivia won the case here in America that I had tried to win in my court battle in England—a ruling about the termination of a contract, no matter how much time had been added on with suspensions. In other words, the jail sentence for the contract actor was over; it could no longer be a life sentence—it ended in seven years, no matter what! We owe Olivia a lot for her fight in the American courts.]*

The Private Lives of Elizabeth and Essex was released with fanfare in December, 1939, but the studio, which had taken full-page ads in the fan books for *Dark Victory, Juarez,* and *The Old Maid,* decided to forgo expense, allowing a rash of publicity releases and interviews to suffice. The magazine articles were varied. *Photoplay* commissioned the famous John Erskine to do a fictional piece ("The Queen's Office Hours," an imaginary romantic episode in the life of Elizabeth and Essex) illustrated with photos. Other articles were bylined by Davis, and many pieces dealt with the production difficulties of bringing the historical drama to the screen. A portfolio of stills and data was distributed to schools and colleges for study groups in history classes.

The New York Times on December 2, 1939, said, "Bette Davis's Elizabeth is a strong, resolute, glamour-skimping characterization against which Mr. Flynn's Essex has about as much chance as a beanshooter against a tank."

It must be said in Flynn's defense that he was not especially anxious to appear in a film that, no matter how exploited, would turn out to be another "Bette Davis picture"—anathema to many male stars cast opposite her. *[Interestingly enough, I never worked opposite the big box office male stars of those years. Theirs were*

Bette Davis and her mother, Ruthie, in 1940. (*Photograph by Warner Bros., from the collection of Whitney Stine.*)

After *The Private Lives of Elizabeth and Essex.* Notice wig and penciled brows. (*Photograph by Elmer Fryer, Warner Bros.*)

Bette Davis as Charlotte Lovell and Miriam Hopkins in *The Old Maid*, 1939, in the latter part of the film when they were both elderly. (*Photograph by Warner Bros.*)

Miriam Hopkins, assistant director Jack Sullivan, director Edmund Goulding, and Davis relax on set of *The Old Maid*, 1939. (*Photograph by Warner Bros.*)

stories about men, mine were stories about women. When a film called for even distribution of male and female roles, I was fortunate—Charles Boyer, Leslie Howard, Claude Rains, Paul Henreid, Herbert Marshall, James Cagney, Edward G. Robinson—all superb actors and stars but not the box office sex symbols.] Jezebel *and* Dark Victory, with her name *alone* above the title, were all that was needed to bring her legion of fans into theaters all over the world. She was billed above Miriam Hopkins in *The Old Maid* and Errol Flynn in *The Private Lives of Elizabeth and Essex*, but Paul Muni received top status in *Juarez*.

From Easter to Thanksgiving, 1939, every critic in the country—and most of Hollywood—believed Davis would win her third Academy Award, but in December *Gone with the Wind* was released. Judith Traherne, in her victory over the dark, lost Oscar to a southern belle named Scarlett O'Hara.

11

> *I came into your house, my dear friend, and in your unhappiness, you reached out your hand for help, and in my loneliness, I took it. We have such a friendship that is given to very few.*
>
> BETTE DAVIS AS HENRIETTE DELUZY DESPORTES
> IN *All This and Heaven Too*

Davis was exhausted after completing *The Private Lives of Elizabeth and Essex,* her sixth major film in a row. She left for a six-month holiday. *[With Mrs. Ogden, a friend of mine, I started off on a motor trip through my beloved New England. This was something I'd been dying to do for years. I saw all of the old landmarks. I found out one thing on that trip, you can't go home again—Thomas Wolfe wrote a book about this.*

After two weeks of roaming, seeing old friends whom I no longer had anything in common with, nor they me, I went to an inn in Franconia, New Hampshire, that Ruthie had told me about before she left California. It was called Peckett's. During my stay there I bought a home on Sugar Hill and met my future husband, Arthur Farnsworth. The home I bought had always been called Butternut. I kept the name. I completely rebuilt the house that was standing there—eventually also built a caretaker's cottage, stables, and a house on the hill above the little white house. The house on the hill was a replica of a barn on the outside, silo and all. This was the first home I had ever planned and built. My first own land—200 acres of it. I have always called it my Shangri-la. This is where I lived off and on for seventeen years. Whenever I wasn't working, I stayed at Butternut. It broke my heart when I sold it.]

THE KING AND QUEEN ARE CROWNED

In charts of the top ten motion picture box office stars from 1936 to 1945 in *Motion Picture Herald*'s annual survey a schism appears between performance and critical acclaim. Shirley Temple headed the list in 1936, 1937, and 1938; Mickey Rooney in 1939, 1940, and 1941; Bud Abbott and Lou Costello in 1942; Betty Grable in 1943; and Bing Crosby in 1944 and 1945. Davis made her first appearance in 1939, placing sixth; she was ninth in 1940, eighth in 1941, missed the list in 1942 and 1943, and barely made number ten in 1944. During this nine-year period Davis was listed four times, but it is interesting to note that Greta Garbo, Katharine Hepburn, Carole Lombard, Ronald Colman, and James Stewart never made the list, and Joan Crawford and Claudette Colbert only scored once (in 1936).

In 1940 Mickey Rooney and Davis were proclaimed king and queen of the movies by columnist Ed Sullivan. Davis traveled to Metro for the award ceremonies. *[Rooney refused to wear his crown—I think because it overpowered him, as he was not very tall. I still have mine in my home in Westport, Connecticut. The crowns were ermine trimmed. No doubt about it, Rooney was, is, and always will be one of Hollywood's great acting talents.]*

With all the awards, both foreign and domestic, Davis was often referred to as the First Lady of the Screen, and it was generally acknowledged that among all the actresses in Hollywood she was the most outstanding in performance after performance. She was called the Fourth Warner Brother and the Queen of the Warner Lot.

She was the first woman elected president of the Academy of Motion Picture Arts and Sciences. The year was 1942. She resigned after learning she was expected to be a figurehead only. She felt that she should have been elected to serve in a very real capacity as president.

THE DUCHESSE DE PRASLIN MURDER CASE

The plot of *All This and Heaven Too,* the best-selling novel by Rachel Field, which the studio had purchased from galley proofs in 1938 for the sum of $100,000, dealt with the employment of Henriette Deluzy Desportes as a governess and the murder of the duchesse de Praslin by her husband.

Life magazine on July 1, 1940, was most interested in the background of the lady who was the most notorious woman in Europe in 1847:

> . . . to Victor Hugo, she appeared a "rare woman . . . at once wicked and charming." To the *London Times,* she served as a text against the corruption of Parisian royalist society. Partly because of her a nation revolted and brushed a king from a throne. In the annals of crime she is coupled with a murder as gruesome and enigmatic as the Lizzie Borden case (1893), the Hall-Mills case (1922) or the Gray-Snider case (1927) . . .
>
> At daybreak on August 18, 1847, the duchesse de Praslin was found hacked to pieces in her bedroom. Henriette Desportes was arrested as an accomplice, thrown into prison, reviled as a siren. The duke's suicide further enraged the populace against Louis Philippe's regime. Though Henriette won her acquittal in court, she watched during the following February the abdication of a king and the revolt of the people on the barricaded boulevards of Paris.

[Rachel Field based her book on the fact that Henriette was innocent of any blame in the murder of the duchesse de Praslin—or any actual affair with the duc. She had access to the court records of the trial, which convinced her of this fact. The opposing opinion was a book called L'Affaire Henriette *by the marquis de Sade. I believed thoroughly in Miss Field's opinion of this famous murder case. She gleaned her material not only from the records of the trial but also from the stories she heard of her great-aunt Henriette and her husband, Henry Field. These stories, even more than the trial records, convinced her that Henriette was never, by any actual deed or act, involved in the murder of the duchesse de Praslin.]*

The studio signed Charles Boyer as her costar. *[I couldn't have been more thrilled with the prospect of working with Charles Boyer, this romantic, beautiful actor. Henriette was an extremely difficult part for me to play. Her calm, her understatement in everything she said and did, was a challenge to me as an actress. Without the smoldering passion portrayed by Boyer as* le duc, *this could have been a* very *dull relationship with Henriette.]*

Barbara O'Neil, the mother in *Gone with the Wind,* was brought over from Selznick to portray the tempestuous, wildly jealous duchesse. *[Barbara O'Neil's test for the part of the duchesse was remarkable. She portrayed her in the test as she was written in the book and the script—a frowsy, unkempt, utterly unattractive woman. Mr. Litvak insisted she be the opposite in appearance for the film. No urging by Miss O'Neil or by me would change his mind. It was heartbreaking to Barbara, as it robbed her of a far greater performance. It also made Mr. Boyer have much less sympathy from the audience. His hatred of her seemed less plausible—this we all, including Miss O'Neil, were aware of.]*

Casey Robinson wrote the screenplay. He made use of flashbacks, creating a prologue and an epilogue. The picture begins in an exclusive girls' school in New York, where the former governess, under an assumed name, is employed as a French teacher. When the snobbish students confront her with her true identity, as a supposed murderess, she tells her story. At the finish the girls sympathetically gather around her, apologizing for the way they had misjudged her.

Rachel Field said, in "Surprise Ending" for *Photoplay,* " 'You won't know your book,' people told me. 'Be prepared for the worst,' which may be the reason why I was rewarded with a happy surprise. . . . So, I was amazed to read Mr. Casey Robinson's script and find that in spite of the necessity for compression and shifts in time and scenes, he had kept as closely as possible to my original in spirit, in characterization, and even in much of the dialogue.''

[Rachel Field and I became great friends during the filming, and afterward remained so. She had such a great writing career ahead of her. She lived only a few years after All This and Heaven Too—*she died of cancer at a very young age. She also wrote many books for children. They are classics as far as I am concerned.]*

Members of the exceptional cast were Harry Davenport, Helen Westley, Walter Hampden, Henry Daniell, George Cou|ouris, Montagu Love, and Janet Beecher. The children of the de Praslin household (reduced from ten in the book to four) were June Lockhart, Virginia Weidler (borrowed from MGM, to whom the studio paid her salary, plus 10 percent), Ann Todd, and Richard Nichols. Nichols, a frail, beautiful child of four, played the sickly Raynald. *[I adored this child. We became great friends during the shooting of the film.]*

Thirty-eight-year-old Tola Litvak had not changed in the two years since he had directed Davis in *The Sisters.* If anything, his penchant for endless rehearsals and many takes had increased. His painstaking efforts labeled him a fine craftsman. Each morning he arrived on the set with the complete blueprint for shooting that he had worked out the night before. Each shot was set up exactly as he had envisioned. *[More times than not, not the way I had envisioned it. He was a very stubborn director.]*

The budget for the picture was set at $1.37 million and listed approximately $1,000 each for the thirty-five costumes designed for Davis by Orry-Kelly—all simple and underplayed, from a gray traveling dress worn with a paisley shawl, to a black two-piece suit worn with a black bow tie for the schoolroom sequences, to a simple jacket with scalloped collar and pockets over a dark wool skirt for the prison-courtroom scenes. "I especially wanted for the opera sequence," Davis told an interviewer, "to wear a copy of one of the gowns described in the book, preferably the green silk that Henriette liked. But green is a dull color in black and white, so Kelly designed for me a lovely pale blue silk with a touch of heavy white lace around the wide revers that sloped down to the low neck. With it, I wore a gold chain with a cameo, and a gold bracelet. . . . What excitement when I lost the brooch! It wasn't at all valuable, but a gang of workmen spent an entire night shoveling and sifting a whole 'snowstorm' until they found it. The point was that it showed in a lot of close-ups and would be missed in subsequent scenes. They shifted half an acre of 'snow.' "

Art director Carl Jules Weyl designed some sixty-five exterior sets and thirty-five interiors, the majority of which were contained in the duc's mansion at 55 Rue du Faubourg Saint-Honoré in Paris, which was three stories high. Other interiors were located in the Louis Philippe palace, a wine shop, and an attic bedroom. Exteriors included cobblestone streets, a prison courtyard, and the beautiful de Praslin château at Melun with miles of staircases. The duc's bedroom featured padded gold damask walls with deep crimson panels, while the duchesse's pink satin bedroom included a $1,200 gold-leaf bed with head and footboard covered with hand-embroidered satin panels.

Weyl searched southern California museums for authentic antiques of the Louis Philippe period, gathering some 12,000 separate items, from rare harpsichords to half-ton chandeliers.

Davis knitted between scenes and had long chats with Rachel Field. There were fun moments on the set. *[In those days there were always fun moments on the set. It helped us to relieve the tension of*

strenuous filming. This is one of the saddest differences between filming then and now, no time while shooting for gags and fun. I miss it.] Boyer danced with O'Neil to the tune of the harpsichord and helped the children with their homework under the vigilant eye of the studio tutor. Litvak, although a week behind schedule, shouted, "It's a hep, heppy day!" when a long involved scene went well. Davis worked on her autobiography, *Uncertain Glory,* which was to be published in the *Ladies Home Journal,* and autographed copies of the motion picture edition of *All This and Heaven Too* featuring her portrait on the blurb.

A dramatic scene near the end of the picture involved Henriette's being brought from prison by gendarmes to the bedroom of the duc, who lies dying of self-administered strychnine. Litvak found the scene difficult to stage, what with the agonized whispers of the duc, the rustling uniforms of the gendarmes, the solemn priests, and Henriette's archenemy, the father of the duchesse, glowering from the head of the bed—all with lines and bits of "business." The scene was rehearsed, changed, and rehearsed again. With the actors' nerves at fever pitch, the gendarmes opened the door to bring in their hostage, who suddenly threw up her hands and screamed in delight. Assembled on the set was the entire cast with an enormous birthday cake. Davis gaily cut the cake, which commemorated her thirty-second birthday.

After the picture was in the can, Davis and associate producer David Lewis held a party for the children in the film at the Beverly Tropics restaurant with Hawaiian decor and food. Bright-colored leis were passed around by Davis, who was dressed in a flowered island dress. It was a gala affair. Shortly after she vacationed in Honolulu, before returning to begin work on *The Letter.*

A full-page ad featured in the fan books showed Davis in a strapless, out-of-character evening dress with the coiffure from *Dark Victory;* Boyer held her hand, something he never did in the picture! *[Another example of the deception of the studios in planning their advertising campaign. First of all, again their fear of a "costume picture" and, in this case, a fear due to the fact that Henriette and the duc never had any physical contact in the film. I always used to say, "Why did they make the picture? When they bought the story, they knew this lack of physical contact was an integral part of the story. Why be afraid afterward?"]*

On May 9, 1940, Louella Parsons announced in her syndicated column:

WARNERS IN DILEMMA OVER 23-REEL PICTURE

ALL THIS AND HEAVEN TOO Seemed Too Good to Cut, So They Want Public to Help Decide Its Fate!

Warners are in a quandry and they'd like to ask your advice—Mr. and Mrs. Public. *All This and Heaven Too,* previewed today, runs 20,000 feet in length— approximately twenty-three reels. Bette Davis and Charles Boyer and Jeffrey Lynn are so good that Warner bosses hesitate about cutting a foot from Rachel Field's book. What to do is the question.

*[It is hard, in the light of the length of present-day films, to realize what doing this took on the part of the studio. This was truly revolutionary for Warner Bros. at that time. There had been others—*Gone with the Wind *was the perfect example in this breakthrough of length of film.]*

The film was released at two hours and twenty minutes and debuted at Radio City Music Hall in New York. Bosley Crowther's review in *The New York Times* on July 5, 1940, praised the film, although he felt it was long, tedious, and somewhat old-fashioned.

Alert to the opportunity, Miss Davis and Mr. Boyer put all the "soul" they possess into the playing . . . Under the slow-paced direction of Anatole Litvak, they carry through mainly on one somber key—Miss Davis with her large eyes filled with sadness and her mouth drooping heavily with woe; Mr. Boyer with his face a rigid mask, out of which his dark eyes signal pain. Barbara O'Neil as the termagant duchess considerably overplays the part, but genuine and tender performances are given by Virginia Weidler, June Lockhart, Ann Todd, and Richard Nichols as the lively Praslin brood. Frankly—and this is commentary—we'd a great deal rather know whatever became of them than what became of the governess.

A SECOND DATE WITH MAUGHAM

Robert will be away for the night. I absolutely must see

you. I shall expect you at eleven. I am desperate and, if you don't come, I won't answer for the consequences.

BETTE DAVIS AS LESLIE CROSBIE
IN *The Letter*

There is a deathly calm spread over the rubber plantation. The Malay moon is full, and its brilliant white light filters down through the palm and rubber trees, creating gigantic shadows. There is no air at all; the very stillness portends things to come. The Malay boys in the bunkhouse, drowsing in hammocks, are beaded with perspiration. The sultriness of the night envelops the atmosphere in a hot embrace—almost passionate in intensity. The closed curtains of the shadowy bungalow hint of the evil taking place inside. The moon shifts behind a cloud. Suddenly a shot is heard; a man runs from the veranda. A beautiful woman follows, another shot is heard, and another, and the man falls. She pumps shot after shot into his inert body sprawled on the path. *[This long opening shot in* The Letter *is, in my opinion, the finest opening shot I have ever seen in a film. This was due to the genius, and I use the word advisedly, of William Wyler, our director.]*

Gladys Cooper, Britain's most beautiful actress, had first portrayed Leslie Crosbie in the play, which opened in the West End in spring, 1927, with Nigel Bruce as the husband. That fall Katharine Cornell brought the play to Broadway, and two years later Jeanne Eagels performed the role in the Paramount film, with Herbert Marshall in the bit part of Hammond, the lover who is killed in the first scene. When Warner Bros. purchased the property for Davis, Marshall was again employed—this time for the meaty part of the weak husband.

Davis was reunited with Wyler for the first time since *Jezebel* and was again photographed expertly by Tony Gaudio. Wallis assigned Robert Lord as associate producer. The cast was notable: James Stephenson, Frieda Inescort, and Gale Sondergaard. *[Gale Sondergaard's performance in* The Letter, *as the Eurasian wife of the man Leslie Crosbie killed, was breathtakingly sinister. I was so lucky that she was cast in this part.]* Also included were Bruce Lester, Cecil Kellaway in a part cut to bits, Elizabeth Earl, and Doris Lloyd. Sen Yung, who had made a career out of playing Number Two Son to Sidney Toler's Charlie Chan, was the evil go-between, the man who originally uncovers the fateful letter. He would achieve a new career in middle age as cook Hop Sing in the long-running television series "Bonanza."

When Leslie Crosbie confronted the Eurasian woman to retrieve the letter, Orry-Kelly designed for her a long white lace mantilla. The other gowns were simple, exactly the sort of wardrobe the English wife of a Malayan rubber plantation owner would wear: skirts, blouses, a gray chiffon evening dress, a starched white piqué dinner gown, a dark suit, and a wide straw hat. Davis wore rimless glasses when doing her crocheting.

Wyler was his usual irascible self during production, requiring many takes of each scene and demanding perfection from each member of the cast. When the shadows shifted on the rubber-plantation set, he ordered the property department to *paint* shadows on the floor of the sound stage.

Stephenson had problems with Wyler, especially in the long courtroom harangues. Stephenson lost his temper many times and walked off the set. [*Every time Jimmy would leave, I would run after him and make him come back, saying, "It will be worth it, Jimmy— don't go. You will give the great performance of your career under Wyler's direction." He would go back on the set. The day the notices appeared in the New York papers, he received much personal acclaim. We were both having lunch in the Green Room at Warner Bros. He came to my table and said, "Bette, I'll thank you all my life for making me stay on the picture." Willie believed in one thing while directing a film. It didn't matter how many differences of opinion or how many upsets occurred during filming—the only thing that mattered was the finished product, what was on the screen after the film was completed. I personally, after Jezebel, would have jumped into the Hudson River if he had told me to. That's how much belief I had in his judgment as a director.*] As a gag birthday gift Davis had an enormous horseshoe wreath designed with vegetables, fruit, and flowers for Wyler, who obligingly posed with the offering—a la Santa Anita—around his neck.

A crucial sequence occurs when Leslie accompanies the go-between to the shop of the Eurasian wife. Wyler insisted that the scene be charged with emotion barely hidden under the surface. The confrontation scene was abnormally difficult because the Eurasian wife does not speak English, only guttural Malay; hatred must emanate from every pore. Her contempt is shown when she drops the letter to the floor and Leslie must bend down at her feet to retrieve it. Wyler did not want Max Steiner to use theme music for the sequence, and, instead, he provided contrapuntal accompaniment to the dramatics by the sound of a wind chime, which jingles ominously. The scene had the same sort of suspense that Wyler had infused in the Comos Ball sequence in *Jezebel*.

Screenwriter Howard Koch found one disturbing element in the story. In the original stage play the wife, although still in love with the man she murdered, lives out the rest of her life with her husband. *[The play ended with Leslie's confession to her husband. The line was, "With all my heart, I still love the man I killed." This obviously was the worst punishment Leslie could receive.]* But the Hays office demanded that she pay for her crime in a flagrant, overt way.

Wyler, Lord, and Koch were forced to obey the production code. Controversy raged; obviously the leading character could not go to prison or the carefully wrought courtroom scenes would fall apart. A fatal accident would be ridiculous. The only other solution would be murder—but how and by whom? The husband could not kill her or the story would disintegrate into absurdity. After many discussions it was decided that the Eurasian wife, out of jealousy and hate, had the proper motivation. But then they would be left with the same predicament. How would *she* then pay for *her* crime? It was a fierce and almost unsolvable round robin.

But Wyler was not yet licked. He had painstakingly created the sultry mood of the tropics; he had established Leslie Crosbie's morbid attraction for the moon. He hit upon the solution. At a party held in celebration of the acquittal, Leslie becomes bored and listless and goes to her room to work on her lace. After a stormy scene with her husband she goes out on the terrace. She walks slowly through the garden, looking right and left, compelled to seek the reason for her intuitive feeling of misgiving. She comes to the patio wall and too late sees the Malay boy. He grabs her roughly, clamping a hand over her mouth. She struggles valiantly, twisting, turning, finally looking up into the Eurasian's inscrutable face. A knife flashes in the moonlight. She falls to the ground, fatally wounded. A policeman shines a light over the scene, illuminating the features of the Malay boy and his mistress. The camera moves through the garden again; a piano heralds the start of a dance. Leslie Crosbie's crochet work on a chair in her room is fluttered by a sudden breeze.

Although the ending incorporated an artistic compromise, the Hays office was satisfied.

James Stephenson was immediately cast in a hospital drama, *Shining Victory,* based on A. J. Cronin's novel *Jupiter Laughs.* Dialogue director Irving Rapper was promoted to full-fledged director. *[I disguised myself as a nurse and appeared on the set as an extra. Rapper did not recognize me for the first few takes. I had a ball. Imagine daring to do this today!]* When the picture was released, not one critic noticed that the most famous star on the Warner lot had made a "good luck" appearance in the opening scene of the movie—as a nurse who hands a letter to the receptionist in the doctor's office.

The Letter opened at the Strand on November 22 on a stage bill featuring Ozzie Nelson and his orchestra, with Harriet Hilliard, Harris and Shore, Ray and Trent, and Roy Davis. Bosley Crowther wrote the next day in *The New York Times,*

> Director William Wyler was remarking recently that the final responsibility for a picture's quality rests solely and completely upon the shoulders of the man who directs it. His, said he, is the liability if an actor's performance is at fault; he is the one to censure—or to thank—for the finished effect, since it is the director, after all, who makes the picture and okays it.

[I completely agree with Mr. Wyler. The motion picture is the director's medium. He is completely responsible for the "finished effect." He is the person "who makes the film and okays it." What Mr. Wyler cannot say is that there are few great directors that the actor can completely rely upon for his or her performance, to say nothing of the finished product. Many a film has been murdered by the lack of judgment in editing our work after it is finished.]

> Mr. Wyler spoke at a most propitious moment. For seldom has this theory been more clearly and more flatteringly supported than it is by his own screen version of Somerset Maugham's play, *The Letter.* . . . Indubitably Mr. Wyler must be grateful to Bette Davis, James Stephenson, Herbert Marshall, and an excellent cast for doing as he told them . . .
> . . . But the ultimate credit for as taut and insinuating a

melodrama as has come along this year—a film which extenuates tension like a grim inquisitor's rack—must be given to Mr. Wyler. His hand is patent throughout.

But Pauline Kael brought all the reviews to a nucleus; she felt that Wyler got from Davis "what is very likely the best study of female sexual hypocrisy in film history."

Both *Calamity Jane* and Dostoevski's *The Gambler* were scheduled for possible films. *Calamity Jane* was eventually turned into a musical for Doris Day in 1953. *[Would have adored to play this character. Always one of my dreams, one that didn't come true.] The Gambler,* first made in 1929, was permanently shelved.

Both *All This and Heaven Too* and *The Letter* were nominated for the best picture of the year by the Academy, and Davis was a nominee for the latter.

12

That child is mine. Your part was finished the minute you gave that baby to me. From that day on, I had only one purpose in my life, to make that baby mine and forget you ever existed.

BETTE DAVIS AS MAGGIE PATTERSON
IN *The Great Lie*

Since *Jezebel* Davis's films had been stories, for the most part, of women's problems. The most important female star at Warner Bros., she fought for the best directors and for the most talented actors and actresses to support her. A case in point was her search for an actress to play the role of concert pianist Sandra Kovak in Polan Banks's best seller *January Heights,* which Henry Blanke was preparing from a screenplay by Lenore Coffee titled *Far Horizon,* which would be changed to the release title, *The Great Lie.* Davis was to portray Maggie Patterson, a Maryland society girl, and George Brent was to play Peter Van Allen, a flier.

Director Edmund Goulding had tested a number of actresses for Sandra, when Ernst Lubitsch suggested Mary Astor, who he knew was a musician.

"I'll be happy to test," Astor told Goulding, who called her in Palm Springs. Knowing the camera always added ten pounds, she had already started to diet when she appeared at the studio. Wardrobe gave her a spangled dress for the test, which was unsatisfactory. She looked fat. Davis recommended another test in a more becoming gown. Orry-Kelly also suggested that Astor pull her shoulder-length hair back from her face. Astor cut her hair and started a new hair style all over America. *[I insisted she play*

Sandra. Plus Astor was in her own right a skilled pianist.]

Davis had twenty-two costume changes, and Astor had eighteen—twelve of which were glamorous creations. The physical production incorporated some seventy-two sets, scattered over several sound stages. The plantation kitchen wing and huge yard (including "darkies" portrayed by the Hall Johnson Choir singing spirituals as in *Jezebel)* took all of Stage Eleven. The location scenes were filmed at Victorville, which doubled as Arizona. Burbank Airport was used for the landing and taking-off scenes, which licensed pilot Brent performed himself.

Among the supporting players and production crew were five Oscar winners. Besides Davis were Hattie McDaniel, cameraman Tony Gaudio, assistant director Jack Sullivan, and art director Carl Jules Weyl. The cast also included two babies—Timony Tennyson, aged three months, and Billy Eugene Ferris, aged nine months—who shared the key role of Little Pete. Ferris had his own movie-within-a-movie, a typical 16 mm "home production," for an amusing sequence. Twenty beagle hounds made up the plantation hunting pack.

"Before I started *The Great Lie,"* Davis told Jack Holland, "I wasn't very excited about it. . . . I had just come back from a vacation in New Hampshire. The studio wanted some retakes for *The Letter."* *[After Wyler saw* The Letter *completed, he felt the audience would have no sympathy for its heroine. He had many scenes rewritten to give her sympathy. I was heartbroken, as I felt, after reading the rewrites, that my performance could be ruined with these additions. I asked Willie if I could see the film before doing the retakes. To my horror I was crying at myself at the end of the showing. There was dead silence in the projection room when the lights came up. I said, "If we film these retakes, we will lose the intelligent audience. It is impossible to please everyone with any one film. If we try to accomplish this, we can lose* all *audiences." Plus, to my shame, even though* I *played the part, I deeply sympathized with Leslie Crosbie. We only made one small addition to the original film. Wyler had agreed with me. Thank God!]*

Davis continued, "I was still wondering what to do when I got some of my fan mail. A lot of it ran in this vein, 'Why can't you be nice for a change?' I also remembered someone, while I was in New Hampshire, said, 'Why, you're *young!'* Everyone apparently had the idea that I was an old woman due to the many older characters

I'd played. . . . I guess I do need happier roles for a change. I don't kill anyone in this picture, and I play a young girl." *[Also Maggie was one of the few times I played a character basically like myself off the screen. This was the second opportunity. Dallas in* So Big, *as I've said before, was the first, and Kit in* Old Acquaintance *was to come.]*

Davis led Holland to a graceful staircase. "You know," she said, "this is the same stairway that was used in *Jezebel, Dark Victory,* and *The Old Maid.* This is my ghost room," she continued as they came to a secluded set on a sound stage. "I made my entrance in *Jezebel* in this room, died here in *Dark Victory.* This time, I make love to George Brent in it."

There were some peculiarities in the film. Brent comes back from a stretch in the South American jungles (in Brazil) after a plane crash with gray hair and lines in his face although gone less than a year! And Orry-Kelly designed a white chiffon evening gown for Astor with a cape with a design that bore a striking resemblance to a similar outfit he made for Davis a year later in *Now, Voyager.* The Tchaikovsky Piano Concerto no. 1 in B-flat gained renewed popularity after the film was released.

According to Mary Astor in one of her autobiographies, *A Life on Film:*

> One morning Bette said to me in a very peremptory manner, "Hey, Astor! Let's go talk a minute!" We went to her portable and she closed the door and I had the old "what have I done now!" feeling. She flopped on the couch and said, "This picture is going to stink! It's too incredible for words." Well! She went on, "I can't get anywhere up front unless I have something to offer that will make it better. You've got to help." How? "You and I, really just us, because I've talked to the writers and to Eddie, and everybody's satisfied but me, so it's up to us to rewrite this piece of junk to make it more interesting. All I do is mewl to George about 'that woman you married when you were drunk' and to 'please come back to me' and all that crap. And that's just soap opera." What wasn't soap opera, she went on to explain hopefully, was simply a different point of view: a constant conflict between Sandra and the, so far, sappy southern

gal who had lost her childhood sweetheart. That would be the story. A declaration of war between the two women and a negotiable but tenuous peace.

The "rewriting" went on and on. Goulding was delighted. The two actresses, by showing understanding of females in general, infused their scenes with a kind of bitchery seldom encountered— but it was the bitchery of *nuance*.

For the concert scenes a full orchestra was assembled on stage, and the famous concert pianist Max Rabinovitch sat huddled over a piano off screen. Astor took her cues from the conductor, expertly fingering her dummy piano, matching notes with Rabinovitch until perfect synchronization was achieved. Later Norma Boleslavsky filmed the close shots of the hands playing. Ralph Dawson cleverly edited the diversified takes into a smooth, foolproof sequence. One member of the cheering audience was pianist Jose Iturbi, who was dumbfounded. He told Astor, "How could you *not* be playing? I have played the concerto many times, and you were right in there!" *[Even though it was a dummy piano, Mary was really playing. She had worked hours memorizing every note of the concerto. These concert scenes of Mary's were the most believable ever seen on the screen—because she really* was *a pianist par excellence. Freddy Martin made the popular hit song "Tonight We Love" after seeing our film.]*

A long sequence occurs when Maggie takes Sandra to Arizona to await the birth of the illegitimate baby fathered by Brent. She is her sole companion for the last few months of pregnancy, since Astor cannot be seen *enceinte* in public. The Davis-Astor collaboration included many "bits of business" that Goulding felt were inspired. One scene found them playing double solitaire, and Sandra asks for a drink. "Okay, the doctor said you could have some brandy—just an ounce."

Sandra makes a face.

"It needs more protest than that," Davis says. "Sandra wouldn't be satisfied with less than a pint—she probably never heard of an ounce of anything in the liquor line. That's it! Why don't you say, 'Whoever heard of an ounce of brandy!' and growl it like you do, Mary."

Later, Davis wanted to wear riding clothes as she paces outside the cabin where Astor is giving birth. But Goulding thought the audience would laugh, conjuring up the picture of a husband pacing the floor of a hospital. "Let them," Davis said. "A laugh at this point is fine." Goulding at other times would say, "Well, ladies— if you're ready—would you kindly inform me as to what you are going to do?"

The director acted out various scenes for the actors, as was his custom, showing Hattie McDaniel ("It's Mr. Pete flying down from the sky like a messenger from de Lord!") how to roll out pastry and giving Lucile Watson tips on answering the telephone. He balked, however, at showing Davis how to pin the baby's diapers. He kidded, "If there are any changes in this scene, you'll make them!"

Mary Astor won an Oscar for her supporting role in *The Great Lie*, incredibly her eighty-sixth film. At the Academy banquet she thanked only two people, Davis and Tchaikovsky.

THE TREK TO NEW HAMPSHIRE

Premieres of motion pictures held away from Hollywood not only entailed great expense, but arranging transportation, radio coverage, and accommodations for the press and dealing with local bigwigs could be almost more trouble than the junkets were worth. The studio usually arranged for festivities to be held at the Carthay Circle Theatre in Los Angeles or the Hollywood Theatre in New York. Exceptions were few and far between, as in the case of scheduling the premiere of *Dodge City* in Dodge City, Kansas, on April 5, 1939.

Now, two years later to the day, the historic value of holding the premiere of *The Great Lie* in Littleton, New Hampshire, on April 5, 1941, was slightly more esoteric as it was Davis's thirty-third birthday. *[Warner Bros. did this for me at my request. The purpose of the premiere was to raise money for the Littleton Hospital, near Butternut, where Farney and I were living at the time.]* Charles Einfeld used all of his experience in the publicity field to garner as much nationwide publicity as possible. He ensconced many reporters from both Hollywood and New York at Littleton's version of the Ritz—the Thayer Hotel.

The only other Davis film to be premiered in New England was *The Virgin Queen* in Portland, Maine, fourteen years later for the benefit of the Children's Theatre of Portland, the first children's theatre in America. This also was her territory, for Davis was living at that time in nearby Cape Elizabeth.

Einfeld set up a special NBC coast-to-coast "Your Happy Birthday" salute, arranged for Luce correspondents to do a *"Life* Goes to a Party" feature, and made sure that all local outlets were tapped for publicity—Littleton Township Band, Boy Scouts, Sea Scouts, Boys from the Civilian Conservation Corps, local clubs, and, of course, the local gendarmes.

Everyone from Senator Styles Bridges and Governor Robert O. Blood to newswoman Mary Margaret McBride either showed up for the "Sugaring Off" party held at Cannon Mountain, beside the still waters of the Ammonoosuc River, or rode horse-drawn sleighs in a torchlight cavalcade through picturesque Franconia Notch.

A bugler, instead of the town crier, summoned the 4,571 townspeople and several hundred visitors to the various activities planned jointly by the city council and Warner Bros.

Davis, in a white blouse and felt skirt, and Farnsworth, in a plaid shirt and brown corduroy suit, hosted a cocktail party at the Iron Mine Inn in the afternoon, then donned evening clothes for the opening that night at the packed 676-seat Premiere Theatre.

It is probably that the small township of Littleton had never before known such excitement. Special editions of *The Daily Record,* as well as dailies flown in from New York, publicizing the star and the film were hawked in the streets by youngsters proudly displaying huge Bette Davis badges. Several Happy Birthday banners were stretched across the busiest intersections as the crowds gathered.

In a black crepe dress topped by a full-length white ermine coat, Davis cut a huge six-tiered birthday cake on the stage of the town hall, in front of a painted backdrop of Butternut painted by Tony Russo, the manager of the theater.

"Never a devotee of Hollywood society," *Life* magazine on April 28, 1941, duly reported, "Miss Davis supremely enjoys her Yankee house, Yankee husband, Yankee neighbors. Littletonians have been friendly, uninquisitive, and amiably responsive to her terrific interest in community affairs and community gossip. The birthday gifts she most appreciated were cookies, candy, and preserves bestowed upon her by Littleton people. Butternut Miss Davis keeps jealously to herself. It is open to friends and neighbors but not to photographers."

Bosley Crowther's mood in *The New York Times* on April 12, 1941, was not too enthusiastic about *The Great Lie:*

Little girls who tell stories sometimes get themselves into jams—not always too perilous predicaments, but ones they'd do better to avoid. And it is such an inconsequential quandry in which Bette Davis finds herself in the Warners's somewhat overstated drama, *The Great Lie,* now at the Strand. . . . So the only excuse to be found for this thoroughly synthetic tale is that it gives Miss Davis an opportunity to display her fine talent for distress, to be maternal and noble, the "good" woman as opposed to the "bad" . . . And Mary Astor as the "other woman," a resplendent concert pianist, provides a beautiful contrast of cold and poisonous conceit. One sequence, which finds the two squared off in an Arizona cabin, where Miss Astor is to give birth to the vexatious child, crackles with sardonic humor and is by far the best stretch in the film . . . In short, the acting is impressive. The direction of Edmund Goulding makes for class, but the story is such a trifle that it hardly seems worth the while. However, the women will probably love it, since fibs are so provocative of fun.

[Mr. Crowther did not use the opening line, The Great Lie *is a great lie indeed, but he said as much and bore out everything I had felt about the story from the beginning.]*

FOR THE FIRST TIME SINCE FOG OVER FRISCO, *A MADCAP HEIRESS*

In 1940 James Cagney finished his contract and resolved to go into production with his brother William. But independent producers in those halcyon days before World War II were looked upon with dismay. Cagney decided to wait for a more propitious time and signed with Warner Bros. for two more years. While he was popular at the box office, J.L. believed a change of pace was indicated, and it was Wallis's bright idea to cast the little fighter with the other fighter on the lot in a comedy, *The Bride Came C.O.D.* Critics and fans alike had complained about the heavy roles Cagney and Davis had undertaken so often.

The Great Lie had finished shooting a few days before Christmas, and *The Bride Came C.O.D.* was scheduled to go before the cameras in January. Apparently all was peaceful at the studio over the holidays until J.L. received the following telegram on January 1:

> ARTHUR FARNSWORTH AND I WERE MARRIED
> AT EIGHT O'CLOCK TUESDAY EVENING AT THE
> RANCH OF MR. AND MRS. JUSTIN DART IN
> ARIZONA.

The studio, and Hollywood, were aghast. How could Davis, so open about her personal life, pull such a *coup*? It was comparable to Lindbergh flying across the ocean without anyone knowing. Actually, a number of people *did* know. Both Bernard Newman at I. Magnin's, who designed the white jersey wedding dress, and Bertie Strauser, the saleswoman, were aware of the event. Also in on the secret were Davis's agent and friend, Lester Luisk, the florist who made up the white lilies-of-the-valley bridal bouquet, her family, and a few invited guests.

Since her contract forbade flying and Davis was afraid that taking the train to Arizona would attract unwanted attention, she decided to drive the 450 miles from Hollywood to Rimrock, Arizona, where the Darts lived [the former Jane Bryan] and where Farnsworth was waiting, having flown in from Vermont.

Three cars left Los Angeles on Monday morning, December 30, occupied by Davis, Ruthie, hairdresser Margaret Donovan, her boyfriend Perc Westmore, dog Tibby, Lester Luisk, cousin John Favor, and house guest Ruth Garland. They picked up the marriage license in a driving rain in Prescott, Arizona. The weary travelers finally drove into the ranch on Tuesday afternoon. Sister Bobby and her husband flew in from Los Angeles with Dart in his private plane. The wedding was held that night.

Farnsworth, the startled press learned, was thirty-four years old. For a time he had played the violin in a classical trio. The son of a Vermont dentist, he had managed Peckett's Inn, located near Butternut in New Hampshire. Divorced in 1939 from Betty Jane Adeylotte, a Boston socialite and aviatrix, Farney, as Davis called him, was interested in flying himself and would later go to work for Minneapolis Honeywell.

Since there was only ten days' respite between finishing *The Great Lie* and beginning *The Bride Came C.O.D.*, the newlyweds returned to Riverbottom.

The Bride Came C.O.D. was produced by Wallis in association with Bill Cagney and directed by William Keighley, known for his fast shooting schedules. The cast members—Jack Carson, George Tobias, Eugene Pallette, and Harry Davenport—were taken to a ghost town near Death Valley for two weeks of location work.

The screenplay by the Epstein brothers (Julius J. and Philip G.) was based upon a story by Kenneth Earl and M. M. Musselman. Madcap heiress Joan Winfield (Davis) is abducted by airplane pilot Steve Collins (Cagney) in return for a $10 per pound freight rate on instructions from her father (Pallette) so that she cannot marry bandleader Allen Brice (Carson). The plot thickens when the plane develops engine trouble on the California-Nevada border and Davis parachutes into a cactus patch near a ghost town inhabited only by Pop Tolliver (Davenport).

The shooting was fast and furious, impeded not at all by an invasion of newshawks to the desert location who gleefully distributed pictures of "the dignified Mr. James Cagney removing cactus quills from the *derrière* of America's top dramatic actress, Miss Bette Davis." *[Plus, as Farney and I had just been married, there was great curiosity to see what he was like. Farney managed all of it very well considering this was his first exposure to any press people ever.]*

The cast and crew lived at the Furnace Creek Inn and got up at 5:30 A.M. in order to be on location, forty miles away, by 8:30. They worked in the high heat until 5:30 P.M. and were back at the hotel by 7:00.

When Cagney complained about the temperature, Keighley laughed. "We're shooting in January, and it's only 100 degrees. Thank God we aren't out here in July when the mercury climbs to 130!"

Back at the studio Davis knitted socks for Farnsworth between scenes, and Cagney took guitar lessons from the property man. The high point was a birthday party held for seventy-six-year-old Harry Davenport, who had played in many Davis pictures. *[The beauty of Harry Davenport as a human being and as an actor will never be forgotten by any of us who worked with him. His glowing performance in* All This and Heaven Too *gave this film such added stature. Even in* The Bride Came C.O.D., *a truly ridiculous film, he gave his moments stature. Without doubt, Mr. Davenport was one of the truly great supporting players of all time. Any of us were lucky when he was cast in one of our films.]*

After the party on the set on the last day of shooting—with Cagney directing the last scene to be shot—Davis and Farnsworth went back to Butternut to vacation.

One of the best things about the picture was the humorous and delightfully satiric music by Max Steiner, who "Mickey Moused" each movement, adding fine counterpoint to the shenanigans of the principals.

13

Ah hope you die. Ah hope you die very soon. I'll be waitin' for you to die.

BETTE DAVIS AS REGINA GIDDENS
IN *The Little Foxes*

"Once or twice a year the major Hollywood studios gamble on producing 'a prestige picture,' " *Life* magazine reported on September 1, 1941, "with no certainty of earning money. It is made because it brings prestige to the studio who films it. Last year such films included *The Long Voyage Home, Our Town, Abe Lincoln in Illinois,* none of which were money-makers. This year another candidate for the prestige list is Sam Goldwyn's *The Little Foxes.* Commercially, its handicap is that it is a stinging and unromantic story about a greedy southern family. Its assets are Bette Davis in the star role."

Goldwyn always financed his pictures with his own money. He believed in the axiom Put up or Shut up, and money was no object. His intuitive reaction was almost always right. An aide told him that the play was extremely "caustic." "To hell with the cost," Goldwyn replied, "I want it!" He paid J.L. $385,000 for Davis's services, and the studio somewhat reluctantly handed over the total amount to the star—upon her "steely" request. *[My first motion picture test was made in 1929 for a Ronald Colman picture,* Raffles, *to be made by Sam Goldwyn. When the test was shown to Mr. Goldwyn, he bellowed, "Who did this to me?" Now I was doing something to him—he had to pay a lot of money for me. I couldn't help but gloat a little, to myself, of course!]*

The story line concerns the snakelike Hubbard brothers, who

want their sister, Regina Giddens, to put up $75,000 to their like amount to build a cotton gin at Paltou. By hiring little more than slave labor, they will make a fortune. Regina's ill husband, Horace, an honest banker, will not go along with the scheme. While he is in the hospital, their bank-teller nephew, Leo, steals $75,000 worth of bonds from the Giddens's safety-deposit box. Horace discovers the theft and tells Regina that he will act as if the money was "borrowed" because he wants no part of the unscrupulous venture. When Regina withholds his heart medicine and Horace dies, she triumphantly tells the brothers that she will take 75 percent of the profits or divulge the fact that Leo stole the bonds.

Director William Wyler worked closely with Lillian Hellman, the author of the play, who also wrote the screenplay. Arthur Kober and husband-and-wife team Dorothy Parker and Alan Campbell wrote additional scenes and dialogue, creating the character of David Hewlitt (Richard Carlson) as the love interest for Alexandra (the daughter of Regina and Horace) and "social commentator" about the community of Paltou.

Dorothy Parker, a close friend of Hellman, had suggested the title in 1938, from the *Song of Solomon:* "Take us the foxes, the little foxes, that spoil the vines, for our vines have tender grapes."

The enormous exterior set of the town of Paltou, designed by art director Stephen Goosson, was a mélange of ingeniously fashioned "houses" arranged around a grassy square, complete with rusty cannon and spreading live oaks hung with moss. Each separate set was composed of a parlor, kitchen, dining room, staircase, and upper bedroom. *[I was not in accord with the Goldwyn set for* The Little Foxes. *It was not decaying grandeur, as it should have been for reasons included in the script. The settings were so opulent, the family automatically seemed to be rich, and, therefore, there appeared to be no reason for Regina to have to go to Chicago for monetary reasons.]*

Innovative cinematographer Gregg Toland, fresh from his triumph with *Citizen Kane,* collaborated expertly with Wyler, inaugurating a luminous, low-key feeling that presented an aura of southern decay. Paint-impregnated gauze was hung over the tops of interior sets, enabling players to be photographed in deep focus from low angles where the ceiling was visible.

Wyler's imaginative roving camera in the opening, establishing shot of Paltou probed into the activities of awakening households, going about morning routines. Davis is first seen cutting flowers in her garden, precise, beautiful, and filled with deadly charm.

Five members of the original stage play were brought to Hollywood for the film: Dan Duryea, the nephew-thief; Patricia Collinge, the drunken Aunt Birdie; Charles Dingle and Carl Benton Reid, the scavenger brothers; and John Marriott, the faithful black servant, Cal. Teresa Wright, from the Broadway production of *Life with Father*, was signed for the important role of the daughter, Alexandra, and Herbert Marshall was picked as the dying banker-husband, Horace Giddens.

Davis seldom forgot players in her films. It was not unusual to see performers like Virginia Brissac, who often played maids, in a succession of Davis pictures. (She played a seamstress in *The Little Foxes*.)

Perc Westmore was brought over from Warner Bros. to do Davis's makeup, a masklike white. She wore false eyelashes to narrow her eyes and a mouth made up thinner than usual to give the look of a woman of forty. Her hair was worn in a pompadour, the fashion of the day.

The striking Edwardian costumes designed by Orry-Kelly ranged from a dove-gray embroidered suit with a frilly high-necked blouse to a black velvet jet-beaded evening gown worn with a black *point d'esprit* scarf. Because California conservation laws prevented the use of stuffed birds on hats, Orry-Kelly borrowed a huge white dove, the epitome of taxidermist art, from the Louisiana Museum. He perched the snowy fowl on a huge picture hat that featured a large dotted veil. *[Orry-Kelly was requested to dress Regina in the height of fashion of that day—1900—the Gibson era. He also felt as I did about the set. A certain worn-out look from a few years back should have been the way to dress Regina.]*

Wyler and Davis, for the first time, were in disagreement about how she should play the part. He wanted a softer characterization and endlessly criticized her harder interpretation of the role. She was adamant that Hellman had so defined Regina that she could be played only one way. She argued that, if her performance was similar to Bankhead's, it could not be helped, as the Broadway actress had played the part as written.

Adding to the production woes was the fact that Los Angeles was experiencing the worst heat wave in some years, aided and abetted by hot, driving Santa Ana winds. As the temperature rose on the set, the players, complicated with extra pounds of period clothing, grew irritable, despite primitive air-conditioning. On May 12, after a hot morning spent rehearsing a difficult scene, Davis left the set.

Immediately rumors flew all over Hollywood. (1) She was pregnant. (2) She was divorcing her husband. (3) She was feuding with Wyler. (4) She was feuding with Sam Goldwyn. (5) She was being replaced by Miriam Hopkins. (6) She was being replaced by Katharine Hepburn. (7) She was taken off the film because she could not stack up to the original New York actors. (8) It was 100 degrees on the sound stage, and the star collapsed from the heat. (9) She walked off the set because Wyler disliked her long eyelashes.

Among the nine rumors two were correct. She *was* feuding with Wyler over the interpretation of Regina, and it was 100 degrees on the sound stage. *[It was the only time in my career that I walked out on a film after the shooting had begun. I was a nervous wreck due to the fact that my favorite and most admired director was fighting me every inch of the way as regards my interpretation of Regina. I just didn't want to continue. I felt there was no way I could give even a presentable performance under these circumstances. I went to Laguna Beach, where I was renting a house at the time, and flatly refused to come back to work. It took a little courage, to say the least. Goldwyn had it in his power to sue me for the entire cost of the production.]*

While columnists were having a field day printing gossip, *Movie-Radio Guide* sent a reporter and a photographer over to *The Little Foxes* set the latter part of May and subsequently ran a story entitled "The Truth about Bette Davis's Collapse":

> No, . . . Bette wasn't a quitter. She was physically and mentally tired and consequently unable to do her work. She was threatened by a physical and possibly nervous breakdown. That was why, in the words of Dr. Moore, plus those of Dr. Dorrell G. Dickerson, examining physician for the Lloyds of London Insurance Company, Bette was ordered to rest. The newshawks should have known, when Lloyds, insurers of the Goldwyn film, agreed that Bette Davis should rest, that the truth was being told, for Lloyds do not want to pay staggering sums to Goldwyn for "losses incurred by delay."

Dr. Dickerson realized I was truly upset by all the circumstances. He knew I was not physically exhausted. I was emotionally exhausted—sometimes a far greater problem. Approval by my director was always a necessity for me if I was to give a good performance. Dr. Dickerson, sympathetic as he was, told me to rest a few days and then return to work. He said, "Every day you finish work, mark it off on a calendar, and the days will pass, sooner than it seems to you now." Back to work I went.]

Teresa Wright posed for *Movie-Radio Guide* with a huge thermometer that read 100 degrees; technicians were shown manipulating the giant coils of the cooling machine that sped cold air to the sound stage; and Davis's black evening gown, petticoats, and underwear were dramatically draped over a hanging scale to show that indeed her dress weighed almost ten pounds.

Goldwyn hired five famous photographers to shoot publicity pictures: George Hurrell, Paul Hesse, James Doolittle, Charles Kerbee, and Willinger. *[George Hurrell for many years shot some magnificent pictures of the characters I played. His photographs of Regina were the best of them all. Hurrell was—and is—a true artist in his work.]* The color and black-and-white photographs were widely published, not only in the fan books but in such diversified periodicals as *Esquire* and *Ladies Home Journal.*

Davis retreated to Warner Bros. when the picture was finally completed, feeling that she had given one of the worst performances of her career Wyler told an interviewer for *The New York World Telegram,* "I'm not knocking Bette, for she is a great actress, but I am relieved the picture is done. Maybe she is just as relieved." *[Tragically enough, I was relieved. To be happy to have a film with Wyler as the director finished was indeed a heartbreak for me. He has never asked me to be in one of his films in all these years. I have few ambitions left—one is to do one more film with Willie before I end my career.]* However, the film was an enormous personal success for Davis, who was nominated for an Academy Award.

The Little Foxes opened at Radio City Music Hall on August 21, 1941, and Bosley Crowther's review in *The New York Times* ran peculiarly hot and cold:

> *The Little Foxes* leaps to the front as the most bitingly sinister picture of the year and as one of the most cruelly realistic character studies yet shown on the screen . . . And Miss Davis's performance in the role which Tallulah Bankhead played so brassily on the stage is abundant with color and mood. True, she does occasionally drop an unmistakable imitation of her predecessor; she performs queer contortions with her arms like a nautch-dancer in a Hindu temple, and generally she comports herself as

though she were balancing an Academy "Oscar" on her high-coiffed head. But the role calls for heavy theatrics: it is just a cut above ten-twent'-thirt'. Miss Davis is all right . . . *The Little Foxes* will not increase your admiration for mankind. It is cold and cynical. But it is a very exciting picture to watch in a comfortably objective way, especially if you enjoy expert stabbing-in-the-back.

[No comment, Mr. Crowther—"'ten-twent'-thirt'" indeed, sir!!!]
But, if Crowther nit-picked, other critics did not; Britain's Dilys Powell thought it was "enormously helped by its chief player: Bette Davis has never given a finer performance than as the cold murderess."

The last shot remains in memory. After being rejected by her daughter, Regina slowly climbs the stairs; the house seems alive, about to envelop her in evil. From her bedroom window she watches Alexandra and David run out into the rain-drenched street. The camera focuses on her haunted face through the water-beaded window pane as the camera pulls back slowly.

"THE BEARD," "THE NOSE," AND "THE OOMPH GIRL"

While on holiday in New York Davis attended the hilarious hit Broadway comedy *The Man Who Came to Dinner,* by George S. Kaufman and Moss Hart, and felt the part of Maggie Cutler, the patient secretary to viperish author-lecturer Sheridan Whiteside, would be an excellent change-of-pace role. She suggested to J.L. that the studio purchase the property for John Barrymore and herself.

Warner Bros. paid $250,000 for the play and assigned the script to the Epstein brothers. The changes in turning the play into screen material dealt mainly with transitions and additional scenes to expand the action from the drawing-room set. The new ending found Eleanor Roosevelt on the phone, speaking in that distinctive way, "Hello, Sheridan, hello."

Barrymore was tested for Whiteside but was having difficulty with the lines, which he read from cue cards placed outside of camera range. *[I've always said that I'd take Barrymore's adlibbing rather than make the film with anyone else.]* The upshot was that Monty Woolley, who had created the part, was brought out from New York for the picture.

Warner Bros. publicity people latched on to a new gimmick; stars were referred to by that portion of the anatomy that had made them famous. It all started when Marie McDonald was tabbed the Body and Betty Grable the Legs. Even S. Z. Sakall, famous for his paunchy jowls, became Cuddles. When Woolley started preproduction work on *The Man Who Came to Dinner,* he became the Beard. Also in the handpicked cast was Ann Sheridan, the Oomph Girl, and Jimmy Durante, the Nose. Also signed were Billie Burke, Reginald Gardiner, and newcomer Richard Travis as Davis's vis-à-vis.

The characters in *The Man Who Came to Dinner* were thought to be based on real people. Whiteside was apparently vitriol-tongued critic Alexander Woollcott, who actually played the role in a revival; Lorraine Sheldon was Gertrude Lawrence; Banjo was Groucho Marx; and Beverly Carleton was Noel Coward. William Keighley directed in a hard, brilliant laugh-getting style, and Jerry Wald, Sam Harris, and Jack Saper produced under Wallis's supervision. *[I felt the film was not directed in a very imaginative way. For me it was not a happy film to make—that it was a success, of course, did make me happy. I guess I never got over my disappointment in not working with the great John Barrymore.]*

The Man Who Came to Dinner opened at the Strand Theatre in New York on January 1, 1942, to excellent reviews. Bosley Crowther reported in his *New York Times* review the next day: ". . . here in the space of something like an hour and fifty-two minutes is compacted what is unquestionably the most vicious but hilarious cat-clawing exhibition ever put on the screen. . . . One palm should be handed to Bette Davis for accepting the secondary role of the secretary, and another palm should be handed to her for playing it so moderately and well."

SNOW WHITE AND ROSE RED

I hate you. I hate the day I married you. I hate everything about you—you and your righteous airs. Why don't you go back to Roy where you belong. She's just fool enough to have you!

BETTE DAVIS AS STANLEY TIMBERLAKE
IN *In This Our Life*

Howard Koch, who had done such a fine job on *The Letter,* was given Ellen Glasgow's Pulitzer Prize novel *In This Our Life* to turn into a screenplay. It was not an easy task, since there was a conglomeration of characters and subplots other than the two sisters with boys' names, who were to be given prominence. The younger sister, Stanley, self-centered and volatile, was to be played by Davis, while the older sister, Roy, sensible and calm, was to be portrayed by Olivia De Havilland. *[The book by Miss Glasgow was brilliant. I never felt the script lived up to the book. As to casting, particularly as regards casting me as Stanley, it could have been better. I was not young enough for the part. It was John Huston's second directing assignment. I felt he, as a writer, was not in accord with the script either. There was, however, a first in this film. The Negro boy, played by Ernest Anderson, was written and performed as an educated person. This caused a great deal of joy among Negroes. They were tired of the Stepin Fetchit vision of their people.]*

The story had two rather explosive elements: an incestuous desire for the younger girl by rich old Uncle William and a touch of racial discrimination in the treatment of a black blamed for the fatal hit-and-run accident Stanley commits. At last a workable script was turned over to Wallis and associate producer David Lewis.

Davis had her usual meeting with Perc Westmore; their collaboration turned up a cupid's-bow mouth—her own slightly exaggerated—and a hairdo with fluffy bangs. Westmore piled De Havilland's hair high on her head to make her look older. Since the family was not wealthy, Orry-Kelly designed simple skirts and blouses for Davis: a red flowered frock; a lavender chiffon dress, worn with a big hat; a dressmaker's suit sporting a pert, veiled pillbox; and a couple of flowing nightgowns. To point up the difference in the girls' characters, he designed a more severe wardrobe for De Havilland.

In the role of Lavinia, the invalid mother of the girls, Huston cast Billie Burke, in her first serious role since playing Katharine Hepburn's mother in *A Bill of Divorcement* ten years before.

The character that caused the greatest difficulty casting-wise was the role of Negro Parry Clay, toiling at night and going to law school by day. Huston looked at the few black actors available, but none seemed to have the right quality. One day Davis noticed Ernest Anderson, who was a waiter in the Green Room restaurant at the

Arthur Farnsworth and Davis cut the wedding cake after the marriage ceremony at Justin Dart's ranch at Rimrock, Ariz., December 31, 1940. (*Photograph by Davis's cousin John Favor, Acme Newspictures, Inc.*)

Property men rig parachute for Davis's landing in rubber cactus patch in *The Bride Came COD*, 1941. (*Photograph by Bert Six, Warner Bros.*)

Bette Davis dons a nurse's uniform and takes the place of an extra in the opening sequence of *Shining Victory*, 1941, to wish Irving Rapper well on his first directorial assignment. (*Photograph by Madison Lacy, Warner Bros., from the collection of Bill Roy.*)

Bette Davis chats with W. Somerset Maugham on *The Little Foxes* set at Samuel Goldwyn Studios. (*Photograph by Samuel Goldwyn Studios, from the collection of Bette Davis.*)

Bette Davis as Maggie Cutler in *The Man Who Came to Dinner.* (*Photograph by Bert Six, Warner Bros.*)

Bette Davis as Regina Giddens in *The Little Foxes,* 1941. (*Photograph by George Hurrell, Samuel Goldwyn.*)

Uncle William Fitzroy
(Charles Coburn) entertains
incestuous thoughts about
his niece Stanley Tim-
berlake (Bette Davis) in *In
This Our Life*, 1942. (*Photograph by Bert Six, Warner
Bros.*)

Bette Davis on the set of *In This Our Life*, with Tibby and Mike; latter
Scottie was a present from husband Arthur Farnsworth. (*Photograph
by Bert Six, Warner Bros.*)

Bette Davis as the repressed, guilt-ridden Aunt Charlotte in *Now, Voyager*, 1942. (*Photograph by Bert Six, Warner Bros.*)

Bette Davis as the liberated Charlotte Vale in *Now, Voyager.* (*Photograph by Bert Six, Warner Bros.*)

Kurt Muller (Paul Lukas, in his Academy Award-winning role) and Sara Farrelly Muller (Bette Davis) in *Watch on the Rhine*, 1943, say goodbye for the last time before he illegally enters Germany to fight the Nazis. (*Photograph by Bert Six, Warner Bros.*)

studio. Impressed with his sensitive face and serious demeanor, she pointed him out to Huston, who went to Wallis. A screen test was made, and he won the part. *[Ernie gave a beautiful performance.]*

Bosley Crowther, in the May 9, 1942, issue of *The New York Times*, said,

> Apparently, the Warners were afraid that Bette Davis's role in *The Man Who Came to Dinner* would inspire for their mordant Duse a bit too much public sympathy. Miss Davis was far too agreeable as Sheridan Whiteside's patient secretary. So, the Burbank Brothers have quickly cast the young lady back into one of her familiar characterizations of an out-and-out troublemaking shrew. And that is what she plays as poisonously as only she can.
>
> . . .
>
> *In This Our Life* opened yesterday at the Strand on a program with Jimmy Dorsey's band. The youngsters who came early to stomp remained at the end to cheer.
>
> But Miss Davis, by whom the whole thing pretty much stands or falls, is much too obviously mannered for this spectator's taste. "I'd rather do anything than keep still," she bitterly complains at one point. And that's the truth; she is forever squirming and pacing and grabbing the back of her neck. It is likewise very hard to see her as the sort of sultry dame that good men can't resist. In short, her evil is so theatrical and so completely inexplicable that her eventual demise in an auto accident is the happiest moment in the film. That, indeed, is what probably provoked the audience to cheer.

The full-page ads in the fan books showed head shots of Davis and De Havilland with the headline caption, "Sister against Sister!" and "Love Made Them Hate Each Other." Bette says, *"What I want I go after—and I get it!"* Olivia says, *"I'm going to be hard—just as hard as she is!"* An engraved card reads, "A sensational novel throbs to life! The cast is one of Warner Bros. best—the picture is one of Warner Bros. biggest!"

[As a finished product In This Our Life *was mediocre. It was a real box office failure. I met Miss Glasgow not long after we had finished transferring her prize-winning book to the screen. She minced no words about the film. She was disgusted with the out-*

come. I couldn't have agreed with her more. A real story had been turned into a phony film.]

FRUMP INTO GLAMOUR GIRL

Oh, Jerry, we have the stars, let's not ask for the moon.
                    BETTE DAVIS AS CHARLOTTE VALE
                    IN *Now, Voyager*

In 1970, when work began on *The Summer of '42*, the producer wanted to show a sequence from a representative movie of that year for a scene where the adolescent boys take their girl friends to the Saturday matinee. *Now, Voyager* was fondly remembered and Davis was asked if the ending sequence from the picture could be used. She agreed, and arrangements were made with the releasing corporation. Wherever the film was shown, the Davis-Henreid scenes were greeted with applause.

This was an instance where a film grew in stature over the years. The studio had purchased the Olive Higgins Prouty best seller in 1941, announcing that Irene Dunne would be on loan-out from Columbia for the role of the troubled Bostonian. Davis went to Wallis. "I'm under contract here—why can't I play Charlotte Vale? As a New Englander, I understand her better than anyone else ever could." Wallis went to J.L. and she was given the part.

In discussing the various "disagreements" between the stars and his studio J.L. said thirty years later, "When you're dealing with talented people, I guess you have to expect some trouble, and friction. You never hear a peep from the duds."

The property dealt with a segment of the fictional Vale family, which Prouty had started with *White Fawn* (1936), followed with *Lisa Vale* (1938) and *Now, Voyager* (1941), and continued with *Home Port* (1947)—in one of the heartiest foursome of sequels since *The Forsyte Saga*. Casey Robinson was assigned script duties, and Irving Rapper, who had completed *The Gay Sisters* with Barbara Stanwyck two weeks before, was given the directorial reins. *Now, Voyager* was a big hit in South America as *Tears of Long Ago*.

Wallis cast a handsome Austrian actor, Paul Henreid (formerly Paul von Hernfeid, who worked for Max Reinhardt in Vienna), in the key role of Jerry Durrance, the architect who meets Charlotte on a cruise to South America and, through his love for her, proves to be the liberating force in her life. Henreid had just finished filming *Joan of Paris* with Michele Morgan, a story about the French underground. *[I was very upset that the actor given the part of Jerry Durrance was not an American, as he was in the book. But, to make matters worse, Paul Henreid in his makeup test appeared to be the typical Valentino hero. His hair was like patent leather; he also wore a satin smoking jacket. In appearance he was everything wrong for the part as written. It was obvious he would ruin the picture if allowed to play the part.]* Henreid confided to Davis that he did not like the test. She went to Wallis and received permission for another test to be made as he believed he should look as the character. The second test was approved. Henreid was thirty-four, the same age as Davis.

Irving Rapper told interviewers Charles Higham and Joel Greenberg in their book *The Celluloid Muse* in 1969, "My great teacher Michael Curtiz was originally supposed to have directed this picture but didn't like it as a subject and preferred to do an action picture. I insisted upon casting *Now, Voyager* myself; I was starting to sail high, and they gave me my head. So I hired Claude Rains to play the psychiatrist, and Gladys Cooper, whom Hal Wallis had never heard of, to play the mother." *[Irving, you said it, I didn't. Can scarcely believe Hal had never heard of Gladys Cooper. Anyway, Miss Cooper's contributions to* Now, Voyager *were wondrous. What a thrill working with her. She will always be one of the few actresses I felt privileged to play a scene with. I adored her, not only for her work but as a person.]*

What saved the rather lachrymose plot was that the heroine is turned from an ugly duckling into a butterfly by the use of psychoanalysis—which was being newly explored by films at that time. Claude Rains played the psychiatrist, Dr. Jacquith, who takes Charlotte to his sanitarium, Cascade, where she is given therapy, placed on a diet, and eventually sent on a cruise to the Caribbean and South America with Walt Whitman's admonition:

> Untold want, by life and land 'nere granted,
> Now, Voyager, sail thou forth to seek and find.

Prouty had given her characters an interesting ceremony with a cigarette, which Robinson carried over into the screenplay. Rapper patiently rehearsed the action. Henreid took a cigarette, which

Davis lighted with a match. He handed the lighted cigarette back to her. She handed the lighted match to him so that he could light his own cigarette. The timing was off from the beginning. The matches would burn out before the rite was concluded, or they would run out of dialogue while transferring the cigarettes. "This just won't work, Irving," Henreid complained. "It's too awkward. Why can't I just place the two cigarettes in my mouth, light both from the same match, then hand one to Bette?" Rapper acquiesced, and the take was completed smoothly. *That* is how the famous business with the cigarette originated. After the film was released, lovers all over the world copied the smoking ritual established in *Now, Voyager.*

Ilka Chase, who played Davis's sister, Lisa, in one of her autobiographies described her impression of Davis on the set:

> Bette Davis took a passing reference to herself in good part and grinned when we met. "You said I used to swear when I blew up in a scene. Well, damn it, I did, but I broke myself of the habit. I saw some of those muffed shots once. Sounded like hell."
>
> Miss Davis is a fine, hard-working woman, friendly with members of her cast, forthright and courteous to technicians on her picture, and her director's heaviest cross. She will argue every move in every scene until the poor man is reduced to quivering pulp. The result on him, I suppose, is the same, but, as far as I could judge, she does not do this out of orneriness. She has had years of experience, she is a perfectionist, and she is what atomic energy draws on when it wants really to gather its forces. To make a picture quietly, a procedure so wearing that it leads many others to the doors of a sanitarium, would exhaust Miss Davis about as much as a bout with a six-year-old contender in the PAL would tire Joe Louis.
>
> Her work is not where the strain lies. Like most people who have reached the top, I think she finds that the staying is harder than the climb.

For the early sequences Davis wore padding to make her look heavier. She also added heavy fake eyebrows and wore glasses. For her first entrance in the film, elaborately built up by conversation between Cooper, Chase, and Rains, the camera focuses on the foyer staircase as Davis's legs come into view. The camera tilts up to disclose the lumpy figure and finally comes to rest upon the ungainly face. Later a similar shot is set up aboard ship, where everyone is waiting for the appearance of the passenger who has closeted herself throughout the voyage. The camera rests below the ladder as her high-heeled, two-toned shoes come into view. The camera tilts up slowly, showing the trim legs, then the svelte figure clothed in a dark suit, and lastly the glamorized face—dark lipstick, tweezed brows, hair upswept under a white panama hat. The audience cheers at the startling transformation.

Wallis provided the film with a magnificent production, and Rapper brought a great sense of taste to the direction. Art director Robert Haas contributed authentic atmospheric sets.

Davis personally worked on the screenplay, determined to use Prouty's original situations and dialogue. While the Cascade shots could have been faked on the back lot or filmed near the studio, Wallis insisted that a real lake and trees would better contrast with the slick interiors of the Beacon Street house. The unit traveled to Lake Arrowhead. Davis became friends with Janis Wilson, who played Henreid's disturbed daughter Tina, and took an interest in her career. When *Watch on the Rhine* was cast, she remembered her for the part of daughter Babette. Davis sported white harlequin-shaped sunglasses on location and was full of pep and vigor—always her reaction to the deep woods much like her own New England forests.

Orry-Kelly designed twenty-two wardrobe changes besides the fussy, middle-aged costumes for the fat Charlotte. For the transformed character he created a casual oatmeal tweed suit; a three-piece outfit with a green wool skirt; a fuchsia blouse and a green, fuchsia, black, and white striped coat; a white crepe dinner dress with an all-over design of bugle beads; a black crepe dinner gown with long tight sleeves and a black velvet sash (worn with gardenias Henreid sends on her first night back in Boston, giving Charlotte the courage to face her mother after she has been liberated from the family tyranny). For a key scene aboard ship she wears a flowing white chiffon evening dress. Since she is supposed to be a butterfly emerging from her chrysalis, Orry-Kelly created a red wool cape with sequined butterflies on the shoulder.

When the rough cut of *Now, Voyager* was shown to Wallis, he made minute changes. He removed a scene showing Charlotte being taken by Lisa to a beauty parlor for the transformation, leaving the shipboard shot for her first introduction as a beauty.

Also deleted was a fanciful silent dream sequence experienced by the young Charlotte during a flashback, where she is romanced by the ship's young officer, who invites her to dance among pillars reaching to the sky. The scene was too long and not sufficiently motivated.

Max Steiner, delighted with the film, was inspired to create a memorable score reminiscent of Tchaikovsky's *Symphonie Pathétique*. He won an Academy Award for his work. The popular song "It Can't Be Wrong"* was derived from "Charlotte's Theme."

Kim Gannon wrote the lyrics:

Wrong, would it be wrong to kiss,
Seeing I feel like this,
Would it be wrong to try?

Wrong, would it be wrong to stay,
Here in your arms this way,
Under this starry sky?

If it is wrong,
Then why were you sent to me,
Why am I content to be,
With you forever?

So, when I need you so much,
and I have waited so long,
It must be right,
It can't be wrong.

In 1971 on the "Dick Cavett Show," Davis admitted that she did not often think about what happened to characters in her films after the story was told but in the instance of *Now, Voyager* felt that Charlotte eventually married Jacquith and helped him with his work at Cascade. *[As in the case of Gladys Cooper, I always felt privileged to work with Claude Rains, who played Jacquith. He was truly a great actor. I mourn the fact I will never have that privilege*

---

again. He also gave me his admiration and friendship. This made me truly proud.]

The full-page ad in the trade magazines proclaimed, alongside a close shot of the lovers in each other's arms, "From Joan of Paris to Bette of Warners!—Better than *In This Our Life*—By the author of Stella Dallas—Made to be Bette's best!" *[For once an ad told the truth. Indeed, it was a better film than* In This Our Life. *I am often asked what are my favorite films?* Now, Voyager *is one of them. Not only did Gladys Cooper and Claude Rains give beautiful performances, so did Paul Henreid. Claude, Paul, and I worked together again later on, much to my delight. Paul's family and mine have been best of friends from the time of* Now, Voyager *all during these years that have followed.]*

A true "woman's picture," *Now, Voyager* was a tremendous box office hit. But, more than a *succès d'estime*, it has survived the carping of various critics to remain a representative picture of its time. *[The fan mail I received after* Now, Voyager *was released was more than rewarding—truly hundreds of letters from children of possessive mothers, whose lives had been ruined as was Charlotte's before meeting Jacquith; also many from mothers admitting their similar mistakes with their children.]* In 1970 Richard Gertner and Martin Quigley, Jr., in *The Fifty Greatest Films* chose *Now, Voyager* as their selection for 1942.

THE HOLLYWOOD CANTEEN

John Garfield, feeling the great need for a servicemen's center for enlisted men in Hollywood, spoke to Davis about helping him form a canteen. The Los Angeles area was the embarkation point for thousands of men who wanted to see Hollywood stars while in the area. Since Davis had been represented by Music Corporation of America since 1938, she was a friend of its president, Jules Stein. *[Jules Stein, up to this time, was seldom ever seen. Few people even knew what he looked like. He preferred to live this way. It was a big decision when he said he would head the financial committee. He would have to alter his way of life. Without his hard work, advice, and investments of our funds the Hollywood Canteen could not have been successful, to say nothing of the work of his wife, Doris, who I asked to be the head of the committee for the hostesses necessary for dancing partners for the servicemen. When the canteen was no*

It happens in the best of families
But you'd never think it could happen to her!
WARNER BROS.
present their new dramatic triumph
BETTE DAVIS
more exciting, more radiant than ever—with her new co-star
PAUL HENREID
in
Now, Voyager
A story that surpasses 'Stella Dallas', by its author, Olive Higgins Prouty
A HAL B. WALLIS PRODUCTION
with
CLAUDE RAINS
GLADYS COOPER · BONITA GRANVILLE · ILKA CHASE · Directed by IRVING RAPPER · Music by Max Steiner

*longer needed after V-J Day, $500,000 remained in the canteen
account. These monies were the result of Jules's ideas. A great
source of revenue came from a film he urged Warner Bros. to make
called* Hollywood Canteen, *a large percentage of which was
allotted by Mr. Warner to the canteen itself. With the remaining
monies a foundation was formed, and to this day contributions are
made to worthy projects dealing with the armed forces.]*

Columbia gave the proceeds ($6,500) of the premiere of *Talk of
the Town,* starring Ronald Colman, Jean Arthur, and Cary Grant, to
the project. *[The first monies conscripted for the canteen. This was
due to the generosity of Harry Cohn, head of Columbia Pictures.]*

A former livery stable and nightclub, the Old Barn, located at
1451 Cahuenga Boulevard, off Sunset, was leased for the duration
of the war. Materials for necessary repairs and decorations, to say
nothing of the actual labor, were donated by members of the
fourteen guilds and unions of the industry, which comprised the
board of directors of the Hollywood Canteen, with Davis as president and Garfield as vice-president. Artists and cartoonists painted
murals on the walls, and kitchen equipment was donated. *[Chef
Milani was in charge of the food at the canteen. Due to his energies
a great deal was donated by different organizations, but much we
had to pay for. Our average weekly food bill was $3,000.]* The
canteen charged $100 to sit in the bleachers for opening night,
October 3, 1942. *[This also was Jules Stein's idea. The canteen
made $10,000 that night from the bleacher seats. It seemed
thousands of men entered the canteen that night. I had to crawl
through a window to get inside.]*

At the opening Davis made the welcoming speech, although
plagued with a bad case of laryngitis. *[All concerned in making the
canteen a success, and it would be impossible to name them all,
were exhausted by the time we opened, including myself . . . thus
the Laryngitis.]* Coast Guardsman Rudy Vallee led the band in the
grand march.

14

I don't like being alone at night. I guess everybody in the world has a time they don't like. With me, it's right before I go to sleep. Now it's going to be for always—all the rest of my life.

BETTE DAVIS AS SARA MULLER
IN *Watch on the Rhine*

[When I was filming the above speech, I had a sixth sense this would be true of me one day. I was right!]

Perhaps more than any other studio, Warner Bros. had great success transferring stage plays into films in the later 1930s and early 1940s. And when J.L. decided to purchase Lillian Hellman's *Watch on the Rhine,* it was with double-edged purpose. Patriotically the property was important. As *Newsweek* on March 27, 1944, commented, "Miss Hellman wrote her play before the United States was at war, but her incisive surgical analysis of fascism— both at home and abroad—is as urgently topical now as it was two years ago. She makes her point through credible human relations, rather than by indulging in the furies of oversized heroes and ideological utterances of the anti-Nazi tract."

But the play, which lasted 378 performances on Broadway, was also a fine drama and had won many awards, including the New York Drama League's coveted Delia Austrian Medal for 1941's most distinguished performance, that of Paul Lukas, and nine out of nine votes in the critics' poll conducted by *Weekly Variety.*

Wallis asked Davis to do the secondary role of Lukas's wife, Sara

Muller. Her name would help this type of film at the box office. She accepted the part because she felt the message of the play was a vital one. She agreed wholeheartedly that no one is ever safe from a creeping political cancer such as fascism.

For forty-one-year-old Sara Muller Davis wore a simple hairdo and little makeup. Orry-Kelly contributed a worn-looking dark dress, coat, and felt hat for the opening sequence, where the family is admitted at the Mexican border. A skirt and blouse and two evening dresses—one white and one black—completed the wardrobe. There was no star introduction scene for Davis and Lukas; they appear in the first shot.

Herman Shumlin, who had directed the Broadway play, was brought out to do the film but found motion picture techniques foreign to his way of working. He was at odds with Merritt Gerstad, the cinematographer assigned to the picture. Shumlin was on the verge of quitting when Wallis asked veteran cameraman Hal Mohr to finish the film. The director would rehearse a scene as he would on the stage; then, with the camera in mind, Mohr would block the action with stand-ins. Shumlin would make suggestions and refine the blocking. By the time the stars were called to the set, the blueprint had been sufficiently worked out to shoot.

Besides Lukas, four other members of the New York cast were brought to Burbank: Lucile Watson as Fanny Farrelly, who delivers the most famous line in the play, "We've been shaken out of the magnolias"; George Coulouris as the evil Teck de Brancovis; Donald Buka as Joshua, the older son; and Eric Roberts as the precocious younger boy, Bodo. Geraldine Fitzgerald was signed for Marthe de Brancovis (her first Davis film since *Dark Victory*); Donald Woods was to play David, Sara's brother; and, in a complete switch, Beulah Bondi portrayed Anise, the French seamstress and companion of Mrs. Farrelly. Janis Wilson was cast as Sara's daughter, Babette, a role that Ann Blyth had played on the stage.

Dashiell Hammett, who had never adapted one of his own mystery stories for the screen, was scriptwriter along with Lillian Hellman, who wrote a few extra scenes to augment the major portion of the play, which takes place in the Farrelly drawing room. Besides the opening border shot, she created a new sequence on a train, Fanny Farrelly in a Washington office, the interior of a cab, an orchard scene with Davis and her brother spraying trees, scenes at the German Embassy, and a couple of exteriors of the

Washington mansion. In a new "coda" Joshua tells his mother that, if his father does not return, he will follow him to Europe and carry on his fight against the Fascists.

Watch on the Rhine opened at the Rialto Theatre in New York on August 27, 1943. The *National Board of Review* magazine felt: ". . . Paul Lukas here has a chance to be indisputably the fine actor he has always shown plenty signs of being. Bette Davis subdues herself to a secondary role almost with an air of gratitude for being able to at last be uncomplicatedly decent and admirable. It is not a very colorful performance, but quiet loyalty and restrained heroism do not furnish many outlets for histrionic show, and Miss Davis is artist enough not to throw any extra bits of it to prove she is one of the stars. . . ."

FINIS—THE SLAVE CONTRACT

In September, 1943, Olivia De Havilland took a step that could have finished her career as an actress. Fortunately she had great intestinal fortitude. In her seven years at the Warner stable she had weathered a variety of blows like a shock absorber, blows that would have downed an ordinary female. After *In This Our Life* and her bit in *Thank Your Lucky Stars* she refused to do *George Washington Slept Here* with Jack Benny and was replaced by Ann Sheridan. After *Princess O'Rourke,* a weak comedy, she appeared opposite Sonny Tufts in *Government Girl* on loan-out to RKO. Incensed at the role, she was even more furious to learn the deal had been consummated in a very roundabout way. The studio wanted Ingrid Bergman, whose contract was held by David O. Selznick, for *Saratoga Trunk.* Selznick loaned Bergman to Warner Bros. in exchange for De Havilland, whose commitment he then sold to RKO!

After making *Devotion,* De Havilland assumed that her seven-year contract was completed but was informed that six months still remained because of the length of five suspensions added to the end of the pact. Furious, she brought suit for declaratory relief. Then, because she could not work while the courts were deciding her fate, several USO tours were set up.

All Hollywood waited with bated breath. Davis, thinking back to her trial in England seven years before over the same disagreement, eagerly looked forward to the decision.

Finally, seven months later, on March 14, 1944, the Superior Court in Los Angeles ruled that a studio might not discipline a player by suspension without salary for an indefinite period and also add that time to the end of the contract. The court proclaimed that the studios were guilty of "virtual peonage for employees" or even a "life of bondage." *[Olivia won the case I had lost in England. Actors will forever owe her a debt of gratitude for releasing us from jail, from a "life of bondage."]*

De Havilland was free and signed a contract with Paramount. In the next few years she won two Oscars. *[I consider three performances that Olivia has given classics:* The Heiress, To Each His Own, *and* Snake Pit. *The pity was that Warner Bros. never gave her a chance to prove how really talented she was. Thank God Paramount and Twentieth Century-Fox did.]*

THE SPIDER AND THE FLY

Millie remembers the same things I do. That's important. For one thing, she's the only one I know who remembers when I used to be called Chunky.

BETTE DAVIS AS KATHERINE MARLOWE
IN *Old Acquaintance*

Comedy-dramas were in short supply during the early war years. Seeking a Davis property, Warner Bros. turned to Broadway once more and bought John Van Druten's *Old Acquaintance,* which had closed May 17, 1941, after 170 performances. Edmund Goulding, the director, wanted Miriam Hopkins for the Peggy Wood part of the bitch, Mildred Drake. Davis, who was to play the heroine, Kit Marlowe, following Jane Cowl, agreed with Goulding, although she knew how difficult Hopkins could be on the set.

Opening in 1924, the picture covered a nineteen-year span, switched through a montage to 1932, and ended in 1943. Perc Westmore cut Davis's long shoulder-length hair to a medium-short bob for the young girl and placed an inch-wide streak of gray in her updo as the older woman. For the opening scene, when she is seen sleeping on the seat of a train, Orry-Kelly designed a simple dark suit with a white blouse, worn with a narrow man's tie. For the older Kit he designed smart woman-of-the-world clothes. In one scene Davis wore a man's pajama top as a nightgown. *[This was a first. It*

*resulted in quite a vogue for young girls at that time. It really was
the beginning of the shorty nightgown still so popular today. It also
shocked many of my fans. They felt it totally undignified for my type
of serious actress to appear in such a garb!]*

Davis thought that Kit Marlowe was more like her in real life than
any role she had ever played. Goulding was taken off the picture to
direct *The Constant Nymph* with Charles Boyer and Joan Fontaine,
and thirty-seven-year-old Vincent Sherman was given the
assignment under Henry Blanke. *[Miriam was her usual difficult
self—Vincent Sherman said he felt like the umpire in a fight ring.
The day we shot the scene in which Kit has finally had enough of
Millie's tomfoolery and slaps her, the set was jammed with
onlookers from other stages. I can, in all honesty, say I never lost
my temper with Miriam on the set. I kept it all in until I got home at
night. Then I screamed for an hour at least!!! I truly felt sorry for
Miriam. She was too good an actress to indulge herself in jealousy
of another performer. It was not necessary. She was more than
capable of holding her own. She finally ruined her career because
of this. No one would work with her. It was too exhausting.]*

Davis's leading man was young actor Byron Barr, who had
changed his name to Gig Young, a character he played in *The Gay
Sisters;* also in the cast were Philip Reed, Roscoe Karns, Anne
Revere, and Esther Dale.

Franz Waxman's musical score was finely balanced, and Kim
Gannon added lyrics to the main theme which was published in
sheet music form.

Bosley Crowther wrote on November 3, 1943, in *The New York
Times,*

> Unless there is some strange fixation in female psycholo-
> gy which this reviewer does not ken, there is plainly no
> basis in nature for such endurance as is shown in this film.
> And that brings us down to this logic: The Warners were
> out to give Miss Davis another workout over an emotional
> obstacle course—and they have done so in a film parallel-
> ing, as closely as possible, her and Miss Hopkins's *The
> Old Maid.* Only the obstacles erected in this one are
> pointless and contrived, and the emotion generated is as
> phony as a spray-gun sweat.

[Always felt this would have been a super film if we had only

Bette Davis as Katherine Marlowe and Miriam Hopkins as Mildred Drake in the ending sequence of *Old Acquaintance*. Their friendship having outlasted teen-age trials, illicit romance, an unfulfilled husband, and an errant daughter, the two novelists end up toasting each other with champagne. (*Photograph by Bert Six, Warner Bros.*)

Bette Davis as the sophisticated, fortyish Katherine Marlowe and Gig Young as young naval officer Rudd Kendall in *Old Acquaintance*, 1943. (*Photograph by Bert Six, Warner Bros.*)

Bette Davis as the young Kit Marlowe in *Old Acquaintance*. (*Photograph by Warner Bros.*)

*filmed the Van Druten play. The addition of the early life of the two
characters was definitely contrived and movie-ish.]*

Under the circumstances, Miss Davis's acting, in her
customary style, is fluid and full of contrivance—but it
doesn't mean a thing. Only when she dresses up
expensively, as a fortyish woman of the world, with a
curiously lacquered complexion and a streak of gray in
her hair, does character coincide with performance. . . .
. . . Vincent Sherman has directed in a manner which
ignores the axiom of the two points and the straight line,
and Mr. Van Druten and Miss Coffee have written such
dialogue as features brittle, pretentious plays. As a sample (and commentary): "There comes a time in every
woman's life when the only thing that helps is a glass of
champagne."

*[I, as a woman, have had many such moments. However, I prefer
scotch. Maybe, had Mr. Crowther been a woman, he would have
understood these two women better. Many of my reviews had the
same complaint—"a woman's picture!" Have always felt the average male had little understanding of women—on or off the
screen. Critics were no exceptions!!!]*

DAVIS SINGS A TORCH SONG

After *Old Acquaintance* was in the can, producer-columnist Mark
Hellinger brought an idea to J.L. about doing a musical film similar
to *The Broadway Melody,* which had been such a hit at MGM,
wherein each Warner star would do a "turn" far different from their
usual characterizations. The studio had a commitment with Eddie
Cantor, whom Hellinger promised to use in developing the story
line.

James Panama, Melvin Frank, and James V. Kern were asked
to turn out an original screenplay, which was finally entitled *Thank
Your Lucky Stars*. David Butler was signed to direct. A dual role
was written for Cantor, who played himself *and* a bus driver for a
movie tour guide. Since the stars had separate numbers, the picture
was shot on as many as six stages at the same time. The stars agreed
to turn over their salaries to the Hollywood Canteen. *[Each of us*

was paid $50,000 by Warner Bros. The whole idea of contributing our salaries to the canteen was Jules Stein's.] Errol Flynn sang a rakish Irish pub song, Hattie McDaniel performed a jivey Harlem number called "Ice-Cold Katie," and Ann Sheridan torched a wryly blue song, "Love Isn't Born—It's Made" to youngish Joyce Reynolds and a bevy of Warner beauties. Olivia De Havilland and Ida Lupino were zany gum-chewing vaudevillians, Alexis Smith was seen in a ballroom dance routine, and other Warnerites had similar chores.

Davis was approached to do a song called "They're Either Too Young or Too Old,"* which described the plight of a woman whose beau is in the army. She had never done a musical number and was petrified to try it. Frank Loesser wrote the lyrics, and Arthur Schwartz the music. *[This song, "They're Either Too Young or Too Old," was Frank Loesser's first big hit. It was the top song on the "Lucky Strike Hit Parade," a very famous radio show of the time, for almost a year. I have sung it many times professionally since. It was fun to be identified with a song hit—a new experience for me.]* Orry-Kelly designed a pink print two-piece evening gown, worn with pearls and aqua gloves. Her "props" were an evening bag and a pink chiffon handkerchief.

Conrad Weidel, who had won several jitterbug contests, was chosen to propel Davis through the number. He appeared on the set wet with perspiration, scared to death of the queen. "Just forget who I am," she said, "and do it!" The cameras were set up so that it would be unnecessary to shoot more than one take. The jitterbugger manfully tossed her up in the air, down and around. The Davis number was the highlight of a somewhat ordinary picture.

Davis enters a club in search of companionship to find the place crowded either with balding oldsters or young men too young to be drafted. She dances first with a grandfatherly type, then with a pimply adolescent:

> They're either too young, or too old,
> They're either too gray or too grassy green,
> The pickings are poor and the crop is lean.
> What's good is in the army,
> What's left will never harm me.

They're either too old or too young,
So, darling, you'll never get stung.
Tomorrow I'll go hiking with that Eagle Scout unless,
I get a call from grandpa for a snappy game of chess.

I'll never, never fail ya,
While you are in Australia,
Or off among the Rooshians,
And flying over Egypt.
Your heart will never be gypped,
And when you get to India,
I'll still be what I've been to ya.
I've looked the field over
And lo and behold!
They're either too young or too old!

They're either too bald or too bold,
I'm down to the wheelchair and bassinet,
My heart just refuses to get upset.
I simply can't compel it to,
With no Marine to tell it to.

I'm either their first breath of spring,
Or else, I'm their last little fling.
I either get a fossil or an adolescent pup,
I either have to hold him off,
Or have to hold him up.
The battle is on, but the fortress will hold.
They're either too young or too old.

Thank Your Lucky Stars was a triumph for Mark Hellinger—
until the ads came out. No mention of his name appeared anywhere.
According to Jim Bishop, in his book *The Mark Hellinger Story,* he
wrote a furious note to Charles Einfeld, who was in charge of
advertising, and an even more vitriolic letter to J.L., in which he
enclosed the offending ad material.

However, J.L., Einfeld, and Hellinger survived the various blue
and pink memos that flew back and forth between their offices.
Hellinger went on to produce four other hit films, but it was during
the shooting of *The Doughgirls,* with Jane Wyman, Ann Sheridan,
Eve Arden, and Irene Manning, that he threw in the sponge. But,

before he left Warner Bros., he suggested that J.L. turn the producing reins of the war comedy over to his writer-friend James V. Kern. Surprisingly, J.L. did and the picture made money.

When Hellinger went on to make *Brute Force* at Universal, his name was featured in the same type of large print as the title—everyone in Hollywood knew why.

15

Job says that a woman is beautiful only when she is loved!
BETTE DAVIS AS FANNY TRELLIS SKEFFINGTON
IN *Mr. Skeffington*

Eighteen feature films, all "A" products, were scheduled for production by the studio in 1944. Davis was thirty-six, and her popularity was at its height. She felt compelled to continue to appear in films that offered her an opportunity for greater development as an actress. After *Old Acquaintance,* she vacationed in Mexico. *[My trip was of long duration. Prior to going to Mexico I was in contractual difficulty with Warner Bros. I hud never demanded a salary raise or limitation of films per year, and I felt the time had come. I informed the studio I would not return until my contract met these demands. This was my only other walkout from Warner Bros., aside from suspensions—the first, of course, being the trial in England. Warner Bros. eventually acceded to my demands.]*

When Davis returned to the studio, *Mr. Skeffington,* from the book by "Elizabeth," had been prepared for her by the Epstein brothers, who were also to produce. Davis requested Vincent Sherman to guide her through the picture, but he was in the midst of *In Our Time.* Another compatible director was sought.

The part of Fanny Trellis Skeffington was one of the most difficult roles that Davis had ever attempted. To point out the ultrafeminine aspects of the character, she raised her voice a full octave. *[The most difficult aspect of the character of Fanny was the fact she was a famous beauty of her day. I was far from being beautiful. My genius hairdresser, Maggie Donovan, who had been my hairdresser for years, designed the stunning hairdo I wore as Fanny. It took an hour each morning but was worth it. It gave me the illusion of beauty.]*

The film begins in 1914, and Fanny, through careful living and the aid of cosmetics, stays youthful until 1940, when a bout with diphtheria causes her to age almost as drastically, although not as quickly, as the little Chinese girl in *Lost Horizon. [Ernie Haller was again my cameraman. He was also responsible for making me beautiful in this film. Warner Bros. had me make a color test for* Mr. Skeffington. *Natalie Kalmus, technical consultant for her husband, who owned Technicolor, did not believe in pastel colors for Technicolor. I wore a white dress with a pale blue sash for the test. Mrs. Kalmus told me that, if the picture was photographed in color, I could not wear pale colors. I said, "Mrs. Kalmus, if we do* Mr. Skeffington *in color, I will wear many pale colors!" In the long run Warner Bros. decided to use black and white. Color makes everything look prettier—sets, costumes, people—especially Fanny. I would have looked prettier. Few people knew I had blue eyes and blonde hair. My ash-blonde hair, in black and white, often gave the impression I was a brunette. My eyes looked brown. The only color film I had ever made was* The Private Lives of Elizabeth and Essex. *I hardly was made up as myself in that—red hair, etc. I was disappointed.]*

The scenes concerning the ravaged Fanny posed a problem for Perc Westmore. He finally used rubber pieces, which had to be applied each day. The process took two full hours, and Davis found the makeup very uncomfortable and hot. Since Fanny had lost her hair due to diphtheria, Davis wore a wig, which in one shot is seen on a wooden stand in close-up. The camera pans to Fanny having breakfast in bed. She is almost bald, with short, thin, and very fuzzy hair. This was the first time Davis had been photographed with a bald "skin piece"—the second time would be eleven years later when she portrayed Elizabeth I again in *The Virgin Queen.*

Orry-Kelly designed some forty costumes to carry Fanny over the twenty-six-year period called for in the script, from the hobble skirt of 1914, through the flapper age, into the modernistic 1930s and contemporary 1940s. Shortly after completing the wardrobe, Orry-Kelly, forty-one, to his surprise was drafted into the army. *[Warner Bros., for me, without Orry-Kelly was as if I had lost my right arm. His contribution to my career was an enormous one. He never*

*featured his clothes to such a degree that the performance was
overshadowed. His clothes for* Mr. Skeffington, *his absolute
dedication to what was the style of the day, was, in my opinion, the
greatest of all the wardrobes he designed for me.]*

Orry-Kelly returned to do the costumes for *The Doughgirls* a year
later and found politics changed at the studio. He fought with J.L.,
and, when great friend Ann Warner failed to repair the breach, he
looked elsewhere for employment. Darryl Zanuck offered him
$30,000 a year to do the costumes for Betty Grable at Twentieth
Century-Fox, which would allow him time to open an atelier on the
side.

In the middle of August, 1943, makeup and costume tests were
commencing on *Mr. Skeffington,* and sets were being readied for a
September starting date. On Monday, August 23, Farnsworth set
out for a day of appointments. He ordered a leopard stole for Davis
at I. Magnin's, then called upon friend and attorney Dudley Furse in
Hollywood to discuss a real estate deal. Going back to his car, he
suddenly screamed and fell to the sidewalk in front of a tobacconist
at 6249 Hollywood Boulevard. The proprietor, David Freedman,
summoned an ambulance, which took the unconscious man to a
nearby receiving hospital.

Davis was at home when the hospital called at 4:15 P.M. She
called her personal physician, Dr. Paul Moore, who immediately
ordered that Farnsworth be taken to Cedars of Lebanon Hospital,
where X rays and the usual tests were taken. Davis sat at his bedside
all that night and the next day, Wednesday, still unconscious,
Farnsworth died.

The accident was investigated by the police because it was known
that Farnsworth was engaged in secret war work with Minneapolis
Honeywell. For a time foul play was suspected, but his briefcase
was examined and all papers found in order. Farnsworth's mother
requested an autopsy, which showed a previous injury in the cranial
area.

Through the studio Davis issued a statement that during the
previous June at Butternut he had fallen down half a flight of stairs.
"He struck the back of his head and quite severely scraped his
back," she recalled. "He suffered the usual lameness for several
days, but said nothing about it, so I thought no more about it."

The funeral was held at 2:30 P.M. on Saturday, August 28, at the
Church of the Recessional at Forest Lawn, and another service was

held in Rutland, Vermont, his home town, the next week. Davis then went to Butternut.

Vincent Sherman had finished *In Our Time* and was waiting to begin work on *Mr. Skeffington*. J.L. told Davis over the phone to stay away from work as long as she chose. [*I'll always remember J.L.'s kindness to me upon this occasion. I told him I was returning in a week to start filming, as I felt work was the only way to get over the state of shock I was in due to Farney's death.*] Warner Bros. cast Claude Rains as the Jewish Job Skeffington, whom Fanny marries because her brother has bilked him out of $25,000. Fanny continues to see her beaux all during her marriage. When she divorces Job, he takes their daughter, Fanny, Jr., to Europe while Fanny continues to dazzle New York society.

Richard Waring, from the stage production of *The Corn is Green,* had been signed to re-create the role of Morgan Evans in the film version, which was on Davis's schedule. Davis, of course, was to play Miss Moffat, following Ethel Barrymore's famous interpretation of the brilliant English schoolteacher. In *Mr. Skeffington* Waring was assigned the part of Trippy, Fanny's temperamental brother. Added to the cast was Walter Abel as Cousin George; George Coulouris as an amusing psychiatrist, Dr. Byles; Marjorie Riordan as Fanny, Jr.; Dorothy Peterson as the faithful maid, Manby; and Fanny's suitors, all of whom age with her: Robert Shayne as MacMahon, John Alexander as Conderley, Jerome Cowan as Morrison, Peter Whitney as Forbish, Bill Kennedy as Thatcher, and Johnny Drake as Johnny Mitchell. Broadway's Dolores Gray sang "It Had to Be You" in a scene set in a speakeasy.

The film opens with a long introductory scene with Cousin George conversing with Fanny, who is dressing behind a draped doorway. At the climactic moment she pops her head through a curtain—young, lovely, gay, and charming.

The Epstein brothers furnished an excellent adaptation of "Elizabeth's" book. [*With one exception Elizabeth tells her story in flashback. At the beginning old Fanny is having tea with a friend and talking about her life. This helps the reality of the sudden loss of beauty after the sailing accident, as you have already met Fanny as the ravaged older woman.*] A running gag is that Fanny is always breaking dates with Janie Clarkson, a character who is never seen. At the end of the film Fanny, old and decrepit, solicitously helps the blind Job up the staircase. She turns to Manby and says, "Telephone Janie Clarkson and tell her that I can't possibly have lunch," which takes the bathos out of the scene. The camera pans slowly to the portrait of the young and beautiful Fanny for the fade-out. (Davis had the picture for many years and finally loaned it to Westmore to hang in his Hollywood salon.)

A bare six weeks after returning from Butternut Davis cut the cake for the first anniversary of the Hollywood Canteen. Dressed in a simple black suit and dark snood, her mourning costume relieved only by a white orchid corsage, she spent the evening in ceremonies involving Kay Kyser, George Burns and Gracie Allen, John Garfield, Leopold Stokowski, Patricia Morison, Bob Hope, Joan Leslie, Marlene Dietrich, Jane Wyman, and other members of the movie colony.

Around the first of the year she impersonated Groucho Marx, with Westmore transforming her into the comic in front of the soldiers, sailors, and marines gathered around the bandstand. Then a husky soldier was selected from the audience and turned, by Westmore, into a voluptuous woman with the help of gourds for breasts, a scrub mop for hair, and a sheet for a dress. Lipstick, mascara, and inch-long false eyelashes completed the hilarity. The high point of the sketch was when Davis, as Groucho, smoked a cigar and asked the enlisted man to dance.

Another "turn" that always brought howls of disbelief involved Davis's being hit in the face with a pie. Her gaiety, unpretentious personality, and graciousness was impressive to the boys, all of whom thought of her as a serious dramatic actress.

The ad department was in a quandary as to how to sell the picture. It was decided to release only two or three stills of the elderly Fanny and concentrate on the romantic aspects of the story. A glamorous head shot of the star was used in the upper right-hand corner of the full-page ads taken in the fan books. To the right was a resume:

WORKING GIRL

Name: Bette Davis

Occupation: Actress

Employer: Warner Bros.

Nature of duties: Helping us maintain the Warner standard of great entertainment.

Remarks: We, at Warner Bros., have been proud of Bette Davis, of her magnificent artistry and enormous talent, ever since she came to work with us (and, no matter how easy it looks on the screen, "work" is the word—with a very large "W"!). But we've never been so proud of Bette as since we (and she) finished making MR. SKEFFINGTON!

MR. SKEFFINGTON is the enthralling story of a very rich man and a very beautiful woman, and of their life together . . . and apart. A love story? We think that, even when you've seen it, you won't be sure!

But you *will* be sure that MR. SKEFFINGTON is one of the finest motion pictures ever made—by anybody, anywhere . . . and that Bette Davis has no peer among screen artists!

You'll be sure, too, that the company which produced MR. SKEFFINGTON can be counted on always for the *best* in entertainment!

great as only

BETTE DAVIS   MR. SKEFFINGTON
she can be in

Another full-page ad featured Davis in a love scene from *Now, Voyager,* but with Paul Henreid "air-brushed" out and Claude Rains substituted with the following legend: BETTE DAVIS is crazy about MR. SKEFFINGTON and so's everybody else! *[Dear God! If ever a woman did not love a man, it was Fanny Skeffington. She loved only herself, until the end of the film.]*

Time magazine on June 5, 1944, wrote, "This story . . . provides a two-and-one-half-hour field day for cinemactress Bette Davis. As a ruthless Gramercy Park beauty, vintage 1914, she has studied such archaic cinebelles as Anita Stewart to startling advantage. As a cloche-hatted bar-prowler of the 1920s, she is even more sharply evocative. But, as the divorcee, she runs to caricature.

Her makeup as an ex-beauty is a stentorian overstatement." *[This was my point about the necessity for a flashback formula of script. My makeup did seem as if it were a "stentorian overstatement" due to the necessary suddenness of it.]*

The review in *Commonweal* on June 9, 1944, said, *"Mr. Skeffington* is a hollow kind of film on which Bette Davis, the makeup and costume departments, and director Vincent Sherman have ganged up to do some excellent things. . . . Miss Davis transforms herself with great effect into a girlish tantalizing prettiness with a high petulant voice that is the best part of the portrait. . . . You are teased with the idea of a love affair between Fanny and her brother, and the problem of a daughter who has a Jewish father and a Gentile mother. You are illuminated almost not at all about either fact, just as you are left in a rather suggestive fog about everything else concerning the Skeffingtons." *[Because our bosses were of the Jewish faith, they were very sensitive about any character in any film who was Jewish. We had many requests from the front office during the filming of* Mr. Skeffington *to add lines that would make Job appear a "saint." Claude and I fought the good fight. We were never forced to say these lines.]*

Directly after *Mr. Skeffington* was completed, Davis played herself in *Hollywood Canteen,* which the studio made with virtually every player on the lot.

Delmer Daves wrote the original story, which was produced by Alex Gottlieb and photographed by Bert Glennon. The plot was thin, with emphasis on the stars who appeared at the canteen and the thirteen musical numbers. The story dealt with two soldiers who come to the canteen (Robert Hutton and Dane Clark) during sick leave. Hutton perchance happens to be the millionth GI to cross the threshold of the canteen, and the prize is a date with Joan Leslie. The picture was a huge success.

THE LADY AND THE CORPORAL

After filming was completed, Davis spent a month in Georgia, interrupted by a trip to Washington, D.C., to see her idol, President Roosevelt, who invited her to Warm Springs for dinner. The southern trip would have caused no stir in Hollywood except for the fact that she was linked romantically with Cpl. Lewis A. Riley, 168th

Signal Photo Company, Second Army, stationed at Fort Benn
When last in Hollywood he had taken her to dinner at both Chas
and La Rue—where they were photographed.

Newshen Pauline Swanson covered the story, down to the
detail, even obtaining a photo of Davis's rented home in Phen
City, Alabama, directly across the border from Georgia.

> Autograph seekers by the scores came to camp at Bette's
> gate once the address of her vacation home was printed in
> the papers [Miss Swanson reported in the January, 1945,
> issue of *Photoplay*]. Even the padlock and the owner's
> four dogs roaming the premises failed to daunt their
> enthusiasm. One enterprising fan made friends with one
> of the dogs—a collie—and sent a note to Bette attached to
> its collar. Bette has a sense of humor, and such enterprise
> deserves recognition, so she sent the dog back to the gate
> bearing the coveted autograph.
>
>   Otis Taft, a Columbus grocer, bragged that Bette had
> ordered supplies from his store. By nightfall everyone in
> town knew that Miss Davis had ordered "twenty-five—
> dollars worth of groceries for one day! Fancy groceries,
> too!"
>
>   Bette's sister Bobby was in Georgia with her. She tried
> valiantly to discourage the reporters and photographers
> who descended on the house—but Bette at last had to
> make an appearance and posed for photographs wear—
> ing a red and white plaid shirt and navy knee-length
> shorts. . . .
>
>   . . . Bette took to the life in Phenix City like a native.
> She carried wood from the back yard for the fireplace and
> the wood-burning cook stove. She learned to make
> biscuits on the old iron stove without burning them and
> mastered a wood-smoked steak. She bought hip boots and
> overalls and joined her farmer neighbors in fishing
> expeditions and coon and possum hunts.

Davis made a personal appearance at Fort Benning, intro
by Riley, before going to Warm Springs. After a quick trip ba
Phenix City and then to New York she came back to Burbank,
to tackle one of the most difficult assignments of her career

THE LADY AND THE MINER

> *The mine is dark. If the light comes into the mine, the*
> *rivers in the mine would run fast with the voice of many*
> *women. The walls will fall in, and it will be the end of the*
> *world. The mine is dark, and, when I walk through the*
> *. . . shaft, I can touch with my hands the leaves on the*
> *trees and underneath where the corn is green. There is a*
> *wind in the shaft, not the carbon monoxide that they talk*
> *about . . . It smells like the sea, only not as if the sea has*
> *fresh flowers lying about—and that is the way I spend my*
> *holiday.*

BETTE DAVIS AS MISS MOFFAT
IN *The Corn Is Green*

The plump, middle-aged school mistress, dressed in a severe gray
dress, circa 1900, sidled up to the young Welsh miner and, batting
her eyelashes, said in a husky, insinuating voice, "Don't you think
I'm attractive?"

The "plump" matron—with thirty pounds of padding—was
none other than Bette Davis, cutting up between scenes of *The Corn
Is Green* with John Dall, humorously placing him at ease before a
difficult scene. Dall, a six-foot-two Broadway actor *(The Eve of St.
Mark)* won the role after Richard Waring was drafted. *[How sad we
all felt for Richard Waring—to have to give up this great part that
he had originated on the stage. His motion picture career never
recovered from losing this opportunity. Good as he was in* Mr.
Skeffington, *the part was not a "star-making" role. It was just
rotten luck. Warner Bros. tried in every way to postpone his date
for being drafted—to no avail.]* The studio made an arrangement
with a monastery in New York State to allow old-time silent-film
actor Gareth Hughes, a Welshman with a particularly good voice, a
Hollywood sabbatical to coach the players on the difficult dialect.
Dall, whose straight hair was permed for the role, also made some
thirty tests with actresses in line for the role of Bessie Watty, played
on the stage by Thelma Schnee. The role eventually was claimed by
Joan Lorring, who had made only two films, *Song of Russia* and
The Bridge of San Luis Rey.

The Corn Is Green by Emlyn Williams had first been performed
in England by Dame Sybil Thorndike in the role of the English

schoolteacher, Miss Moffat, and later brought to Broadway with Ethel Barrymore, who played the role some 477 times. *[Seven years later, while filming* Another Man's Poison *in England, Emlyn introduced me to the real schoolteacher he wrote about in* The Corn Is Green, *Miss Cooke. The play is the true story of Miss Cooke and Emlyn himself.]* The screen adaptation was the work of Casey Robinson (his last writing job for Davis) and Frank Cavett. Jack Chertok was the producer, Irving Rapper the director.

Instead of creating the Welsh village of Glansarno on the back lot—impractical because of winter and fog effects—all of Sound Stage Seven was used for both interiors and exteriors. Four hundred cubic yards of dirt were placed on strong compoboard, then rolled to make an even surface for lorries, carts, and surreys. Twenty tons of grass sod made up the meadows and had to be fed, watered, and mowed to keep in the peak of condition. When gypsum "snow" for winter scenes was spread over the lawn, blades of grass grew up through particles and had to be recovered! A few building facades and a bridge were built and trees planted in strategic places—all overseen by art director Carl Jules Weyl. *[This set and many others of that day designed by men of genius, and I use the word advisedly, such as Carl Jules Weyl, are living proof of the stupidity, in my opinion, of traveling hundreds of miles, as they do today, to the actual locations. The discomfort for the performer in the outdoor weather is agony, plus the time wasted when it rains, snows, blows, and the company has to wait until the good weather returns.]* Five special-effects men were required to keep the trees moving with wind machines and the clouds (Britt solution) in the sky shifting realistically. The haze of a mining village was created with smoke. A hundred goats had to be fed constantly so they would not nibble on the grass. Ten thousand props, from an ancient church bell to authentic slates and books, were amassed.

Ezra Goodman reported in the April 1, 1945, edition of *The New York Times,*

> There is a dirt road and large crude Pendarth House, a stable, a well and a shed, and the interior of the school room, all mounted on a tremendous platform against a cyclorama of blue sky. . . .
> Just beneath this platform, in her attractively furnished dressing room, sat Bette Davis . . . typing at a portable

machine and transacting some Hollywood Canteen
business by telephone during her lunch hour. She was
now eating a meal consisting of vegetable soup, an egg
and spinach, and a cup of coffee. She took time out to
discuss her role . . . "Four members of the New York
cast of the play are appearing in the picture," she pointed
out, "Rhys Williams, Gwenyth Hughes, Mildred
Dunnock, and Rosalind Ivan. This is the third picture in
which I have appeared with many of the original members
of stage casts. . . . I find that it makes for a better picture
when many of the performers are intimately familiar with
their roles. I also have the same feeling . . . as I did about
the other two—namely, a healthy respect for the actress
who originated the part. . . . The critics," Miss Davis
complained, "are always referring to me as a she-
monster. They forget that I've played more or less normal
women in pictures like *The Petrified Forest, The Old
Maid, Dark Victory, The Man Who Came to Dinner, Old
Acquaintance,* and many others."

Said E. Arnot Robertson in England's *Picture Post,* "As the
school mistress . . . only Bette Davis, I think, could have combated
so successfully the obvious intention of the adaptors of the play to
make frustrated sex the mainspring of the chief character's interest
in the young miner. This would have pulled down the whole idea of
their relationship into something much simpler and more banal—
more suitable to the sillier film audiences—than the subtle interpretation she insisted on giving. Drab outwardly, the school
mistress, in her hands, became someone consumed by inward fire,
by the sheer joy of imparting knowledge."

Orry-Kelly came back from Twentieth Century-Fox to design the
nine turn-of-the-century costumes, which were slightly padded to
add a middle-aged girth to the Davis figure. She tested in the
wardrobe in the Pendarth House setting in her own hair, which was
styled in a simple, off-the-face coiffure. She did not look old
enough for the role, so Westmore designed a high red wig with
strands of gray, which added the necessary age. The wig saved her
life one day, softening the blow when a light fell from a catwalk
onto the set.

Actual shooting began in June with rehearsals of the miners, interspersed with the Saint Luke Choristers, under the musical direction of Robert Vreeland, coming back from the mine singing a Welsh folk song. *[A professional Welsh choir was wrong in my opinion. It made the film very "Hollywood." A direct recording of the actors who played the miners, many of whom did not have perfect voices, would have given reality to the songs.]* John Dall told Dorothy Hasking in the August, 1945, issue of *Movie Story,*

> I was simply petrified at the thought of working with Bette. As far back as I can remember, I've worshiped her. I've seen all of her pictures several times . . . Many people began warning me, "You'll suffer. Playing with that woman!" Since then I've realized that no one who talked like that had worked with her. Actually she was wonderful. Every time I played a scene with her, I felt strength coming to me from her. In that scene where I had to tell her off, for instance, in some shots the camera was on me alone. But Bette always stood right behind the camera, facing me, giving the scene the same acting as if she were before the camera. She really listened to what I was saying and fed me my lines with the same intensity she would have if the camera had been on her.

Irving Rapper said in *The Celluloid Muse,*

> Bette Davis, in particular, had a marvelously probing intelligence, which gave great strength to the director working with her.
>
> Sometimes, of course, you'd have to correct her. I remember . . . at the end of the second act, which we retained in the film, there is a moment when the schoolteacher in the Welsh mining village conveys to the audience that she has dreamed, that she somehow clairvoyantly knew, that her star pupil's main historical question in the big examination would be all about Henry VIII. . . .
>
> Bette tossed the moment away, and there was a bit of an argument. I simmered down for five days, and finally I said to her, "Bette, I saw the cut stuff, and I am very sorry to tell you that wasn't the way it should have been done." And she said, "Do you really think so?" And I said,

"Yes." And she agreed to do it again. You could get through to her even though she had enormous power at the studio; she was its queen.

After the film was edited and Max Steiner had contributed a distinguished score that made use of Welsh folk melodies, Warner Bros. executives looked at the picture and were in a quandary as to how to handle the advertising copy. Why stress the fact that Davis was playing the role of a fifty-year-old woman? Outside of one brief love scene between Dall and Lorring there was no sexual interest in the film. Art work was prepared showing Davis in a décolleté evening gown. She went to J.L.: "This is absolute misrepresentation," she argued. "Can't the ad department come up with an honest representation of the character and the story?"

The full-page ads that appeared in the fan books later *did* show a modern head shot of her and a legend that could be taken two ways: "In her heart of hearts she knew she could never hold him." The ad also featured a shot of John Dall in a contemporary suit, but the newspaper advertisements showed her in period costume as she appeared in the film.

The Corn Is Green opened at the Hollywood Theatre, New York, on March 29 to excellent reviews. After three smash months, the film went into general release. Louella Parsons wrote in her July 14, 1945, review in *The Los Angeles Examiner,* "The drab schoolteacher is an unusual role for a star of Bette's fire and polish . . . Davis, I believe, is at her greatest when she is the creator and not following in a pattern established by some other outstanding personality." *[I was hardly conceited enough to try to imitate Miss Barrymore—this great star of the theater. My performance was a totally different conception. As a matter of fact, Herman Shumlin, who directed the play, had little praise for my performance. This he told me personally. Miss Moffat is a part I would like to play again now I am older. I think I could do a much better job than I did at the time.]*

FINIS TO THE HOLLYWOOD CANTEEN

On November 22, 1945, the Hollywood Canteen staged a farewell party. *[Kay Kyser's band had never missed giving its services every Saturday night since the opening of the canteen on October 3, 1942.*

I think the greatest contributors of any union to the entertainment for the servicemen in our canteen was the musicians' union. There were few nights without music. Without music for dancing we would have had no canteen. We could not possibly have afforded to pay musicians—we never had to—plus our guests, the servicemen, heard all the great bands of the day. Kay Kyser and his band were unbelievable in their weekly appearances. Harry James and Betty Grable met at the canteen. We were always proud of this fact. As you know, they married each other.] The Hollywood Canteen had entertained, with the highest-priced talent of the land, more than three million servicemen and servicewomen.

Davis, nostalgic and almost tearful, led the festivities. Flanked by Sgt. Jim Scanlan and Francis Ashley MM 3/c, each kissing her cheek, she posed for pictures. Ingrid Bergman and Jack Benny performed a skit, and other stars did a "turn"; Bob Hope was master of ceremonies.

MARRIAGE AND A PRODUCTION COMPANY

At a party in Laguna Beach Davis met a young artist, William Grant Sherry. After a month's acquaintance they were married on November 29, 1945. The ceremony took place in the chapel at the historic Riverside Mission Inn. Ruthie, a recent bride herself, and now Mrs. Robert Palmer, took the usual wedding pictures. Davis wore a simple light-blue suit with silver nail heads and a hat that Louella Parsons reported was composed of goose feathers! After the reception the newlyweds motored to Mexico where Davis was to receive a medallion from the government.

Davis formed B.D., Inc., a production company, to film six pictures. Twentieth Century-Fox put out feelers for her to do the role of the English schoolteacher in *Anna and the King of Siam* with Rex Harrison, a role she coveted, but the studio refused to loan her to the Westwood lot. *[One of the really great disappointments of my career. I loved the role of Anna—and a chance to work with Rex Harrison. I have always been a real fan of his. I consider him one of the most attractive men I have ever met. I also consider him a truly great actor. His performance as Higgins in* My Fair Lady *was utter perfection, both on the stage and on the screen.]* For the first independent picture she chose to remake an Elisabeth Bergner

British film, *A Stolen Life* (from a novel by Karel J. Benes), which had been released by Paramount in 1939. Directed originally by Paul Czinner, that story dealt with identical twin sisters: Martina, who is demure and sweet, and Sylvina, who is feline and immoral. The climax took place when the sisters go boating and the craft is capsized in a storm. The bad twin drowns, and the good twin takes her place.

Catherine Turney, who had written the screenplay for *Mildred Pierce,* which had won an Academy Award for Joan Crawford, was signed to turn Margaret Buell Wilder's (of *Miss Boo* fame) adaptation into a script under the supervision of Davis and director Curtis Bernhardt. She changed the names of the twins to Kate and Pat Bosworth and switched the locale to New England. Kate, an artist (with actual paintings by Alexander Rosenfield), is lonely and withdrawn, while Pat, a playgirl, is gay and impetuous. When Kate begins a romance with lighthouse inspector Bill Emerson (Glenn Ford), Pat lures him into marriage. The boating accident occurs, and Kate discovers her sister is on the brink of divorce. Emerson eventually discovers the identity switch, and Kate and he live happily ever after.

Curtis Bernhardt told an interviewer (as recorded in *The Celluloid Muse),*

> We were offered several highly touted young leading men but did not find the quality in any of them that we wanted until Glenn Ford returned from the Marine Corps. He came to my office, spent five minutes with me, and I was convinced he was our man. I sent him to see Bette, and she knew at once our search was over. It worried her for a while that she might look too old for him, but after the shock of hearing an actress refer to herself in those terms wore off, we were able to convince her there was nothing to worry about on that point.
>
> . . . It's not difficult to get along with Bette, provided you know her moods and the proper time to approach her with ideas. It's fatal to ask her something at the wrong time, although you *do* get an answer, even then; it usually consists of some interesting and explosive variations of the word "NO."
>
> . . . I recall a particularly rough day while we were

shooting . . . the tension had built up to a high point, and I told Bette she was a tough babe to get along with. The barometer fell rapidly, and there was a chill in the air. She gave me a dirty look and said, "And what do you think you are? When you blow your top, nobody dares to raise his voice until you cool off." That cleared things up. We both laughed like mad and calmly went back to work. There's solid satisfaction in working with one who can absorb punches and punch right back.

The small cast included Dane Clark in the role of artist Karnock; Charles Ruggles as Cousin Freddy; and Bruce Bennett as Pat's lover, Jack Talbot. Walter Brennan played the lighthouse keeper, Eben Folgor. *[One of the rewards of making comments on Mr. Stine's book is my opportunity to acknowledge publicly my good fortune to have worked with many great actors. Walter Brennan was one of them. He has had a phenomenally successful career due to his great talent. How lucky any of us were to have him in our films. A Stolen Life was no exception. What a joy he was to play scenes with. What a joy to have known Walter Brennan as a person.]*

Enthusiastic as a new producer, Davis invited Hedda Hopper to the studio for lunch in the Green Room. Hopper reported in the June 9, 1946, edition of *The Los Angeles Times,* "Writers," says Bette, "get some of the worst breaks in town. . . . And the story is the foundation for any successful film. Yet producers often become impatient, yank a writer off the story after he's been on the script for a few weeks, put him on another one. . . . Sometimes we've had as many as thirty writers on one story, and each new writer, in order to live up to his reputation and salary, has to throw most of his predecessor's stuff out and begin all over again. He can't admit it's good for fear the producer will say, 'I didn't put you on this story to praise it, but to fix it.' "

Hopper continues, "Bette has another beef with the major studios in matters of casting." Davis told her, "With a stable of stars under contract, studios like to keep them busy. You can't blame them. But whether or not the stars fit the roles, they're likely to be shoved into them. This is bad for the actor, bad for the picture, bad for the audience—which, after all, is the final payoff. If stars and producers had a free hand in picking their casts and parts, you'd see fewer actors floundering around in parts that fit them about as well as the well-known sack."

Curtis Bernhardt said in *The Celluloid Muse:*

> Despite what she claims in her autobiography she did *not* produce the picture, although it was made by her production company. I'll face her any day on that. It had, in fact, no official producer. I was stuck with both ends of the thing, with producing and directing—which I don't like, because it's too much unnecessary bother.

[Curt, we were coproducers. Never realized you felt "stuck with both ends of the thing." Judge the "thing" you refer to was the movie. If you felt this way about me, why were you my copartner in a film years later?]

> It started out with a tremendous clash between Davis and me on the first running of her wardrobe tests. The tests were all done by her favorite designer.

[Did not have Orry-Kelly to help me on this film. I felt the clothes were very inferior for the character of Kate—in fact, a hodgepodge, with a few exceptions. The dress and hat for Pat's wedding were attractive. Pat's clothes, I still feel, were right for the part.]

> We all sat in a little projection room, about twenty people, looking at those wardrobe rushes.
>
> I hardly knew Miss Davis at that time, and I thought one test was more horrible than the other. . . .
>
> At the third costume I said carefully, "Now, Miss Davis, don't you think these things are a little theatrical?"
>
> To which she replied, "Let's cut this *theatrical* talk. Nobody can ever say that things connected with me are theatrical. . . ."
>
> I thereupon became hot under the collar and saying, "Goodbye, Miss Davis," I got up and walked out.
>
> "Where are you going?" she asked.
>
> "I'm going home," I said.

"What do you mean?" she called after me.

"You don't need a director," I said. "You need a yes-man, Miss Davis, and I'm not cut out to be a yes-man."

[This interview must be full of misquotes, as interviews often are. I never believed in yes-men. I despised them. I also never believed in clothes that were "theatrical"—not suitable to the character I was playing.]

Although *A Stolen Life* was set in New England, all the location work was done north of here at Pebble Beach, near Carmel and Monterey; nothing was done in New England, which the locations closely resembled. Most of the film, however, was shot on studio stages.

[The lighthouse was built offshore in Laguna Beach, which is where I lived at the time. The town grew very fond of it and didn't want us to take it down after we finished shooting.]

Because of the difficulty of the trick photography both Sol Polito and Ernie Haller shared cinematography credit. Bernhardt was determined to perform stunts that had never been attempted before in connection with a dual role. *[No compliments can be too much for the dual-shot scenes planned by Bernhardt. I have people still ask me how they were done. They were completely real—filmed as if two actors were in the scenes instead of the same actress playing both parts.]* Optical printing—the method by which both girls could be seen simultaneously in the same shot—had long been in use but in simpler forms.

Usually in connection with twins played by the same actor one twin stays in one-quarter or one-half of the frame and the other in the remaining three-quarters or one-half; the two parts are then combined in the laboratory. This is accomplished by shooting the scene with one portion of the camera aperture covered, with action confined to the exposed film area. The film is wound back through the camera and the scene shot again; this time the portion that has already been exposed is covered.

But new tricks were worked out by lensers Willard Van Enger and Russell Collings, with other special effects created by William McGann and E. Roy Davidson. In the dual scenes Davis, as Kate, first plays a scene with double Sally Sage, in an identical costume, playing Pat; then the scene is shot again with the roles reversed. The two negatives are cut and placed together in the lab in exact alignment. The completed print from the composite negative then contains perfect illusion. Dubbing of the voice allows the two girls to talk to each other.

Both the camera and the furniture must be bolted to the floor, because with double filming of the same scene the slightest movement of camera or props spoils the reality when the films are combined.

One scene shows Kate lighting Pat's cigarette—a very tricky business, requiring absolute perfection of timing. The following action was worked out by Bernhardt: Pat is seen in a highbacked wing chair; Kate stands beside the chair and lights the match. Pat surreptitiously rests her arm on the arm of the chair (to steady her hand) and takes the match. On film only a slight jerkiness could be discerned when the match exchanged hands. Another scene called for Pat to be fussing with Kate's collar—the line of demarcation taking place in the fuzzy fur that Pat is wearing. The girls also talk in bed, converse in a garden, greet each other at a cottage door, stand side by side when Pat is marrying Emerson, and dance at a party— either within a hairbreadth of each other or touching.

One sequence causing a great deal of discussion was the scene at the wharf when Pat is first mistaken for Kate. There were totally different wardrobes for each girl. Kate is seen mostly in simple suits, slacks, and sweaters, while Pat wears showier clothes. In this scene Pat wears a white slack suit, somewhat Oriental in fashion, that was simple enough for Kate but stylish enough for Pat! To Emerson Kate looks dressed up and not out of character.

The storm sequence, where Pat is swept overboard and Kate assumes her identity, was shot in the new studio "tank." The sailboat was anchored from below by wires. With the wind and wave machines creating havoc and the boat bobbing up and down against a turbulent seascape projected on the screen behind the action, the effect was very real. Davis first performed as Kate, then changed clothing and portrayed Pat being carried off by a wave. Davis submerged and did not come up. It became apparent to everyone that she was caught on the wires underneath the boat. Emergency men in rubber suits standing by dived in and brought her sputtering to the surface.

Curtis Bernhardt further commented, "It's not true that Bette had anything to do with the lighting of her close-ups." *[To this day I*

*know nothing about lighting or camera angles. I never interfere
with cameramen. That, as Mr. Bernhardt says, is the director's
department. In later years, when I was being badly photographed, I
wished I had learned some of the fundamentals about how to
photograph me.]* He also said,

> Compared with Bette Davis, Joan Crawford, whom I
> subsequently directed in *Possessed,* was as easy to work
> with as can be. She was naturally a little subdued because
> she was the studio's second-ranking star, Bette being
> number one. She threw her handbag at me several times
> when, having just done a picture with Bette, I called her
> Bette by mistake.
>
> The chief difference between Crawford and Davis is
> that, while Bette is an *actress* through and through, Joan
> is more a very talented *motion picture star.* That means
> that, while she is just as professional, she is also simpler.
>
> Granted, she's not as versatile as Bette. If Bette has an
> emotional scene, she tackles it completely consciously,
> and, when you say "Cut," she might ask, "Do you think
> that was a little too much this or a little too much that?"
>
> But, when Crawford plays an emotional scene, you
> have to wait twenty minutes until she comes out of it after
> you have said "Cut," because she is still crying or
> laughing or whatever; she's still going.

A Stolen Life was shown to the press at the studio on April 26,
1946, and opened in Washington, D.C., on July 25. Tom Donnelly
wrote in *The Washington Daily News,*

> *A Stolen Life* at the Earle is a double helping of hokum
> and Bette Davis. It packs enough problems to wear Mr.
> Anthony right down to the rim, and enough high-powered
> mush to set millions of impressionable females purring
> happily over their after-matinee tea. . . . This cliché
> foundation is liberally decorated with cliché garnishes.
> During cod-scented, chowder-thick New England fog,
> Miss Davis (as Kate) murmurs, "It's just like the end of
> the world." Possibly discouraged by this speech,
> assistant lighthouse keeper Ford is soon assuring Patricia
> that he loves her because "she's like a cake with frost-

ing'' whereas her sister is just a cake. Poor Kate tries to forget her unsugared state by plunging into art. She is going down for the third time when she hooks up with one of those relentlessly rude young painters I had thought must be out of fashion, even in the movies. This fellow, Dane Clark, gets off one of the most-quoted lines of the season: ''Man eats woman and woman eats man; that's basic.'' He is just about to eat Bette, when the scenario writers decide he's said quite enough for one film, and he drops out of the proceedings as inexplicably as he dropped in. . . . In the Elisabeth Bergner version of this story the good twin actually took over the marital duties of her defunct sister. This would have been unthinkable by current U.S. censorship standards, and the 1946 *Stolen Life* turns black in the face in its efforts to keep the imposter from getting into any serious clinches with the husband.

[Dear Mr. Donnelly: Nothing but the people came. A Stolen Life made a fortune, which made me very happy as it was the first film for my own company—B.D., Inc.]

John Hobart said on July 4, 1946, in *The San Francisco Chronicle,*

[Davis] is doing the same tour de force that Elisabeth Bergner did some years back in an English picture of the same name—only she is doing it better. Miss Bergner, as I remember, resorted to strikingly different hairdos, costumes, and makeup to differentiate between the two sisters. Miss Davis is much subtler about it; her sisters look exactly alike, but they are different in the way that they walk and talk. In short, Miss Davis assumes two separate personalities. . . . *A Stolen Life* does have a vitality of its own, thanks to the literacy of the writing, the smoothness of Bernhardt's direction, and, of course, Miss Davis's brilliant doubleheader performance.

[Thank you, Mr. Hobart. This review, which I have never seen until now, makes me very happy.]

When the Treasury Department issued the list of the ten highest-paid females in the United States in 1947, Davis topped the list with

$328,000, nudging out Deanna Durbin's $323,477. Bogart was the highest-paid male with a whopping $467,361. The next year Davis would do even better with $364,000, with Dennis Morgan at $315,476.19 and Henry Blanke at $244,666.67. Only Louis B. Mayer made more—a cool $733,024.

During these years she regularly appeared on radio, re-creating many of her famous screen roles as well as performing in many outstanding original plays. She did *Elizabeth the Queen* with Brian Aherne, *The Small Servant* with Rex Harrison, and *Dark Victory* for the "Hollywood Players," as well as *June Bride* with James Stewart on the "Screen Directors Playhouse," and *Jezebel* with Fay Bainter on the "Academy Award Theatre." Kirk Douglas was her costar in *Alien Corn* on the "Theatre Guild on the Air" (memorably announced by Norman Brokenshire), and she did *Skylark* on the "Ford Theatre" and *Now, Voyager* with Gregory Peck for the "Lux Radio Theatre." *[What a nightmare! We always had audiences in the studio for these performances. Peck was madly worshiped by his fans—especially his female fans. Every time he read a line, they squealed and screamed with joy. We felt sorry for Peck. There was nothing he could do about it. It certainly made our radio performance of* Now, Voyager *anything but ideal.]*

She played in many of Arch Oboler's original radio plays. *[I was indeed privileged to have been chosen for Mr. Oboler's radio plays. They were written especially for radio. Often the plays we were in were visual and hard to portray with just a voice—which was your only tool for radio, performance-wise. Mr. Oboler wrote only for a listening audience. I received more acclaim publicly from two of his plays than from many of my films. One was titled* Alter Ego, *in which I played two characters—and with only the use of my voice this was a tremendous challenge. The other was* Beloved Friend, *a play about Tchaikovsky and Madame von Meck. He wrote every speech to match the Tchaikovsky music that was being played in the background—a brilliant job of writing. Hans Conreid played the composer with me. He was marvelous.]* Davis appeared on the "Screen Actors Guild Theatre" many times over the years. The $10,000 paid to each star on this show was turned over to the Motion Picture Relief Fund. Many of her costars were men with whom she had never appeared in pictures: Ronald Colman, Walter Huston, Jean Hersholt, Melvyn Douglas, George Murphy, Bob Hope, and Clark Gable.

FAREWELL TO A FRIEND

One morning Davis, preparing to go to the studio, could not find
Tibby. After searching the house, the little pet was found near the
road, where she had crawled off to die. Davis was devastated;
Tibby had been her great friend for twelve years.

She called J.L. "Tibby is dead. I just can't bear coming to work
today." *[Again, Mr. Warner was utterly understanding of my
feelings.]*

Tibby, in a little brown velvet casket filled with gardenias, made
the long trip back to New Hampshire once more—to be buried on a
hill overlooking the Butternut cottage.

THE ETERNAL TRIANGLE

*Forgive me, my darling, forgive me. I was afraid I'd lose
you if I told the truth. After the first lie, I had to go on and
on.*

BETTE DAVIS AS CHRISTINE RADCLIFFE
IN *Deception*

In 1927 Louis Verneuil wrote a two-character French play called
Monsieur Lamberthier, then *Satan,* and finally *Jealousy,* which
Eugene Walter rewrote the next year for the new Broadway season
to star Fay Bainter and John Halliday. Paramount filmed the
property in 1929 with Jeanne Eagels and Fredric March. Seventeen
years later Eugenic Leontovich and Basil Rathbone revived the
vehicle, now called *Obsession* and updated by Jane Hinton, on a
national tour that eventually led to Broadway, where it played
twenty-six performances.

The plot concerned the mistress of the rich old man of the original
title—never seen on stage—who marries an artist and tries un-
successfully to conceal the previous affair. The climax occurred
when the husband strangled the lover offstage.

Warner Bros. bought the screen rights and assigned the script to
John Collier and Joseph Than, who made a number of startling
changes, beginning with the resurrection of the third character, now
famous composer-conductor Alexander Hollenius, played by
Claude Rains. Davis was cast as Christine Radcliffe, a concert

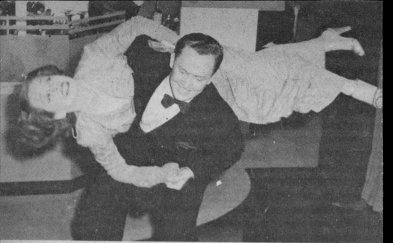

Jitterbug king Conrad Weidel whirls Bette Davis around in "They're Either Too Young or Too Old" sequence from *Thank Your Lucky Stars*, 1943. (*Photograph by Warner Bros., from the collection of Whitney Stine.*)

Dancer Johnny Coy hit Davis with a lemon pie in a comedy slapstick sketch before 8,000 soldiers at Camp Cooke, Calif., on August 18, 1945. (*Photograph by Acme Newspictures, Inc.*)

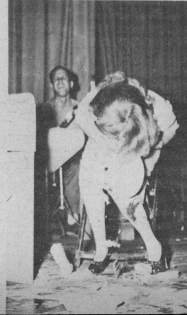

Bette Davis as the young Fanny Trellis in *Mr. Skeffington*, 1944. (*Photograph by Morgan, Warner Bros.*)

Bette Davis in Fanny Skeffington's "middle period." (*Photograph by Morgan, Warner Bros.*)

Bette Davis as the elderly Fanny Skeffington. (*Photograph by Morgan, Warner Bros.*)

Wardrobe test for *The Corn Is Green,* 1945, shows Bette Davis in her own hair. Perc Westmore fashioned a pompadour wig that helped Davis look older for the role of the middle-aged schoolteacher. (*Photograph by Warner Bros.*)

As in real life, Davis presides over the film version of *Hollywood Canteen*, 1944. A large portion of the profits was donated to the servicemen's center by J.L. Warner. (*Photograph by Warner Bros.*)

Sgt. Jim Scanlan and Francis Ashley, MM 3/c, kiss Davis at the closing ceremonies of the Hollywood Canteen, November 22, 1945. (*Photograph by Associated Press.*)

Bette Davis goes over costume sketches with designer Orry-Kelly, 1945. (*Photograph by Morgan, Warner Bros.*)

Bette Davis relaxes at a football game, November 19, 1944, in Columbus, Ga., with Cpl. Louis Riley, stationed at nearby Fort Benning, and Mrs. Ellis Arnall, wife of Georgia's governor. (*Photograph by Associated Press.*)

Ruthie prepared to shoot wedding photo. *Left to right:* Ruthie's new husband Robert Woodbury Palmer, best man Seymour Fox, William Grant Sherry, Davis, Bobby. Ceremony took place at the Mission Inn, Riverside, Calif., November 29, 1945.

pianist, set up in a lavish Leonard Bernstein-type penthouse in New York, designed by art director Anton Grot. Paul Henreid became Karel Novak, a brilliant cellist, conveniently separated from his vis-à-vis by World War II. *[I pleaded with Warner Bros. to keep the motion picture a two-person film as Mr. Halliday and Miss Bainter performed it. The idea was ahead of its time. Warner Bros. could not imagine a film with only two characters and the third character at the end of a telephone, unseen ever by the audience. Today it would be attempted. I also once suggested at this time a film of three one-act plays—called* An Evening with Bette Davis—*in which I would play three different parts. It was done many years later with three of Somerset Maugham's plays but by different groups of actors in each play. I still think my idea was an original and box office idea.]*

Bernard Newman's costumes were chic but simple; the addition of a sable cape, a fully let-out mink, and a floor-length white ermine evening coat added the right touch of grandeur. Margaret Donovan designed two hairstyles, a casual long bob and a sophisticated hair-parted-in-the-middle-with-a-chignon-at-the-nape coiffure.

Davis, who had learned to play the piano as a child, began rehearsing Beethoven's *Appassionata* Sonata three hours a day. When the professionally recorded number, by Shura Cherkassky, was played back for the take, Davis achieved exact synchronization. She had originally wanted to record the number herself, but director Irving Rapper said, "Why bother, Bette? No one will believe you actually performed the number anyway!" *[Rapper was so right. The public was so "movie wise" as to photographic tricks that I'm sure no one believed I could actually play this difficult piano solo. In the finished film one saw so little of it that my efforts were not worth it.]*

For the cello-playing scenes (before 1,175 dress "soup and fish" extras in the concert hall set) Rapper tied Henreid's hands behind his back. A breakaway coat was then buttoned in place. *Two* actual cellists were used for the medium close shots; one placed his *right* hand through Henreid's right sleeve and used the bow, while the other placed his *left* arm through Henreid's left sleeve and performed the fingering. Ernest Haller angled the camera into a three-quarters view, blocking out the two men, and the perfect illusion of Henreid playing was achieved.

In *The Celluloid Muse* Irving Rapper said of the filming,

Deception ends with Bette shooting Claude dead and going to prison, but it should have been concluded as a comedy, and the writer, John Collier, intended it that way. It was supposed to have a gay, light, natural, "So what?" ending. The three people walk off as friends. But Bette wanted a dramatic conclusion; she insisted on it; and I didn't care very much either way, so I gave in. The dramatic scene gave her a greater chance, and I will say she seized on it!

[Irving R.: I never wanted a script written a certain way to give me a better scene to play. Deception was a phony, contrived script from beginning to end. The only worthwhile thing in the finished film was the great performance of Claude Rains.]

For *Deception*, I used Ernest Haller as my cameraman instead of Sol Polito, my usual one. The late Sol Polito was a no-nonsense technician, whereas Ernest Haller is almost a cosmetician's cameraman, very concerned with making the stars look beautiful.

[I was not as young anymore, thirty-nine to be exact, and I insisted on Haller—plus I was overweight, due to the fact, as I found out during filming, I was pregnant. I needed him. Irving had nothing to say about it. Thank God cameramen like Haller could make us look better than we did. Why did Irving Rapper resent this? He should have been grateful!!!]

Composer Erich Wolfgang Korngold created the Hollenius Cello Concerto (as well as the remainder of the score) performed by Henreid. When Davis became pregnant during the filming of *Deception,* she jokingly renamed the film *Conception.*

Opening at the Hollywood Theatre in New York on October 18, 1946, *Deception* made money, but the reviewers carped. *Weekly Variety* said on October 23, 1946, that the "role given Miss Davis is less neurotic than most of her recent assignments. She plays it to the hilt, using full dramatic talent in the reading to please her large fan following. It's not all her show, though. Claude Rains, as her elderly teacher and sponsor, walks off with a considerable portion of the picture in a fine display of acting ability." *[To sum up all the* Deception *reviews, it was an unreal script—and the critics were not the only ones who knew it. So did Paul, Claude, and I.]*

Aline Mosby, UP press correspondent, wrote, "That old censor rule that movie heroines pay for their sins took the salt out of many a Davis film." Davis said, *"Deception* was completely ruined by censorship. We wrote the last scene, in which I had to confess my crime, ten thousand ways, but they all were so phony we never did get a solution. A similar scene in *The Letter* was done artistically, but it would still have been greater without censorship. . . . What could Garbo play on the screen today? She couldn't play the parts anymore that made her famous." *[My one regret about the era in which I made films was the lack of freedom to be honest. Due to censorship, we constantly had to prostitute our scripts—and thus hurt the honesty of our performances.]*

THE HEIRESS APPARENT

The Sherrys went to Butternut to await the birth of the baby, but the winter was so severe they returned to California where medical help would be nearer if an emergency occurred. They purchased a new home on Wood's Cove in Laguna Beach.

Time magazine reported the birth in its May 5, 1947, issue:

> Born. To Bette Davis, 39, high-strung cinemactress, and painter (ex-boxer) William Grant Sherry, 32, her third husband: her first child, a girl, on May Day, which Bette Davis chose for her cesarean section; in Santa Ana, Calif. Name: Barbara Davis Sherry. Weight: 7 lbs.

The hospital was loaded with flowers, turning Davis's room in Santa Ana Hospital into a bower.

The studio had several scripts waiting. Reported Louella Parsons in her May 28 column: "I pinned Jack Warner down at dinner the other evening and learned that Bette Davis's first picture since she had her baby gets going August 15. Two stories are on tap. Rebecca West's *The Return of the Soldier* and *Winter Meeting* by Ethel Vance. Said Jack, 'We'll leave it to Bette, herself, which one she wants to do, but, whichever she decides on, Henry Blanke will produce.' When Queen Bette gets back, the velvet carpet will be rolled out for her on account of Jack has a tremendous liking for the Davis gal. The last time Bette and I sat down for a talk, she told me

how beautifully everything had worked out for her with Warners—
the company she fought tooth and nail in England a few years ago.''

*[Jack Warner sent my daughter the beginnings of a string of real
pearls, to be added to each birthday. He remembered for many
years.]*

THE VIRGIN AND THE PRIEST

> *I like the way your mouth moves. It's fascinating.*
> BETTE DAVIS AS SUSAN GRIEVE
> IN *Winter Meeting*

Davis returned to the studio to do preproduction work on the
decided-upon *Winter Meeting,* a two-character study. Catherine
Turney had completed the screenplay under Blanke's direction. At
the helm was Bretaigne Windust, a Broadway director *(Life with
Father, Arsenic and Old Lace, State of the Union).* To gain film
experience he had been occupied on the lot as dialogue director and
"observer" on the recently completed *Stallion Road* with Ronald
Reagan and Alexis Smith. *[Winter Meeting was a great book. A
study of a non-Catholic, Susan Grieve, and a devoted Catholic,
Slick Novak. We should never have tried to make it. This is where
censorship really hurt us. We were not allowed to be honest about
the differences of opinion between a Catholic and a non-Catholic. It
was, therefore, a dull and meaningless film.]*

The role of the former submarine commander, her vis-à-vis, was
the most difficult to cast. Among the leading men available was
Richard Widmark, whom Davis did not feel was right for the part.
Among the thirteen actors tested was Missouri-born James Davis,
six foot three and weighing 185 pounds, who had played a hillbilly
in Metro's *The Romance of Rosy Ridge.* His test was exceptional,
and he won the part. *[Because of the overanalytical approach of
Bretaigne Windust, our director, Jim Davis never again during
filming showed any signs of the character he portrayed in the test
that made me want him for the part. No help I tried to give him could
offset the effect of the detailed direction of Windust. He was lost and
openly admitted it.]* Others in the cast were Janis Paige as the sexy
secretary Peggy Markham; John Hoyt as Stacy Grant, a dilettante
socialite; and Florence Bates and Walter Baldwin as the Castles,
caretakers of Susan's farm. *[After performing for a week on the*

actual sets, there was a complete dress rehearsal. Not since the George Arliss days had such involved preproduction rehearsals taken place.]

Davis's wardrobe was selected at I. Magnin's. *[Bertie Strauser for some twenty years helped me choose my personal wardrobe at I. Magnin's. One could say she taught me how to dress. I bought my first expensive evening dress from her. It cost $325. It was made of pale pink lace. We are still close friends. Strauser has retired from I. Magnin's. How they must miss her.]*

Art director Edward Carrere supervised the construction of the sets, the most elaborate of which was Davis's New York apartment, filled with New England antiques. The back lot was used for the exterior country winter scenes at the farm house, which included a snowy road suitable for a sleigh ride. Windust requested two gnarled oak trees with "character" for the front of the cottage, which Ernie Butterworth, head of the green department, found in his tree pile and whitened with snow.

The title was switched from *Winter Meeting* to *Strange Meeting* and back again to *Winter Meeting* before the film was press previewed at the studio on March 31, 1948.

On Thursday, April 8, Warner Bros. took out a full-page ad in the trade magazines:

WE'RE PROUD
of
BETTE DAVIS
BRETAIGNE WINDUST
and HENRY BLANKE
They've just finished *Winter Meeting.*
Now the members of this great star-
director-producer combination are building
high comedy with *June Bride,* costarring
ROBERT MONTGOMERY
Next they'll do *Ethan Frome* from
the Edith Wharton classic.
Three such pictures, from such a creative
trio, are something to shout about!

The shouting was premature. *[Give the studio credit. Their shouting was not premature. We all knew we had made a dog of a film. The ads were whistling in the dark! Why did they go on about future films? Hoping everyone would eventually forget* Winter Meeting.] *Winter Meeting* won a frozen reception in New York. There were those around town who rejoiced; Bette Davis had finally appeared in a turkey.

On April 1, *Daily Variety* reported, "Miss Davis tries hard, but script and the part and its treatment are against her, and the role assigned [James] Davis opposite her is too much for him."

Bosley Crowther wrote on April 8 in *The New York Times,* "Under Bretaigne Windust's direction, she actually catches at times some sense of a woman's deep disturbance at a most puzzling turn in an affair of love. And never, let's say to her credit, does she nibble the scenery as of yore." *[Mr. Windust had a deep ambition during the filming of* Winter Meeting *to present a completely different Bette Davis. This meant totally unemotional. I had just given birth to my first child and couldn't have been happier. I was putty in his hands, said yes at every turn. A little of my former emotional approach might have pepped up the proceeding no end, Mr. Crowther. Just a little nibbling of the scenery as of yore could have accomplished miracles!]*

Time magazine on April 26, 1948, reported: "The best thing that can be said about *Winter Meeting* is that its attempt to articulate Ethel Vance's obscure theme is a thoroughly honest failure and that Bette Davis's talents are great enough to be sometimes apparent even in the midst of such unrewarding mediocrity."

In an interview with Thomas M. Pryor in *The New York Times* titled "Lament from a Star" Davis said she felt that censorship was stifling honest expression in American pictures:

> After taking two critical lambastings, Miss Davis has turned to comedy in her latest picture, *June Bride,* and she says that she will stick with pictures which are no censorship problem to make. Two-time winner of the Academy Oscar and generally recognized as the screen's first lady of drama, Miss Davis freely acknowledges that her two previous pictures, *Winter Meeting* and *Deception,* were legitimate targets for critical arrows.
>
> Censorship, by the industry's own self-regulatory production code and by state and municipal boards, has now encroached to the point where "vitality and honesty" no longer exist in pictures. "Anyone who attempts to

A NEW CHAPTER IN GREAT SCREEN DRAMA... Now!
In her hands a note that was soiled, in her heart a yearning for an answer...
The most esteemed actress on the American screen
BETTE DAVIS
in a performance more powerful than any you've known in
"WINTER MEETING"
THE NEW WARNER BROS. SUCCESS
WB

do something that hasn't been previously tested and approved soon finds out that you can't do this because Mr. Binford (Lloyd T. Binford, chief censor in Memphis, Tennessee) or somebody else won't approve.''

Miss Davis says she knows the restrictions of censorship from personal experience, that being the dismal *Winter Meeting*. She insists that the story as written by Ethel Vance would have made an engrossing film drama, but unfortunately much of the novel had to be bowdlerized to meet production code requirements. She admits the mistake here was in attempting ''to get around a problem'' and added that others in Hollywood are dissipating their talents and energies in similar fruitless endeavors.

. . . Miss Davis says that the Johnson office has nixed production of George Sklar's novel *The Two Worlds of Johnny Truro* on the grounds that it would be ''indecent'' to involve a ''thirty-five-year-old woman and a twenty-year-old boy'' in a screen romance. The studio tried several treatments of the novel, she said, but finally put it aside when they couldn't beat this problem without committing a major distortion.

[Imagine anyone objecting to this today!]

If anyone has a nice, harmless comedy that is guaranteed to constitute good entertainment without causing any problems, Miss Davis, no doubt, will be interested.

FEATURE FOR JUNE

Oh, it's incredible, utterly incredible. Perched up on that pinnacle of masculine ego, looking down at poor, weak, defenseless females—and pitying them—because they don't have beards!

BETTE DAVIS AS LINDA GILMAN
IN *June Bride*

The script of *June Bride* was rich in comedic wit and situation. The publicity department began to create a "new Bette Davis." Fan book writers were lined up for interviews and stunning color photographs were taken of the star in her new bouffant hairdo. Warner Bros. hired Edith Head, on a nonexclusive contract with Paramount, to design Davis's "new look" wardrobe. The clothing was so glamorous that she found herself doing her first fashion layout for the fan books since *Now, Voyager*. *[This was my first introduction to the brilliance of Edith Head's work. I had desperately missed Orry-Kelly as my designer in the past years. I found that Edith was also a selfless designer, like Orry-Kelly. She was only interested in clothes that suited the character you were playing. The clothes for Linda Gilman were of necessity chic. Edith Head designed some of the most beautiful modern clothes I had ever worn. I bought most of them for my personal use when the film was completed. This was the first of many films in which I was fortunate enough to have my wardrobe in her genius capable hands. I also admire Edith so much as a person.]*

The part of Carey Jackson was played by Robert Montgomery, and the screenplay, the work of Ranald MacDougall, was based on the play *Feature for June* by Eileen Tighe and Graeme Lorimer.

Richard L. Coe in his November 12 review in *The Washington Post*, reported, "Bette plays the hardboiled 'I-Can-Live-Without-Love' career-woman editor of one of those women's magazines which goes into detail on how our countrymen live. Assigned to her staff is a war correspondent without a war—Robert Montgomery— a wisecracker who once stood Bette up at dinner because he thought Berlin was safer than marriage. . . . For her June issue, Bette plans to give a small-town Indiana wedding the works. Since it's December, this means all sorts of picture shooting around the snow and redoing of the family in *Home Life*—circulation 5 million— pattern. It turns out that the bride and bridegroom aren't in love at all, a matter clear to Bob, annoying to the deadline-minded Bette."

Art director Anton Grot had a field day in creating the interior of the Brinker family's turn-of-the-century "McKinley stinker" house. Warner Bros. "Gingerbread man" Harry Platt was in charge of the numerous curlicues that were modernized by the staff from *Home Life*. "Years ago," he commented to Lowell E. Redelings in *The Hollywood Citizen News*, "we started making patterns of interior wood and plaster trims. From these patterns we can make unlimited quantities of carved moldings, wood door trimming, relief work, and cornices . . . There must have been a ton or more ornamental plaster used in the decoration of the Brinker home. It was a mess." One of the delights of the film was the gradual refurbishing of the home, which served as a background for most of the action.

There was a bit of double entendre concerning the bust of Julius Caesar, which Mrs. Brinker had acquired by accumulating soap coupons. The staff does not know how to disguise the eyesore, which means a great deal to Mrs. Brinker. The following dialogue involving Linda (Davis), Rosemary (Mary Wickes), and Mr. Brinker (Tom Tully) takes place around the kitchen table, while they are partaking of an alcoholic jasmine tea, thoughtfully provided by Wickes via a thermos bottle:

Davis (conversationally): "By the way, Rosemary, Mrs. Brinker wanted me to ask you something. She's a little worried about her bust. You didn't throw it away, did you?"

Wickes (contemplatively): "What would I do with it? I know—I put it out in the garage."

Davis (concerned): "Is it safe?"

Tully (questioningly): "What's it doing out in the garage?"

Wickes (firmly): "I'm going to paint it."

Tully (gulp!): "You ARE?"

Wickes (earnestly): "I thought I would paint it black. I thought it would be very effective that way "

Tully (thoughtfully): "Yeah, I can see where it would be."

Wickes (meditatively): "I might even drape a rich gold turban on it. What do you think?"

Davis (smoothly): "Oh, perhaps you'd better not. It's pretty battered, but it seems to have a certain sentimental value."

Tully goes into a paroxysm of wild coughing, of course later finding out they're speaking about the bust of Julius Caesar.

Since the film would be released during the 1948 presidential elections, one line by Mary Wickes in the script was shot both ways: "How can I convert this McKinley stinker into a Dewey modern?" Just in case, the line was also shot with "Truman" substituted, but the Dewey line was in the released version. When Truman was unexpectedly elected, a revised reel was rushed to theaters.

At the traditional party on the last day of shooting Davis appeared dressed in the wedding gown from *A Stolen Life.* Presents were handed to cast and crew, and the star received a white leather makeup case from her coworkers.

The reviews were excellent.

Ethan Frome, Helen Deutsch's screenplay of Edith Wharton's classic New England book, which had been announced as Davis's next picture, was reviewed by the studio. *[It had also been a great success as a play in New York with Raymond Massey, Pauline Lord, and Ruth Gordon.]*

The drama concerned Frome and his carping wife Zenobia, who take in her impoverished niece Mattie as a servant girl. Ethan and Mattie fall in love, but, since they cannot escape the rigid morals of New England life, they decide to commit suicide and purposely run their toboggan into a tree. They are not killed but horribly maimed. The denouement: Zenobia, now cowed, takes care of the embittered Ethan and the crippled, whining Mattie. The trio tragically live out their lives on the remote farm.

Davis, who was to play Mattie, wanted Gary Cooper for the part of Ethan, but he felt the theme was too tragic for his image. *[Mildred Natwick was tested for Zenobia and was perfect for the part.]* English actor David Farrar was finally signed as costar, but, when he arrived in the States, the picture had been shelved. The studio paid off his contract. *[Ethan Frome has never been made into a film. Today, Jimmy Stewart as Ethan, Liv Ullman as Mattie, and I as Zenobia—I have never given up hope that one day I will make this film. Columbia Pictures now own the rights.]*

SOMETHING FOR THE BIRDS

If I don't get out of here, I'll just die! Living here is like waiting for the funeral to begin. No, it's like waiting in the coffin for them to carry you out!

BETTE DAVIS AS ROSA MOLINE
IN *Beyond the Forest*

Lenore Coffee turned in the screenplay for *Beyond the Forest,* based on Stuart Engstrand's best seller. Henry Blanke knew the material was controversial and hoped they would have no problems with the production code.

Rosa Moline, disgusted with her Wisconsin small-town life and her weak husband Lewis, has an affair with millionaire Latimer (David Brian), who has a lodge on a nearby lake. After collecting past-due bills from her husband's patients to finance the trip, Rosa visits the millionaire in Chicago, only to be told that he is marrying a socialite. Humiliated, she returns to Fleming, and her husband reluctantly takes her back. Latimer returns and decides he wants her after all. On a hunting trip she shoots and kills Moose (Minor Watson), a friend of Lewis's, after he inadvertently discovers that she is pregnant and has scheduled an abortion.

There is a dramatic, spine-chilling ending. Striken with peritonitis and delirious after the abortion, Rosa painfully gets out of bed and in a crazed kind of stupor throws on her clothes. *She must get to Chicago*. She drags herself to the mirror and, reaching for her makeup, goes through the ritual of fixing her face. The mascara runs; she misses her lips with the lipstick. Disheveled and grotesque, she staggers to the railway station as the train bound for Chicago chugs to a stop. The train leaves. Rosa lies dead in the dust near the tracks—her hand outstretched in one last plaintive gesture of yearning. *[This is without doubt the longest death scene ever seen on the screen. Night after night I crawled along the road leading to the railroad station. It was agony and in my opinion completely unbelievable. I don't think any actor could have made this believable.]*

Davis told Arkadin in Britain's *Sight and Sound* magazine in 1965 that *Beyond the Forest* was a "terrible movie":

> It didn't have to be; primarily it was terrible because I was too old for the part. I mean, I don't think you can believe for a moment that, if I, as Rosa Moline, was so determined to get to Chicago, I wouldn't just have upped and gone years ago. I told them they should have put Virginia Mayo in the part—she would have been great. It was all a great pity, because the book is very good and could have made a marvelous movie. The husband, for instance, is supposed to look like Eugene Pallette and be an absolute monster. So what do they do? They cast Joseph Cotten, who is so attractive and kind—why should any wife want to get away from him? The one interesting thing Vidor did in the film was to make the train into her lover; that bit was good. But all the rest was just crazy.

Arkadin continued,

> Well, I said, maybe; but, even if wildly miscast, she

did play Rosa Moline all out, and so gave her a sort of weird believability, whereas Joan Crawford, say, might have just coasted through on star quality. "Oh, I would never do that. Would? I never *could* do that. For one thing, if you really don't want to play a part, or really don't think you can, then you just don't take it in the first place. If for some reason you are forced to play it, then you do all you can with it, because that's your job, that's what you're paid for. That is the only way I can do things; the more truth I can find in a role, the more fully I can act it, the easier it is for me."

She made one last call on J.L. and begged him not to cast Cotten in the part of the husband.

Davis wore a black wig as Rosa. Edith Head designed the wardrobe—all with low necklines. For the seduction scene, set around a billiard table in Latimer's lodge, she wore a white terry-cloth bathrobe—ostensibly borrowed from her lover.

Director King Vidor (who had just finished *The Fountainhead* with Gary Cooper and Patricia Neal) sought to shoot the exteriors in a locale similar to Wisconsin. Location man Kenneth Cox was dispatched to the Pacific Northwest to hunt for location sites that would pass for Wisconsin. Twenty-six hundred miles and eight days later he returned to the studio with photographs and ideas about how the film should be shot. He had visited some forty towns and lakes as far north as Eugene, Oregon. Later Vidor, a studio cameraman, and Cox left for Lake Tahoe, where, by touring the lake in a motorboat, they finally found the perfect hunting lodge, the property of Mrs. John Drum.

"We picked for the town of Loyalton a hamlet about seventy miles from Tahoe for the town scenes," Cox told Lowell E. Redelings in an October 24 interview in *The Hollywood Citizen News,* "and, although all 925 inhabitants were interested in the filming, we managed to clear the streets of people, cars, dogs, and cats at noon on a Saturday for a scene we needed. That was real cooperation. The company, made up of ninety cast and crew, arrived two weeks before the summer season opened."

There was difficulty at Lake Tahoe. Davis contracted tick fever, then suffered a bruised eye when a rifle recoiled. The unit came back from location, and shooting on the lot resumed. "I waited until the picture was three days from completion," she told Robert

Graham in the December, 1972, issue of *After Dark*. "Then I phoned J.L. and said, 'You want this picture finished? Then let me out of my contract.' It still had ten years to run. Ten years! I'd already been with Warner Bros. for eighteen . . . I was tired of fighting, and I thought, why should I if they keep putting obstacles in my path! If, after all these years, I'm still being given scripts like *Beyond the Forest*, then to hell with it." *[Before I returned to the studio next morning J.L. had given me my release from my contract, and I finished the film. My last professional act on the Warner lot after all those years was recording a line for the film—Rosa Moline saying, "I can't stand it here anymore." Truer words were never spoken! I couldn't stand it at Warner Bros. any longer.]*

On July 25, 1949, every newspaper in the country carried the news that Davis was leaving Warner Bros. Hollywood was taken by surprise; stars all over town began to review their contracts with a jaundiced eye. "Nothing has been signed yet concerning the termination of my contract," Davis said from Laguna Beach, "but, when and if anything is signed, I am sure it will be completely mutual and a happy agreement."

The Hollywood Citizen News reported,

> Miss Davis has been having trouble with Warner personnel since the start of her current picture, *Beyond the Forest*. She appealed to Jack Warner to uphold her arguments and demands, but Warner backed up his executive personnel instead.
>
> She had trouble with a publicist assigned to her picture, a veteran of many years with the Warner publicity department, and to appease her another publicist was assigned to her film. Then she had trouble with various others associated with the picture, resulting in her decision to ask for her release.
>
> It has been known for some time that Warner Bros. executives have been none too happy with the box office grosses of her past half dozen films. And it is believed that this is back of the studio's willingness to grant her contract release.

[This was a statement released by the studio. The fact of the matter was that Warner was forced to give me my release if he wanted to have Beyond the Forest *finished. No studio could afford*

to throw away the money already spent on a film and leave it unfinished. This is the only time I ever threatened to walk off a film during shooting—no, the second—the other was when I got permission for the change in title during the filming of The Private Lives of Elizabeth and Essex!]

Said J.L. in his autobiography,

Bette had disposed of Mike Levee. She was caught on the fly by Lew Wasserman and his associates.

[Dear J.L.: At this point Lew Wasserman had been my agent for years. Mike Levee and I parted company many years before. Lew Wasserman of MCA was one of the great agents of his day—as was MCA the greatest agency of its day.]

Bette began showing up in my office surrounded by the MCA group, and every time we talked about a new script she would say sweetly: "Jack, can I have a copy for Lew?"

"I'd be happy to, honey," I would say, "but I did not engage Lew Wasserman to read scripts. I want *you* to read it."

But Lew would get his copy, and he would come back claiming to have read it and reporting that we flunked our Wasserman test. What he really meant was that his fifth cousin Amanda had read it, or a little old lady on a park bench had read it, and on their recommendation he would decide it wasn't good enough for Bette Davis.

[Dear J.L.: Lew did read them.]

Before long the ten percenters had Bette so confused that it affected her story vision, and she was laying bigger eggs than an ostrich.

[If Beyond the Forest *was a sample of parts you thought I should play, I was hardly confused. My future with your studio looked grim indeed if this part was a sample.]*

I simply couldn't take it. Or them. I finally cracked down and barred the MCA blackbirds from the lot—a move no one had ever dared to make in Hollywood. I kept them outside peeking through fence knotholes for quite a while, but eventually they sneaked in with the connivance of other studio executives, or by conning my brother Harry.

"Jack," Harry said one morning, "you're wasting your energy fighting these guys. You're just bucking a stone wall."

"I'm not bucking anybody," I protested. "They're bucking me, and by God, they're not going to come in here and smash up everything we've built."

Nor did they. When they pushed me too far, I told Bette I was through. We settled her contract, and I was relieved to see her go elsewhere with her cortege.

[I have always felt guilty for doing what I did to Warner when I got my release. It was dirty pool on my part, but I was that desperate. As I read this excerpt from Warner's book, I am relieved of my guilt. He was happy to see me go—that made two of us, J.L.)

This carefully worded telegram was sent by Davis to the press:

MY RELEASE FROM MY WARNER BROTHERS CONTRACT WAS SIGNED YESTERDAY BY THE STUDIO AND MYSELF, EFFECTIVE WITH THE COMPLETION OF MY CURRENT PICTURE THIS WEEK. AFTER EIGHTEEN YEARS TOGETHER THIS "PROFESSIONAL DIVORCE" IS THE RESULT OF MY LONG-STANDING WISH TO BE RELIEVED OF ANY CONTRACTUAL OBLIGATIONS IN ORDER TO HAVE A WIDER CHOICE OF STORIES THAN IS NOW POSSIBLE AT ANY ONE STUDIO. I AM MOST APPRECIATIVE TO MR. J.L. WARNER FOR HIS CONSIDERATION OF MY REQUEST. IT IS WITH CORDIAL FEELINGS AND A SENTIMENTAL REGRET THAT I LEAVE THE WARNER STUDIO. I SHALL MISS THE FRIENDLY ASSOCIATION WITH ALL MY CO-WORKERS TO WHOM I AM VERY GRATEFUL FOR THE WONDERFUL HELP THEY HAVE GIVEN ME AT ALL TIMES.

BETTE DAVIS

[Henry Blanke, my great producer friend; Bob, a sound man who had been on all my films for years, my favorite gaffer; and a property man sat up all night on a set on the back lot on my last day at Warner Bros., and, as the dawn came up—three sheets to the wind—I drove through the Warner gate for the last time. I was crying. I never heard from the studio one word after I left. I remember thinking at the time, not even a diamond bracelet for all those sound stages I built?]

The Hollywood trade papers reported that no financial or other settlement was involved.

Hedda Hopper wrote that British producers Emeric Pressburger and Michael Powell offered Davis an adaptation of V. Sackville West's *All Passions Spent* and Alexander Korda felt *The King's General* was suitable, while Louella Parsons reported that she was to do a Broadway play, *Saucersand,* by Jacques Duval for the Theatre Guild.

Other film prospects were *Affair No. 5* by Ranald MacDougall and *All Our Tomorrows* with James Cagney. The Theatre Guild wanted to sign her for a repertoire of three plays, one of which was Clifford Odets's modern version of *Hedda Gabler.* John Huston was rumored to be after her to play the role of a psalm-singing missionary in *The African Queen* with Humphrey Bogart. Then there was also *Mrs. Lincoln,* a play by Ramon Romero that had interested her for some time and that was later the cause of a lawsuit. Davis returned from Florida, where she had gone for a rest while Sherry painted circus scenes at the Ringling Bros. and Barnum & Bailey winter quarters in Sarasota, and was reading scripts. *Beyond the Forest* brought down the wrath of the critics in the worst reviews of her entire career. *[I was rewarded by these reviews. I knew after reading them I had been right to leave Warner Bros.]* The comments of the Fourth Estate regarding *Winter Meeting* paled in comparison to the reports on *Beyond the Forest.*

A few weeks later Curtis Bernhardt called. "Bette, let's have a talk. I have been working on a script with Bruce Manning called *The Story of a Divorce,* which I think we can peddle. We have an 'in' at RKO."

Beyond the Forest was shown to the press on October 11, 1949. *[Edward Albee in his play* Who's Afraid of Virginia Woolf? *includes a scene where the actress playing Martha imitates Bette Davis. He has her refer to* Beyond the Forest *and has her say,*

"What a dump"—a line of Rosa Moline's in the film. This is the only claim to fame Beyond the Forest *has or ever will have.]*
    The Hollywood Reporter on October 18, said,

> For every one who concludes that Rosa is the nadir of an illustrious career, there are those ready to defend a champion. All are bound to agree that photographically Bette Davis has never looked worse; she affects the most grotesque makeup, and the strands of her stringy black hair hardly belong to a small town belle out to land a man. The actress's performance is bound to stir comment and controversy, an angle that will go a long way toward heightening box office response.
>
> From the viewpoint of a trade paper review, this element cannot be overlooked, even while the inescapable facts remain that *Beyond the Forest* has something of a tragic valedictory to a studio-star partnership which made artistic and box office history.

The New Yorker on October 28, 1949, wrote of the film,

> Miss Davis's interpretation of this role involves more hip-shaking than I've seen since burlesque left Irving Place and the use of a black wig of such formidable length that, when she tosses her head about, her features frequently become as blurred as those of a muzhik behind a head of whiskers. Miss Davis's obsession is to blow town and head for the home grounds of her lover, and, every time she gets to revolving this problem in her mind, which is often, the sound track breaks out with variations on the hymn to the hog-and-corn metropolis that starts, "Chicago, Chicago, that toddling town."

A RUN-IN WITH CENSORSHIP

To add to the current woes the National Legion of Decency placed a condemned "C" rating on the picture. Warner Bros. was willing to compromise by deleting the objectionable sequences. Eliminated was the scene where Rosa jumps from the car driven by her husband

and falls down a mountainside to induce the miscarriage. Also removed was an insert of a shingle outside the doctor's office where Rosa first goes for an abortion. The studio added another insert of a lawyer's shingle—which made no sense whatsoever to the finished product. Satisfied, the legion removed the "C" classification and announced the film was only "objectionable in part."

Margaret Hinxman in an article in the April 22, 1950, issue of Britain's *Picturegoer* expressed the attitude of many members of the press in her piece "Question Mark on Bette Davis":

> Probably no screen actress since Garbo has been so recklessly admired and irrationally disliked as Bette Davis. She is one of those dominating personalities about whom it is almost impossible to be indifferent. Which is, I suppose, as healthy a state of affairs as any star—whose continued success, after all, depends primarily on his or her capacity to arouse the public's interest, both approving and not so approving—could wish for.
>
> And it's been that way for quite a few years now, despite reverses which might have crushed a lesser actress.
>
> But sooner or later all screen stars must reach that point in their career when it is prudent to pause and take stock, to weigh future prospects against past triumphs, and, most important, to get a new slant on themselves.
>
> For the indefatigable Miss Davis that moment has arrived . . . Never a typical ingenue type, she has always needed an intelligent script and firm directorial handling, for she is too much of an individual personality not to succumb, occasionally, to the temptation to over-emphasize and overplay . . . A woman, who, during the whole of her screen life, has never fitted neatly into a Hollywood pattern, she seems at this stage to need the presence in the background of a strong, sympathetic guiding influence to help set her career once more on the right lines.
>
> It is possible, I believe, in her recent films to sense this feeling of unsureness, even though her work has as much verve as ever.
>
> In the unpredictable film world she has traveled a long way since she first earned the praise and blessing of the

late George Arliss while playing a supporting role in one of his American pictures. And still there is much that she can contribute of lasting value to the cinema and our entertainment.

But now, Miss Davis, is the time to pause and ponder.

[I was pondering. I was really, for the first time in eighteen years, professionally on my own. Father—Warner—and his daughter—me—were separated. A contract actor of eighteen years has to have courage to leave the family.]

On October 21, 1949, Davis filed suit for divorce against Sherry. Said Sheilah Graham in a piece entitled "Bette Davis Acts to Rub Out 3rd Marriage" in *The New York Daily Mirror*, "Screen tragedienne Bette Davis chalked up another real-life setback late today when she filed suit for divorce here from her artist-husband William Grant Sherry, accusing the muscular one-time masseur of rubbing her the wrong way."

[This is a typical Sheilah Graham remark. She is the only member of the press I barred from my sets while I was working. She consistently was rude about my life in her column.]

She continued, "The petition, charging cruelty, was not entirely unexpected as rumors have had Bette and her third spouse quarreling for months in their nearby Laguna Beach home. . . . Hubby, who has developed into something of a classic painter since abandoning his rubbing table when he wed Bette four years ago, expected his art subjects to sell faster. Then, too, he has confessed being a victim of the Hollywood malady—being known as Mr. Bette Davis."

When contacted at their Laguna Beach home, Sherry told newsmen he was dumbfounded by the turn of events. "She used to kid sometimes about getting a divorce, but I always told her, 'Just try and get rid of me.' . . . We were made for each other, and I'm not going to let her go . . . When I first heard about the divorce suit, I thought someone was trying to play a joke on me. When I learned it was true, I was just sick. I'm just sick. I'm sure she'll come back when this blows over. . . . It's just a matter of me controlling my awful temper, but I know we can patch this thing up if we can just see each other again."

Davis had obtained a temporary order restraining Sherry from doing bodily harm to her or Barbara. Superior Court Judge Robert Gardner signed the order, which also gave Davis temporary custody of the child. Attorney B. S. McKinney filed the suit, which asked that Sherry be restrained from molesting Davis or the child until the court ruled on Barbara's custody. Davis had not even told Ruthie she was planning the action.

Sherry promised to see a psychiatrist, and Davis returned to live with him in Laguna Beach. The idyll would soon become a nightmare.

16

> *Without me, you're nothing! Less than nothing! And then*
> *you wouldn't be able to afford a . . . a conscience or . . .*
> *to help your indigent, sniveling, whining friends . . . so*
> *called!*

BETTE DAVIS AS JOYCE RAMSEY
IN *Payment on Demand*

The motion picture industry experienced a year of upheaval in 1949. Star contracts were running out at the studios, contracts that had been signed in the great money year 1942. Box office was off to an alarming degree. Male stars, however, were faring better both story-wise and at the wickets. Joan Crawford was portraying a hootchy-kootchy dancer in *Flamingo Road;* Greer Garson was miscast as *That Forsyte Woman*. Marlene Dietrich, Vivien Leigh, Merle Oberon, and Irene Dunne did not make a film in 1949. Claudette Colbert's *Bride for Sale* was not good, and Rosalind Russell's *Tell It to the Judge* was disappointing. *The Lady Gambles,* starring Barbara Stanwyck, and *Lust for Gold,* with Ida Lupino, did nothing for their careers. Among the handful of actresses appearing in hits were Katharine Hepburn in *Adam's Rib*, Ann Sheridan in *I Was a Male War Bride,* Ginger Rogers in *The Barkleys of Broadway,* and Olivia De Havilland, who would win a second Oscar for *The Heiress*.

Curtis Bernhardt had been working with Bruce Manning, tailoring the part of Joyce Ramsey to Davis's talents. Manning was to produce with Jack Skirball at RKO. The budget for *The Story of a Divorce* was set at $1.8 million, a low figure compared to the costs of her films at Warner Bros. Leo Tovar was engaged as cinematographer. The art direction, under Albert S. D'Agostino and Carroll Clark, was especially important because a very different sort of flashback device was to be employed. Curtis Bernhardt said in *The Celluloid Muse:*

> The picture had some very fascinating flashback effects using negatives and transparent sets, incorporating a technical innovation of my own invention. Frankly, I cannot understand why it hasn't been used since.
>
> It was all a play with light. In part of it Bette Davis had to play a thirteen-year-old girl, and I had her sort of impressionistically in the middle ground of the set. When we reverted to the past, the foreground became dark, the background lit up, and the walls disappeared, because the walls were actually transparent. But you couldn't discern that when they were illuminated for foreground action; they were like screens. As soon as you took the light off them and moved into the background, the walls vanished.

Barry Sullivan, who had just finished *The Great Gatsby* for Paramount, was signed for David Ramsey, Davis's husband, along with Kent Taylor, Betty Lynn, John Sutton, Frances Dee, Peggie Castle, and Otto Kruger. Davis's daughter, "B.D.," at three years old appeared as the tiny daughter. Jane Cowl was signed for the important role of Mrs. Hedges, who is first seen as a matriarch and social arbiter whom Joyce imitates and later, after *her* divorce, as a lonely old woman in a Port-au-Prince villa who supports a homosexual poet for companionship. *[I, for years, had seen and admired Jane Cowl on the stage. She was one of my earliest memories as a theater-goer. I was unbelieving that I was playing scenes with her. I was nervous, as I wanted her to feel I was worthwhile working with from her standpoint. I did everything to see she was comfortable on our set. The cast and crew all had such respect for her. How sad I was that she died soon after we finished the film. We had talked about the possibility of working together again one day.]*

The story depicted the plight of a woman whose husband divorces her after twenty years of marriage. In flashbacks she relives her past and in so doing is revealed as a grasping, social-climbing shrew, who will stop at nothing to push her husband forward in a career he hates.

She is awarded almost all of her husband's wealth during the divorce proceedings when she threatens to expose his affair with a pretty university instructor (Frances Dee, with whom Davis had not worked since *Of Human Bondage*).

The original ending to the Manning-Bernhardt script depicted Joyce and David reconciled after the wedding of their older daughter. The last scene showed the couple at breakfast, with Joyce beginning a familiar social-climbing tirade. The audience knows that, even with all she has been through, she is still the same ambitious, overbearing woman, determined to push her husband on to greater career heights.

On April 5 the cast and crew gave Davis a surprise birthday party. She was forty-two years old. She was presented a huge award, the size of an ostrich egg, for being a "good egg." Sherry came by to pick her up at the studio and quarreled with two studio policemen who apparently did not recognize him.

Sherry told newsmen, "I had called the studio for Bette, and they told me the party was over. I hadn't heard from her and was worried. I drove to the studio. I told her I wanted her to come home. She objected and ordered me off the lot. Sullivan came up and said, 'Why don't you have a sense of humor? The company worked very hard, and everybody was just relaxing a little.' I told him to stay out of it. 'I don't want to hit you because you have to be photographed tomorrow.' He said, 'Don't let that bother you!' So, I knocked him down."

Davis called Jerry Geissler, Hollywood legal beagle, and instructed him to reinstitute the divorce proceedings.

Newsweek magazine reported laconically on April 10, 1950, in an account titled "Mr. Housewife":

Last October Bette Davis and artist William Grant Sherry patched up their domestic discord after Miss Davis filed for divorce. But last week they were back in court. Irked because he hadn't been invited to a studio party celebrating Miss Davis's birthday, Sherry slugged Barry Sullivan, her leading man. Then he told the press, "I'm tired of being pushed around. She was the breadwinner and I was the housewife . . . I have dinner ready when

she gets home. I take off her shoes and bring her slippers
and a drink. I press her dresses when her maid isn't here.
But . . . I'm a man who needs a lot of affection. When
she comes home from work, she always says she's too
tired.''

*[Sherry always got a little carried away with the press. If a
divorce was necessary, I never made any statements of particulars
to the press. Sherry constantly did, rather enjoyed it I always felt.
As to dinners ready for me, slippers, shoes off, etc.—if he ever did
these things, which I doubt, it was small recompense for a very
comfortable life at my expense. I never turned any man into a
housewife—was and still am very old-fashioned in this area. A
man's place is* not *in the kitchen.]*

THE QUEEN MOTHER

*Funny business a woman's career. The things you drop
on your way up the ladder—so you can move faster—you
forget you'll need them again when you go back to being a
woman. That's one career all females have in common
whether we like it or not. Being a woman. Sooner or later
we've got to work at it, no matter what other careers
we've had or wanted. And in the last analysis nothing is
any good unless you can look up just before dinner—or
turn around in bed—and there he is. Without that, you're
not a woman. You're something with a French provincial
office—or a book full of clippings. But you're not a
woman. Slow curtain. The end.*

BETTE DAVIS AS MARGO CHANNING
IN *All about Eve*

During the last five days of shooting *The Story of a Divorce* Davis
received a telephone call from Darryl F. Zanuck. She was not really
sure that a prankster was not impersonating his voice. *[At the time of
my resignation as president of the Academy of Motion Picture Arts
and Sciences Mr. Zanuck said, "If you resign, you will never work
in this town again!" So naturally I didn't believe it was actually
Darryl Zanuck calling me.]* He wanted her for the part of Margo
Channing in *All about Eve*. *[Zanuck also said I would have to start*

Bette Davis shakes hands with J.L. Warner, with Albert Warner's approval, after she has signed a contract to produce six pictures under the Warner Bros. banner, 1946. (*Photograph by Warner Bros., from the collection of Bill Roy.*)

Artist Kate Bosworth confronts twin sister, playgirl Patricia, in this split-frame blowup from *A Stolen Life,* a B.D. Production, 1946. (*Photograph by Warner Bros., from the collection of Gunnard Nelson.*)

Christine Radcliffe (Bette Davis) has shot Alexander Hollenius (Claude Rains) in the climactic scene from *Deception*, 1946. (*Photograph by Warner Bros.*)

The "McKinley Stinker" scene from *June Bride*, 1948. Robert Montgomery, James Burke, Betty Lynn, Davis, Mary Wickes, George O'Hanlon, and Fay Bainter. (*Photograph by Morgan, Warner Bros.*)

Rosa Moline (Bette Davis) dreams of taking a trip to Chicago to visit her boy friend in *Beyond the Forest*, 1949; husband Lewis (Joseph Cotton) cannot understand her attitude. (*Photograph by Warner Bros.*)

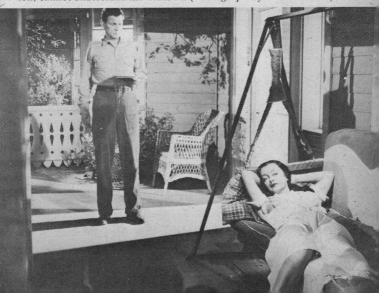

Three-year-old B. D. and Davis on the set of *Payment on Demand* in 1950. B. D. played her mother's daughter in the film. (*Photograph by R.K.O. Studios.*)

On behalf of French trade journals Charles Boyer presents awards to Davis, William Wyler, and Gary Cooper on the set of *June Bride*, 1948. (*Photograph by Warner Bros.*)

"The one Sin no Woman ever forgives"

He strayed...
and he paid!
She saw to that!

JACK N. SKIRBALL and BRUCE MANNING
present

BETTE DAVIS
BARRY SULLIVAN

in

Payment on Demand

with

JANE COWL · BETTY LYNN · FRANCES DEE

Produced by JACK M. SKIRBALL · Directed by CURTIS BERNHARDT · Written by BRUCE MANNING and CURTIS BERNHARDT

the picture in ten days' time. They were in a jam. Claudette Colbert, who was to play Margo, had hurt her back and could not, therefore, be in the film.]

The script arrived, and Davis soon realized that the part of Margo Channing was made for her. Comedy, drama, pathos, all wrapped up in witty and scintillating dialogue. She called Zanuck immediately. Filming was to begin in San Francisco at the Curran Theatre during the only two weeks available out of a season of solid booking.

She had dinner with writer-director Joseph L. Mankiewicz the next night. *[Mankiewicz very succinctly gave the key to the character of Margo Channing: She is a woman who treats a mink coat like a poncho.''*] Davis was given permission to have Edith Head design Margo's wardrobe, which she fitted at night while finishing *The Story of a Divorce* during the day. That week she also did makeup tests with Gary Merrill for the part of Bill Sampson. Zanuck wanted to be sure they looked right together.

Later Colbert told columnist Erskine Johnson, "It's like I told Joe Mankiewicz—every time I read the beautiful notices, a knife goes through my heart. It's fate. I had to break my back so that Bette could meet Gary Merrill and get the role of a lifetime."

The plot was outlined by *Time* magazine on October 16, 1950:

> The movie shows the swift rise of a young Broadway actress, Eve Harrington (Anne Baxter), from a stagestruck unknown to an adulated star. She is seen first at her most triumphant moment, as the theater's elite prepare to honor her with their highest prize for acting. Then, in flashbacks, introduced with narration by three different characters, the story of Eve's success proves her less a Cinderella than a Lady Macbeth.
>
> . . . Actress Davis, who submits herself to deliberately harsh lighting, unflattering camera angles, and messy makeup, gives the picture's showiest role what may be the best performance of her career. A thoroughly convincing theatrical first lady given to spats, rages, and drunken maunderings, she commands sympathy and even admiration for a character whom the audience is prepared to hate. The sensitively modulated playing of

Anne Baxter, one of Hollywood's most versatile performers, makes Eve everything she should be, [and] counts heavily in the movie's effectiveness.

Also in the superb cast were Marilyn Monroe, in the role of "a graduate of the Copacabana School of Dramatic Arts" and Barbara Bates, who played Phoebe, the new viper in Eve's life, bent on repeating Eve's machinations with Margo. She has the ending shot all to herself, posing in Eve's satin cape in front of a three-way mirror, pretending that she is receiving the Sarah Siddons Award, which has been presented to Eve—just as Eve posed in Margo's antebellum gown backstage the year before. Eddie Fisher played the stage manager, a role cut before release.

Sometime after the picture was out, a group of persons interested in the theater formed a real Sarah Siddons Society in Chicago and inaugurated an annual award. Twenty-three years later, in 1973, Davis was presented with the trophy for her years of outstanding achievement.

Milton Krasner photographed expertly, catching dramatic shading and comic nuances in slick high key, imbuing the sets by Lyle Wheeler and George W. Davis with an authentic feel for New York habitats.

It had been years since Davis had been on a picture that was charmed from the first day to the last. It was an extraordinary experience to work with actors and actresses perfectly cast and well satisfied with their roles. There was the pleasure of working with a superb director in a great script. Merrill's growing attachment to Davis was obvious to all on the set. *[Bill Sampson was falling in love with Margo Channing!]*

In the December 24 edition of *The Los Angeles Times* Hedda Hopper entitled an interview with Davis: "Comeback in 'Eve' Proves Bette's Still Film Queen" and began,

Hollywood's most thrilling comeback in 1950 was made by its finest actress, Bette Davis. Just a year ago her long and brilliant career was never in worse shape. A succession of bad, yes, mediocre, pictures had proved that not even the queen was immune to the skids. Thinking that *Beyond the Forest* was the worst thing that she'd ever done, I wrote in my column, "If Bette had deliberately set out to wreck her career, she couldn't have picked a more appropriate vehicle."

. . . Hollywood wondered: Was Bette Davis through? The answer is that a girl like Bette is never through until the last gong has sounded. She's a battler from the word "go" . . . For my money, her performance in *All about Eve* topped anything she ever did, including the two pictures that brought her Oscars. To a brilliantly conceived and written part she gave everything that any director could desire. If the job doesn't get her a third Academy Award, I'll miss my guess. . . .

[My part was exactly right for me. I've played many things harder than Margo Channing. Anne Baxter was the one who really had the diabolically hard job. She went all through the picture. I did my part in three and one-half weeks.]

"I didn't have to worry about my looks," Davis told Hopper. "If you have to be concerned about your appearance, acting goes out the window. Margo Channing was past forty. So was I. I was supposed to look the way I did." Davis continued,

But I see no reason why a woman of forty should be embarrassed by trying to look as well as she can. It's a cliché—and I think Hollywood established it—when a woman at forty is supposed to be a character. It's not true. When we were preparing *The Story of a Divorce,* we had quite a time deciding whether my hair should be graying.

As far as I'm concerned, a seventy-year-old couple decided that matter. When I told them of the part, they said, "Now, you're not going to play a white-haired woman. We get so tired of Hollywood's view of forty."

People get that idea that actresses my age are dying to play younger women. The fact is we die every time we play them. But most pictures are written for younger women. And, as Tallulah Bankhead once said when asked why she took a bad play, "Every now and then you have to earn a living!"

I think Claudette Colbert paid me my greatest compliment. About ten years ago she said to me, "I envy you your career, because you've played older women before

you had to. Now you'll never have to make the age
bridge.''

On July 4 Davis's divorce from Sherry became final, and on July
28 she married Gary Merrill in Juarez, Mexico, with Judge Raul
Orozco performing the rites. They took off immediately for a
honeymoon in the East.

The world premiere of *All about Eve* was held at Grauman's
Chinese Theatre on November 9, 1950, and everyone was there—
more famous names than sometimes attend the Academy Awards.
Davis did not stay for the showing because she had promised to see
the picture for the first time with her husband, who was making
Decision before Dawn in Germany. She joined the studio party at
Ciro's, where she put in an overseas call to Merrill.

Davis had appeared in many unqualified hits before, but never
were the members of the press so lavish in their praise of her, the
picture, and her fellow players. And the most startling attribute of
the performance was that she did not illegitimately steal the film—
the role of Margo Channing was integrated into the whole of the
story and could not be called a vehicle in the same sense as *Dark
Victory, Mr. Skeffington,* or *Now, Voyager.*

Davis has said many times that she has played roles far more
difficult than Margo Channing. Yet the circumstances that
surrounded the picture, the immediate sexual attraction engendered
between Merrill and her, the glamorous wardrobe and makeup, and
the stage setting with which she had been familiar for more than
twenty years contributed to the conception of the role—all aided and
abetted by a producer who had seen her grow from the bitch in
Cabin in the Cotton to her box office triumphs and who was willing
to give her a star part after her critical lambasting in *Beyond the
Forest,* when Hollywood pundits said she was through.

Davis received the New York Film Critics Circle Award for the
best female performance of 1950. *[Finally I had been given an
award by the New York Film Critics. To all of us in Hollywood this
award seemed to be a special compliment. I was pleased beyond
words to have finally been chosen by the New York critics for this
honor.]*

She also received the San Francisco Critics Award—a unique
triumph because these same reviewers had voted her the worst
actress of 1949 for *Beyond the Forest*—the *Photoplay* Gold Medal,

and the *Look* Magazine Medallion. *All about Eve* was selected as the "picture of the month" by both *Redbook* and *Liberty*. But according to Hollywood standards the most belated tribute of all was finally tendered: Davis was asked to place handprints and footprints in cement in the forecourt of Grauman's Chinese Theatre on Hollywood Boulevard. Helped by two marines, S. Sgt. Jack Spencer and T. Sgt. Bert R. Nave, the ceremony was recorded for posterity by Twentieth Century-Fox newsreel cameramen.

Pauline Kael said, "Bette Davis is at her most brilliant. Her actress, vain, scared, a woman who goes too far in her actions and emotions, makes the whole thing come alive."

Dorothy Manners wrote in the November 23 edition of *The Los Angeles Examiner,* "By this time the scuttlebutt should be around that Bette Davis, who portrays this devastating belle, gives a sort of takeoff on Tallulah. For my money, it is the sharpest, truest, most sophisticated and titillating performance of the season." *[Tallulah herself, more than anyone else, accused me of imitating her as Margo Channing. The problem was that I had no voice at all when I started filming* All about Eve *due to emotional stress as a result of the Sherry divorce. A doctor gave me oil treatments three times a day for the first two weeks so that I could talk at all. This gave me the famous husky Bankhead voice. Otherwise, I don't think the similarity to Bankhead in my performance would ever have been thought of.]*

Davis and Merrill took a house at Malibu after returning from the East. They adopted a five-day-old baby, whom they named Margot.

On Monday, December 31, 1951, Davis was reunited on radio with George Brent in the series "Woman of the Year"—a story that MGM had filmed with Katharine Hepburn and Spencer Tracy in 1942. She portrayed Tess Harding, *New York Chronicle* columnist on international affairs, with sports writer Sam Craig played by Brent.

When the Academy Award nominations were released, *All about Eve* scored with a record fourteen, including *both* Davis and Anne Baxter for best actress—the first time two actresses were nominated for starring roles in the same film. Baxter was still under contract to Twentieth Century-Fox; Davis was freelancing. But even with all the voting power of a great studio on Baxter's side it appeared that either Davis or Gloria Swanson in *Sunset Boulevard* would be the ones to beat. Another fateful happening occurred twenty-one years later, when Baxter took over the role of Margo Channing from

Lauren Bacall in *Applause,* the Broadway musical version of *All about Eve.* Unlike Bacall, not afraid of portraying Margo in the same vein as her predecessor, Baxter received rave reviews. Davis watched her performance from backstage one matinee. Among the quick changes, with sets flying upward and moving horizontally over the stage, and with members of the enormous cast making entrances and exits, Davis stood in the wings all during the show. At the end, after the curtain call, she took Baxter in her arms. "You *were* Margo!" she exclaimed.

With *All about Eve* making box office history, Howard Hughes decided to release *The Story of a Divorce.* He changed the title to *Payment on Demand,* and the film was booked into the prestigious Radio City Music Hall on February 15, 1951.

Hughes took another look at the film and decided to change the ending. The last scene at breakfast, where it is revealed that the woman has not changed, seemed harsh and uncompromising. He had originally wanted the wife to invite the husband into the house after he brings her home from the wedding party, thereby making sex the instigator of the action. He called Davis, Barry Sullivan, and Curtis Bernhardt back to the studio on February 13. The new ending had David asking if he might come in and Joyce replying that she doesn't want him to decide now; but, if he wants to come back later, she will be waiting. *[The new ending broke our hearts. The one we had shot was the true ending for our film. We also were brokenhearted over the title change.]*

The scene was processed through the lab, spliced into the last reel, placed aboard a Hughes TWA airlines for New York, and arrived just in time for the sweating projectionist, who had started the matinee run at Radio City Music Hall, to thread up his machine with the new material.

The reviews were excellent. *Hollywood Reporter,* on February 15, said, "If *Payment on Demand* has been withheld from release until the Bette Davis hit in *All about Eve* has been cemented, it wasn't necessary. The picture, completed before the Twentieth Century-Fox comedy drama, stands on its own firm feet and Miss Davis on the powerful range of her acting talent. It's a superb part, and the actress plays superbly, reading nuances of the modern woman into it that her fans will recognize and understand."

A DATE WITH EROS

All right, Fury, I haven't forgotten you . . . Here's your little snack . . . How are you, beautiful, better? Oh, what if I couldn't talk to you every night? Do you think Larry will come? . . . Goodnight, Fury, on this special night.
BETTE DAVIS AS JANET FROBISHER
IN *Another Man's Poison*

Shortly after *Payment on Demand* began to coin money, Douglas Fairbanks, Jr., and Daniel M. Angel, who had formed Eros Productions, with a United Artists release, sent the script of *Another Man's Poison* by Val Guest, based on a play called *Deadlock* by Leslie Sands, to Davis and Merrill. Filming was to take place in England.

The entourage, including Davis's personal maid Dell, B.D., Margot, and two nurses, arrived at Southampton aboard the *Queen Elizabeth* and was met by the press corps. The next day the papers were full of invective, referring to the star as a "middle-aged matron" and calling Merrill "Mr. Bette Davis."

David Marlow in the December 15, 1951, issue of *Picturegoer* wrote of Davis's reactions: "She threatened to catch the next boat back. There were rumors that she refused to have an official press reception. It was even said that she made dark hints about 'putting a stop to this kind of treatment of American stars by the British press,' though there was no intimation of how she intended going about it.

"But the publicists wheedled her around as good publicists must. Eventually she met the press at a Savoy reception. Always the good trouper, she mixed with the reporters, but there was an unseasonable December chilliness about the occasion."

Another Man's Poison, budgeted at £100,000, was scheduled to be shot at Nettleford, England's oldest studio, which was composed of three sound stages at Walton-on-Thames. *[Gary and I were thrilled beyond words when Emlyn Williams accepted a part in our film. Another example of how fortunate I was to work with one of the greats in the theater . . . not only as an actor but as a playwright as well. We also grew to be great admirers of Emlyn as a person.]* Also in the cast were Anthony Steel, Barbara Murray, Reginald Beckwith, and Edna Morris. Irving Rapper, at Davis's request, was brought over from Hollywood to direct. Robert Krasker was the cinematographer.

Davis was to play mystery writer Janet Frobisher, who is having an affair with engineer Steel. When her husband, a convict who has been incarcerated for years, returns unexpectedly with blackmail on his mind, she poisons him. Before she can dispose of the body, a friend of her husband's, Merrill, comes to the house and, suspecting foul play, forces her to reveal the killing. They hide the body in the nearby tarn, and Merrill poses as her newly returned husband. Williams, a kindly veterinarian, suspects the ruse. Davis sends Merrill to the village in a jeep that has faulty brakes, but he escapes unharmed; however, she later manages to poison him. Williams reveals to her that he knew of the impersonation. She faints, and he revives her with the poisoned brandy. Seeing the fateful glass, she knows she is dying and, appreciating the irony of the situation, begins to laugh. The film ends with a close-up of her congested face, frozen in mirth.

The film completed, Davis and Merrill left for home on July 2, 1951, on the *Queen Mary*. A score by John Greenwood was added to the picture but did not contribute to the necessary suspense. Paul Sawtelle, in Hollywood, composed new music to be added to the film before release in the United States. *Another Man's Poison* was previewed at the Gaumont Theatre in London on November 20, 1951.

Frank Hauser wrote in Britain's *New Statesman:* "It is fascinating watching Bette Davis, a superb screen actress if there ever was one, play everything in a blaze of breathtaking absurdity. From beginning to end, there is not a lifelike inflection, a plausible reaction. . . . It is like reading Ethel M. Dell by flashes of lightning." *[We had nothing but script trouble. Gary and I often wondered why we agreed to make this film after we got started working on it. Emlyn rewrote many scenes for us, which gave it some plausibility, but we never cured the basic ills of the story.] Daily Variety,* on December 27, said, "Miss Davis clicks solidly with a dominating performance in the lead spot, deftly shading her unsympathetic role for maximum effect."

The unusual release pattern of the picture garnered some attention. United Artists, foregoing a first-run Broadway house, booked the film into the Metropolitan in Brooklyn on January 16, 1952, where it took in $17,000 the first week and another $150,000 in four days on the Loew's circuit and day-and-date houses in the metropolitan area. United Artists figured that the advertising alone in a first-run house might wipe out the profit for the first week, since heavy booking was called for during the Christmas rush. The film got a bad break, however; first because of the lukewarm reviews and second because the end run coincided with Warner Bros.'s *A Streetcar Named Desire*. With exhibitors having a choice of which film to book, most took *Streetcar*.

Booked into 513 theaters all across the country, the film made production costs back with a little profit.

Davis, at forty-four, was beginning what she would later term ''her ten black years.''

17

*Dull, foolish, vulgar, a clown . . . but not to me. To me
he was a man like a rock—nothing could shake him,
nothing could shake his love. It was from him I learned
what love really was. Not a frail little fancy to be smashed
and broken by pride and vanity and self-pity. That's for
children, that's for high school kids. But a rock, as strong
as life itself—indestructible and determined.*

BETTE DAVIS AS MARIE HOKE
IN *Phone Call from a Stranger*

The Merrills moved from Malibu into a large, rambling clapboard
house, with a pool and a tiny guest house, on the corner of Franklin
Avenue and Camino Palmero in Hollywood. B.D. was enrolled in
the nearby Bluebird Nursery School. Davis was busy being a wife
and mother—and "loving it," as she often told the press.

Merrill was cast in the pivotal role of lawyer David Trask in
Nunnally Johnson's screenplay *Phone Call from a Stranger,* based
on a story by Ida Alexa Ross Wylie. Episodic in form, the film dealt
with Trask, who has left his wife because she has had a brief affair
with another man. Aboard a plane bound for Los Angeles, he meets
three people: an ex-burlesque queen, a doctor, and a traveling
salesman. When the plane crashes, Trask, the sole survivor, takes it
upon himself to visit the families of the victims.

Cast were Shelley Winters as Binky Gay, the runway terper;
Michael Rennie as Dr. Fortness; and Keenan Wynn as Eddie Hoke,
the salesman. Jean Negulesco, who had directed many films at
Warner Bros. before coming to Twentieth Century-Fox, notably

Johnny Belinda, which won an Academy Award for Jane Wyman, was having difficulty casting Marie Hoke, who turns out to be not the sexpot her husband always spoke so lovingly about, but a bedridden paralytic.

[Merrill gave the script to me to read one day. I asked who was playing Marie Hoke? Gary said Negulesco hadn't cast it yet. I told him to ask if I could play it. Merrill was flabbergasted because it was such a small part. I said it would be a change of pace for me. I believed in the part more than its length. I have never understood why stars should object to playing smaller parts if they were good ones. Marie Hoke was such a part.]

Davis actually appeared in five scenes: running away from Hoke with her lover, a bathing sequence in which she injures her head, in bed in a hotel room, in an iron lung in the hospital, and finally her last long scene as an invalid, with Merrill, in which she tells him how her husband took her back after her lover disappeared.

Phone Call from a Stranger won the best screenplay award at the Venice Film Festival; *Another Man's Poison* was showing simultaneously in some cities in the United States.

The reviews were good. W. E. Oliver wrote on February 22, 1952, in *The Los Angeles Herald Express,* "Best scene is by Bette Davis as the crippled wife. Her magic with words brings a lump in the throat as she explains why she loved the jerk who was her husband."

Jimmy Durante, who had a top-rated weekly television show, called Davis about a guest spot. *[Durante said, "C'mon, Bett, you gotta do it." I reluctantly said yes.]*

The critics were less than enthusiastic. Said *Daily Variety,* on April 21, 1952, "Video's newest convert was Bette Davis, and it might be recorded that she broke in reading a commercial—'I'll take two cans of Pet Milk.' Miss Davis was used otherwise in one large scene running close to fifteen minutes. That her coming-out in the channel set was not too auspicious can be traced to an apparent nervousness (people, not cameras) and a lack of sufficient elasticity to 'unbend.' She was no Traubel or Truman, but she outgloried Swanson." *[I was scared to death in my first live TV appearance. That I got through it at all was a source of great wonderment to me!]*

THE OLD HOLLYWOOD

Come on, Oscar, let's you and me get drunk!
BETTE DAVIS AS MARGARET ELLIOTT
IN *The Star*

Months went by, and no film offers were tendered. The Merrills adopted another child, a boy, whom they named Michael. Now there were three children in the household. In summer, 1952, Bert E. Friedlob (married to another Warner alumna, Eleanor Parker) contacted Davis about playing the role of Margaret Elliott in *The Star*, by Katherine Albert and Dale Eunson. When Davis signed, a Twentieth Century-Fox release was set, and a thirty-day shooting schedule was mapped out by director Stuart Heisler.

A special type of leading man was required by the script. He must not look like an actor. *[I suggested Sterling Hayden as the ideal choice to Friedlob and Heisler. They agreed with me, and Hayden was cast as Jim Johannson.]*

Newsweek magazine on February 9, 1953, gave the story line succinctly:

> Hollywood, which is open to contagions of story ideas, seems to have been fascinated recently with the notion of the elderly or worn-out Thespian. Most notable, there was Charles Chaplin's *Limelight* . . . A good deal less notable, there is Red Skelton's *The Clown,* and quite compelling—though somewhat flawed—there is Bette Davis's *The Star,* which her publicity agents are booming as her latest bid for Oscar. . . .
>
> Bette Davis creates an acute, frightening picture of a woman obsessed with her past career and her legend, self-accusing and humble at times, but then again utterly callous to the ordinary and wonderful business of human relations. It is a fine portrait, and imparts a high value to the picture. Regrettably, there is altogether too fast and too contrived an ending to the actress's deep-seated trouble.

The Star, on a 24-day shooting schedule, made use of many actual locations in and around Hollywood and San Pedro, which brought a documentary touch to Ernie Laszlo's photography. Also

in the small cast were Natalie Wood as daughter Gretchen, Warner Anderson as agent Harry Stone, and Minor Watson as producer Joe Morrison, with Fay Baker and David Alpert as Davis's sponging relatives. Starlet Barbara Lawrence played herself—the epitome of young Hollywood fame. Davis used her own Oscar for the wild drunken automobile ride through Beverly Hills where she props the award on the dashboard of the car. *[I have always felt* The Star *was very underrated by critics and the public. Katherine Albert and Dale Eunson had been familiar with the Hollywood scene for many years. Their script was an authentic picture of a "motion picture star," as opposed to the actress-type star. I enjoyed very much playing in their really great script of Margaret Elliott's demise as a Hollywood star and rebirth as a person.]*

After *The Star* was in the can, Hal Wallis sent over the script of *Come Back Little Sheba,* which he was planning to film at Paramount with Sidney Blackmer as the drunken husband. Wallis felt that Davis could do the part of the disoriented, slattern wife. She declined the part. *[One of the really great mistakes of my career. I was, of course, delighted to have this offer from my long-time boss at Warner Bros. I foolishly, as I now realize, felt I was not right for the part, personality-wise—the gorgeous vagueness that Shirley Booth brought to the stage role I felt would not ring true with me. I find it hard to believe I turned this part down for such a senseless reason.]* Shirley Booth was signed for the part opposite Burt Lancaster.

TWO'S COMPANY—AND THREE'S A CROWD

Radie Harris, in a piece called "Bette Davis Tells How She Got Set for Musical Revue," in *The Los Angeles Times,* August 17, 1952, interviewed Davis in the Camino Palmero residence:

It is here in this unfashionable neighborhood that Mr. and Mrs. Gary Merrill and their three enchanting youngsters reside now, and it is here in their large old-fashioned house in the living room (which is really lived in because there is no drawing room!) that I had cocktails with Bette as she talked excitedly of her imminent return to Broadway.

"This whole thing came about by sheer accident—the

same way that most of the important things in our lives happen,'' she started. ''I had been approached to follow Judy Garland into the Palace, and I gave it some serious thought. I knew I didn't want to do the usual 'in-person' appearance of reenacting scenes from my movies, nor did I want to do anything heavy and dramatic. I thought it would be fun to try a variety act—IF I could get the right material. Famous last words! Well, in the midst of all this, Ralph Alswang—you know, the well-known scenic designer—long distanced Gary from New York. They're old pals, and they always phone each other at the drop of a toll call. Well, it seems that Ralph shares his office with two young producers named Jimmy Russo and Mike Ellis, who were about to produce a revue called *Two's Company,* only needed a star like Bea Lillie, Gertrude Lawrence, or Mary Martin, whom they couldn't get.''

And, of course, they knew you were equally unobtainable, I interrupted.

''So they assumed,'' Bette answered as she helped one-and-a-half-year-old Margot on her hobby horse. ''That's why, just as a gag, Jimmy asked Ralph to ask Gary if I would be interested in doing a revue on Broadway. When Gary said yes and they revived Jimmy from the stool he had fallen off, things began to happen. Vernon Duke played me the score he had written to Ogden Nash's lyrics, and I adored it.

''Then I heard Charles Sherman's sketches, and they're absolutely wonderful! I appear in most of them with Hiram Sherman and two other comedians who haven't been cast yet. Jerome Robbins, than whom there is none better, is going to stage the show, and Miles White, who turns everything into a white Christmas with his beautiful creations, is designing my wardrobe. . . . We won't come in until we're sure it's in perfect shape. That's why we're trying it out first in Detroit—far from the Sardi scuttlebutt.''

The Merrills gave up the house on Camino Palmero and rented a penthouse on Beekman Place on New York's exclusive East Side. Rehearsals began. Davis found that she tired easily but put it down to the different and longer hours than the studio working day. After a month of rehearsing the company went to Detroit to prepare for the opening of the show.

Two's Company opened at the Shubert Theatre in Detroit on the evening of October 19, 1952. The 2,050-seat house was sold out for the premiere. The curtains opened on a bare stage, showing the brick back wall of the theater. The only props were a piano and a stepladder. Hiram Sherman appeared and explained that production costs had kept the show spare. As he continued his monologue, elaborate scenery was set in place, and the lights came up to full.

Davis's first entrance was made from a magician's sealed box, to an ovation. She began her number, "Good Little Girls."*

> I don't want me a poor young me-chan-ic
> Not as long as there's a mil-lion-aire named Max,—
> 'Cause Good Little Girls go to heav-en—
> But smart lit-tle girls go to Berg-dorf's, to Bul-lock's, to
> Bon-wit's, to Mag-nin's and Saks.

The second chorus went well, then she started the third:

> I won't be a sub-urb-an com-mut-er . . .

To the surprise of the audience and the horror of the cast, she toppled over, hitting the stage with a bone-jarring bang. As murmurs spread through the audience and the house lights came up, the curtain came down. *[I was singing away; then, all of a sudden . . . a voice was saying, "Get up, Bette, get up." It was Merrill, at the same time assuring all concerned that I would go on with the show. I got up, walked down to the stage apron, smiled, and said, "Well, you can't say I didn't fall for you!" The audience laughed and applauded, and I went on with the show.]*

During intermission Davis said that she had probably fainted because she had not slept for twenty-four hours because of rehearsals. The wire services picked up the story! Davis made front pages across the country.

The reviews were on the good side. Russell McLauchlin on October 20, wrote in *The Detroit News*, "Probably *Two's Com-*

---

pany will be fast and funny and melodious and spectacular in the proper degree, when all the work is done for which it now clamors. . . . Bette Davis is not the world's greatest singer by about twelve city blocks, and she wisely tries no very complex dancing. She is competent on the acting side, certainly, and there is a real distinction in her personality which makes her situation the constant center of the stage. You like her exceedingly and you keep, as you might say, 'pulling' for her, in all the curious adventures which befall the star of a big lengthy review.''

After the show's opening in Pittsburgh on November 10, Kaspar Monahan wrote in *The Pittsburgh Press,* ''The new musical on the whole is disappointing. Its sketches, save for a couple in which Miss Davis wears outlandish getups and a few more in which some lively members of her cast disport, are merely mildly amusing . . . The show is new and in the agonizing stages of being reshaped, rewritten, etc.''

In Boston, with the show in real trouble, play doctor and former Davis mentor John Murray Anderson was brought in to restage the revue. Both John Hoyt and Paul Hartman were briefly added to the cast but departed before the opening in New York. Hiram Sherman thought he might leave the production, then changed his mind. Comedian David Burns joined the cast. New material was added almost nightly, and other sketches and musical numbers were switched around. *[I was never able to do the original opening song again. I was just plain frightened of it after I had passed out on the opening night in Detroit. Jerome Robbins planned a new opening for me finally. We rehearsed it for a day or so and then put it in the show after the Boston opening. It was a success—''Just Turn Me Loose on Broadway'' became my opening number.]*

The show was scheduled to open at the Alvin Theatre on December 4. *[When we arrived back in New York I was very ill—I presumed from exhaustion due to the tryout weeks on the road. Mr. Anderson continued to work on the show in New York. I was too ill to attend rehearsals—stayed in bed trying to get my strength back for the New York opening. The day before I went to the theater, I was rehearsed in all the changes Mr. Anderson had made—and gave a performance in front of an audience that night. Never did know how I remembered all the changes. But Murray Anderson had done wonders for* Two's Company. *I will always feel indebted to him for his great work on my show. I had studied at the Robert Milton-John Murray Anderson School of the Theatre. He told me when he took over the show in Boston that he was doing it for me—his former student—whom he admired. It was too late to make it the show it could have been had he been in charge from the beginning, but I owe him my eternal gratitude.]*

With the changes in the revue Russo and Ellis requested that the critics not attend the opening but wait until December 15 to review. The period from December 4 to December 15 was to be treated as previews, allowing the production to smooth out. The Alvin had already booked thirty-five theater parties, including five matinees, through February 11. A theater party set for December 15 would have to be canceled, since that was the official opening.

Peter de Vries was brought in to help Charles Sherman with the book, and Sheldon Harnick added new lyrics. New sketch writers were Arnold B. Horwitt, Lee Rogow, Nat Hiken, Billy Friedberg, Mort Green, and George Foster; Genevieve Pitot contributed music for the ballet.

Meanwhile the revue, which had originally been budgeted at $175,000, already had a 20 percent overcall, but now Russo and Ellis needed additional money and wired the backers to put up another 25 percent, on a "purely voluntary basis." The new money was to be repaid from the first profits. The show cost about $32,000 per week.

Two's Company was reviewed by *The New Yorker* on December 27, 1952:

> Miss Davis got herself up in more costumes than I recall ever seeing before on one actress, and she worked at least as hard as Ethel Merman did in *Annie Get Your Gun*. The only trouble was that, with the exception of two or three numbers, the material—furnished by eight or nine writers—just didn't seem to be there. The star imitated Tallulah Bankhead lousing up a Bette Davis opening; she impersonated Jeanne Eagels in *Rain;* she was an actress who tangled up with an Italian director, a hillbilly singer on TV, minus a couple of front teeth and smoking a pipe, the female lead in what I took to be a parody of Noel Coward's *Private Lives,* and a slattern in a moderately painful scene based on passion and jealousy in a tenement and having, I guess, something to do with the works of Arthur Miller; and she even sang a kind of torch song toward the end. About half these items ought to be funny,

but there is some quality in Miss Davis's technique that suggests she should confine her talents to Maugham's pale-green and despicable Mildred and leave humor to the girls who just play for quick laughs.

[I had purposely chosen to do this kind of a show for my return to the theater. I felt it was an ideal way to "rebreak" myself into doing theater after twenty-two years. I was someone well known to the public—and spoofing myself, I thought, would be ideal. I felt the critics were angry with me for this decision on my part. They felt cheated. They would much rather have had a go at me in an emotional role in a straight play. At that time there was great critical snobbery about Hollywood stars! I was one of the first to return to the theater. New York critics, I also felt, wanted famous Hollywood people to fall on their faces when performing in the theater. It was truly a wall of prejudice that was almost impossible to overcome at that time.]

Three numbers in the show would be used by Davis many years later on television. On an "Andy Williams Show" she sang her opening number, "Just Turn Me Loose on Broadway"; the "Jealousy" sketch was reincarnated for a "Hollywood Palace," with Bert Lahr as the husband; and she debuted her torchy "Just Like a Man" on the "Sun City Scandals," emceed by Johnny Carson.

The Star was previewed at the Academy Awards Theatre in Hollywood on December 16, 1952, and opened at the Four Star Theatre on Christmas day to qualify for an Academy Award nomination. The requirement being that to be in the running for an Oscar, a film must be shown in the Los Angeles area for at least one week before the calendar year is up. *Picturegoer* on February 28, 1953, said, "This is a one-woman picture, with the limelight fully focused on the character so sensitively and excitingly drawn by Bette Davis. . . . It shows that Bette Davis is still right at the top as a screen star."

Two's Company played to "standing room only" audiences from the beginning. Davis was overly tired much of the time; Dexedrine got her through show after show. She went for frequent checkups, but doctors could find no reason for her unnatural fatigue. Finally on March 7 a wisdom tooth became inflamed. She was treated by Art Carney's brother, a dentist whom she had met the night before backstage. He prescribed poultices, and the next day she went to see Dr. Stanley Behrman, head of dental surgery at New York Hospital. He insisted on extracting the tooth at once, but Davis asked permission to do the Sunday night show because it was an actors' benefit. That night she went to the hospital to have the tooth removed. *[I knew that, if I did not play the actors' benefit, rumor would have it that I was frightened to do the show in front of the greats of the theater.]*

The condition that had been sapping Davis's strength for months was diagnosed as osteomyelitis of the jaw. An extremely difficult operation was required—the jaw had to be scraped and bone tissue removed, which would take a long time to grow back. *Two's Company* closed after eighty-nine performances.

Walter Winchell, who had given the show what amounted to a plug a day ("She makes a very impressive and very persuasive comedienne. She sings in an easy, relaxed voice, dances jauntily and projects her personality convincingly." "Bette is not only the star, she is the chief ticket seller . . . This dept. plans to catch bits of it again every evening"), reported that Davis had cancer of the jaw. Davis and Merrill were thrown into a panic, knowing how worried friends and family would be and how the assertion could adversely affect her career. She sent the following wire to the columnist:

> YOUR RECENT STATEMENTS ABOUT ME ARE UTTERLY WITHOUT FOUNDATION. HAVE AUTHORIZED MY PHYSICIAN AT N.Y. HOSPITAL TO ANSWER ANY QUESTIONS YOU MAY CARE TO PUT TO HIM, AND TO EXAMINE HOSPITAL'S AND PATHOLOGISTS' REPORTS. I AM SURE YOU HAVE NO WISH TO HURT ME. ACCEPT MY ASSURANCES THAT I DO NOT HAVE CANCER. PLEASE RETRACT ON BROADCAST.
>
> BETTE DAVIS

Winchell published the telegram in his syndicated column and added, "The correction (as quoted by news wire services and the star's husband) was recorded here earlier last week. The official report called it osteomyelitis of the jaw. Bette's condition, they added, is 'not malignant.' " *[Mr. Winchell's retraction, as is true of any retraction, does not change the original impression in the minds of the public. For years afterward people would hint about my cancer of the jaw. Mrs. Dorothy Schiff—editor of* The New York Post, *whom Gary found in the middle of the night at her home in Connecticut—ran a front-page story of the untruths of Mr. Winchell's statement. I have never forgotten this understanding and generous offering on her part. It is interesting to note that Mr. Winchell, head of the Damon Runyon Cancer Fund, was just starting his yearly drive for funds!!!]*

Loss on the production, with no hope of Davis continuing, amounted to about $320,000, *Weekly Variety* reported. Some money would probably be salvaged on an insurance claim that Russo and Ellis had taken out on the star.

Davis had no way of knowing that the rehabilitation of her jaw would keep her away from work for three years, an eternity when a career hangs in the balance.

The "Queen Mother" scene from *All about Eve*, 1950. Anne Baxter as Eve Harrington, Bette Davis as Margo Channing, Marilyn Monroe as Miss Casswell, and George Sanders as Addison DeWitt. (*Photograph by Twentieth Century-Fox.*)

Helped by S./Sgt. Jack Spencer and T./Sgt. Bert R. Nave, Davis places handprints and footprints in the cement in the courtyard of Grauman's Chinese Theatre in Hollywood, November 6, 1950, while *All about Eve* was playing. (*Photograph by Twentieth Century-Fox, from the collection of Eddie Brant.*)

Gary Merrill, ten-month-old Margot, Davis, and four-year-old B. D. Sherry enjoy the sun in front of their Malibu home after returning from England where *Another Man's Poison* was shot in 1951. (*Photograph by Associated Press.*)

Bette Davis as paraplegic Marie Hoke in *Phone Call from a Stranger*, 1952, with Gary Merrill as Davis Trask. (*Photograph by Twentieth Century-Fox.*)

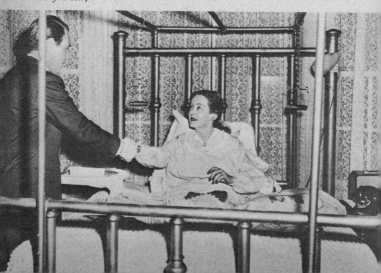

18

*Why should I be served by underlings? You'll sail the
ship yourself! This doesn't mean that I forgive you nor
that slut you married. I want the world you promised me.
And I don't want to dream of a brat crying as I dreamt last
night . . . I'll never see you again unless I need you. And
those cargoes you bring back had best be rich!*

BETTE DAVIS AS ELIZABETH I
IN *The Virgin Queen*

After Davis was well enough to leave the hospital, the Merrill
family went to Maine while she slowly recuperated from the operation. They eventually bought a house by the sea on Cape Elizabeth,
which they named Witch Way. *[We chose this name for our house
because at the time we didn't know which way we were going, and
also a witch lived in the house. Guess who?]*

As her career receded into the background, she and Merrill built a
new life in New England. The children—B.D., 6; Margot, 3; and
Mike, 2—were growing up in the same New England atmosphere as
had their parents. A year later Margot was sent to the Lochland
School in Geneva, N.Y., when it was discovered that she was brain
damaged and was a retarded child. *[Under the guidance of Florence
Stewart, the founder of the Lochland School for Retarded Children,
Margot has improved yearly. She is now twenty-two years old. This
has been her second home. I owe everything to Miss Stewart for the
disciplined way Margot has been brought up. She comes home for
Christmas and for her summer holiday every year. She is a beautiful, loving child, able to cope with her limitations. It, of course, has*

been a heartbreak for all of us, but thank God we found the Lochland School, for her sake and for ours.]

In summer, 1954, Leonard Goldstein of Twentieth Century-Fox sent the script of *Sir Walter Raleigh* to Davis in Maine. Negotiations regarding the film went into fall. Zanuck was anxious for her to do Elizabeth again; Charles Brackett was producing the film, with Henry Koster (Hermann Kosterlitz, the famous German director who had come to the United States to escape Hitlerism in the 1930s) as director. Richard Burton had been mentioned for the title role, but another Richard—Todd—was finally cast, along with Joan Collins as Beth Throckmorton, Jay Robinson (the malevolent Caligula in *The Robe)* as Chadwick, Herbert Marshall as Lord Leicester, Dan O'Herlihy as Lord Derry, and a host of character people.

On February 25, 1955, the press reported that Davis, B.D., and her poodle Tinkerbelle had arrived in Los Angeles by train from New York. A press conference was held at the Bel Air Hotel. Interviewers noticed that she was heavier than in some years—140 pounds.

She told Edwin Schallert in *The Los Angeles Times* (who entitled his interview, on March 1, 1955, "Prefers Housewife Role, Bette Davis Discloses"), "When I was leaving New York, my identity didn't seem to be exactly known by a railroad station attaché, whereas he recognized my husband immediately because he is on television every week. Gary quipped: 'That's one reason she's going to California.' "

Having her family in middle age, after a glowing and satisfying career, she could have the best of two worlds: dividing her time between home projects, the theater and films. Behind the gates of Bel Air mansions aging, unemployed, and disgruntled actresses without children envied her anew.

Sir Walter Raleigh had been written by Mindred Lord and Harry Brown. Brown was pleased that Brackett had let him "mess around" with the Elizabethan idiom; and it turned out so well that even some English critics spoke well of the language in the film.

The picture was to be shot in CinemaScope and Deluxe color by Charles G. Clarke, with Leonard Doss as color consultant. Mary Wills designed twenty-five costumes for Davis and did not hesitate to go into pastels, along with darker, more elaborate royal colors. During an early wardrobe fitting Davis insisted that a nightgown worn in a key scene be lined in silk. She felt the rustle of the material would add authenticity to the period. She also told Brackett and Koster that she wanted to reveal her baldness to rival Joan Collins. Thus, seventeen years after filming *The Private Lives of Elizabeth and Essex,* she was permitted to show the queen without hair. She also asked that Perc Westmore do her makeup. Every morning he shaved her hair back two inches, as he had when she played Elizabeth the first time. For the "bald" scene she wore a rubber cap with a few straggly gray hairs showing.

While still filming *Sir Walter Raleigh,* Davis was asked by the Academy of Motion Picture Arts and Sciences to present the best-actor award. She was in a quandary because of her shaved head. She went to Mary Willis, designer of the clothes for the picture, who made a medieval black velvet dress and a peaked, jeweled Elizabethan cap to cover her shaved hairline.

[I had no idea how I'd be received by the movie bigwigs seated in the theater. I wondered what their reaction would be. Had I been forgotten after three years? Then, through the noise and haze, I heard master-of-ceremonies Bob Hope announce my name. I walked onto the stage and a vast wave of sound rolled over me. I was being welcomed by the town where I had spent most of my life. I couldn't keep the tears from my eyes. The applause went on and on. It was one of the greatest moments of my career. I could hardly speak as I announced the name of the winner of the best actor of the year.]

Davis completed her role in the film in eleven days. Art directors Lyle Wheeler and Leland Fuller re-created the Elizabethan sets with great historical accuracy. The exterior palace and falconing sequences were shot on the back lot, which would soon become what is now Century City.

Davis asked the studio to stage the world premiere of the film, now retitled *The Virgin Queen,* in Portland, Maine. The Strand Theatre was reserved for the occasion, with proceeds going to the local Children's Theatre. It was the first Davis premiere in New England in fourteen years, since *The Great Lie* in Littleton, New Hampshire. The opening was scheduled for July 22. Festivities began at the afternoon clambake given on the shore estate of publisher Jean Gannett for the 100 press representatives and stars flown in from New York, Boston, and surrounding communities. Conrad Nagel, Jay Robinson, Tom Ewell, Jinx Falkenburg, and Faye Emerson made the trek along with Senator Edmund Muskie's executive council.

After the clambake the press and guests were invited to a cocktail party at Witch Way, hosted by the Merrills.

The evening's program started with a buffet dinner at the Eastland Hotel. Crowds had begun to form along the sidewalks from about 6:00 P.M. for celebrity watching. Twenty extra patrolmen and two sergeants took up stations on High Street, down Congress Street, to the Strand. By 8:30 P.M. 10,000 persons milled around in front of the theater and, when the preshowing action began, Davis looked out over the multitude and quipped, ''Hollywood Boulevard was never like this!''

The reviews were glowing. Sara Hamilton reported on August 4, 1955, in *The Los Angeles Examiner,* ''Like a magnificent war horse, breathing fire and brimstone, Miss Davis injects life and action into the tale, seeming to inspire everyone and everything about her. What a queen! What an actress!'' Irene Thirer in her August 5 review in *The New York Post* said, *''The Virgin Queen* comes as one of the year's better pictures of its type. We enjoyed it very, very much.''* [My wardrobe for* The Virgin Queen *was designed by a very talented girl named Mary Wills. The clothes I thought very handsome, quite up to those Orry-Kelly had made for me the first time I played Elizabeth.]*

D.W. in the December 26 issue of Britain's *Picturegoer* also had something to say about her royal gait:

> Whatever you think of *The Virgin Queen,* you must admit the critics were unanimous about one thing: they all said Bette Davis as Elizabeth I walked away with the picture. Literally—for it is the walk of Miss Davis that they all noticed.
>
> The critics had an extraordinary variety of descriptions. ''Rather like an overfed duck walking across a frozen pond,'' said one. ''Like Groucho Marx,'' was the opinion of another.
>
> As though she ''is walking not on one artificial leg, but on three,'' said a third. ''An overhearty lacrosse captain in a red wig,'' was another choice. So was ''a hopalong walk rather like that of a saddle-sore jockey.''
>
> I have a different idea. Bette Davis walks in the picture like Bette Davis having a whale of a time in the hammiest, most outrageously glorious character role of her career.

[I always felt a great propinquity to the character of Elizabeth. In many ways we were very alike. But the power to roll heads—this she had over me. Both times I played her, I had a whale of a time. Elizabeth I was a ham. The script of The Virgin Queen, *I felt, contained a better character study of her than did* The Private Lives of Elizabeth and Essex. *Also I was almost twenty years older and more equipped to play a sixty-year-old woman than I was at age thirty.]*

Several of the advertisements for the film, however, used a glamorous portrait of Margo Channing! The tagline read, "It's here for all to marvel at . . . the voluptuous days and violent nights of history's most dazzling court and most dangerous courting—the love story of Sir Walter Raleigh and the Virgin Queen!" and "CinemaScope spectacularly spreads before you the velvet cape and the violent age of Sir Walter Raleigh and the Virgin Queen!"

But despite the great reviews, the film was nevertheless disappointing at the box office. *[Twentieth Century-Fox did not spend the proper amount of money to sell* The Virgin Queen. *It was snuck out, as if they were ashamed of it. No film, no matter how good, with few exceptions, can make money without money spent on the advertising campaign.]*

THE COMMUNIST DREAM

I have no intention of leaving. I'm going to stay here, and I'm going to help rebuild the library. And, if anybody ever again tries to remove a book from it, he'll have to do it over my dead body!

BETTE DAVIS AS ALICIA HULL
IN *Storm Center*

An August 8, 1956, article in *Weekly Variety* made clear certain pertinent issues in Davis's next film: "That Hollywood is reaching out for 'new and different' story material is evidenced by Columbia's upcoming *The Library,* which focuses on the controversial issues of book burning and the guilt-by-association type of thinking."

Daniel Taradash and Elick Moll had written the original screenplay *(This Time Tomorrow)* several years before, and it had been slated for production at various times. *The Library* was now set to roll September 7 under the aegis of Phoenix Productions, which Taradash set up in partnership with Julian Blaustein, with Columbia financing and distribution. The budget was around $750,000.

"The studios don't want ordinary stories any more," commented Taradash in the above *Weekly Variety* interview. "Themes like the one about the husband getting into trouble because the box of flowers he intended for his wife were delivered to his girl friend—these are on television. The companies are now producing material they wouldn't touch a couple of years ago. . . . I think this is more of an anti-Communist picture than the usual variety of melodramas about spies and little men boring from within. We're telling Russia we can read a book designed to be inimical to democracy and yet not be damaged by it, because we are stronger than Russia."

The article continues, "It's an open secret that some Columbia exec sentiment in N.Y. is against making *The Library,* presumably because of reservations about the box office potential of a pic dealing with a hot issue. Harry Cohn, Columbia president, though, is high on the project. For one thing, he's been impressed with Taradash's and Blaustein's willingness to produce the film, with Taradash also to direct, without salary or guarantee of any payoff. It's to be a straight 50-50 profits plus split between Columbia and the Phoenix unit."

In 1952 Taradash and Moll had first sold the script to Stanley Kramer, who tested Mary Pickford and Irene Dunne for the role of Alicia Hull. But the film was postponed.

Burnett Guffey was signed as cinematographer, film editor William A. Lyon was given the script, and Kim Hunter was cast in the important role of the librarian's assistant—all Academy Award winners.

Taradash and Blaustein selected the community of Santa Rosa, California, 400 miles north of Los Angeles, as the site for the filming, to start in August, 1955. Also in the cast were Brian Keith, Paul Kelly, Joe Mantell, and Sallie Brophy.

Blaustein said in a press release, "I don't expect the picture to be met with acclaim from all quarters—but on the other hand we think people are willing to listen to this side of the argument today. Nobody has objected so far—and in Santa Rosa, the nonregional-looking town we picked for our location, everyone was understandingly cooperative. They even let us remove the palm trees from in front of their library. Turned out they wanted 'em out anyway!"

Upon returning to Hollywood, the cast and crew were assembled for a night scene that involved the burning of the library, which had been recreated, stone by stone and ivy leaf by ivy leaf, on the Columbia Ranch in Burbank. Taking a cue from David O. Selznick, who had placed paid advertisements in local papers when he "burned Atlanta" on the Goldwyn lot for *Gone with the Wind,* the studio took out announcements in the press stating that the nearby citizenry should not be alarmed to see flames shooting from the lot, that the fire was carefully controlled for *Storm Center*—new title for *The Library.*

Davis went back to Maine to spend a few weeks setting Witch Way in order before returning to California with Merrill and the children for Thanksgiving. She had been offered the Thelma Ritter role in the movie version of Paddy Chayefsky's hit television comedy-drama *The Catered Affair,* which Sam Zimbalist was preparing from a Gore Vidal script at MGM. The Merrills rented Fay Bainter's Malibu home to cut down traveling time to the Culver City studio, which had tagged a ten-day shooting schedule on the picture.

Davis regretted that she did not continue to produce films at Warners after *A Stolen Life.* With other stars arranging attractive packages, the Merrills, along with agent William Shiffrin, purchased *The Angel Manager* by John Beradino and Sheldon E. Bonnewell and signed Catherine Turney to fashion the screenplay, which dealt with a nun who manages a baseball team. The picture, costarring Merrill, would be shot in Maine. Banks, however, were hesitant about loaning money for the project.

Another abortive enterprise was *The Stubborn Wood,* Robert Bassing's screenplay, based on a novel by Emily Harvin, which detailed the author's experiences in an insane asylum. Paul Henreid, set to direct, and Davis purchased the property. A tentative deal was made for a United Artists release, but, again, the project was stymied because of tight funds.

THE HOUSEWIFE FROM THE BRONX

You're going to have a wedding whether you like it or not!

BETTE DAVIS AS AGGIE HURLEY
IN *The Catered Affair*

A director known for realism, Richard Brooks was signed for *The Catered Affair,* along with cinematographer John Alton. An unusual musical score was composed by Andre Previn. In the cast were Debbie Reynolds in her first straight acting role, Ernest Borgnine, and Barry Fitzgerald, in his last acting job before he died. Rod Taylor and Dorothy Stickney supported.

Davis wore a matronly wig by Sidney Guilaroff, and Brooks purchased clothing for the female stars from the racks of a local department store. *[Without Sam Zimbalist this film would never have been made the way we made it. After the first day of shooting I was told to change my appearance; no star in a leading role should look like this. Sam and I fought the good fight with the help of Richard Brooks. Aggie Hurley should look the way I did.* The Catered Affair *will always be one of my proudest efforts as an actress. In England, under the title of* Wedding Breakfast, *I received eulogies for my performance in this film.]*

On February 8, 1956, a remade *Phone Call from a Stranger,* now called *Crackup*, was presented on the "Twentieth Century-Fox Hour" on television, listing Davis as "The Queen of Hollywood in Her Dramatic TV Debut!" Actually writer Peter Packer and producer Jules Bricken lifted out the old Davis scenes from *Phone Call from a Stranger* and filmed new scenes with Gary Merrill, now an engineer instead of a lawyer, with new players Barbara Ruick, Virginia Grey, and others—with Jesse White as Eddie Hoke, Davis's husband. Integrated footage was well done; however, as Dave Kaufman in *Daily Variety* mentioned the next day, "Gary Merrill is probably the only TV actor who ever finished a picture four years younger, and it shows. Quality of the old and new film is noticeably different." Davis's performance as the cripple was favorably mentioned.

Butternut, which had been on the market for some time, was finally sold. She had owned the property for seventeen years, during the greatest period of her international fame. Now that she had a home on Cape Elizabeth Butternut was no longer needed.

The preview of *The Catered Affair* took place at the Fox Beverly Theatre, Beverly Hills, California, on April 20, 1956, to good reviews.

Newsweek wrote, "The film's most revealing scene, however, is the climax of a relationship that should have been the major concern of Chayefsky's drama. Left alone in their railroad flat to face the remaining years together, Pa Hurley and his wife are drawn close in companionship for the first time in their inarticulate lives. . . . Mrs. Hurley is a courageous change of pace for Bette Davis and she plays the nagging, middle-class housewife with an understanding that includes a reasonable facsimile of a Bronx accent.''

Wanda Hale in *The New York Daily News* on October 21 said, ''God love her, in a part that only an actress sure of herself would attempt, Miss Davis makes us believe that she is Mrs. Tom Hurley of The Bronx.'' *[Without doubt one of the most against-type characters I ever attempted. When I saw the finished film, I believed myself as Mrs. Tom Hurley. Thank you, Wanda Hale, for agreeing with me. This film was another example of a studio spending no money on an advertising campaign. Metro was obviously ashamed of* The Catered Affair.*]*

The ads for the picture *again* used a portrait of Davis in *All about Eve.* The New York advertising ads featured a shot of Debbie Reynolds in her slip, sitting on the edge of a bed, with the tagline, ''The story of a girl who wanted to lead her own life.'' The full-page ads in the fan books showed a full shot of Ernest Borgnine, sitting on a chair with his arms braced against the back, with the legend, ''THE ACADEMY AWARD-WINNING TEAM DOES IT AGAIN . . . The star and author of famed 'Marty'—Ernest Borgnine and Paddy Chayefsky—with new honors in this wonderful story.''

Storm Center was scheduled to be shown to the press on July 11, 1956. Award-winning artist Saul Bass, who had made a name for himself with the startling and inventive campaign for *The Man with the Golden Arm* the year before, was signed in the same capacity for *Storm Center.* For the main title and the ads he used the background of pages of a burning book with the face of Kevin Coughlin, the child who sets fire to the library, superimposed. The ads carried only one legend: ''What book did they make her burn?''

The controversial columnist Drew Pearson filmed a special trailer with Davis. In addition to narrating film clips he read an excerpt from President Eisenhower's famous ''book-burning'' letter to the American Library Association in July, 1953.

The Catholic Legion of Decency placed the film in a ''special category,'' calling it ''propagandistic'' and stating that ''its specious arguments tend seriously to be misleading and misrepresentative.''

In a rare move the Motion Picture Association of America issued a brochure plugging the picture, accompanied by a letter of introduction from Arthur H. DeBra, head of the community relations department, who said, "You may not agree with its conclusions, but you can't afford to miss this intriguing and entertaining photoplay, which has something important to say." The material also contained a center spread keynoted by President Eisenhower's "don't join the book burners" exhortation during his famed Dartmouth College address in the days when Senator Joe McCarthy still rode high.

Davis and Julian Blaustein flew to Philadelphia for the world premiere of *Storm Center* at the Midtown Theatre on July 31, and then flew to Washington, D.C., to attend the opening at the Playhouse Theatre.

The Hollywood Citizen News on September 24 said of the film, "Bette Davis is an extraordinary actress, as everyone knows, and, if *Storm Center,* the new tenant at the Four Star Theatre, has anything recommendable about it—her name is Miss D. Even Bette is hard pressed to make her role convincing—or even believable— in this film, which runs close to one hour and a half [and] seems interminably longer." *[I was not overjoyed with the finished film* Storm Center. *I had far higher hopes for it. The basic lack was the casting of the boy. He was not a warm, loving type of child. Because of this his relationship with the librarian was totally unemotional and, therefore, robbed the film of its most important factor. Their relationship, apart from the political aspect, was the nucleus of the script.]*

EDWARD R. MURROW AND A 110-FOOT TOWER

Returning to Witch Way and domesticity again, the Merrills were contracted by the popular television program "Person to Person," a show in which Edward R. Murrow, in New York, interviewed celebrities in their homes via a live telecast screen. Late in September, 1956, the New England Telephone Company set up microwave equipment on the estate. A huge 110-foot tower was built to beam the television signal to Portland for retransmission through the network. The morning of the telecast Witch Way was invaded by a CBS camera crew for setups and rehearsals. Davis told local *Portland Press Herald* reporters, "I'm terrified. It's so much harder to be yourself than to play a part." Merrill was calm, "I'm only nervous when I have to remember lines." On the air Davis wore a simple dark dress with pearls and showed her home to Murrow with an easy, gracious air. Any discomfort was not apparent; her "old-pro" background came magically to her assistance.

Said *Time* magazine, in its October 1 issue, "Oscar-winner Bette Davis couldn't resist some real-life emoting on Ed Murrow's *Person to Person* (CBS), on which she volunteered a friend's suggestion for her tombstone ("She did it the hard way"), while Gary Merrill suggested that, if Bette had not become an actress, she would have been president of Lord & Taylor. Best bit: Bette reading from Robert Frost's *Fire and Ice* ('I hold with those who favor fire')."

TV OR NOT TV?

The half-hour program that had brought Davis back to Hollywood, *With Malice Toward One,* was set for March 20, 1957, on the "GE Theatre," a highly rated show that featured as host old Warnerite (and future governor of California) Ronald Reagan. It was filmed at Revue, which later moved to Universal, and Davis found the studio had changed little in the twenty-seven years since she had first stepped on the lot as a contract player.

On March 22 Davis appeared in *For Better or Worse* on the "Schlitz Playhouse." The producer was Frank P. Rosenberg, at Revue. In March she also signed a contract to appear in *If You Knew Elizabeth* on "Playhouse 90," the hour-and-a-half CBS live television show. Merrill, who had made many live TV appearances before, was to play opposite her. The program, to air on April 11, was set for rehearsals on Friday, March 28. But Davis bowed out. Facing the live cameras in a complicated story with many sets and costume changes appeared too difficult a task. She was replaced by her old friend Anne Baxter, who, in turn, also bowed out. Claire Trevor then stepped into the breach.

Her third appearance occurred on April 24 when she portrayed Dolley Madison in *Footnote on a Doll* for the "Ford Theatre."

With her films being shown regularly on television, Davis found herself in the midst of a vogue. Bessie Little, editor of *Screen Stars,* reported that she had been receiving requests from teenagers to run stories and pictures of Davis and other screen stars whose pictures appeared on the tube. Miss Little cited this interest in detailing the error Hollywood made in selling its old films to television. She felt that these pictures would have done exceedingly well if they had been rerun in local neighborhood theaters. For a time it appeared that Davis would host a local TV show from Portland, relating anecdotes about her films on camera in conjunction with showings, but the deal fell through.

She also made her first pilot for a series, "Telephone Time"—the true-life story of a schoolteacher, Beatrice Enter, who in 1940 became stranded in a country schoolhouse during a Minnesota blizzard with her pupils. She kept the schoolroom warm as long as possible by burning papers, chairs, and desks and then, guided by a news broadcast, led her charges through the storm to meet a rescue party. Appropriately enough, the story was called *Stranded,* and the real life Mrs. Enter was on the sidelines during filming.

The "June Allyson Show" also starred Davis (with Leif Erickson) in *Dark Morning.* As the spinster teacher defending an eleven-year-old-girl suspected of murder, the characterization was good, but the plot was motheaten. The reviews were undistinguished.

WHISPERING STREETS, HENREID, AND HALLER

Various motion picture properties were offered, but none seemed quite right. Ketti Frings then submitted her masterfully written stage adaptation of Thomas Wolfe's autobiographical novel *Look Homeward, Angel.* Davis would portray the mother, Eliza Gant, with Anthony Perkins as the son Eugene, along with Arthur Hill, Rosemary Murphy, Florence Sundstrom, Hugh Griffith, and Bibi Osterwald.

Ready to begin rehearsals in the fall, Davis rented a house at 641 Bundy Drive, Los Angeles, for $675 per month on June 23, 1957. On moving day, she opened what she thought was a closet door. It was a basement. She fell down fourteen steps, breaking her back.

As fate would have it, B.D. was thrown from her horse a few days later, breaking her arm. Mother and daughter were both in hospital beds in separate rooms. After four months Davis moved to her sister's house in Laguna and stayed there until she was well enough to return to her home in Maine.

The producers of *Look Homeward, Angel* could not wait for her broken back to heal because of a commitment to open the play at the Ethel Barrymore Theatre in New York on November 28. The role of

Eliza Gant went to Jo Van Fleet, and the Pulitzer Prize went to Ketti Frings. The play, the most outstanding of the season, played 564 performances and did not close until April 4, 1959.

Early in 1958 Davis signed as hostess-narrator for a radio soap opera, "Whispering Streets," to debut March 31. She returned to Hollywood for the tapings. The format was unique—a new story each day, with a moral based on the episode to close the show. Gordon Hughes, the director, told Jon Bruce in the July 5 issue of *TV Radio Guide,* "Bette is so easy to work with, and it's a lot of fun to be with her. I have only one complaint—there's not enough time for the two of us to be together. She comes in once every two or three weeks and tapes her part of the shows. As a performer she is remarkable. She is always entirely prepared, knows all the stories and her narration, and never goofs. She does the whole job in about two and a half hours."

Her second appearance for the "GE Theatre," *The Cold Touch,* was filmed at Revue in January, 1958, to air on April 13. Jack Hellman in *Daily Variety* reported,

> Foreign intrigue, a popular subject for faraway places, requires diligent attention to keep the plot skeins from becoming tangled. This GE whizzer, planted in Hong Kong, turns up so many facets and confused identities that by the time Bette Davis backs off with gun in hand the looker must've started to recap what had passed through his tube, to separate one from the other and the whys and wherefores.
>
> . . . in her state of high excitement and frustration, Miss Davis may be exonerated of overacting and biting deep into the scenery . . . Don Weis, a seasoned hand at these TV short shots, makes it move with fast action and electrified acting.

[Without doubt one of the most unbelievable characters in as unbelievable a script.] The most harrowing sequence was when Davis, in extremely high heels, moves to freedom along the ledge of a building from a locked room.

Two additional TV outings were contracted, both mysteries and both filmed at Revue. The first, *Out There—Darkness,* an "Alfred Hitchcock Presents," was memorable because old friend and costar

Paul Henreid was hired to direct and Ernie Haller, whom she had not seen since *Beyond the Forest,* nine years previously, was to photograph. The result was disappointing.

The second foray, Daphne du Maurier's *Fraction of a Second* on "Suspicion," was even more disappointing. Dave Kaufman in *Daily Variety* felt the story was a masterpiece of confusion: "This 'Suspicion' spends close to sixty minutes telling events that never occurred—events apparently imagined by a woman in the 'fraction of a second' before she's killed by a load of lumber which falls on her. They call this a suspense series, but the only note of suspense arising here is why they ever made the picture."

Later in the year Davis and Merrill appeared in a proposed pilot for a series called "Paula." The segment, *Starmaker,* concerned a theatrical agent who has to dig up an old theater review to set a worried father straight about his son's dramatic debut. *[The night before Gary and I started the actual filming on "Paula," our living room at the Chateau Marmont, where we were staying, caught on fire. Had not someone in a nearby room seen the smoke billowing out our window, we would have been asphyxiated by morning. I often wondered why I was saved. My career at this point was practically nil—only TV offers, scripts of which were mostly inferior. My only desire for living were my children.]* The series was not picked up.

With several tapes of "Whispering Streets" under her belt, Davis left to see the children at Witch Way. On April 26, 1958, Louella Parsons headlined her column "Bette Davis Spain-Bound for *John Paul Jones*":

> Bette Davis had no more set foot in her home in Maine after weeks on the Coast than she started packing to be ready to sail May 6 on the S.S. *Independence* for Spain and *John Paul Jones.*
>
> The bid from producer Sam Bronston for her to play Catherine the Great—$50,000 in nonrecession money—was too much to turn down, although she recently signed a radio contract. She'll do the radio show aboard ship.
>
> Bette has just four days' work as Catherine. It's called a guest appearance, such as Mike Todd introduced in *80 Days.*

Samuel Bronston signed Robert Stack to portray the title role in

John Paul Jones and Charles Coburn to play Benjamin Franklin. Davis's scene, revolving around her appearance at court, was to be filmed in the Royal Palace at Versailles. A magnificent off-the-shoulder gown of black velvet trimmed with sable, worn with white gloves and a scarlet sash, was designed by Phyllis Dalton; a gold-blonde wig with a large sausage curl was fashioned by hair stylist Joan Smallwood. The picture was to be shot in the wide-screen Technirama in Technicolor. Erin O'Brien, Tom Brannum, Bruce Cabot, Marisa Pavan, and a long list of character actors embarked for Spain.

[B.D. and my sister Bobby went with me to Spain. After I finished playing Catherine the Great, we flew to Rome—my first trip to Italy. After a week in Rome we hired a car and spent a week driving to Milan. From Milan we flew to England for the film The Scapegoat, *starring Alec Guinness.]*

19

*Your preliminary information is incorrect. I saw the
deceased after the child did. I was walking around the
corridor toward my daughter-in-law's bedroom, the
child came out and called goodnight and went on upstairs
. . . So you need not trouble the child with your
questions.*

BETTE DAVIS AS THE DOWAGER COUNTESS DE
GUE IN *The Scapegoat*

The idea for *The Scapegoat,* according to Daphne du Maurier in an
article in *The Boston Globe* on August 2, 1959, began in the
following way:

In October, 1955, I went on a pilgrimage to La Sarthe,
that department of northwestern France whose capital, Le
Mans, was made famous half a century ago, because it
was from here that Wilbur Wright made his first controlled airplane flight in public. . . .

I found that I was beginning to think out a modern story
of a man who met his double and through trickery
accepted the challenge of leading his double's life. . . .

The Scapegoat took about six months to write, and,
even before it was finished, I knew that, if it should ever
be adapted to a motion picture, there was only one man
who could play my scapegoat. That man was Alec
Guinness. . . .

. . . Finally, after many vicissitudes, Alec and I

formed a partnership. He was to give his acting. I was to
give my story, and Sir Michael Balcon would produce the
film for us.

Irene Worth, Pamela Brown, and Annabel Bartlett were signed
as supporting actresses.

The budget was high, although the picture was filmed in black
and white. Davis was to portray the cigar-smoking, drug-addict
mother, with all scenes except one to be played in bed. She was
strong and commanding when her hunger for morphine was abated
and whining and crazed when in need. She was to receive costar
billing with Guinness, who was to star as both the schoolmaster and
the count via split screen.

During the first meeting with Guinness, perfectly groomed and
chicly dressed, she saw that he was apprehensive about her young
appearance—they were approximately the same age. Davis allayed
his fears: "I assure you, Mr. Guinness, that when I am properly
made up, I will look old enough to be your mother!"

Wardrobe consisted of several bed jackets, ruffled with lace,
trimmed with marabou feathers, or lavishly crocheted. For the
scene in which the mother comes downstairs to attend her daughter-
in-law's inquest, she wears almost an exact replica of an outfit from
The Little Foxes, complete with hat, bird, and veil. She sported a
disheveled, gray-almost-white wig and blotchy makeup.

FOR THE FIRST TIME IN HER CAREER—A WESTERN

Immediately upon returning to Hollywood after filming *The
Scapegoat,* she was approached by the producer of the TV series
"Wagon Train" to make a segment for that show, *The Ella
Lindstrom Story,* where she would portray a pioneer woman with
seven children, expecting an eighth when her husband dies. *[This
script was written for me by author and director Allen Miner—in
my opinion one of the most talented men through the years in
television. He later wrote another script for me,* The Elizabeth
McQueeny Story, *which we shot as a pilot for a series—I think my
third pilot. These scripts by Mr. Miner were, as regards my TV
appearances at this point, the only two I was proud of appearing in.
He also directed both of them. He was a joy to work with. Ward
Bond never gave a better performance than in* The Ella Lindstrom

Story. *I was so happy that Bond, who had for years played support-ing roles, became a star on "Wagon Train."]*

The kicker to the tale was that she discovers, instead of a baby, that she has a malignant growth. Knowing death is near, she prepares the children to carry on without her on the wagon train. This was the first time that Ward Bond and she had worked together, although they had known each other from her first days in Hollywood, when he lived next door in one of the DeMille cottages on Franklin Avenue. In those days Bond, home from a party in the early morning hours and having imbibed, often mistook the Davis house for his own and had to be shown personally to his own door.

Reminiscing on the western set, Bond treated her like the veteran star that she was. The segment gained good press space and general critical acclaim. Along with Ann Blyth, Virginia Mayo, and Bond she made her first magazine cover appearance in some years in *Look* on October 27, 1959. Ironically the foursome had all worked for Warner Bros. in the old days.

Out of the crop of stars under contract to the studio several had achieved success in nonacting careers. Ida Lupino and Paul Henreid had become directors; Gene Nelson, a choreographer-director; Mary Astor and Ruth Chatterton, writers; Dick Powell and Bonita Granville, TV producers; Marion Davies, a real estate tycooness; and Ronald Reagan, governor of California.

A TV DIET AND A "NEW FIGURE"

Louella Parsons reported in a Sunday supplement, "When I saw Bette last year, . . . I asked her what the secret was of her new vitality and beauty. She looked like a fashion plate in a pretty summer print dress and groomed to the *n*th degree." Her report continued,

> "You probably won't believe it," said Bette, "but one morning I watched a man named Jack La Lanne on TV who was teaching exercises and gymnastics. I tried to do some of them with him, and I was so stiff I couldn't move. But I decided to stick with it and follow him every morning, and I did it faithfully for three months.
> "I also started swimming and playing tennis, and soon felt like a different person," she added. "I had felt so

> miserable with my broken back, which had me in traction
> for six months, and this complicated by osteomyelitis was
> a very trying period in my life.''

In April, 1959, Norman Corwin proposed a tour of *The World of Carl Sandburg,* a collection of readings from the author's works. Since both Davis and Merrill were free of contracts, they accepted the offer, even though it meant a strenuous, back-breaking seventeen-week tour of one and two nighters in sixty-seven cities throughout the country. Armand Deutsch, producing with Judd Bernard, noted in an interview on August 14, 1959, in *Daily Variety* that ''some 30 percent of the stops are universities, and many of the others are sponsored by civic associations, chambers of commerce, and so on. . . . In staging it's along the lines of *Don Juan in Hell* and *John Brown's Body,* except there are more props.''

MCQUEENY 'N' JONES

When writer-director Allen Miner offered her the role of impresario Elizabeth McQueeny on ''Wagon Train,'' who, with her ''girls,'' would dance the cancan, Davis accepted with alacrity. The group of pioneer women on the train look askance at the suspicious brood, and to alleviate their misgivings Davis puts on a show. It was a good outing. The show had originally begun as another pilot, *Madame's Palace,* set in the 1800s in Las Vegas. By placing the story on ''Wagon Train,'' expenses would be pared and exposure guaranteed. The property was not picked up as a series.

The reviews on *John Paul Jones,* which was press previewed at Warner Bros. studios on June 2, 1959, were mixed, with most critics hailing Davis's brief appearance and the spectacular sea action but deriding the ponderous script. Bosley Crowther in *The New York Times* opined, on June 17, that the picture was a dismal comedown for Davis ''who once played good historical roles,'' but Abner Morison in *Films in Review* felt ''pleased to see Bette Davis in a . . . bit as Catherine the Great, expensively costumed amid tasteful decor.''

The press preview of *The Scapegoat* was held at MGM on July 16, 1959. Film critic Paul Rotha put forth an interesting theory in his review in *Films and Filming:*

After a series of wildy improbable and quite unconvincing incidents during which the plot wears more and more
threadbare, this hotchpotch finds its alleged solution first
by Barratt killing his double and then by his seeking
solace in the bosom of the dead man's mistress in her
stable. Every thread of the so-called plot is left tangled in
a way diabolically unfair to the audience, and we languish
in a state of helpless confusion. Seldom has an audience
been more cheated out of a climax. And why was it all set
in France anyway, when England would have done just as
well?

What really puzzles me is how by all that's sane in
British films—and that's precious little right now—how
did the highly intelligent Mr. Hamer; the best box office
name we've got, Sir Alec Guinness; that grand old-time-
used-to-be, Miss Davis; and all these other distinguished
people ever 'come to get mixed up in such an Anglo-
American piece of citizen-paste? What a grisly burning of
brilliant talents—including not only the admirable cast
but first-class art direction and photography as well?

Had this story, I wonder, originally some quality of
fantasy or even the macabre played amid strict reality,
such as made *Les Diaboliques* acceptable, and did in
some ghastly way the whole conception go awry without
anyone spotting it? Did someone—maybe at the
Hollywood end—get cold feet at the last moment and lay
on just about the most unnecessary and fatuous narration
(spoken by Guinness) in an effort to explain it all away? I
am convinced that none of these clever, expensive, and
intelligent people whose names are given above ever took
part in the film at all. They all used doubles.

*[There were many days during the filming when all of the women
in the cast could have wished doubles were doing their work. A
more unhappy set I have never worked on; and a duller film, when it
was finished, would be hard to find. A great deal of the footage in
which I had appeared had been eliminated. If you sneezed while
watching it, I had disappeared!]*

SANDBURG VIA AIR-CONDITIONED SEDAN

The Merrills were to play *The World of Carl Sandburg* in evening clothes. Orry-Kelly designed two evening gowns for Davis, one for each act. Corwin in an interview with San Francisco columnist Paine Knickerbocker, on April 3, 1960: "Davis was apprehensive about the stage. . . . But, as soon as we started working on our script, everything clicked." Knickerbocker continued, "Regarding his two stars, Corwin has found both extremely cooperative, in spite of the reputation Miss Davis has for being difficult. [Corwin added,] 'She accepted the idea of the show on faith. She's a fast study, and an eager worker, and Merrill looks rather like a young Sandburg, which is another advantage.' "

Two previews were scheduled for Merrill's alma mater, Bowdoin College in Brunswick, Maine. Guitarist-balladeer Clark Allen was added to provide appropriate folksongs. The show formally opened in Portland's State Theatre on October 12, 1959, to rave reviews. The production received front-page headlines when Carl Sandburg flew in for the opening and was met by Davis and Merrill. "The 'Face of America' Shines on Portland" was the caption to photos of the airport reception.

Davis told Radie Harris on November 3, 1959, in the *Hollywood Reporter,* "It's a joy to work for a management which only considers the best, not the cost. Deutsch has so set up our production that we never have to worry about new lights and mikes in each town. Our own equipment travels right along with us. Gary takes credit for the wonderful sound system. He recommended a young friend of his in Portland, who had no previous pro experience. Deutsch was willing to gamble on him. The result has been perfect."

During Florida performances of *The World of Carl Sandburg* Tennessee Williams came backstage one evening and spoke about a play he was writing called *The Night of the Iguana,* which was scheduled for Broadway in 1961. He asked Davis to read the play with the idea of doing the part of the gentle lady, Hannah Jelkes, from Nantucket, who has a ninety-two-year-old grandfather. The Williams play had begun as a short story in 1946 and then became a long one-act play, which was performed in Spoleto in 1959, and the expanded version was ready to try out in Miami.

After a long and fruitful tour *The World of Carl Sandburg* opened at the Huntington Hartford Theatre in Hollywood on March 1,

1960, to a sold-out house. The theater had many memories for Davis, since the building had been the setting for radio's "Lux Radio Theatre" for many years. She had given many memorable performances on that stage, but none as memorable as opening night.

Ruthie was in the front row. *[My mother Ruthie, who had cared so much and worked so hard to give me every opportunity financially for a career, was personally in the front row the night of the Sandburg opening in Hollywood. It was the first time in years that she witnessed her daughter once more as "a star." This meant everything to her, more to her than to me. I think she lived a few years longer being present that night and being a part of the enormous success of our show. In the dedication of my book* The Lonely Life *I say, "Ruthie, you will always be in the front row." She always has and always will be, since her death. Her belief in my potential and her guts to provide the financial means made it all possible.]*

Sandburg occupied an aisle seat until autograph hunters chased him backstage. In a curtain speech he said, "This is the moment of a lifetime for me tonight—the audience of my dreams come true. This is theater—anyone who says this is a recital, we're gonna kill them! It's the oldest form of theatrical performance." He turned to Davis, "I would salute you not only for your genius but for endurance." Davis smiled wryly, "One learns that in Hollywood!"—which brought down the house.

Sandburg said thoughtfully, "I have felt humble here tonight." Then Corwin joined him on stage and quipped, "Be happy, kid!"—setting off another wave of laughter and applause, and then the curtain closed. *[I had vowed all my professional life that I would never appear on a stage in Hollywood. The risks were too great. Hollywood, I knew well, was always secretly delighted at any failure of a fellow performer, plus my career had been in the doldrums for the past few years, a fact well known to each and every one in the celebrated opening night audience. But risk it I did. I was proud of the Sandburg show. It had had such a successful tour prior to the Hollywood opening that I really wanted "my town" to see it. What an evening it turned out to be! Gary and I relived that evening many times afterward.]*

The reviews were ecstatic. Patterson Green in *The Los Angeles Examiner* on March 3, 1960, reported, " 'I don't know what this is all about,' said a woman as she battled her way through the foyer crowd to get into the Huntington Hartford last Tuesday night, 'but I want to see HER.' ''

Leo Kovner in *The Hollywood Citizen News* said,

> While the contributions of Merrill and Allen were excellent, this was meant to be Miss Davis's evening, and Hollywood's biggest names turned out in full regalia to make it an event. Miss Davis lived up to the challenge magnificently and the eager—sometimes overeager— audience responded just this side of idolatry. If there were a carriage available, without doubt Miss Davis would have been drawn in triumph up Hollywood Blvd.
>
> Miss Davis deserved most of this applause, even if this particular audience came primed to pay her homage. Time has mellowed, if not quelled, her famed mannerisms.

[A reading is a total departure from an acting performance. You become the servant of the author—in this case, Carl Sandburg. The audience, which you play to in a reading, is one of the characters of the play. Norman Corwin, our director, gave us practically every gesture, every reading. So it was not a matter of time mellowing or quelling my "famed mannerisms"; it was a question of a new, to me, form of theater—a form I grew to love.] After being extended to a four-week run, the show went on to San Francisco to close the tour. Davis went back to Maine, and Merrill started filming *The Great Impostor* at Universal.

On Wednesday morning, May 4, 1960, the headlines in *The Los Angeles Times* proclaimed: ''Bette Davis Asks Divorce.'' The article reported, ''Bette Davis, the Academy Award-winning screen actress, has filed a suit for divorce against her fourth husband, actor Gary Merrill, it was disclosed here yesterday.'' The complaint had been filed in the Superior Court of Cumberland, Maine. The document charged cruelty and requested custody and support for their three children, Barbara, 13, Margot, 10, and Michael, 9.

On Friday, June 17, Davis filed suit in Superior Court, Los Angeles, for injuries suffered in the fall at the Bundy Drive house three years before. The Superior Court jury of eight women and four men awarded her $65,700 in damages for the fall. According to *The Los Angeles Examiner,* ''The Oscar-winning film star burst into tears as the jury's verdict favoring her was read in the courtroom of Superior Court Judge Carlos M. Teran.'' *[The basic reason I sued the owners of the Bundy Drive house and the real estate office that rented it to me was that they did not warn me of the door leading to a cellar. The suit was not for money. It hopefully would establish new law. No such black pit with no lights and no lock or warning on a door leading to such danger would ever be legal again. No doubt about it, I could have been killed in this fall. We won against the owners of the house and the real estate company. Magania, the great personal injury trial lawyer, handled my case brilliantly. I was indeed fortunate to have him. The damages of $65,700 were but a fraction of the salaries I had lost due to the accident.]*

Davis leased a town house in New York on East Seventy-eighth Street near Central Park and prepared for the opening of *The World of Carl Sandburg* on Broadway. *[Barry Sullivan had taken Merrill's place for the southern tour the following year. Leif Erickson replaced Barry on the road and was my costar when we opened in New York.]*

Opening September 14, 1960, at the Henry Miller Theatre, N.Y., there were three affirmative reviews (Walter Kerr, *Herald Tribune;* John McClain, *Journal American;* Howard Taubman, *Times),* two yes-no (John Chapman, *Daily News;* Richard Watts, Jr., *Post),* and two negative (William Hawkins, *World Telegram;* Robert Coleman, *Daily Mirror). The World of Carl Sandburg* took in $14,300 for the first five performances, but the box office dwindled thereafter. Four weeks later the closing was posted. Davis's personal notices were glowing, and Erickson was well received, but the public was apathetic. Davis was crushed. *[Because we were going to be divorced, it was my decision to replace Merrill on the second six months of the tour, which included the opening in New York. I was proven wrong—Gary, with his beautiful voice and his enormous resemblance to Sandburg, plus the fact we were husband and wife, which the audience enjoyed— gave the Sandburg show something that, through no fault of Barry's or Leif's, it never had again. I feel that, had Gary opened in New York, we would have been a success.]*

The years of inactivity in Maine and the expenses that being a star always entail, plus family obligations, even though she lived simply, had depleted the bank account. Many years had passed since she had earned big money. Even in 1946, when she was the highest-paid woman in the United States, a large chunk went for income taxes. In financial straits, she signed a deal with Putnam to write her autobiography, *The Lonely Life. [Being so sure the Sandburg show would have a long run, I had rented the Seventy-eighth Street house for a year and had put the children in schools. I thought it unfair to them to change schools in the middle of the year. The offer to write a book, with the cash advance, was a lifesaver at that point, financially.]*

MADAME LA GIMP, THE SENILE CINDERELLA

She's a lovely girl, isn't she, judge? . . . Suppose the count calls off the wedding? She'll hate me . . . She'll want to know who her father is. What am I going to tell her—that I never was married?

BETTE DAVIS AS
MRS. E. WORTHINGTON MANVILLE (APPLE ANNIE)
IN *Pocketful of Miracles*

Director-producer Frank Capra was remaking *Lady for a Day,* based on Damon Runyon's *Madame la Gimp,* which he had at first filmed with May Robson for Columbia in 1933. He purchased the rights for $225,000 and set up offices on the Paramount lot, assigning the original Robert Riskin screenplay to Harry Tugend to update with Hal Kanter. Jimmy Cannon, a New York sports writer who was familiar with Broadway argot, was later signed to polish and rewrite. The film was made as a co-venture between Capra Productions and Glenn Ford's Newton Productions, with a new company christened Franton. This was the only way that Capra could get the property produced. Helen Hayes, who had originally consented to play Apple Annie, turned the part down because of a State Department tour. When the film was postponed, associate producer Joseph Sistrom suggested Davis for the role, and Capra agreed that she could play Apple Annie.

When Davis arrived on the coast, the cast included Hope Lange, Arthur O'Connell, Peter Falk, Thomas Mitchell, Edward Everett Horton, Mickey Shaughnessy, David Brian, Sheldon Leonard, Ann-Margret, and a host of some of the most respected character actors in Hollywood.

Robert Bronner was signed as cinematographer to shoot in Panavision and Eastman color. Edith Head designed three elegant and sweeping gowns for Davis to wear in the latter part of the film, when she is transformed from the scurrilous Apple Annie into the proud Mrs. E. Worthington Manville.

The picture was fraught with difficulties. Sheilah Graham noted in her May 15, 1961, column, "You could have heard a pin drop when Hope Lange on the set . . . asked to have the dressing room next to Glenn Ford's—because the lady in that room was Bette Davis!" *[Dear Miss Graham: Glenn Ford asked the assistant director to ask me to move—to say he was embarrassed is the understatement of the year. Mr. Ford wanted his girl, Hope, next to him.]* "Hope and Glenn have been 'going together,' as you probably know. But to push the tempestuous Bette from her rightful place! Well, every one expected the studio to cave in." *[Ha! Ha!]*

Graham continued, "Instead Miss Davis said, 'You can put my dressing room at the end of the row if you like; I couldn't care less." *[I said quietly and not tempestuously, "Give me any dressing room you choose—dressing rooms have never been responsible for the success of a film." He was a grateful assistant director at this reaction.]* "Then she added, 'This sort of thing belongs to a Hollywood that's dead and buried.' " *[Naturally the studio gave me the dressing room next to Mr. Ford. I was his costar. It should have been this way. The request for my removal from the "second" dressing room only showed Mr. Ford's bad manners and lack of professionalism.]*

Capra, stricken with blinding headaches, which he hid from the company and crew, was not helped when Ford gave out an interview to the effect that he felt so grateful to Davis for giving him a break in *A Stolen Life,* that he was returning the favor with the part of Apple Annie. Davis was furious and has never forgiven him for this condescending remark. *[When Frank offered me the costarring role at a big salary, I accepted it not too enthusiastically. Apple Annie lacked reality to me. I had to find a way to make it real and yet fit myself into the fairy tale spirit of the picture. It was like walking a tightrope.]*

During the last part of the picture Ruthie died, a terrifying experience for Davis. After finishing the film, Davis flew back to her family in New York.

Rehearsals for *The Night of the Iguana* were about to begin. Having turned down the role of Hannah Jelkes, a part she found dull, she asked Williams if she could play Maxine Faulk, the lusty owner of the Mexican hotel where the action of the play took place,

Elizabeth I (Bette Davis) greets Sir Walter Raleigh (Richard Todd) in *The Virgin Queen*, 1955, shot in Cinemascope and color. (*Photograph by Twentieth Century-Fox.*)

Ruthie visits Davis on the set of *The Virgin Queen* in 1955. (*Photograph by Twentieth Century-Fox.*)

On December 7, 1954, Davis and Merrill are shown rehearsing for a home-town production for charity, *The Junior League Follies*, in Portland, Me. Davis shortly left for Hollywood to star in *The Virgin Queen*. (*Photograph by Associated Press*.)

Aggie Hurley (Bette Davis) and husband Tom Hurley (Ernest Borgnine) discuss the marriage of their daughter Jane (Debbie Reynolds) in *The Catered Affair*, 1956. Role is Davis's favorite. (*Photograph by MGM*.)

Bette Davis as Empress Catherine of Russia in *John Paul Jones*, 1959. (*Photo by Warner Bros.*)

Alec Guinness as the Count de Gue and Bette Davis as the dowager Countess on the set of "The Scapegoat," 1958. (*Photograph by Metro-Goldwyn Studios.*)

"The 'Face of America' Shines on Portland," headlined *The Press Herald* on October 12, 1959, when Bette Davis and Gary Merrill met Carl Sandburg at the airport. The poet flew up to Maine to attend the premiere of *The World of Carl Sandburg*. (*Photograph from the collection of Bette Davis.*)

A gin-soaked Apple Annie (Bette Davis) writes to her daughter Louise (Ann-Margret), fresh out of a Spanish convent, in *Pocketful of Miracles*, 1961. (*Photograph by United Artists.*)

Apple Annie, turned by beauticians into the dowager Mrs. E. Worthington Manville, is greeted by the governor of New York (David Brian) in *Pocketful of Miracles*. (*Photograph by United Artists.*)

Bette Davis with Daniele Aubry on the set of the proposed pilot, *Madam's Palace,* which debuted on Wagon Train. Davis danced the Can-Can with a bevy of beautiful young girls. (*Photograph by Herb Ball, NBC.*)

and he agreed. Maxine was the third part in the play—Davis found the woman fascinating.

The company began rehearsing in New York in October, 1961. Seymour Peck, from *The New York Times Magazine,* dropped by one afternoon and watched peformers Davis; Margaret Leighton, playing Hannah Jelkes; Alan Webb as Nonno, the ninety-two-year-old grandfather; Patrick O'Neal as the Reverend T. Lawrence Shannon; Patricia Roe as Miss Judith Fellowes; and Christopher Jones and James Farentino as the beach boys; going through their paces, scripts in hand, under the guidance of director Frank Corsaro and author Tennessee Williams. "Bette Davis," Peck wrote in his October 29, 1961, piece, "regards her part as 'basically an animal, a good healthy animal.' She wants one thing, guys, and this guy in particular. Working on Maxine, Miss Davis does not find her 'ten-sided, like most Williams characters.' She's fairly direct, down-to-earth, uncomplicated."

The production opened November 21 at the Blackstone Theatre in Chicago for a twenty-eight-day run. The play was going through agonizing changes, and business around the holidays was not good—houses through the week were half empty. It was a painful time of trial and error. One of the first things that particularly bothered the cast about the physical production was the raked stage, since they were used to rehearsing on a flat, conventional stage. The curtains remained open throughout the production, the false-bottom stage was higher downstage than upstage, and the floor timbers of the Costa Verde Hotel jutted out over the orchestra pit.

Davis had a great deal of "business" with a tea cart, which she had to maneuver casually, time her lines and action, and take care that every performance the cart did not career into the audience. Also the raked stage caused imbalance, and Davis thanked her moccasins, which she wore for the character Maxine, for never falling on her face in front of the audience.

Time magazine in its December 8, 1961, issue dealt with the Chicago run. Entitled "Gobbledygook," the piece ran, "A big, ugly, edible lizard called the iguana is, in Mexico, more or less what Thanksgiving turkey is in the U.S. Mexicans catch iguanas, fatten them up, and serve them on festive occasions . . . from all indications last week, despite impressive performances from Margaret Leighton and Bette Davis, it is indeed a massive turkey."

[Mr. Williams had never had a critics' failure in Chicago. This was where his beautiful The Glass Menagerie *won him fame and*

fortune when it was tried out there many years before. We were all heartbroken for him, and the cast was discouraged for the future success of the play once it opened in New York.]

Meanwhile, the sneak previews for *Pocketful of Miracles* were so excellent that United Artists decided that a big push could launch one of the biggest money-makers in history. The film was a natural for the holiday trade. On December 18 the film opened in 650 theaters throughout the country in an unprecedented mass release. The ads were spectacular, showing Ford, Davis, and Lange with the tagline "YOU HAVE TO SEE IT TO BELOVE IT! Frank Capra's mob is taking over the town . . . lock . . . stock and barrels of laughter! Meet the barons of Broadway and their babes—and the funniest plot that ever copped your heart." The mass release did not bring the customers in to see the picture. Capra felt the film should have been booked into smaller theatres where word-of-mouth would have increased attendance.

The reviews were extraordinary. James Powers in the November 1, 1961, edition of *The Hollywood Reporter* wrote that it was "a Christmas sockful of joy: funny, sentimental, romantic. A gay and gaudy Yule attraction . . . But it is Bette Davis, frightfully frumpish as the apple-seller, but regal as a duchess in her metamorphosis, who walks—or stalks—off with the picture. Miss Davis always gloried in these changeling roles, and she makes this part one of the screen's most memorable characterizations. She is a street brawler, a genuine lady for her day, but essentially she is still and always a woman."

TENNESSEE WILLIAMS STRIKES AGAIN

The New York critics liked *The Night of the Iguana*. On December 29, 1961, Walter Kerr in *The New York Times* reported, "Nor is Miss Davis's role altogether substantial. Still, in the coarse and blowzy effrontery of her overpainted presence, in the moral indifference of her flat-footed walk, in the arrogance with which this slattern raises a cocoanut shell as though it constituted the full glory of the future, there is some tattered and forlorn splendor." John McClain in *The New York Journal American* wrote, "Bette Davis, displaying an unbuttoned shirt, a shock of flame-colored hair, and the most raucously derisive laugh this side of a fish wharf, is marvelously brash and beguiling."

Radie Harris, who had indicated in her column that Davis was dissatisfied with some aspects of the play, ran a long interview in her column in *The Hollywood Reporter:* ''Shelley Winters will replace Bette Davis in *The Night of the Iguana* when Bette leaves the cast starting April 4 (when she has an 'out' vacation clause in her contract), instead of waiting until the end of June, as she had originally planned. Bette has been none too happy with her Tennessee Williams assignment because of her dissatisfaction with leading man Patrick O'Neal, and, since Williams IS satisfied, and so is Maggie Leighton, Bette has decided not to cope with the situation any longer.''

Davis told Louis Calta in the March 15, 1962, edition of *The New York Times,* ''I feel that I have done it long enough for my book. . . . I don't want to go on for another six months. I'm going to rest and walk in the country for about a hundred miles a day.''

20

I wonder if you can guess who I am? . . . I'm Baby Jane Hudson. I'm going to revive my act exactly the way I used to do it. Of course, some of the music will have to be brought up to date. . . . And you know, they're desperate for new acts, television, Las Vegas and the clubs. Well, there's a lot of people who remember me, lots of 'em!

BETTE DAVIS AS BABY JANE
IN *What Ever Happened to Baby Jane?*

Before leaving the cast of *The Night of the Iguana,* Davis had been approached by producer-director Robert Aldrich about playing the title role in *What Ever Happened to Baby Jane?* In a piece for *The New York Times* published on November 4, 1962, Aldrich gave a candid description of the origins of the film:

While in the throes of directing a rather vast spectacular, *Sodom and Gomorrah,* in Europe, I received from Miss Hersey [a secretary] a copy of *What Ever Happened to Baby Jane?* a suspense novel by Henry Farrell, the story of two sisters, both former film stars, living together and hating one another in an old Hollywood mansion. With it was a letter saying Miss Hersey's present employer had taken an option, and that she felt it would make a great picture. The price for the movie rights was $10,000.

. . .After reading the book and agreeing wholeheartedly with Miss Hersey, I sent the novel to Joan Crawford, who for several years had urged me to find a suitable story to team her and Bette Davis.

Joan's prompt and enthusiastic response only heightened the suspense of waiting while Miss Hersey's employer made up his mind. . . . She cabled me that he had let his option lapse and the property was available, but no longer at the $10,000 figure. Inevitably during the forty-day period speculators had learned of interest in *Baby Jane* as a film possibility and had moved to cut themselves in on the action. The price was now $61,000.

Since I was working . . . with Joe Levine, a money man with a gambling instinct . . . he and I bought the film rights . . . and hired Lukas Heller to write the script.

Shortly thereafter the Levine-Aldrich honeymoon terminated. . . . I decided to buy his interest in *Baby Jane*, but by this time the price was $85,000, which included Heller's screenplay.

My immediate problem was to get Bette Davis and Joan Crawford to make *Baby Jane* for what I could pay them, a figure far below their going salaries. From my rapidly narrowing slice of the pie I offered each actress a piece of the picture plus some salary. . . .

Four major companies declined even to read the script or scan the budget. . . . Three distributors read the script and looked at the budget and turned the project down. Two of these said they might be interested if I would agree to cast younger players. . . .

At this point a second lifesaver bailed me out of what loomed as a sinking proposition. Eliot Hyman of Seven Arts Productions read the script, studied the budget, and told me candidly, "I think it will make a fabulous movie, but I'm going to make very tough terms because it's a high-risk venture. But I feel that it's a picture that should be made by you and with Davis and Crawford."

The publicity from the signing of the contract was tremendous. There was much interest generated about the possibility of a "feud" between the two actresses. On July 19, 1962, J.L. Warner held a luncheon at Warner Bros. for the stars in the Trophy Room. This was the first time that Davis had been on the lot in fourteen years. Hazel Flynn reported in a July 20 article in *The Hollywood Citizen News* that Davis admitted J.L.'s courage was remarkable.

> She further stated that, while she had had many difficulties with Papa Jack, she felt he was the man who gave her her start and was responsible for her career, and that she would forever be grateful to him.
>
> Jack, in fine fettle, joyously accepted the tribute, which sounded sincere.
>
> Joan also spoke: "I can't exactly call you my father, Mr. Warner," she kidded, "because I have to give that credit to the late Louis B. Mayer, but you are my second father. . . ."
>
> Both actresses arrived on time and smiling for the press reception. . . . Joan wore a colorful print and had her auburn hair up in a sort of Oriental or Spanish bun. Bette was in black to set off her blonde locks, worn long. . . .
>
> I talked to Ernest Haller, the noted cinematographer. He had made fourteen movies with Bette Davis . . . He also had made several with Joan . . . It will be up to Haller to record the great performances both actresses will probably give. He admitted the whole thing may develop into a battle royal.

"Hollywood TNT" was the title that Murray Schumach tagged on his article in *The New York Times* on July 29. "According to Miss Crawford, during the three or four years when she and Miss Davis occupied adjoining dressing rooms at Warner Bros., they rarely held any conversation more personal or prolonged than 'Good Morning' or 'Good Night.' . . . Mr. Aldrich was aware of the dangerous possibilities of directing the stars. He must never favor one or the other."

"On the *Baby Jane* set," wrote Mike Connolly in the August 22, 1962, edition of *The Hollywood Reporter*, "one last quote on the feud: 'We wouldn't have one,' says Bette. 'A man and a woman, yes, and I can give you a list, but never two women—they'd be too clever for that.' "

Davis, after thoroughly studying the seriocomic aspects of Jane, decided to do her own makeup. She chose a dead-white pancake makeup, which she applied every morning, along with rimming her eyes with black kohl, painting her mouth into a slash, and adding, as the pièce de résistance, a beauty mark on her cheek. A blonde, Mary Pickford-type wig completed her appearance. *[I've always loved character parts. My joy in working was never just playing the heroine. It started with Mildred in* Of Human Bondage, *one of the first despicable heroines on the screen. I got the part only because no one else would play this bitch-heroine. Jane's appearance, I felt, was fascinating—and just exactly the way she would look. I felt Jane never washed her face, just added another layer of makeup each day.]*

Interiors and a few exteriors were filmed on the small Producers Studio lot on Melrose Avenue. Besides the house location in the Wilshire district, Western Costume Co., *The Hollywood Citizen News* office, a local bank, and a seedy apartment court were also utilized. The production could not afford process screen work, that is, the technique used when interior car shots are photographed with a screen in the rear of a break-away auto showing background flying by. Davis drove around Beverly Hills one whole day with Ernie Haller either sitting in the back seat of the car shooting over her shoulder or reclining on the front fender, photographing street scenes. A portion of Santa Monica beach was used for the ending, with Davis staying at the Holiday House Motel in Malibu.

Since B.D. at age three had appeared in *Payment on Demand* as a memento of her childhood, Davis asked that she be cast in the small role of a neighbor's daughter to document her maturity at fourteen.

Aldrich cast Julie Allred and Gina Gillespie, respectively, as the young Jane and the young Blanche in the 1923 prologue. The young Jane sings a maudlin song, "I've Written a Letter to Daddy," before an adoring crowd of vaudeville aficionados. The eerie song is later reprised by the elderly Jane in one of the most harrowing sequences in the film.

The long prologue establishing the relationship between the girls as children and then as grown-up stars, which took place before the main titles, is usually cut in the shortened TV version of the film.

When the film jumped to 1932, Aldrich chose scenes from *Parachute Jumper* and *Ex-Lady,* which were viewed by producers as current Baby Jane films too bad to release. For an important scene involving Blanche, who is watching herself on television in an old movie, he chose scenes from *Sadie McGee.*

Aldrich continued in his article in *The New York Times:* "We finished shooting on schedule on September 12. Exactly one month

Artists

MOTHER OF THREE - 10, 11 & 15 -
DIVORCÉE. AMERICAN. THIRTY
YEARS EXPERIENCE AS AN
ACTRESS IN MOTION PICTURES. MOBILE
STILL AND MORE AFFABLE THAN RUMOR
WOULD HAVE IT. WANTS STEADY EM-
PLOYMENT IN HOLLYWOOD. (HAS HAD
BROADWAY.)
Bette Davis, c/o Martin Baum, G.A.C.
REFERENCES UPON REQUEST.

later, we held our first sneak preview, at the State Theatre in Long Beach, California. That we were able to get the picture in shape in this incredibly short time is due to a group of dedicated craftsmen who performed above and beyond the call of duty—and almost beyond physical endurance—who worked virtually around the clock to meet our schedule.''

On September 21 all Hollywood—and consequently the world, because the story was picked up by the wire services—was shocked to open the daily trade papers and see the full-page ad on page 310.

[Actually the ad was tongue-in-cheek, but a deep dig as well. The ad was half playful and half serious. After all, I had left a hit play, had finished What Ever Happened to Baby Jane? *and my book* The Lonely Life *was just out, so my career was not in jeopardy. If I was truly unemployed, I could never have taken the advertisement. But I wanted Hollywood and the money men who finance pictures to know that, unless they gave me a chance in good films, how could I be box office again?]*

On election day, November 6, Davis began her first personal appearance with a film since *Storm Center,* turning up at seventeen New York theaters in three days for the multiple showings of *What Ever Happened to Baby Jane?* Joseph Morgenstern reported in the November 11, 1962, edition of the *Herald Tribune,*

> She ranged as far as White Plains and as wide as Astoria. She subjected herself, not merely willingly but gleefully, to a sightseeing tour of New York by day and night, on which she saw the same sights seventeen times; movie palaces in various states of decayed splendor suddenly came alive again with throngs of fans who had paid to see a fabled chatelaine in the flesh.
>
> "It is awesome," Miss Davis said at midtour, "the interest in Hollywood. . . . The tour is good for the picture, and important to me because people get a terrific surprise to find that I'm not ninety, despite the fact that I've been around for a thousand years."
>
> . . . She gave the audience advice on how to imitate her. "Puff the cigarette like mad, roll the left elbow like mad, and say Petah," a Davisism invented by Arthur Blake in his imitation of her.

In another account of the tour Vincent Canby in *Weekly Variety,*

November 14, wrote, "One of the gimmicks at each theater was Miss Davis's announcement from the stage that a Baby Jane doll would be given to the patron who found 'the lucky envelope' under his seat. Her view from the stage of the ensuing rumpus in the auditorium always delighted her. 'It's as if I had just shouted "bottoms up," ' she said, though at the more posh RKO 58th Street Theatre, she remembered, people started off by genteelly feeling around under their seats as if they just dropped a glove."

The reviews on *What Ever Happened to Baby Jane?* indicated favor at the wickets. Paul V. Beckley in *The New York Herald Tribune* on November 6, 1962, said, "If Miss Davis's portrait of an outrageous slattern with the mind of an infant has something of the force of a hurricane, Miss Crawford's performance as the crippled sister could be described as the eye of that hurricane. . . . Both women are seen in the isolated decay of two spirits left to dry on the desert by the receding flood of fame. 'I didn't forget to bring your breakfast because you didn't eat your din-din,' Miss Davis tells Miss Crawford. She then howls a witch's laugh that would frizzle the mane of a wild beast. It is the mingling of baby-talk and baby-mindedness with the behavior of an ingenious gauleiter that raises the hackles."

The Hollywood Reporter headline on page one read " 'Jane' Recoups Cost in 11 Days," followed by the subhead "First Film Shown under TOA's 'Hollywood Premiere' Plan Makes Hollywood History." The article said, *"What Ever Happened to Baby Jane?* made film history by amassing through the weekend $1,600,000 in film rental, putting the Warner-Seven Arts Association and Robert Aldrich picture into the profit column in less than two weeks. Negative cost was $825,000; the rest went for prints, advertising, and other expenses."

On December 5, 1962, Warner Bros. sent out the following press release: "Because of the success of *What Ever Happened to Baby Jane?* Jack L. Warner has announced plans for another film to star Bette Davis. The new property, titled *Dead Pigeon,* will be developed by writer Al Beich from an original story and will be produced for Warner Bros. by William H. Wright."

Meanwhile she was a hot property. Immediately after her tour of the theaters in New York, she appeared on Jack Paar's "Tonight Show," hoarse but game. Apologizing for her laryngitis, she promised that she would do another show for Paar when her voice returned. After Paar told of the fabulous success of the film, Davis croaked, "I must say we are gloating. When Aldrich tried to interest the studios in Joan Crawford and myself, the moguls said, 'We wouldn't give you a dime for those two old broads,' " whereupon the audience applauded wildly. *[I was given a message from Miss Crawford not to refer to her that way again. I didn't call her that—I was quoting the money men.]*

Jonathan Winters, also on the show, imitated Davis's hoarseness, and she turned to him and said, "Go to hell!"—which delighted the fans, but the show quickly switched to a commercial.

What Ever Happened to Baby Jane? would eventually gross in the neighborhood of nine million dollars.

THE LONELY LIFE

For some years, various publishers had hounded Davis about doing her autobiography. Finally, in the fall of 1960, a contract with Putnam was signed. Writer Sanford Doty was given the task of doing research and acting as collaborator. She named the book *The Lonely Life*.

Brooks Atkinson in his "Critic at Large" column in *The New York Times* on September 18, 1962, compared three books by contemporary female stars—Crawford, Davis, and De Havilland: "If Bette Davis and Joan Crawford come to blows during the promotion of their joint film *What Ever Happened to Baby Jane?*, it is now possible to make book on the probable winner, Bette Davis. Each of these movie queens has a good right cross and left hook, and both are formidable in-fighters. But Bette Davis is the more aggressive. She can take out an opponent with one punch." *[To my credit I have never indulged in physical punches, only verbal punches.]*

William K. Zinsser (who often encountered the passions of Bette Davis in his years as a movie critic) in *Saturday Review* wrote, "It has many of the ingredients of the films that Miss Davis played so indomitably on the screen—it is maudlin, intensely feminine, and often tedious in personal detail. It is also absolutely candid. Miss Davis blames herself more than anybody else, and her story comes to an ending that any scriptwriter for one of her movies, but nobody else, would envy: 'I have always said I would end up a lonely old woman on a hill.' " *[I haven't yet, but I still feel I will.]*

Time magazine said, "When Bette Davis first arrived in

Hollywood, she was (by her own account) a mousy, twenty-two-year-old virgin with knobby knees, a pelvic slouch, and cold blue bug eyes that radiated intelligence.'' *[A typical* Time *magazine account. This magazine was always anti-Hollywood. Twenty-two-year-old virgin—yes. Knobby knees—no. Cold blue bug eyes—ye gods! Mousy—never!]* The article continued,

> But in three overworked decades and some seventy over-wrought roles, Bette earned two Oscars, $3,000,000, and a reputation as the first U.S.born actress to make the movie moguls respect talent and independence in a star. In an age of camps she became the Compleat Vixen. But in this autobiography Bette can (and does) brag: ''I brought more people into theaters than all the sexpots put together.''
>
> With the ruefulness implicit in her title, but also with honest and bitchy bonhomie that seldom adorns such Sunset sagas, Bette Davis, now fifty-four, pictures herself as Mother Goddam, a tamable shrew who never found her Petruchio. . . .
>
> Today, living in California and Maine, Mother Goddam admits that she has been ''uncompromising, peppery, untractable, monomaniacal, tactless, volatile, and ofttimes disagreeable.'' In a line that only Bette Davis could deliver, on or off screen, she concludes, ''I suppose I'm larger than life.''

The Lonely Life in hardback went into three printings, had hefty sales as a paperback, and was serialized in the *Ladies Home Journal* and in newspapers all over the country.

THE SMALL TUBE—AGAIN, AND AGAIN!

On December 20, 1962, Davis appeared in glamorous makeup on the ''Andy Williams Show.'' She opened the show with ''Just Turn Me Loose on Broadway'' from *Two's Company,* joined her host and the New Christy Minstrels in a folk song from *Jezebel,* and then performed a rock-and-roll version of a new song entitled ''What Ever Happened to Baby Jane?''

She also signed to appear in a segment of ''The Virginian'' with Doug McClure, in which she played Della Miller, a bank teller not above blackmail. She would also portray a woman lawyer in the title role of *The Case of Constant Doyle* in the January 31, 1963, episode of "Perry Mason" when regular star Raymond Burr was scheduled to be hospitalized for minor surgery.

On January 7, 1963, *Newsweek* magazine in a piece entitled "Bette for Burr" said, "Miss Davis, who had made only four previous television shows, stepped into the 'Mason' breach without ever seeing a script." *[Four TV shows? Nearer forty!]* " 'That wasn't necessary,' she said last week as the film was being cut. 'It's a formula show, and I knew the formula.' The formula was flexible enough for writer Jackson Gillis to tailor the script specifically to Miss Davis. Every inch a lady lawyer, she wins her case by demonstrating that the murder victim's trench coat was buttoned by a woman (right over left), not by her male client."

The article continued, "Miss Davis had no trouble fitting in with the show's regulars. 'Just because they've been working together for a long time,' she said, 'doesn't mean they're enemies.' Still, the pace of the weekly show left her gasping. 'There aren't even any rehearsals,' she marveled. 'I have always thought this madness, but they really don't need them; in a series the formula is there. I might one day do a series myself.' " *[I have been trying to find a series ever since.]*

With her career in a new whirlwind of activity and money in the bank Davis contacted real estate agents. She had not owned property in Los Angeles since the Toluca Lake house, which she had sold after her divorce from Sherry, but now with her new success she began to think about establishing roots again in Hollywood. She found a lovely, New England-style house a few blocks from the Bel Air Hotel at 1100 Stone Canyon Road.

What Ever Happened to Baby Jane? placed Davis back among the box office stars. Her ten black years were over.

OSCAR NIGHT

Davis won an Academy Award nomination for *What Ever Happened to Baby Jane?* in a year when most of the nominees were in other parts of the world on various film projects. She sat backstage with Olivia De Havilland, who held her hand as the winners were announced. She told Joyce Haber in an interview in *The Los Angeles Times* of October 11, 1970: "I was positive I

would get it. So was everybody in town. I almost dropped dead
when I didn't win. I wanted to be the first actress to win three times,
but now it's been done (by Hepburn), so I may as well give up.''
Haber went on,

> She lost on *Jane* to Anne Bancroft, of *Miracle Worker*,
> whose performance she calls "brilliant." "But," she
> adds, "I have a theory that someone who's played a play
> on Broadway for three years and then puts it on the screen
> has a definite advantage. I think it's more difficult to start
> from scratch and create a character for a film."
>
> "And, of course," she said, "the fact that Miss
> Crawford got permission to accept for any of the other
> nominees was hysterical. Miss Crawford was being in-
> terviewed and photographed by the press, clutching Miss
> Bancroft's award. I was nominated, but she was receiv-
> ing the acclaim. It would have meant a million more
> dollars to our film if I had won. Joan was thrilled I
> hadn't.''

A trip with Robert Aldrich was scheduled for London from May 7
to May 10, 1963, to promote the picture, then they were to go to the
Cannes Film Festival on May 10, when *What Ever Happened to
Baby Jane?* was to be screened for competition. B.D. accompanied
her on this trip. *[I saw the film for the first time at Cannes.]* Aldrich
told *Cinema* magazine, "She, more than I, decided on her *Baby
Jane* makeup, that ugly chalky mask. I'd say that was 80 percent
Davis and 20 percent Aldrich."

After Cannes Davis appeared with Steve Allen on his television
show, where a parody of *What Ever Happened to Baby Jane?* was
staged by Allen, with Louis Nye in dirndl and curls as Jane, called
What Ever Happened to Baby Fink? Davis took the show with good
humor.

Meanwhile, J.L. reported that *Dead Pigeon* was ready to start
shooting. It was the story of murderous twin sisters, filmed once
before with Dolores Del Rio in Mexico, in 1946, as *La Otra*. After
sixteen years Bette Davis, who had affected her era much more than
her era had affected her, was returning to Warner Bros.

A *MACABRE* A STOLEN LIFE

Remember—remember, when we were children, you were the only one I really loved.
> BETTE DAVIS AS MARGARET DE LORCA
> IN *Dead Ringer*

Love? You never loved anyone but yourself.
> BETTE DAVIS AS EDITH PHILLIPS
> IN *Dead Ringer*

Robert Aldrich asked Davis to appear as a guest star in a western, *Four for Texas,* starring Frank Sinatra and Dean Martin, but J.L. rescheduled *Dead Pigeon,* now called *Dead Ringer* (or *Dead Image* in Britain), for August so a first-of-the-year release could be scheduled. Davis had been off the screen a year, and the studio wanted to take advantage of her hit comeback in *What Ever Happened to Baby Jane?* Aldrich released her from *Four for Texas.*

J.L. surrounded her with the same sort of plush production for *Dead Ringer* that she had enjoyed when under contract to the studio. The budget was set at $800,000—but with the studio overhead rose to $1.2 million, which included the split-screen work.

William H. Wright was the producer, and Paul Henreid the director. Karl Malden, Peter Lawford, Philip Carey, Jean Hagen, George Macready, Estelle Winwood, Cyril Delevanti, and others were cast in important roles. A young designer, Don Feld, was signed to do the clothes. Gene Hibbs was her makeup man, and Ernie Haller was her cameraman. It was his last assignment. Rupert Allen, Davis's press agent, had insisted a year or so before that she wear professional makeup for her appearances on TV talk shows. He introduced her to Gene Hibbs—famous for making older actresses look younger. *[Gene certainly made "this" older actress look younger—and still does. He was trained by Perc Westmore at Warner Bros. I first knew him there when he was a kid. He is a genius. He paints a face as if he were painting a portrait. As the years go by, he paints me more and more.]* He has been her makeup man ever since.

Interviews with magazine and newspaper reporters were set, and a documentary film, *The Unsinkable Bette Davis,* would be filmed during the actual shooting of the picture—a segment of

"Hollywood and the Stars." On September 4, 1963, Davis complained to newshawk Bob Thomas about Hollywood money-man problems, "Ralph Nelson wanted me for *Lilies of the Field*. He flew to New York to try to talk United Artists into it. No, they wouldn't go for it. I wasn't box office. *Baby Jane* was a freak. Haw!

"Oh, if they could only learn! It's still names that sell movies— names that have established a reputation with the public by past performances. Those are the ones who sell tickets, not the so-called names who are used in picture after picture even though they don't draw flies at the box office."

Henreid told interviewer Don Alpert in *The Los Angeles Times* about his relationship with Davis: "We stayed good friends over the years . . . We bought a book, but unfortunately it was impossible to finance a film on her name—or mine for that matter." Then he spoke about his craft:

> I believe you direct ahead. You don't direct when you come to the scene but a day or two before. This comes from my experience as an actor. It's terribly difficult for an actor to be confronted suddenly by a director. It's better that two people search out the possibilities rather than the director alone. . . . With Bette my ideas were complemented by ideas of hers—and, my God, we all know she has great ideas . . . I think a girl like Bette Davis or Katharine Hepburn, there should be a way to give them continuous employment. They may have a string of bad luck, but they remain excellent actors, and they prove it time and time again.

"I arrive on Sound Stage Eighteen at Warner Bros. Studios," recounted Harrison Carroll in the August 4, 1963, edition of *The Herald Examiner,* "just in time to see the Academy Award winner do the 'impossible.' She's going to kill her twin sister, portraying both the murderess and victim." He continues,

> They're about ready to shoot the murder scene in Bette's shabby apartment that is supposed to be above a bar that she owns. The slaying is the climax to twenty years of bitterness between sisters over a man they both loved.
>   Director Henreid explains to me that in order for Bette to kill and be killed, cameraman Ernest Haller is shooting

on a split-screen basis. Bette will commit the murder, and they'll shoot another take of her being murdered. Then the film will be processed as a single take.

Although the actress will be seen doing both on the screen, a double is required to establish the mood. The double is Connie Cezon, an actress who has impersonated Miss Davis on stage for years. The two look enough alike to be twin sisters.

I notice that all the furniture (bed, overstuffed chair, and dresser) is chained to the floor. Assistant director Lee White spots my observation and says, "We can't afford to take a chance of anything moving an inch because both takes have to match exactly."

Miss Davis's double takes her place in the overstuffed chair. Bette, wearing a bright red dressing gown, is standing by a doorway.

"Action," says director Henreid.

Bette moves over to the chair and sarcastically tosses a note (it's supposed to be a suicide note) in the double's lap.

"This is why I told you to come," Bette snaps and then briskly goes behind the chair. She removes a .32 caliber pistol from the dresser. While the other woman is reading the note, Bette places the pistol to her head and pulls the trigger.

"Cut!" calls director Henreid.

Quickly Bette goes into her dressing room to change into the costume of the other sister. She emerges less than five minutes later, wearing a black gown and hair arranged differently.

This will be the toughest part. The double will have to emulate, to the second, the movements of Bette in the previous shot in order for the split-screen process to work.

Director Henreid calls for the playback of the previous action.

The recording starts, as this time Bette is sitting in the chair, and Miss Cezon in the red robe approaches. Bette's dialogue on the playback is repeated, and so is the noise of the pistol being picked up.

Then comes the "click" of the gun—moments before

the double pulls the trigger. Naturally they'll do it over again until the timing is perfect. Bette is a little upset because the double was apprehensive about pushing the gun into her temple.

"Don't worry about hurting my head," Bette tells her. "Push it up hard. Don't hesitate. This is the way I want you to kill me."

. . . As I was leaving the set, I met Bette's double. She tells me that she once impersonated the actress in Ken Murray's Blackouts. [A review that ran for seven years at the El Capitan theater in Hollywood.]

"And once," she laughs, "I was asked by the New York Chamber of Commerce to meet Gary Merrill at the airport . . . Even he thought I was Bette Davis."

There were certain similarities to *A Stolen Life*. Margaret de Lorca's dead husband's dog, who has never warmed up to his mistress, is immediately taken with Edith. There is again the complication of a lover whom Edith does not know about, and of course the maid is suspicious. The latter role was played by Henreid's daughter Monika, whom Davis had known since childhood.

In the August 11, 1963, edition of *The Los Angeles Times* Art Seidenbaum wrote of Greystone, the location mansion, located in Beverly Hills: "In the mid-1920s, when the estate was built, the Doheny family owned 450 acres—where Trousdale Estates are now dug in. . . . The definite Miss Davis, out of costume and craven character, toured the house and proclaimed it indeed a landmark worth preserving."

Greystone eventually was given to the American Film Institute, an organization that preserves and restores films from the past and collects data on Hollywood history, among other worthwhile activities.

Henreid and Davis brought the film in four days under schedule. Warner Bros. insisted that the ending be changed. Originally Edith, as Margaret, goes up the stairs at Greystone, and the audience knows she will be apprehended for the murder of her sister. The new ending saw Edith picked up by the sergeant, which left nothing to the imagination of the audience.

Dead Ringer was previewed at the studio on January 14, 1964. The next day, *The Hollywood Reporter* said, "Miss Davis is careful not to overdo the roles. She is simple and credible in both parts without making sharp or superficial distinction between the characters.''

The New York Times on February 19, 1964, reported, ''Remember that celebrated Warner Bros. ad a few years ago that proudly claimed, 'Nobody's as good as Bette Davis when she's bad? Well, Bette Davis is back, and she is very, very bad. . . . Her mammoth creation of a pair of murderous twin sisters not only galvanizes this uncommonly silly little film, but it is great fun to watch.'' *[The original script of* Dead Ringer *was appallingly bad. Paul and I worked very hard to make it plausible at all. We did not completely succeed. We also were forced by Warner Bros. to change the ending we first filmed. The Warner ending was so ordinary. Paul Henreid did a beautiful job as director, especially the way he shot the split screen. It was even better thought out than the split screen in* A Stolen Life, *plus Connie Cezon was such an unbelievable double for me—we could actually use her in some of the scenes.]* ''The vehicle may be creaky on the plot track, but it has all the extra accoutrements the studio used to supply in her dramatic heyday. Paul Henreid, Miss Davis's most dependable cigarette lighter, is on hand this time as director, to guide her through a swanky array of sets, costumes, and men friends.''

While exploiting the film in various media, Davis *[an Aries]* appeared on the ''Johnny Carson Show'' with astrologist Sydney Omarr, a Leo. She revealed that she believed in astrology—however, not on a ''checking chart,'' day-to-day basis. She found the traits attributed to the various twelve signs of the zodiac very helpful in getting to know people by their signs.

EXISTENTIAL MOMISM

Many happy returns, ma' darlin' son! . . . Ya' know I could spend hours lookin' at plants 'n' flowers jest for the sheer joy of it. I was browght up that-a-way. In ma' grandfather's howse in New Orleans, the-ah were the most bea-u-ti-ful flowers . . .

BETTE DAVIS AS DINO'S MOTHER
IN *The Empty Canvas*

Davis was scheduled to do *Faster, Faster* in England for producer

Jack Deitz, from a screenplay by William Marchant, but the project never materialized. Soon afterward Joseph E. Levine and Carlo Ponti offered her the mother role in Damiano Damiani's screen version of Alberto Moravia's novel *La Noia (Boredom)*. Retitled *The Empty Canvas,* the film was shot in Rome with Horst Buchholz as the son.

The Empty Canvas, Time magazine reported tongue in cheek,

> is one of those "international" movie projects that have been dreamed up by the principals (during a transatlantic jet flight?) in a spirit of reckless unity. . . . Directed by Italy's Damiano Damiani, the film stars the U.S.'s durable Bette Davis, Germany's Horst Buchholz, and Belgium's Catherine Spaak. It is chiefly notable for the fun of watching Davis breast the New Wave plot with bitchy authority.
>
> In a blonde Dutch-boy bob, Bette looks like a degenerate Hans Brinker, and she plays a wealthy old skate who lays out plenty of silver to keep son Horst from nipping off. She offers him an Austin-Healey, a luxuriantly upholstered housemaid ("or find a nice married woman in your own world"), and cold cash. Horst uses the money to set himself up as a Bohemian artist in Rome, but he can't fill his life or his canvas because "there is nothing worth painting." Ultimately he finds redemption through fleshly enslavement to Catherine, an amoral part-time model and full-time hetaera who makes him feel love, jealousy, and suicidal impulses. This, of course, means that he is alive again.
>
> Stretched too far to be believable, *Canvas* is the kind of overdrawn foolishness that frequently proves diverting. Its existential blend of sex, symbolism, and comedy reaches a bizarre climax when Horst takes Catherine to a party at his mother's villa. In his mother's bedroom, crowning a marriage proposal to the girl whose favors can be had for the price of an espresso, he generously covers her nude body with some of mama's 10,000-lire banknotes. The door opens. In sails Bette, rococo-eyed, jewels a-jangle, a one-woman spectacular. She sees her darling at play, drops into her deep-fried Southern drawl, and issues what must be the last word in ultrapermissive

momism: "Please put the money you don't want back in the safe—I don't want the maid to find the room in this curious state."

[When I accepted the part in The Empty Canvas, I knew the script needed lots of work, especially the part I was to play. I was promised by the producer, Mr. Ponti, that more scenes for me would be added to the script. I arrived in Italy to find that nothing had been done to the script at all. In desperation I decided to use a southern accent to give some kind of flavor to this extremely dull woman. The blonde wig was also my idea, a further attempt to make her at least a noticeable character in the film. My costar, Horst Buchholz, was anything but easy to work with; in fact, he went out of his way to thwart me at every turn. No doubt about it, mincemeat was made of Mr. Moravia's classic book about an Italian family. I was certainly anything but an Italian mother. I actually never understood why I was asked to be in The Empty Canvas at all—an American star, I guess—I was little help with the part being so sketchily written.]

A FAMILY MARRIAGE AND A NEW MOVIE

Two main events were in the offing: the first personal, the second professional. B.D., now sixteen, had fallen in love with Jeremy Hyman, twenty-nine, whom she had met at the Cannes Film Festival. He was the nephew of Eliot Hyman, president of Seven Arts Productions—which in another of Davis's strange coincidences was the company that had put up the money for What Ever Happened to Baby Jane? Davis's friends raised eyebrows when her engagement to Hyman was announced, because she was "only sixteen." [It was the hardest thing I ever did, giving my permission for B.D. to marry Jeremy. I didn't want to lose her so early in her life. But one thing I believed, she was mature enough at sixteen to know her own mind. In many ways she was ninety. They have been married for ten years and have a son, Ashley, four years old. It is a marriage of mutual love and respect. What mother could hope for more for her daughter?]

The second event was that she was to start preproduction work on her mother role in Where Love Has Gone, from the explosive best-selling book by Harold Robbins, which Joseph E. Levine was producing for Paramount. For the second time in her career she would costar with another female—this time with Susan Hayward.

B.D.'s wedding took place at the Beverly Hills Episcopal Church on January 5, 1964. Just before Christmas Seven Arts transferred Hyman to the New York office. He was upset because the London flat had been newly furnished in preparation for his marriage. His mother-in-law-to-be commented, "Think nothing of it. B.D. has moved so many times in her life she can make a home anywhere in five minutes flat."

Louella Parsons, in her syndicated column on January 8, noted, "Leave it to Bette Davis not do do anything traditional at daughter B.D.'s wedding to Jeremy Hyman. Bette herself gave the bride away, which may give a turn to social arbiters." *[It is allowed in the Episcopal Church for the mother to give the bride away, if there is no father involved in the ceremony. B.D. had gone to court a year before and received permission to change her adopted name, Merrill, to her real father's name, Sherry. Actually it was a most proper, conventional wedding in every sense of the word. One paid a price being a star in Hollywood. How the press loved to make fun of us and our doings. In the case of B.D.'s wedding no member of the press was invited—that was the really unconventional thing I did—thus the Parsons article about the wedding. She was not invited.]*

Parsons went on, "And it was the unconventional mother of the bride who decided against using a familiar wedding march. Instead the beautiful B.D. met her bridegroom at the altar of the chapel of the Episcopal Church in Beverly Hills to the brand new strains of 'March Triumphant,' composed by Wilbur Chenowith. Even the floral decorations were different. There wasn't a satin ribbon nor a lily of the valley in sight. The floral arrangements were of pine boughs ('a New England touch!' according to Bette) and pink carnations. And when the bridal couple took off for New York and their honeymoon apartment on Monday, Bette did not toss any rice." *[As to tossing rice, when the Hymans left the wedding reception at the Beverly Wilshire Hotel, they were pelted with rice!!! Each guest also had a wrapped piece of wedding cake to take home—very conventional!]*

When Hyman toured the South in his new job to sell a package of old features to television stations, the first film he had to peddle was his new mother-in-law's *The Star*. *[Made at the time B.D. was four years old.]*

THE MOTHER SYNDROME, A CLEF

*It is unthinkable that such a thing could happen in the
Hayden family . . . I'm not unsympathetic to Dany, I love
her very much, but to have one hundred years of social
standing brought to earth in a—a—mass of—of
scattered feathers is horrifying. Thank heavens Valerie's
father is not alive to know about it.*

BETTE DAVIS AS MRS. GERALD HAYDEN
IN *Where Love Has Gone*

Time presented the premise for *Where Love Has Gone* in its
November 16, 1964, review, " 'Somewhere along the line the
world has lost all of its standards and all its taste,' says Mrs.
Hayden. But don't let her dictum fool you. Miss Davis is merely
throwing in the opening ball for a few innings of big-league smut
scraped together from the best-selling novel by Harold Robbins
(The Carpetbaggers). " The article continued,

> This time Robbins's story bears certain unmistakable
> but less than libelous resemblances to the real-life tragedy
> of 1958, in which Lana Turner's teenage daughter,
> Cheryl, killed her mother's lover. Producer Joseph E.
> Levine has dressed it up as what used to be called "a
> woman's picture," amidst sumptuous settings supposed-
> ly inhabited by the *haut monde* of San Francisco. Heroine
> Susan Hayward plays a world-famous "sculptor, pagan,
> alley-cat" who detests her domineering mother (Davis),
> betrays her war-hero husband, unwittingly shares a
> gigolo with her daughter, until one calamitous night when
> the kid picks up a chisel and . . .
> What follows is a custody battle, some gamey
> dialogue, and numerous untidy revelations, none of them
> very interesting. "With you," observes one of Susan's
> playmates, "art and sex go hand in hand." Maybe so, but
> in movies like *Where Love Has Gone* they efficiently
> cancel each other out.

Edward Dmytryk was signed as director of the John Michael
Hayes screenplay, with photography by Joseph MacDonald in
Technicolor and Techniscope. Davis's wardrobe was designed by

Edith Head. Wally Westmore contributed a white wig, very similar in style to Miss Moffat's in *The Corn is Green.* For a key scene where Hayward rips into a portrait of her mother with a sculptor's knife, Clem Hall, president of the California Water Color Society, painted an oil portrait of Davis, posed grandly in a white wig and evening gown.

CANVAS, LEVINE, AND A NUDE GIRL

After previewing *The Empty Canvas,* the Catholic Legion of Decency tendered a "C"—"Condemned"—classification, stating that the film was "a peep-show excursion with a special appeal to the prurient-minded," and the picture ran into advertising problems in Los Angeles when it opened on March 10, 1964. According to one trade paper report, headlined "Levine Lashes L.A. Downtown Papers for Censoring Ad,"

> "I'm shocked and amazed, Next time, if I have a picture with a bold theme, I'm certainly not going to open it here. This is something you'd expect from some small, provincial town, not Los Angeles."
>
> Shaking with anger, Joe Levine yesterday ripped into both *The Los Angeles Times* and *The Los Angeles Herald-Examiner* for refusing to run ads which had been prepared for his Embassy Productions' *The Empty Canvas.* "Had I known this was going to happen, I would have pulled the picture out," he thundered. "These ads have been taken all over the country. There is no reason for anybody to refuse them."
>
> One of the nixed ads included a rear view of Catherine Spaak posing, unclad, for an artist played by Horst Buchholz. In another the actress is "nude" on a bed covered by a blanket of bank notes. In yesterday morning's *Times* a slip had been superimposed on Miss Spaak. . . .
>
> But, rather than continue with the touched-up ads, Levine instead elected to take his case to the public. Announced ads running today in both the *Times* and *Herald-Examiner,* "Because of the character of its frank approach to modern life, this newspaper will not accept

advertising showing scenes from *The Empty Canvas.*"

Included in copy both papers refused to run were the following lines: "They cannot satisfy themselves or each other" and "In a villa . . . in a garret . . . in a car . . . in a park . . . on a couch . . . on a beach . . . they are six reasons why this is the most startling film that you will ever see."

Levine says that he is rerouting what coin he can of the film's $25,000 local advertising budget into other media and that he intends to spend a minimum of money in L.A. newspapers in the future in preference to TV and radio blurbing.

Meanwhile, back at Paramount, Michael Connors, Joey Heatherton, Jane Greer, DeForest Kelley, George Macready, Anne Seymour, and other players were signed for *Where Love Has Gone.* A title song was written by Sammy Cahn and James Van Heusen, which Jack Jones recorded to sing over the main credits—a vogue of the times.

Davis knew that the script was maudlin, but she was paid $125,000 for her few key scenes. *[I also accepted this part in order to be able to give B.D. the elegant wedding she wanted. Her veil was made for her in Marseilles. Her wedding dress was designed by Stella of I. Magnin's. Her trousseau came from I. Magnin's, as did her bridesmaids' and matron of honor's dresses. Her wedding reception was at the Beverly Wilshire Hotel, with an orchestra and all the trimmings. All this was extremely expensive, and I was thrilled to be able to give her the best of everything.]*

GHOULS RUSH IN . . .

Damn you! Damn you! Get off my property. . . . Get off my property or I'll shoot!

BETTE DAVIS AS CHARLOTTE HOLLIS
IN *Hush . . . Hush, Sweet Charlotte*

Robert Aldrich had been looking for a property that would reunite Davis with Joan Crawford. Writer Henry Farrell came up with an original story, *What Ever Happened to Cousin Charlotte?*, a blood relative to *What Ever Happened to Baby Jane?*, which he turned into a screenplay with the help of Lukas Heller. *[I wildly objected to this title. Comparisons can be odious, and I felt it was cheap to have the same title as* What Ever Happened to Baby Jane?, *except for the name of the leading character. Through a lucky break I was allowed by Aldrich to have the title changed to* Hush . . . Hush, Sweet Charlotte. Aldrich arranged a Twentieth Century-Fox release. Interiors were to be filmed on the home lot, and exteriors were to be shot in Louisiana. A June 1 start was planned to enable Davis to segue directly from Paramount to Twentieth Century-Fox.

Also signed were Joseph Cotten as Drew, a doctor who has had an affair with both cousins, Davis as Charlotte, and Joan Crawford as Miriam; also Agnes Moorehead, Cecil Kellaway, and Victor Buono, along with twenty-three other supporting players. Gene Hibbs was again to do Davis's makeup, and costumes were to be designed by Norma Koch, who had won an Oscar for *What Ever Happened to Baby Jane?* The picture was to be shot in black and white on wide screen by Joseph Biroc.

The film begins with a long prologue, set in 1927, which establishes the tenuous relationship between the cousins and shows the cleaver-murder of John Mayhew, with suspicion cast upon Charlotte. The action then switches to the present day, with a group of boys daring a new member of the gang into entering Hollis House, where Charlotte lives. He knocks over a music box, which plays the title song. Davis picks up the box and goes out on the veranda. The main titles fade in on the left side of the frame as the camera holds on a close-up of Davis on the right, crying silently as she listens to the music box. It was an effective, character-building star entrance.

In the end, with Charlotte driven almost insane by the efforts of Drew and Miriam, with the hodgepodge of the past that they have effectively recreated, she overhears them planning to commit her to an insane asylum while they share the riches of her inheritance. Hiding in the shadows of a balcony, she peers below as they move close for an embrace. She quickly pushes an enormous cement planter-pot over the edge, crushing them together.

Barbara Stanwyck was first sought for the key part of Jewel Mayhew. Mary Astor, who had become a best-selling author and had unofficially retired when she had "died" in a Ben Casey segment, was finally signed for the role. With 108 films behind her she wrote in her autobiography, *A Life on Film,*

I read the script. The opening shot described a severed head rolling down the stairs. . . . I skipped to my few pages—a little old lady sitting on her veranda waiting to die. There was a small kicker to it, inasmuch as it was she who was the murderess in her youth and had started all the trouble. And then in the story she died. Good! Now I'd really be dead! And it was with Bette, which seemed sentimentally fitting.

. . . The locale was the deep South, and we went on location to Baton Rouge, and it was hellish hot. We worked at one of the magnificent, decaying, old, pillared mansions, with an avenue of moss-hung trees leading down to the levee. It was an hour's drive from the hotel, and we had to get up at the crack of dawn—naturally!

The first day of shooting I was, as always, full of anxiety tremors. Every actor worth his salt has them, and you *never* get over it. I had lots of dialogue in a southern accent, and I had never worked with director Bob Aldrich. Bette was not in the scene and so naturally had the day off. But she had the sensitivity and courtesy to take the long drive out to the location and be a friendly, familiar face on the sidelines. "Hi, Astor!" she said. "You look great!" and I knew that *she* didn't mean the usual Hollywood flattery. She took a quick look at my costume, listened to my accent, watched a rehearsal, and said to Aldrich, "Turn her loose, Robert, you might learn something!"

Back home I went through the process of retiring without any nonsense. I simply turned in my union cards and moved out of town.

Boxoffice magazine on Monday, June 15, 1964, put a current dilemma succinctly in a headline, "Drama, Confusion Too, in Joan-Bette Affair." The article continued,

A two-pronged decision issued Friday (June 12) in superior court forbids Bette Davis from appearing in any picture until she first completes added scenes in Paramount's *Where Love Has Gone* and at the same time requires Paramount to put up a bond of $175,000 to be used to pay Miss Davis's salary in the event she is prevented from working in Robert Aldrich's *Hush . . . Hush, Sweet Charlotte* underway at Twentieth-Fox.

Miss Davis already has received the first $125,000 on payment of $200,000 pledged by Aldrich.

Meanwhile, an upper respiratory infection landed Joan Crawford, who also stars in *Charlotte,* in the Cedars of Lebanon Hospital.

Both events focused attention on the "Joan Crawford/Bette Davis Day" luncheon at the Twentieth-Fox commissary, which Mayor Sam Yorty had proclaimed in honor of the two actresses for Monday, the 15th. Robert Aldrich was host at the affair, a bit confused perhaps, but the luncheon went on despite the absence of Miss Crawford.

The added scene required avis to go mad. She protested that had she known Mrs. Hayden was supposed to go insane, she would have given a different interpretation to the role. She felt the new ending would be ridiculous.

Filming around Crawford was resumed, and Davis won a round in the district court of appeals, staying the Paramount injunction, and the court set a hearing for June 29, probing the matter further. Davis subsequently won her point. The court upheld her artistic point of view; she would not be forced to do the new ending for *Where Love Has Gone.* It was a victorious battle for integrity.

Robert Aldrich in *The Celluloid Muse* said,

> There's no doubt in the world that Crawford was sick, seriously sick. If she'd been faking, either the insurance company would never have paid the claim or she would never have been insurable again. Insurance companies here are terribly tough; there's no such thing as a made-up ailment that they pay off on.
>
> While Crawford was in the hospital, we finished all Davis's scenes in which Crawford didn't appear. When she came back to work, she was so exhausted that she could only do about two or three hours' filming a day. Even that proved too much; she returned to the hospital and became worse. At that stage the insurance company offered us the alternatives of finding a replacement for

Miss Crawford within two weeks or scrapping the picture.

As you can well imagine, there were great arguments about whom we should get. A number of ladies were considered, all of whom, for a variety of reasons, were not acceptable to all parties. There was also a contractual problem in that Davis had star approval. Until then it had been academic because she had approved Crawford, but it now became vitally important.

Obviously the ideal candidate would have been Vivien Leigh. . . . I won't say that Olivia (De Havilland) was the third choice, but Olivia was the first choice that was acceptable.

I guess if Davis has a friend who's a real lady, it's De Havilland; they're very close. She tried to persuade Olivia to do the part, helped me talk with her on the phone. No good. So I went off to Switzerland to try to convince De Havilland in person. It was terribly difficult. I'm not sure why, but I think it has to do with Miss De Havilland's opinion of what her image is vis-à-vis what it *may* be.

De Havilland told newshawk Harrison Carroll on October 20, 1964, "I didn't want to play a murderess . . . I did it once before when I played a dual role, including the evil twin in *The Dark Mirror*. I never hated anybody as much in my life as I did Terry, the bad twin in that picture." Carroll goes on, "When producer Aldrich flew to Switzerland, he was very clever, Olivia admits. 'We were sitting on top of a mountain,' she laughs. 'Doesn't the ambivalence, the duality of the character, challenge you?' he demanded. 'The upshot was I promised to read the script again. I accepted the role.' "

On Tuesday, August 27, 1964, Radie Harris in her column in the *Hollywood Reporter* reported,

Joan Crawford is sizzling at Robert Aldrich for not giving her the courtesy of calling her before announcing that Olivia De Havilland had replaced her in *Hush . . . Hush, Sweet Charlotte*. Said Joan from her hospital bed at Cedars of Lebanon, "Aldrich knew where to long distance me all over the world, when he needed me. But he made no effort to reach me here to alert me that he had signed Olivia. He let me hear it for the first time in the radio release—and, frankly, I think it stinks.''

The original budget for the picture was $1.3 million, but with Crawford's illness delay the cost would rise to $1.9 million, although about $634,000 was expected from the Crawford insurance and Aldrich intended to spend from $85,000 to $90,000, out of a total of $200,000, to publicize the March release.

Shooting resumed on September 29, after De Havilland had contracted a bad cold, which delayed shooting for two days; still the studio expected to have a print ready for showing in the Los Angeles area in December, in time to qualify for Academy Award consideration.

Where Love Has Gone was previewed at Paramount Studios on October 5. The next day, James Powers in *The Hollywood Reporter* wrote, ''Susan Hayward and Bette Davis may seem like a sure-fire combination for a highly charged melodrama, but unfortunately Miss Hayward and Miss Davis are two actresses who need material to match their intensity. Neither gets it.''

Said Bosley Crowther in the November 3, 1964, edition of *The New York Times,*

it ensnares Bette Davis in a grossly preposterous role. Never mind Susan Hayward. We've become quite accustomed to seeing her expending her pyrotechnic talents on lurid and fatuous roles. But to see the respectable Bette Davis, who has won two Academy Awards and has been rather careful with her talents (except in the horrendous *What Ever Happened to Baby Jane?),* is to see a fine talent go down the drain. To be sure, she may merit some forgiveness. It is a thoroughly thankless role she has to play . . . No wonder, you may say, that Miss Davis resorts to histrionic extremes. She has to do something excessive to give authority to this grotesque character. The only thing is that the authority she gives is florid and absurd. It is as phony as the inky eye makeup and the platinum-silver hair Miss Davis wears. That is to say, she strikes poses. She speaks with profound solemnity—except when she has to holler, and then she shrieks and bellows like a shrew. Her hairdos and clothes are as lacquered as the sets in this polished color film, and her manners are as synthetic as her emotions. The same must be said of the other actors.

[Can't imagine why my eye makeup was called inky. As to the white hair, Paramount insisted I wear it. When I made my makeup test, I wore a short bob and hair my own color. I felt Mrs. Hayden would have her hair dyed and never allow herself to look like a white-haired old lady. The studio felt the white hair necessary to establish a definite age difference between Miss Hayward and me.]

Judith Crist in *The New York Herald Tribune* reported, "Now, mommy's mommy, I must hasten to point out, is Bette Davis, replete with white hair, haute couture, and her full powers as the grande dame of Sturm und Drang. And she sinks her teeth into her role as the ruthless tycooness and domineering mama and devours it with a style glorious to behold."

A TAKEOFF ON A LULLABYE

Frank DeVol wrote the music, and Mack David the lyrics, for a haunting lullaby, "Hush . . . Hush, Sweet Charlotte,"* which was sung by Davis to harpsichord accompaniment. Patti Page's recording of the song was high on the charts for months upon release of the picture.

Hush, hush, sweet Charlotte
Charlotte, don't you cry;
Hush, hush, sweet Charlotte
I'll love you till I die.

Oh, hold me, darling, please hold me tight
And brush the tear from your eye;
You weep because you had a dream last night,
You dreamed that I said goodbye.

The ad campaign featured a head shot of Davis screaming. The taglines were takeoffs of the original lyrics, some of which were sung by a group of boys over the main title:

> Hush, hush, sweet Charlotte
> Charlotte don't you cry
> Chop, chop, sweet Charlotte
> A faithless man must die.

or

> Hush, hush, sweet Charlotte
> Suppress that piercing scream
> Your lover's blood on yonder rug
> Gives substance to your dream.

or

> Hush, hush, sweet Charlotte
> Charlotte don't you cry
> I'm going to cut off your lover's head
> And both his hands and bake them in a pie.

"No more macabre films for me after this one," Davis said. "My macabre era is over." She planned to do personal appearances with De Havilland; they were booked for an in-tandem dramatic reading on the TV show "Hollywood Palace."

Arthur Knight in the January 23, 1965, issue of *The Saturday Review* wrote, "Once again he [Aldrich] is aided immeasurably by the gutsy, free-wheeling performance of Bette Davis, with her incredible ability to abandon all consciousness of self in the full realization of a role that ranges from youthful, wide-eyed innocence to the stark terror of a middle-aged woman helplessly in the grip of a nightmare, both real and imagined. And she can still spit out, with savored venom, a line like 'What do you think I asked you here for—company?' "

Kenneth Tynan, the British critic, said, "An accomplished piece of Grand Guignol is yanked to the level of art by Miss Davis's performance as the raging, aging southern belle; this wasted Bernhardt, with her screen-filling eyes and electrifying vocal attack, squeezes genuine pathos from a role conceived in cardboard. She has done nothing better since *The Little Foxes.*"

After touring twenty theaters in the New York area, where the grosses were very large, Davis and De Havilland took off for Chicago. Clifford Terry wrote on March 17, 1965, in *The Chicago Tribune,*

> At the end of the large square table in Maxim's, Olivia De Havilland, elegant in what might be described as, er, a very nice orange dress, drinking "a whisper of gin and a whisper of soda," charming, talking enthusiastically about her family and home in Paris.
>
> At the opposite end, Bette Davis, wearing a very nice light blue dress, drinking Scotch-on-the-rocks, fending off unending questions about her celebrated feud with Joan Crawford, smoking cigarette after cigarette (inhaling with a finality that seems to defy the smoke to seep out), calling her own shots, outspoken, gutsy, Finally, the answer, unequivocal: "The only thing I will say about Miss Crawford is that, when Olivia replaced her in the film (Miss Crawford had virus pneumonia), Crawford said, 'I'm glad for Olivia—she needed the part.' Joan issued these daily releases from her oxygen tent!"

21

Master Joey, why are you afraid of me?

BETTE DAVIS AS NANNY
IN *The Nanny*

''In my new film I play an English nanny,'' Davis told a BBC radio interviewer.

> It's a problem between a nanny and a young boy. That's the contretemps . . . I don't consider this a horror movie. I made a tour of theaters in New York City with *Charlotte,* and I suggested to the audience, when they asked me about horror films, to start reading Shakespeare again. You know, everybody acts in the press today as if anything that involves any kind of murder, legitimate or not, or any kind of tragedy is a ''horror'' movie.
>
> *Charlotte* was not a horror film. It was the study of a very sad woman who had a terrible thing happen in her life. And I'm not saying this was written like Shakespeare. *The Letter* was never criticized as a horror film—was it? Well, at the start of *The Letter* I'm plugging a man with six bullets. *The Little Foxes* was never called a horror film, and I let a man die of a heart attack.

The Nanny was produced by Jimmy Sangster and directed by Seth Holt from a screenplay by Sangster from the novel by Evelyn Piper. The usual conference was held on makeup and wardrobe. Designer Rosemary Burrows suggested cotton dresses for the character. Davis, who was to wear a parted-in-the-middle wig and heavy eyebrows, insisted on the traditional uniform and was amazed when told they were in short supply. Shooting on the film was delayed because she contracted a bad case of flu. During her illness the proper uniform was found—a dark gray woolen long-sleeved dress with a white, Peter Pan collar; a white apron to be worn in the kitchen; and a dark gray coat and gray felt hat, very masculine in shape, worn with her uniform for street wear.

She had been working only a few days when a woman came up to her on the set and exclaimed, "Oh, it's a pleasure to meet you, Miss Davis. You look great." Davis laughed to friends, "I almost killed her!" Davis went on in the BBC interview,

I have always believed in an enormous variety of parts. Much more than I've been given credit for. *The Nanny,* for instance, is a complete departure from anything I've ever played. It is very easy to say, "Well, you know, she's always the same." This is not true. This I will never accept from any critic . . .

. . . We don't always make films for critics. We know full well when we make a film whether or not criticism should be involved. Some films are made just for people to enjoy. We're not always as surprised as the critics think when they pan us . . . We know ahead of time basically what we're in for. . . .

One of the things over the years that critics have repeatedly referred to have been my "mannerisms." Well, that depends on what part I'm playing. I can show you just as many parts where I didn't flutter one eyelid, ever. It's a terribly easy thing for a critic to say. They forget the parts in which you don't flutter eyelids or do any of your usual things; some parts require this; some parts are more suited to what your actual personality is.

Davis flew home after the picture was in the can, determined to move to the East Coast. The Bel Air house seemed empty with B.D. married. She found a clapboard house in Westport, Connecticut, on the west branch of the Saugatuck River. She proceeded to install her much-moved antiques and personal effects—which had been carted across the continent more times than she could count. She named this house Twin Bridges.

The Nanny opened at the Normandie Theatre and selected neighborhood houses in New York on November 3, 1965. *Time* magazine wrote, ''*The Nanny* is a small sedate British thriller, based on the assumption that one good squirm deserves another. Having mopped up in three earlier bloodletters, moviedom's Ace Bogeywoman, Bette Davis, now goes about her grisliness with quiet, unruffled efficiency. *The Nanny* is her definitive essay on the servant problem, and may be taken as antidote by those who found *Mary Poppins* too sweet to stomach.''

The film took in $263,000 at the twenty showcase theaters in New York alone, one of the best runs of the year.

MIKE DOUGLAS AND MARSHAL DILLON

The rest that Davis had planned was longer than anticipated; no new roles of any consequence were offered to her. In April, 1966, she flew to Philadelphia to cohost a week-long series of Mike Douglas television shows, where she performed in sketches, sang, and introduced new talent. At the conclusion of the week's work, after a big buildup and with a straight face, Douglas presented a birthday cake. She was touched. *[This was a first, having a birthday party on television.]* Leaning toward the cake, she took a deep breath and blew again and again and again. Finally it occurred to her that the candles were of the ''relighting'' variety. She broke up both the audience and the crew by shouting to Douglas, between laughs, ''You *bastard!*'' It was the highlight of the week's work.

In July she portrayed Etta Stone, the widowed mother of four grown sons, on a segment of ''Gunsmoke.'' In *The Jailer* she slapped Amanda Blake and fired a shotgun several times. Recalling the old days at Warner Bros., she told an interviewer, ''There is something about doing a show quickly, but I think doing an hour show in six days is cutting it a little close.''

The program was beamed on October 1, and six days later Davis appeared on the ''Milton Berle Variety Show,'' looking chic in a smart wardrobe. She did a screwball takeoff on a Raymond Chandler whodunit, *The Maltese Chicken.*

Jacqueline Susann's best seller *Valley of the Dolls* had been purchased by Twentieth Century-Fox, and the authoress spoke to Davis about the possibility of her doing the older-actress role of Helen Lawson. Judy Garland was finally signed for the part but was replaced after a few days' filming with Susan Hayward. Other properties discussed at this time were Robert Aldrich's *The Killing of Sister George,* which eventually went to Beryl Reid, and an account of the Beverly Aadland affair, *The Greatest Mother of Them All,* which was shelved.

ROCK OF AGES

> *You're right, of course; I have only one eye . . . One hot day in August, when Terry was a little boy, he crept into Henry's bedroom and took Henry's air pistol. He ran up to me in the garden. He was so excited that he pressed the trigger with both his little hands. He shouted, "Bang, you're dead, Mummy." And he laughed and laughed until he saw the blood spurting out.*
>
> BETTE DAVIS AS MRS. TAGGART
> IN *The Anniversary*

During summer, 1967, Hammer Productions sent the script of Bill McIlwraith's hit, *The Anniversary,* which had opened in London's West End in April, 1966, with Mona Washbourne starring as the monstrous Mrs. Taggart. Three members of the supporting cast were to be transferred to the screen version: Sheila Hancock, Jack Hedley, and James Cossins, with new cast members Christian Roberts and Elaine Taylor. Davis turned down the property, but Jimmy Sangster, who had done the screenplay for *The Nanny,* did a rewrite and resubmitted the material.

Before leaving for England in July, Davis bought two costumes, a wig, and several self-adhesive eye patches necessary for the role. *The Anniversary* was to be produced by Sangster, directed by Canadian Television director Alvin Rakoff, and photographed by Harry Waxman in Technicolor at Elstree Studios.

The story concerned an emasculating mother whose husband, a successful housing contractor, has been dead for ten years. The film takes place in one day and evening as the clan gathers for the traditional annual observance of their mother's wedding anniversary. Mrs. Taggart has a possessive hold over her three sons. The older one, Henry, is a transvestite. ("Get that stuff off, Henry. There's a dear. You can't go to dinner dressed like that. You know nylon brings you out in a rash!") The middle son is married to

Bette Davis poses before the Fanny Skeffington portrait at her New York townhouse, 1961. (*Photograph from the collection of Will Henderson.*)

"Sister, sister, oh, so fair, why is there blood all over your hair?" was the catchline for *What Ever Happened to Baby Jane?*, 1962, with Joan Crawford as Blanche Hudson and Bette Davis as Baby Jane Hudson. (*Photograph by Warner Bros.*)

Bette Davis as the faded southern belle Chär-
lotte Hollis shoots the ghost of her childhood
lover in *Hush...Hush, Sweet Charlotte*, 1964.
(*Photograph by Twentieth Century-Fox, from
the collection of Gunnard Nelson.*)

Rich twin, Margaret de Lorca, in a rare mood of largesse, offers cast-
off clothing to her poor sister, tavern owner Edith Phillips, in *Dead
Ringer*, 1964. (*Photograph by Warner Bros., from the collection of
Gunnard Nelson.*)

a shrew. ("What about the money, then? The 5,000 quid, 1,000 pounds in fivers every time you tell me that Karen is pregnant?") Of course Karen has a reported "heart condition," and mother hopes that she will die in childbirth. However, Karen's heart is sound, and she is saving the 5,000 quid to emigrate to Canada. The third boy, Tom, brings a new girl home each year, only to have "mum" break up the affair. ("You belong to me. If I could stuff you, I'd put you in that cabinet there, along with my other beautiful possessions—and that's love!") However, this time the girl, Shirley, is pregnant. ("My dear, would you mind sitting somewhere else? Body odor offends me.") Later, when Tom and Shirley attempt to make love in mum's bed upstairs, Shirley finds her glass eye under the pillow——which almost induces a miscarriage.

Furiously Shirley tells her prospective mother-in-law, who has discovered that she has deformed ears, "Find someone who can stand up to you and you don't like it, do you? Tom and I are going for a walk now, and, when we come back, I don't want to hear any more talk about the wedding, because it's been settled . . . Tom and I are getting married and, if you start up again, I'll poke your other eye out!"

The ending finds her planning another anniversary party for the next year and toasting the portrait of her dead husband, whom she always hated. She then takes Tom's gift, a small replica of The Pissing Boy, which is equipped with a bulb full of water, and proceeds to "spray" the room, indicating to all the sundry ghosts, living and dead, exactly what she thinks of them.

Davis felt the emasculating mother was more typically American than British and felt stateside actors would be more convincing, but Sangster disagreed. She found that the eye patch affected her balance in much the same way as the raked stage did in *The Night of the Iguana.*

She began to have difficulty with director Rakoff when he said, "Now count two and cross to the mirror, pause two beats and move the lamp!" She replied, "What's that? That's not acting, that's television. What you want is a dummy. Why hire me to count chalk marks?"

Rakoff was replaced by Roy Ward Baker after a week, and Hammer films issued the following statement: "It was a conflict of personalities and in no way reflects on Mr. Rakoff's indisputable talents as a director." [*What a cop-out by Hammer Productions. Mr. Rakoff didn't have the first fundamental knowledge of making a*

A few days ago, the whole family
got together to discuss what to do
for Mom for Mother's Day. Taking
into consideration her love, demeanor,
the way she brought us up, the way she
accepted our sweethearts, the fond
memories, the happy hours...
WE DECIDED TO KILL HER!

Bette Davis in *The Anniversary*

Now Filming A Seven Arts-Hammer Production
For 20th Century-Fox Release

*motion picture, let alone what an actor was all about. Mr. Baker
saved this film. He not only changed the set so we could work in it,
he changed the total conception of the characters. The actors from
the stage play fought me tooth and nail. After all, the motion picture
script, as I finally accepted it, was a total departure from the play.
A slapstick comedy was being played by me as a comedy drama.]*

The Anniversary was previewed at the Rialto Theatre in London
on January 11, 1968.

The New York Times on March 21, 1968, reported: "Bette
Davis's seventy-eighth movie, *The Anniversary,* is a horror film for
faint-hearted horror movie fans. It has no horror music. . . . It is not
scary. . . . *The Anniversary* is not a distinguished example of the
Terrifying Older Actress Filicidal Mummy genre." *[The Anniversary was not a horror film. The mother that I played was a
horrific character, as all possessive mothers of sons are. Loathing
this kind of mother, I feel portraying one might change the ways of
mothers who see these films, who are like the character I'm playing.
There are so many of these mothers of sons! These mothers ruin
their lives.]*

Davis plugged the picture on the "Johnny Carson Show" and
brought the host, who was suffering from an eye ailment, a patch
similar to the one worn in the film.

There were no offers for parts for some months, and once again
she settled into Twin Bridges and busied herself with housekeeping
and cooking. She enjoyed her seclusion. B.D. and Hyman moved
from New York to nearby Weston, Connecticut.

Early in 1969, Davis decided to do *Connecting Rooms* in London
for producers Harry Field and Arthur Cooper. She told UPI
correspondent Maris Ross, in the April 19, 1969, edition of the *Los
Angeles Herald-Examiner,* "I first saw this script two years ago. I
liked the fact that it was not a film of violence. It was a complete
change of pace for me. You could work every week of the year if
you're willing to play murderesses because that's just as much a
vogue as salaciousness in films, but I've determined I will not do
another of them."

In *Connecting Rooms,* a story about the generation gap, she
played the role of a fifty-year-old cellist who lives in a seedy
boarding house in London along with Sir Michael Redgrave, a
former professor kicked out of his job because of homosexuality,
and a young no-good pop singer, Alexis Kanner. The film got under
way as scheduled on February 7, 1969, with Franklin Gollings

directing his own screenplay based on a play by Marion Hart. For the cello-playing scenes Davis remembered how Rapper had tied Henreid's hands behind his back in *Deception* and had brought in two real cellists to do the bow and fingering work. Contracted to do the actual playing for her was Ian Fleming's sister, Amorlis, who showed up on the set not having been told she was to do the fingering and bow work positioned behind Davis. After many difficult rehearsals the scene was shot.

22

> *This is—a—stickup. I've got a gun in my purse. How*
> *would you like your guts spilled all over the floor? . . . If*
> *you don't put all the money you've got in this paper bag,*
> *I'm going to open you up like a can of tomato soup.*
>
> BETTE DAVIS AS BUNNY O'HARE
> IN *Bunny O'Hare*

Davis returned to Twin Bridges. After a short career lull she accepted a guest-starring role in a segment of Robert Wagner's hit television series "It Takes a Thief." She would portray a retired safecracker troubled with arthritis in her fingers, who is brought back into the limelight by Alexander Mundy for a spectacular caper. The "changeling" role in *A Touch of Magic* allowed Davis to be transformed from a seedy inmate of a convalescent home to a glamorous dowager, who in one scene is disguised as a nun to escape detection.

Wagner, although reaching prominence in the 1950s as the star system was disappearing from the Hollywood scene, respected the old order and rolled out the red carpet for his star at Universal, where his series was shot. A limousine was placed at her disposal, a deluxe dressing room was set aside, and her own makeup man, Gene Hibbs, was in attendance. For the first time since "Wagon Train" she was given the accoutrements of a star. The hour teleplay was well received.

When J.L. "officially" retired from Warner Bros., Ted Ashley, new board chairman and chief executive officer of Kinney National Services, who had made the latest purchase of the studio, invited

Davis to sit on the dais at the affair honoring Warner. Cocktails were served on Stage Seven—the enormous great hall where *Camelot* had been filmed. Then the thousand-odd guests were taken to Stage One. The entrance had been redesigned as an exact duplicate of the Cascade Nickelodeon at New Castle, Pennsylvania, where the Warner brothers first got their start.

"It was by any standards an historic evening," wrote *The Los Angeles Times* film critic, Charles Champlin. "The audience was a Who's Who of surviving giants of Hollywood's most golden era and those of newer eras." He continued,

> Busby Berkeley and Ruby Keeler were there, and Mae Clarke and Billie Dove, Jack Oakie, Pat O'Brien, Miriam Hopkins, Joan Blondell, and Otto Kruger. Dennis Morgan was on hand, as was his long-time companion in the Warner Bros. stock company Governor Ronald Reagan . . . and dozens of others.
>
> Frank Sinatra was master of ceremonies. Mervyn LeRoy, Bette Davis, and Rosalind Russell were on the dais, along with Edward G. Robinson and Efrem Zimbalist, Jr., who narrated a stunning pastiche of the great Warner movies from *The Jazz Singer* to *Camelot,* by way of Dooley Wilson singing "As Time Goes By" in *Casablanca* and Judy Garland singing "The Man That Got Away" in *A Star Is Born.*
>
> The audience, sniffling a bit in the darkness now and again, watched Gary Cooper meet Ingrid Bergman in *Saratoga Trunk* and Errol Flynn die bravely as Custer in *They Died with Their Boots On.*
>
> Edward G. Robinson, to keep things in salty perspective, noted that the studio also had to its credit *Dames* and *Code C of the Secret Service.* "I knew Jack Warner when he had gray hair," said Robinson, in an affectionate tribute to Warner's presently brown locks.
>
> Bette Davis said, "The room is so full of people who knew each other so well, and so few of us are left." She asked for a silent standing tribute to the great company of players no longer present. And, indeed, the evening was witness to the time of man and the timelessness of film.
>
> It was, as Warner proudly noted, an unprecedented evening, for no retiring president has been so honored

previously in Hollywood. It also was an evening unlikely to be duplicated ever again, for this was a valedictory banquet for the age of the unabashed impresario.

"Can you imagine going to a banquet in honor of a conglomerate?" Edward G. Robinson asked rhetorically, and the point is you can't.

Davis said, "The Hollywood that I knew came to an end the night of our tribute to Jack Warner." *[Sitting on the dais, looking around at all that was so familiar and dear to me, I thought, "This is the end of it. This is the end of all of it as I knew it. It will never come back." And I said my little private farewell.]*

Meanwhile American International Pictures submitted the script of *Bunny and Billy,* a rather charming comedy about a middle-aged widow who, in a vendetta against the bank that has foreclosed on her home in Albuquerque, teams up with Ernest Borgnine as a man wanted by the police. Together, dressed as hippies, they rob banks. Two elements of the script were attractive—the role was completely different from any part she had ever played, and the idea of Bette Davis riding a motorcycle seemed amusing.

Bunny and Billy went through several title changes before the final selection, *Bunny O'Hare.* The film featured a screenplay by Stanley Z. Cherry and Coslaugh Johnson from an original story by Cherry.

The ending was memorable: the widow O'Hare, after having put up with her inconsiderate, demanding children—indeed, having robbed several banks to keep them in funds throughout five reels—when asked by Borgnine what she intends to do about them, replies briskly, "Fuck them!" She and Borgnine then take off in a camper to live in Mexico, where he is affectionately called "Señor Toilet," because he sells secondhand bathroom appliances to his friends south of the border.

Davis flew to Los Angeles in October, 1970, for Phyllis Garr wardrobe fittings and several press conferences. New-time newsdoll Joyce Haber and old-time newshen Dorothy Manners were sufficiently respectful in their interviews. Haber, in the October 11, 1970, edition of *The Los Angeles Times,* wrote, " 'Although the basic theory about my career was that I played evil women,' says Bette, 'I never was typed. I played every kind of part known to man. But to my basic wonderment I think I do have a special ability to play a bitch. If you are one, you know, you refuse to play one honestly—and,' Bette laughs, 'I won't name the many who are—and won't. No one who's really a bitch dares to expose herself.' "

Said Manners in the October 18, 1970, edition of *The Los Angeles Examiner,* "La Davis was a star in Hollywood in the days when great film stars were treated like royalty, and it clings to her aura, as gracious and charming as she is. No shoddy attire for this lady. She looked smashing in a red-and-white pants outfit, perfectly groomed. When she lighted a cigarette, she smoked it elegantly, as though Paul Henreid had lighted it for her. Her gallant career has earned this actress her royal scepter."

Production on *Bunny O'Hare* began in November in Albuquerque, under the direction of Gerd Oswald for producer Norman T. Herman and executive producers James H. Nicholson and Samuel Z. Arkoff. Michael Dugan was in charge of the second-unit photography in New Mexico, and Loyal Griggs and John Stevens were the cinematographers.

Although both Davis and Borgnine had doubles for the motorcycle stunts photographed in long shot, many of the chases, intercut with medium shots, required Borgnine to drive the cycle with Davis perched precariously behind him. The facilities on location were primitive. Albuquerque, while warm of day, was cool of night, and many sequences were shot in the frigid dawn. *[Many were also shot in rain, snow, and sleet. This was my first all outdoor-location film. I will never again attempt it. The real scenery is heaven to the modern film director. He will sacrifice life, limb, and talent to find the perfect sky or tree or perfect anything scenically to be in the background of the actors playing the scene. No time for any rehearsals, no chance to give any kind of a pro performance—it is all catch as catch can. There is no reason why Borgnine and I weren't killed in some of the shots up and down those New Mexico mountain roads.]* When *Bunny O'Hare* was finished, she flew to Westport to spend the Christmas holidays with her children.

Gerd Oswald turned his cut of the picture into American International Pictures. The producers took a long look at the film and immediately scheduled added scenes. There were subsequent rumors around Hollywood that *Bunny O'Hare* was being completely recut.

The press preview of the film was held at the Picwood Theatre in Los Angeles on June 24, 1971, where *Shinbone Alley,* a full-length cartoon, was playing. The showing was poorly attended, probably because many Davis admirers were attending a Gay Liberation

The monstrous Mrs. Taggart (Bette Davis) shows what she thinks of her children—and the world in general—in the ending scene from *The Anniversary*, 1968. (*Photograph by Twentieth Century-Fox.*)

Disguised as hippies, fugitive from justice Bill Green (Ernest Borgnine) and the widow O'Hare (Bette Davis) set out to rob a series of banks in *Bunny O'Hare*, 1971. (*Photograph by American International Pictures.*)

Davis starring in a projected TV pilot, *Hello Mother, Goodbye*, at MGM, January, 1973, is joined by James Stewart, filming a TV movie. Banner in the background surprised both stars. (*Photograph by MGM.*)

Parade on Hollywood Boulevard at the time of the unreeling. Some of the crowd, who had come to see the cartoon feature, left before the preview. It was the wrong audience for the film.

A TOUCH OF MOTHER GODDAM

Music is food for the hungry soul; don't you agree, Mr. Lawrence? The world of sound vibrations is relatively unexplored. I find it endlessly rewarding. In art it has the power to soothe, but in science it has the power to hurt.

BETTE DAVIS AS MADAME SIN
IN *Madame Sin*

Robert Wagner, with the assistance of Sir Lew Grade, the British multimillionaire, put together a "Movie of the Week" package, *Madame Sin,* as a possibility for a television series to star his new friend Bette Davis. The hour-and-a-half teleplay would be released as a feature film in Europe.

Wagner commissioned Edith Head to do Davis's wardrobe, made up of black gowns relieved by interesting pieces of jewelry. The female James Bond had a black Rolls-Royce and a black palace, and her sense of humor was also on the black side.

During a supposed filming of a promotion for *Madame Sin* with Wagner and Edith Head at John Engsted's photographic studio Davis was surprised by Ralph Edwards for his "This is Your Life" show. *[Wagner and Head knew of the deal. I was in a state of complete shock. Told both Wagner and Head I was going to murder them.]* Guests were William Wyler; Olivia De Havilland (who flew in from Paris especially for the appearance); Victor Buono; sister Bobby from Phoenix; Sally (Sage) Hutchinson, her stand-in on thirty-seven pictures; and impressionist Barbara Heller, who said that she had earned her living for the past twenty years by doing Davis impersonations. Also on the program were Ted Kent, who had edited *Bad Sister,* and Benny Baker, who had given Davis her first stage kiss in 1929.

Jay Robinson, who had worked with Davis in *The Virgin Queen* and *Bunny O'Hare,* greeted her warmly. He had been convicted of a drug charge and had gone to jail. Edwards remarked that Davis had made some statements to Dwight Chaffin of *The Los Angeles*

Times, who had put them in letter form: "I first met Jay Robinson in 1955 and not again until we worked on *Bunny O'Hare.* His drug involvement was over in 1960. He is one of our very fine actors. I have only admiration for his having overcome his problems. He is in a fine position to encourage others. Jay never talked about what happened to him. I know he's been through his own private hell. I think we should forget about it; I believe his life experiences have enhanced his talent, and I believe that, given the opportunity, he can go on to much greater things."

Before Davis left for England and *Madame Sin,* De Havilland and she had luncheon together in the Green Room at Warner Bros. Looking around at the tables filled with TV actors, Davis said in a nostalgic mood, "Oh, Livvie, what ghosts there are in this room!"—to which De Havilland replied laconically, "Yes, and wouldn't you just know, we'd outlive them all?"

The budget for *Madame Sin* was set at a high for TV, $1.7 million —which included extensive location work in Scotland and some expensive special effects. Julian Wintle and Lou Morheim produced for Wagner's 2 X Productions in association with the Lew Grade organization, with a screenplay by Barry Oringer and Davis Greene, from an original concept by Lou Morheim and Barry Shear. Tony Richmond was signed as cinematographer; the music, some of which was electronic, was the work of Michael Gibbs. Besides Wagner the cast was made up of Denholm Elliott, Gordon Jackson, Dudley Sutton, Catherine Schell, and Piksen Lim, among others.

The Eurasian look was accomplished with makeup, using false eyelashes and silver-blue mascara that turned her eyes into almonds. Since Madame Sin was to have black hair, she remembered the wig Sophie had made for *Juarez* and contacted Warner Bros. The wig was found and given to Sophie to copy for *Madame Sin.*

Davis took a house in Ascot, near Pinewood Studios, where the interiors were scheduled to be shot. Wagner put a Silver Cloud Rolls-Royce at her disposal. A long introductory scene—like the old days—was written for her first appearance. Wagner, as the ex-CIA agent, is kidnapped and sent to Madame Sin's Scottish castle, where he is summoned into her presence. The camera rests in close-up on a sting ray in a huge tank, then pans slowly to Davis in profile. There is a cut to a medium long shot as Davis moves into view from the shadows, then comes dramatically forward. It was her best introductory scene since *The Corn Is Green,* when she first appeared riding a bicycle in from Glansarno.

When Davis arrived in Glasgow, Scotland, on her way to the Isle of Mull, she was met by many white-haired women. *[Their polished, shining faces looked up at me with tears in their eyes. Each carried a spray of white heather, the good luck flower of Scotland. I was very touched, realizing they were fans of long standing who had never thought they would ever see me in person.]*

The filming progressed smoothly, except for one almost disastrous incident. One morning a bee flew up Davis's dressing gown sleeve and stung her twice in a *vein*. The poison raced through her body, and, by the time a doctor was located, her arm and upper lip had swollen to twice their normal size. The doctor told her that the sting of an insect in a vein, which sends the venom directly into the bloodstream, can be fatal. An antidote was administered at once; it was a close call.

Davis discovered that the reports about *Bunny O'Hare* were true; the film had been entirely recut, with many scenes added. On August 23, 1971, she filed suit in New York Supreme Court against American International Pictures for $3.3 million, contending that AIP made fraudulent misrepresentation to induce her to star in a film designed to be a social documentary with humorous undertones and, after the film was finished, transformed it into a substantially different film. The complaint sought $500,000 exemplary damages "as a result of the willful nature of the defendant's wrongdoings." On November 1 the producers of *Bunny O'Hare* countered with a $17.5 million damage suit against *her*.

Meanwhile the picture had been released October 10, 1971, to odd reviews. Kathleen Carroll in *The New York Daily News* said, "It would be difficult to improve upon Miss Davis's own review of *Bunny O'Hare* . . . Miss Davis called her latest picture 'a broad, tastelessly, inartistically assembled slapstick production . . .' The criticism is justified certainly from Miss Davis's point of view. Wearing the most unflattering clothes and makeup, she looks simply pathetic as the senior-citizen Bonnie who joins forces with a has-been Clyde."

Vincent Canby in the October 19, 1971, edition of *The New York Times* wrote,

> Bette Davis's motion picture career, which began about forty years ago, has been recycled more often than

the average rubber tire, often with results—like *The Nanny* and *The Annivesary*—that convince you there is a definite limit to the number of times any organic resource can be profitably reclaimed. I say that quickly and ruthlessly because not recently (certainly not since *What Ever Happened to Baby Jane?)* have I admired the star's wit, courage, discipline, talent, and guts in quite the same degree as I did yesterday, watching her in a silly, foolishly entertaining movie that may well disappear before anyone sees it . . . *Bunny O'Hare,* directed by Gerd Oswald, a man whose strengths have never been in comedy, is a gimmick comedy, unusual in the fact that to be told its gimmick is to know the very worst there is about the film. Everything else is an improvement. As I said, the gimmick is dreadful. Miss Davis, however, gives a performance that may be one of the funniest and most legitimate of her career, which has been spectacular for mannerisms that overwhelmed every character she's ever played, with the notable exceptions of Leslie Crosbie . . . Regina Giddens . . . and Margo Channing.

Film Facts, volume 19, commented,

Reportedly, after Miss Davis finished her sequences in New Mexico, additional footage was later shot in Hollywood featuring John Astin and Reva Rose; since Astin was credited as "Creative Consultant," these scenes were presumably written by him. And he may also have directed this material since Gerd Oswald said he was "100 percent with Bette Davis in her suit. I feel that they mutilated the picture completely after I turned in my final cut. They made a different film from that which we had conceived."

A call from Universal Studios brought her back to Hollywood for a pilot film for another potential series. She played retired Judge Meredith who was stricken with hypochondria in *The Judge and Jake Wyler.* The role had originally been written for a man, but producers Richard Levinson and William Link, who did the teleplay with David Shawn made the character over without changing a line of dialogue except reference to gender. The pilot was not sold for a series, but it was finally shown as a full-length TV movie a year later. *[By the time Universal added enough scenes to make it run for two hours, there was no similarity to the pilot film we shot. The judge's part was a bit part in comparison to her importance in the film I accepted. This is a new gimmick practiced often by the TV companies. You can't win!!!]*

Said *Daily Variety,* on December 4, 1972,

> Bette Davis as a detective? . . . With a pair of parolees—Doug McClure and James McEachin—on her lease to help her solve crimes without her having to stir out of her humidified old house? . . . Miss Davis sternly admonishes her charges now and then, issues orders cryptically . . . Eccentricity is the key to characterization in the film. Miss Davis plays poker at a table divorced from the other players, eats dill pickles, and won't open a window because fresh air has germs in it. . . . David Lowell Rich attempted to put style into the banal script with his direction, but too much was against him. Gil Melles's score couldn't disguise the poverty of the project. Film was not world premiere's two finest hours.

Davis played the judge with an auburn wig and horn-rimmed glasses and was photographed competently by William Margulies.

She returned to Westport the night before Christmas. Mike was home from college, and Margot was at home from the Lochland School. B.D., Hyman, and grandson Ashley came to Twin Bridges for Christmas. Davis cooked the dinner herself, including the traditional goose always served to her family at Christmas.

LESE MAJESTY

Madame Sin (ad catchline, "Even the diabolical Dr. No would have to say yes to Madame Sin") was released on "ABC Movie of the Week" on January 15, 1972, to excellent reviews. The theatrical version was premiered in London in the middle of May. *Connecting Rooms* was released at the same time. Said the June, 1972, issue of *Sight and Sound,* "Bette Davis in Bayswater bedsitter territory, and her most sympathetic performance in years as a musician who befriends Michael Redgrave, the down-at-heel schoolteacher in the next room. Otherwise an old-fashioned piece of schmaltz, camped up, laced with pop, and laid on rather thick.''

Looking glamorous in a blue beaded evening gown, Davis appeared on television on March 13 singing ''Just Like a Man'' from *Two's Company* on ''Johnny Carson Presents the Sun City Scandals '72.''

After the Carson show, she went for three weeks to the spa at La Costa, a health resort near San Diego. While there she was sent a script by Dino de Laurentis for a film called *Lo Scopone Scientifico (The Scientific Cardplayer* or *The Game)*. On twenty-four-hour notice, she flew to Rome with a one-night stopover at Twin Bridges. The technical artists on the picture sounded like alphabet soup: director, Luigi Comencini; screenplay, Rodolfo Sonego; camera, Eastmancolor, Giuseppi Ruzzolini; art director, Luigi Scaccianoce; music, Piero Piccioni; in the cast, Alberto Sordi, Silvana Mangano, and Joseph Cotten.

At the airport Davis was met by the Italian stars of *The Game*, all of whom spoke English, but was startled to find on the first day of shooting that the dialogue was to be recorded in *Italian*. An interpreter translated directions from Comencini. Wearing a white wig and elegantly gowned, she played all of her scenes in a wheel chair. *[My name for Alberto Sordi was Alberto Sordid. It was unforgivable of him to refuse to speak English with me, especially as he spoke very good English.]*

Returning to Westport, she rested throughout the summer, enjoyed her family and friends, and granted an occasional interview. The Italian version of *The Game,* destined to take in $1 million in Italy alone, opened at the Fono Roma Theatre, Rome, on October 16, 1972. Hank Werba in *Daily Variety* wrote,

> *The Scientific Cardplayer,* in the vein of an O'Henry short story, is built around a Latin card game (scopa) for its sentimental, dark comedy situations. With Alberto Sordi topbilling, the CIC entry should do strong biz at home in Latino markets, but despite excellent name performances by Bette Davis and Silvana Mangano, scopa and *Scopone* are a bit remote for other markets.
>
> Miss Davis plays an old American millionairess with a passion for card playing and spends her dwindling years at it with George (Joseph Cotten) as her faithful, cowed partner. In Rodolfo Sonego's clever screenplay parable

of class conflict, she finances and invariably recoups her money from slum card table opponents. In Rome her annual victims are Peppino (Alberto Sordi) and his wife Antonia (Silvana Mangano). Game also provides a golden mirage for the entire slum suburb.

Social comment is subservient to comedy suspense. Stakes stir futile hopes of sudden wealth—always followed by dramatic despair. Peppino's oldest daughter, Cleopatra, ends the proletarian rat-trap. Before the old, rich eccentric planes away (with her bankroll intact), Cleopatra bakes and presents her with a cake full of venom.

. . . Bette Davis dominates with a neat thesp display of egomania and cruelty beneath a stance of gracious dignity.

A COMMAND PERFORMANCE

On November 10, 1972, Davis was invited to make an appearance in New York before a congregation of film aficionados. Addison Verrell wrote in *Weekly Variety,* on November 12,

In an era when the wispiest Warhol transvestite is billed as a "superstar," definitions have certainly crumbled, but New York's New School of Social Research got a glimpse of the real thing . . . as Bette Davis made a rare assault on the groves of academe. Miss Moffat *(The Corn is Green)* would have approved. . . .

La Davis is no aging screen goddess out to prove in grande dame manner that she still has what it takes. She is, and the audience knew it, upfront, a vital, intelligent professional whose long career is a tribute not only to a versatile talent and an imposing film presence but to a fierce independence on screen and off.

Warmed by an audience whose affection could clearly be felt, the veteran actress held little back, frankly responding to questions ranging over her forty-plus-year career and some that touched on her personal life. Results, in box office terms, were socko. . . .

. . . Miss Davis bristled at interviewer [John] Gruen's

statement that she was known as a "monster" on the set, saying that, until the tag is stuck on an actress, she is never really a star. Her battles, she insisted, were waged with the bosses who denied her decent scripts and directors and were never aimed at technical crews or coworkers. As to her four marriages and the effect of her star status on them, she said, "If I was a fool in my private life, I can't blame my profession for that."

The actress was especially eloquent about the difficulties faced by the aging female screen star, pooh-poohing an adoring fan who suggested she get her face lifted—"Who the hell would I be kidding?"—and speaking of the pleasures derived from her three children while growing old with grace, still realizing there are choice parts now forever out of reach.

"HELLO MOTHER, GOODBYE," JIMMY STEWART AND DEAN MARTIN

In early December Harris L. Katleman, vice-president of MGM-TV, signed Davis to star in a half-hour comedy pilot, "Hello Mother, Goodbye," for NBC. The story line by Jack Sher and Bud Freeman cast her as a possessive mother of two grown sons. The pilot was not picked up for the 1973 season.

When she reported for work at MGM, driving through the gate on the Culver City lot, she looked up in amazement. A huge banner was stretched from sound stage to sound stage.

WELCOME BETTE AND JIMMY

[I was finally costarring with Stewart, who was on the lot for a TV movie, even if only on a banner—plus we had a date for lunch. I told Jimmy I had waited forty years for a date with him. One must never give up one's dreams! They do come true!]

She would return to the coast on September 27, 1973, for a taping of "The Dean Martin Show" to be shown on October 19. In a laugh-getting segment, she was "roasted" by Henry Fonda, Joyce Haber, Kay Medford, Howard Cosell, Vincent Price, Nipsey Russell, Barbara Heller, and Pat Buttram. Wearing a green print dress sparkling with glitter which set off her pageboy hairdo, she took the barbs with good humor. After a protracted ovation, she admitted that she had "had a lot of fun here tonight," then looking around at the star-studded dais and the banquet hall decor, she ended her rebuttal with a quip, "Quoting a line from one of my movies: *What a dump!*"

After the taping of the twenty-minute segment of "The Dean Martin Show," she was preparing to return to Weston, when Universal TV producer Lou Morheim asked her to "guest star" in an NBC suspense Movie of the Week called *Scream, Pretty Peggy.* The part was small but interesting, inasmuch as she would portray Mrs. Elliott, the alcoholic mother of a psychopathic murderer (Ted Bessell) in the teleplay by Jimmy Sangster and Arthur Hoffe. All of Davis's scenes were filmed on location at the old Noah Dietrich stone mansion above the Sunset Strip in Hollywood. Gene Hibbs did her makeup and Peggy Shannon styled the high, blonde wig which transformed Davis into the attractive Mrs. Elliott, who finally shoots her tormented son in the fadeout.

A LEGENDARY LADY

On February 11, 1973, she was the first actress honored in a series of tributes to "Legendary Ladies of the Movies." On February 16, *The New Yorker* magazine, which had pecked snobbishly at some of her most triumphant screen roles, turned benevolent:

> The scene on West Forty-third Street in front of Town Hall . . . looked like something from an old movie—the opening night, perhaps of another Broadway triumph for Margo Channing, the character Bette Davis played in *All about Eve.* Black limousines were jammed bumper to bumper along the curb, and honking yellow taxis discharged excited-looking passengers. On the sidewalk a smoothly dressed crowd jostled its way toward the box office and entrances of the staid old theater. Flashbulbs popped. Movie cameras cranked.
>
> In fact, the occasion *was* a Broadway triumph for Bette Davis, but this time she was playing herself.
>
> Inside, the crowd was in a happy mood. The first half of the program consisted of excerpts from Miss Davis's

films, and there were cheers when the first clip—from *All about Eve*—appeared on the screen. There were more cheers when she delivered her first line on the screen— "Peace and quiet is for libraries."

The film clips showed Miss Davis in an immense variety of roles—from the sweet blind girl of *Dark Victory* to the disintegrating hag of *What Ever Happened to Baby Jane?*, from the fiery southerner of *Jezebel* to the Bronx mama of *The Catered Affair*. A clip from Edward Albee's *Who's Afraid of Virginia Woolf?*, in which Elizabeth Taylor badgers Richard Burton to remember what movie Bette Davis says, "What a dump!" in, was followed by the scene in question (from *Beyond the Forest*). In every excerpt Miss Davis's nervous intensity dominated the screen. The clips showed the qualities that made her a kind of pre-women's-liberation feminist heroine: pride, wit, intelligence, defiance, anger, worldliness, and a powerful will.

Eighty-four films lay in the background of a career that had survived forty-three years of changing mores—690,570 feet of film, 7,673 minutes if shown continuously, 128 hours of entertainment. It would take five days and eight hours to view her creative output. Film had truly been her life. *The New Yorker* continued,

> The last clip, like the first, was from *All about Eve*. Margo Channing drams her drink, climbs halfway up the stairs, turns, and says to her guests, "Fasten your seat belts—it's going to be a bumpy night." The screen went dark, the lights went up, and Miss Davis walked from the wings out to the center of the Town Hall stage. The audience stood and applauded. There were shouts of "Bravo!" Miss Davis wore a gown of black velvet and white satin. Her hair was blonde and bobbed in pageboy style, and her mouth was bright red. She held out her arms to accept the cheers, and, when at last the crowd quieted, she said, "What can I say?"

[All the blood, sweat, and tears of forty-three years were suddenly worth it for a reception like this.]

On May 13, 1973, Davis flew to Chicago to accept the Sarah Siddons Award. On May 19 son Michael was married to Chou-Chou Rains in Westport. Gary Merrill flew in from California for the wedding, and Davis and he stood side by side at the head of the reception line.

As she says, "All of the chicks are gone." She leased Twin Bridges and moved to a smaller house. She is starting a new life and has no idea where it will lead her. "At least," she says, "it is looking ahead, not looking back." *[This was one of the great things Ruthie taught me. With all our ups and downs, and there were so many, she never bemoaned the past—she went on to the future. I will always miss living with, and being needed by, my children. These years were the happiest of my life. Now I must find a new life. I am truly fortunate that I have my work. I have decided that work is the one great hope, the one anchor for a satisfying life.]*

STAGE APPEARANCES

(Stock) Davis acted in *Excess Baggage* with Miriam Hopkins, *Yellow* with Louis Calhern, and *The Squall* and *Broadway* and other plays for the George Cukor-George Kondolf Stock Company at the Temple Theatre, Rochester, N.Y., for the 1928 fall season.

(1) *THE EARTH BETWEEN*—a play in two acts by Virgil Geddes. Produced by James Light and M. Eleanor Fitzgerald. Opened Provincetown Playhouse, March 5, 1929. 27 performances.

(Cast) William Challee, Bette Davis, Carroll Ashburn, Janne Burbie, Warren Colston.

(Stock) Davis portrayed Hedvig in *The Wild Duck* and also appeared in *The Lady from the Sea,* both by Ibsen for the Blanche Yurka Company on tour for the 1929 fall season.

(2) *BROKEN DISHES*—by Martin Flavin. Staged and produced by Marion Gering. Opened Ritz Theatre, N.Y., November, 1929. 178 performances.

(Cast) Donald Meek, Bette Davis, Ellen F. Lowe, Etha Dack, Eda Heineman, Reed Brown, J. Francis-Robertson, Duncan Penwarden, Josef Lazarovici. After Broadway, play went on tour. *Broken Dishes* was purchased by Warner Bros. and filmed as *Too Young to Marry* in 1931 with Loretta Young in the Davis part, and again as *Love Begins at Twenty* in 1936 with Patricia Ellis, and a third time as *Calling All Husbands* in 1940 with Lucille Fairbanks.

(Stock) Davis played the role of Dinah and sang "I Passed by Your Window" in *Mr. Pim,* starring Laura Hope Crews, for the Cape Players, Dennis, Mass., for the 1930 spring season.

(3) *SOLID SOUTH*—a satirical comedy in three acts by Lawton Campbell. Produced by Alexander McKaig. Opened Lyceum Theatre, N.Y., October 14, 1930. 31 performances.

(Cast) Richard Bennett, Elizabeth Patterson, Bette Davis, Jessie Royce Landis, Georgette Harvey, Owen Davis, Jr., Richard Huey, Moffat Johnson, Lew Payton.

(4) *TWO'S COMPANY*—a musical review by Charles Sherman. Presented by James Russo and Michael Ellis. Directed by Jules Dassin. Music by Vernon Duke, lyrics by Ogden Nash, additional lyrics by Sammy Cahn. Sets and lighting by Ralph Alswang. Costumes by Miles White. Sketches by Charles Sherman. Ballet music by Genevive Pitot and David Baker. Choreography by Jerome Robbins. World premiere, Shubert Theatre, Detroit, Mich., October 19, 1952.

(Cast) Bette Davis, Hiram Sherman, Nora Kaye, Bill Callahan, Stanley Praeger, George Irving, Pete Kelley, Maria Karnilova, Ann Hathaway, Nathaniel Frey, Robert Orton's Teen Aces, plus singers and dancers.

After two weeks in Detroit, the show moved to the Nixon Theatre, Pittsburgh, Pa., then opened at the Shubert Theatre, Boston, Mass., where Paul Hartman and John Hoyt (who did not go on to New York) were added to the cast, as well as David Burns, Ellen Hanley, Buzz Miller, Oliver Wakefield. Many changes were made with John Murray Anderson brought in as production supervisor. Sheldon Harnick provided additional lyrics, and new sketches were added, written by Peter De Vries, Arnold B. Horwitt, Lee Rogow, Nat Hiken, Billy Friedberg, Mort Green, George Foster. Opened Alvin Theatre, N.Y., December 15, 1952; closed March 8, 1953, after 90 performances because of Davis's illness (osteomyelitis of the jaw).

(5) *THE WORLD OF CARL SANDBURG*—a two-part platform reading, adapted from the works of Carl Sandburg. Presented by Armand Deutsch, in association with Judd Bernard. Directed by Norman Corwin. Gowns by Orry-Kelly. Scenic consultant, Virginia Johnston.

(Cast) Bette Davis and Gary Merrill, with guitarist-balladeer Clark Allen.

World Premiere State Theatre, Portland, Me., October 17, 1959 (after two preview performances at Bowdoin College, Brunswick, Me.). Presentation toured for 17 weeks prior to opening at the Huntington Hartford Theatre in Hollywood, March 1, 1960, for four weeks. Tour closed at the Alcazar Theatre, San Francisco. Barry Sullivan replaced Merrill on Southern tour. Show reopened at Ogunquit Playhouse, Ogunquit, Me., September 5, 1960, then opened at the Henry Miller Theatre, N.Y., September 14, 1960, with Leif Erickson.

(6) *THE NIGHT OF THE IGUANA*—a two-act drama in three scenes by Tennessee Williams. Staged by Frank Corsaro. Presented by Charles Bowden. Associate producer Violia Rubber. Scenery by Oliver Smith. Lighting by Jean Rosenthal. Costumes by Noel Taylor. Audio effects by Edward Beyer.

(Cast) Bette Davis, Margaret Leighton, Alan Webb, Patrick O'Neal, Patricia Roe, Christopher Jones, James Farentino, Bruce Glover, Laryssa Lauret, Heinz Hohenwald, Lucy Landau, Theseus George, Lane Bradbury, Louis Guss.

World premiere Blackstone Theatre, Chicago, Ill., November 21, 1961. Opened Royale Theatre, N.Y., December 28, 1961. Davis left the show on April 3, 1962, and Shelley Winters took the part of Maxine Faulk.

(7) *BETTE DAVIS IN PERSON AND ON FILM*—a history of the career of Bette Davis. Produced by John Springer, presented by Columbia Artists Theatricals Corp. Opened Denver Auditorium Theatre, Denver, Colorado, March 11, 1974. Presentation toured Northeast, South and Northern U.S.A. and ended at Hartford, Connecticut, April 6, 1974. After thirteen excerpts from her films, Davis answered questions from the audience in a forty-five minute segment.

(8) *MISS MOFFAT*—a two-act musical in twelve scenes by Emlyn Williams and Josh Logan, based on *The Corn is Green,* a play by Williams. Staged by Josh Logan. Presented by Eugene V. Wolsk, Joshua Logan and Slade Brown. Music by Albert Hague, lyrics by Emlyn Williams. Musical staging by Donald Saddler. Scenery and lighting by Jo Mielziner. Costumes by Robert Mackintosh. Musical director, Jay Blackton; orchestrations, Robert M. Freedman; associate producer, Jim Milford.

(Cast) Bette Davis, Dody Goodman, David Sabin, Marion Ramsey, Nell Carter, Lee Goodman, Avon Long, Anne Francine, Gil Robbins, Dorian Harewood, plus singers and dancers.

World premiere Shubert Theatre, Philadelphia, Pa., October 7, 1974, after two previews. Closed October 18, 1974 after 15 performances because of Davis's illness (pinched nerve in back and leg which had caused her to be hospitalized for two weeks during rehearsals). Show was to have toured for nine months before Broadway premiere during 1975 Fall Season.

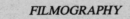
FILMOGRAPHY

(1) *BAD SISTER*—a Universal Picture. Carl Laemmle, Jr., in charge of production. Directed by Hobart Henley. Screenplay by Raymond L. Schrock and Tom Reed, with additional dialogue by Edwin Knopf, based on the novel *The Flirt* by Booth Tarkington. Photographed by Karl Freund. Edited by Ted Kent. Working titles: *Gambling Daughters, What a Flirt.* Davis played the good sister. Opened Globe Theatre, N.Y., March 29, 1931.

(Cast) Conrad Nagel, Sidney Fox, Bette Davis, Zasu Pitts, Slim Summerville, Charles Winninger, Emma Dunn, Humphrey Bogart, Bert Roach, David Durand.

(2) *SEED*—a Universal Picture. Carl Laemmle, Jr., in charge of production. Produced and directed by John M. Stahl. Screenplay by Gladys Lehman, based on the novel of the same name by Charles G. Norris. Photographed by Jackson Rose. Edited by Arthur Taveres. Davis appeared in only a few scenes. Opened Rivoli Theatre, N.Y., May 14, 1931.

(Cast) John Boles, Genevieve Tobin, Lois Wilson, Raymond Hackett, Bette Davis, Frances Dade, Zasu Pitts, Richard Tucker, Jack Willis, Don Cox, Dick Winslow, Kenneth Selling, Terry Cox, Helen Parrish, Dickie Moore.

(3) *WATERLOO BRIDGE*—a Universal Picture. Carl Laemmle, Jr., in charge of production. Directed by James Whale. Screenplay by Benn W. Levy, with continuity and additional dialogue by Tom Reed, based on the play of the same name by Robert E. Sherwood. Photographed by Arthur Edeson. Edited by James Whale. Remade by MGM in 1940 with Vivien Leigh and Robert Taylor and again in 1956 as *Gaby* with Leslie Caron and John Kerr. Opened RKO Mayfair Theatre, N.Y., September 4, 1931.

(Cast) Mae Clarke, Kent Douglas (Douglass Montgomery), Doris Lloyd, Ethel Griffies, Enid Bennett, Frederick Kerr, Bette Davis, Rita Carlisle.

(4) *WAY BACK HOME*—an RKO Picture. Produced by Pandro S. Berman. Directed by William A. Seiter. Screenplay, *Other People's Business* by Jane Murfin, based on radio characters created by Phillips Lord. Photographed by J. Roy Hunt. Davis was well photographed for the first time. Max Steiner,

unbilled, provided the musical score. Opened RKO Mayfair Theatre, N.Y., January 15, 1932.

(Cast) Phillips Lord, Effie Palmer, Mrs. Phillips Lord, Bennett Kilpack, Raymond Hunter, Frank Albertson, Bette Davis, Oscar Apfel, Stanley Fields, Dorothy Peterson, Frankie Darro.

(5) *THE MENACE*—a Columbia Picture. Produced by Sam Nelson. Directed by Roy William Neill. Screenplay by Dorothy Howell and Charles Logue, with additional dialogue by Roy Chanslor, based on the novel *The Feathered Serpent* by Edgar Wallace. Photographed by L. William O'Connell. Edited by Gene Havelick. Working title: *The Squeaker*. Picture was disappointing, but Murray Kinnell suggested to George Arliss that Davis might be right for the role of Grace in *The Man Who Played God*. Opened Beacon Theatre, N.Y., January 29, 1932.

(Cast) H. B. Warner, Bette Davis, Walter Byron, Natalie Moorhead, William B. Davidson, Crauford Kent, Halliwell Hobbes, Charles Gerrard, Murray Kinnell.

(6) *HELL'S HOUSE*—a Capital Films Exchange Release. Produced by Benjamin F. Zeidman. Directed by Howard Higgins. Screenplay by Paul Gangelin and B. Harrison Orkow, based on a story by Howard Higgins. Photographed by Allen S. Siegel. Edited by Edward Schroeder. Also released as *Juvenile Court*. Opened Strand Theatre, N.Y., January 30, 1932.

(Cast) Junior Durkin, Pat O'Brien, Bette Davis, Junior Coughlan, Charley Grapewin, Emma Dunn, James Marcus, Morgan Wallace, Wallis Clark, Hooper Atchley.

(7) *THE MAN WHO PLAYED GOD*—a Warner Bros. Vitaphone Picture. Produced by D. F. Zanuck. Directed by John Adolfi. Screenplay by Julien Josephson and Maude T. Howell, adapted from a short story by Gouverneur Morris and the play *The Silent Voice* by Jules Eckert Goodman. Photographed by James Van Trees. Edited by William Holmes. Also in the cast: Ray Milland and Hedda Hopper. Davis was so good that she was given a Warner Bros. contract. Orry-Kelly created the costumes, Perc Westmore the makeup. One of the least distinguished remakes of all time, Liberace's *Sincerely Yours*, was filmed by Warner Bros. in 1955. Opened Warner Theatre, N.Y., February 10, 1932.

(Cast) George Arliss, Violet Heming, Ivan Simpson, Louise Closser Hale, Bette Davis, Donald Cook, Paul Porcasi, Oscar Apfel, William Janney, Grace Durkin, Dorothy Libaire, Andre Luget, Charles Evans, Murray Kinnell, Wade Boteler, Alexander Ikonikoff.

(8) *SO BIG*—A Warner Bros. Vitaphone Picture. Production supervisor, Lucien Hubbard. Directed by William A. Wellman. Screenplay by J. Grubb Alexander and Robert Lord, based on the novel of the same name by Edna Ferber. Photographed by Sid Hickox. Edited by William Holmes. First filmed by First National Pictures in 1925 with Colleen Moore and again by Warner Bros. in 1953 with Jane Wyman. Davis felt her role of Dallas O'Mara was very

much like her own personality. Opened Strand Theatre, N.Y., April 29, 1932.

(Cast) Barbara Stanwyck, George Brent, Dickie Moore, Bette Davis, Guy Kibbee, Mae Madison, Hardie Albright, Robert Warwick, Arthur Stone, Earl Foxe, Alan Hale, Dorothy Peterson, Dawn O'Day (Anne Shirley), Dick Winslow, Elizabeth Patterson, Rita LeRoy, Blanche Friderici, Lionel Bellmore.

(9) *THE RICH ARE ALWAYS WITH US*—A First National Picture, released by Warner Bros. D.F. Zanuck in charge of production. Production supervisor, Ray Griffith. Directed by Alfred E. Green. Screenplay by Austin Parker, based on the novel of the same name by E. Pettit. Photographed by Ernest Haller. Edited by George Marks. First film in which Davis was photographed by Ernest Haller, her favorite cameraman. Opened Strand Theatre, N.Y., May 15, 1932.

(Cast) Ruth Chatterton, George Brent, Adrienne Dore. Bette Davis, John Miljan, Mae Madison, John Wray, Robert Warwick, Virginia Hammond, Walter Walker, Eula Gray, Edith Allen, Ethel Kenyon, Ruth Lee, Berton Churchill.

(10) *THE DARK HORSE*—a First National Picture, released by Warner Bros. D. F. Zanuck in charge of production. Production supervisor, Ray Griffith. Directed by Alfred E. Green. Screenplay by Joseph Jackson and Wilson Mizner, based on an original story by Melville Crossman, Joseph Jackson, and Courtenay Terrett. Photographed by Sol Polito. Edited by George Marks. This political satire was timely and was received well. Opened Winter Garden Theatre, N.Y., June 8, 1932.

(Cast) Warren William, Bette Davis, Guy Kibbee, Frank McHugh, Vivienne Osborne, Sam Hardy, Robert Warwick, Harry Holman, Charles Sellon, Robert Emmett O'Connor, Berton Churchill.

(11) *CABIN IN THE COTTON*—a First National Picture, released by Warner Bros. D. F. Zanuck in charge of production. Production supervisor, Hal Wallis. Directed by Michael Curtiz. Screenplay by Paul Green, based on the novel of the same name by Harry Harrison Kroll. Photographed by Barney McGill. Edited by George Amy. Davis sang "Willie the Weeper," an old folk song. Opened Strand Theatre, N.Y., September 29, 1932.

(Cast) Richard Barthelmess, Bette Davis, Dorothy Jordan, Henry B. Walthall, Berton Churchill, Walter Percival, William Le Maire, Hardie Albright, Edmund Breese, Tully Marshall, Clarence Muse, Russell Simpson, John Marston, Erville Anderson, Dorothy Peterson, Snow Flake, Harry Cording.

(12) *THREE ON A MATCH*—a First National Picture, released by Warner Bros. D. F. Zanuck in charge of production. Production supervisor, Ray Griffith. Directed by Mervyn LeRoy. Screenplay by Lucien Hubbard, based on an original story by Kubec Glasmon and John Bright. Photographed by Sol Polito. Edited by Ray Curtiss. Sheila Terry sang "My Diane." Remade by Warner Bros. in 1938 as *Broadway Musketeers,* with Marie Wilson in the Davis part. Opened Strand Theatre, N.Y., October 28, 1932.

(Cast) Joan Blondell, Warren William, Ann Dvorak, Bette Davis, Grant Mitchell, Lyle Talbot, Sheila Terry, Glenda Farrell, Clara Blandick, Buster Phelps, Humphrey Bogart, John Marston, Patricia Ellis, Hale Hamilton, Frankie Darro, Dawn O'Day (Anne Shirley), Virginia Davis, Dick Brandon, Allen Jenkins, Jack LaRue, Edward Arnold.

(13) *20,000 YEARS IN SING SING*—a First National Picture, released by Warner Bros. D. F. Zanuck in charge of production. Production supervisor, Ray Griffith. Directed by Michael Curtiz. Screenplay by Wilson Mizner and Brown Holmes. Adaptation by Courtenay Terrett and Robert Lord, based on the book of the same name by Warden Lewis E. Lawes. Photographed by Barney McGill. Edited by George Amy. James Cagney was originally set for the male lead. Remade in 1940 by Warner Bros. as *Castle on the Hudson* with John Garfield and Ann Sheridan. Opened Strand Theatre, N.Y., January 9, 1933.

(Cast) Spencer Tracy, Bette Davis, Lyle Talbot, Arthur Byron, Sheila Terry, Edward McNamara, Warren Hymer, Louis Calhern, Spencer Charters, Sam Godfrey, Grant Mitchell, Nella Walker, Harold Huber, William Le Maire, Arthur Hoyt, George Pat Collins.

(14) *PARACHUTE JUMPER*—a Warner Bros. Picture. D. F. Zanuck in charge of production. Production supervisor, Ray Griffith. Directed by Alfred E. Green. Screenplay by John Francis Larkin, based on the story *Some Call It Love* by Rian James. Photographed by James Van Trees. Edited by Ray Curtiss. Opened Strand Theatre, N.Y., January 25, 1933.

(Cast) Douglas Fairbanks, Jr., Leo Carrillo, Bette Davis, Frank McHugh, Claire Dodd, Sheila Terry, Harold Huber, Thomas E. Jackson, George Pat Collins, Pat O'Malley, Harold Healy, Ferdinand Munley, Walter Miller.

(15) *THE WORKING MAN*—a Warner Bros. Vitaphone Picture. D. F. Zanuck in charge of production. Production supervisor, Lucien Hubbard. Directed by John Adolfi. Screenplay by Maude T. Howell and Charles Kenyon, based on the story *The Adopted Father* by Edgar Franklin. Photographed by Sol Polito. Art Direction by Jack Okey. Edited by Owen Marks. Davis was delighted to work with mentor Arliss again. Opened Radio City Music Hall, N.Y., April 20, 1933.

(Cast) George Arliss, Bette Davis, Hardie Albright, Theodore Newton, Gordon Westcott, J. Garrell MacDonald, Charles Evans, Frederick Burton, Edward Van Sloan, Pat Wing, Claire McDowell, Harold Minjir, Douglas Dumbrille.

(16) *EX-LADY*—a Warner Bros. Vitaphone Picture. D. F. Zanuck in charge of production. Production supervisor, Lucien Hubbard. Directed by Robert Florey. Screenplay by Davis Boehm, based on an original story by Edith Fitzgerald and Robert Riskin. Photographed by Tony Gaudio. Edited by Harold McLernon. A remake of a Warner Bros. picture, *Illicit*, 1931, with Barbara Stanwyck. Davis was embarrassed by the story, the dialogue, and the seminudity. The film was not a success as her first starring role. Opened Strand Theatre, N.Y., May 14, 1933.

(Cast) Bette Davis, Gene Raymond, Frank McHugh, Monroe Owsley, Claire

Dodd, Kay Strozzi, Ferdinand Gottschalk, Alphonse Ethier, Bodil Rosing.

(17) *BUREAU OF MISSING PERSONS*—a First National Picture, released by Warner Bros. Production supervisor, Henry Blanke. Directed by Roy Del Ruth. Screenplay by Robert Presnell, based on the book *Missing Men* by Police Captain John H. Ayers and Carol Bird. Photographed by Barney McGill. Edited by James Gibbon. Opened Strand Theatre, N.Y., September 8, 1933.

(Cast) Bette Davis, Lewis Stone, Pat O'Brien, Glenda Farrell, Allen Jenkins, Ruth Donnelly, Hugh Herbert, Alan Dinehart, Marjorie Gateson, Tad Alexander, Noel Francis, Wallis Clark, Adrian Morris, Clay Clement, Henry Kolker, Harry Beresford, George Chandler.

(18) *FASHIONS OF 1934*—a First National Picture released by Warner Bros. Production supervisor, Henry Blanke. Directed by William Dieterle. Screenplay by F. Hugh Herbert, Gene Markey, Kathryn Scola, and Carl Erickson, based on the story *The Fashion Plate* by Harry Collins and Warren Duff. Photographed by William Rees. Songs by Sammy Fain and Irving Kahal. Dances by Busby Berkeley. Edited by Jack Killifer. Davis was glamorized almost beyond recognition. Opened Hollywood Theatre, N.Y., January 19, 1934.

(Cast) William Powell, Bette Davis, Frank McHugh, Verree Teasdale, Reginald Owen, Henry O'Neill, Philip Reed, Hugh Herbert, Gordon Westcott, Nella Walker, Dorothy Burgess, Etienne Girardot, William Burress, Spencer Charters, Jane Darwell, Arthur Treacher, Hobart Cavanaugh, Albert Conti.

(19) *THE BIG SHAKEDOWN*—a First National Picture, released by Warner Bros. Production supervisor, Samuel Bischoff. Directed by John Francis Dillon. Screenplay by Niven Busch and Rian James, based on the story *Cut Rate* by Samuel Engel. Photographed by Sid Hickox. Edited by James Gibbon. Charles Farrell, who had starred with Janet Gaynor in eleven pictures, was the leading man. Opened Mayfair Theatre, N.Y., February 11, 1934.

(Cast) Charles Farrell, Bette Davis, Ricardo Cortez, Glenda Farrell, Allen Jenkins, Henry O'Neill, Philip Faversham, Robert Emmett O'Connor, John Wray, George Pat Collins, Adrian Morris, Dewey Robinson, Samuel S. Hinds, Matt Briggs, William B. Davidson, Earl Foxe, Frederick Burton.

(20) *JIMMY THE GENT*—a Warner Bros. Vitaphone Picture. Production supervisor, Robert Lord. Directed by Michael Curtiz. Screenplay by Bertram Milhauser, based on the story *The Heir Chaser* by Laird Doyle and Ray Nazarro. Photographed by Ira Morgan. Edited by Tommy Richards. Working title: *Always a Gent.* Opened Strand Theatre, N.Y., March 25, 1934.

(Cast) James Cagney, Bette Davis, Alice White, Allen Jenkins, Arthur Hohl, Alan Dinehart, Philip Reed, Hobart Cavanaugh, Mayo Methot, Ralf Harolde, Joseph Sawyer, Philip Faversham, Nora Lane, Howard Hickman, Jane Darwell, Joseph Crehan, Robert Warwick, Harold Entwhistle.

(21) *FOG OVER FRISCO*—a Warner Bros. Vitaphone Picture. Production supervisor, Henry Blanke. Directed by William Dieterle. Screenplay by Robert

N. Lee and Eugene Solow, based on an original story by George Dyer, *The Five Fragments*. Photographed by Tony Gaudio. Edited by Harold McLernon. Davis liked her role of the thrill-mad debutante. Remade by Warner Bros. in 1942 as *Spy Ship* with Irene Manning in the Davis role. Opened Strand Theatre, N.Y., June 6, 1934.

(Cast) Bette Davis, Donald Woods, Margaret Lindsay, Lyle Talbot, Arthur Byron, Hugh Herbert, Douglas Dumbrille, Robert Barrat, Henry O'Neill, Irving Pichel, Gordon Westcott, Charles C. Wilson, Alan Hale, William B. Davidson, Douglas Cosgrove, George Chandler, Harold Minjir, William Demarest.

(22) *OF HUMAN BONDAGE*—an RKO Radio Picture. Produced by Pandro S. Berman. Directed by John Cromwell. Screenplay by Lester Cohen, based on the novel of the same name by W. Somerset Maugham. Photographed by Henry W. Gerrard. Art direction by Van Nest Polglase and Carroll Clark. Edited by William Morgan. Gowns by Walter Plunkett. Max Steiner, unbilled, wrote the poignant score. Remade by Warner Bros. in 1946 with Eleanor Parker (to whom Davis sent a note, "I hope Mildred does for you what she did for me") and Paul Henreid and by MGM in 1964 with Kim Novak and Laurence Harvey. Opened Radio City Music Hall, N.Y., June 28, 1934.

(Cast) Leslie Howard, Bette Davis, Frances Dee, Kay Johnson, Reginald Denny, Alan Hale, Reginald Owen, Reginald Sheffield, Desmond Roberts.

(23) *HOUSEWIFE*—a Warner Bros. Vitaphone Picture. Production supervisor, Robert Lord. Directed by Alfred E. Green. Screenplay by Manuel Seff and Lillie Hayward, based on an original story by Robert Lord and Lillie Hayward. Photographed by William Rees. Edited by James Gibbon. Made before *Of Human Bondage* but released afterwards. Opened Strand Theatre, N.Y., August 9, 1934.

(Cast) George Brent, Bette Davis, Ann Dvorak, John Halliday, Ruth Donnelly, Hobart Cavanaugh, Robert Barrat, Joseph Cawthorn, Phil Regan, Willard Robertson, Ronald Cosbey, Leila Bennett, William B. Davidson, John Hale.

(24) *BORDERTOWN*—a Warner Bros. Vitaphone Picture. Production supervisor, Robert Lord. Directed by Archie Mayo. Screenplay by Laird Doyle and Wallace Smith, adapted by Robert Lord, based on the novel of the same name by Carroll Graham. Photographed by Tony Gaudio. Edited by Thomas Richards. Made before *Of Human Bondage* but released afterwards. Remade by Warner Bros. in 1941 as *They Drive by Night,* with Ida Lupino in the Davis role. Opened Strand Theatre, N.Y., January 23, 1935.

(Cast) Paul Muni, Bette Davis, Margaret Lindsay, Gavin Gordon, Arthur Stone, Robert Barrat, Soledad Jiminez, Eugene Pallette, William B. Davidson, Hobart Cavanaugh, Henry O'Neill, Vivian Tobin, Nella Walker, Oscar Apfel, Samuel S. Hinds, Chris Pin Martin, Frank Puglia, Jack Norton.

(25) *THE GIRL FROM TENTH AVENUE*—a First National Picture released by Warner Bros. Production supervisor, Henry Blanke. Directed by Alfred E. Green. Screenplay by Charles Kenyon, based on a play by Hubert Henry

Davies. Photographed by James Van Trees. Edited by Owen Marks. Opened Capitol Theatre, N.Y., May 26, 1935.

(Cast) Bette Davis, Ian Hunter, Colin Clive, Alison Skipworth, John Eldredge, Philip Reed, Katherine Alexander, Helen Jerome Eddy, Gordon Elliott, Adrian Rosley, Andre Cheron, Edward McWade, Mary Treen, Heinie Conklin.

(26) *FRONT PAGE WOMAN*—a Warner Bros. Vitaphone Picture. Production supervisor, Samuel Bischoff. Directed by Michael Curtiz. Screenplay by Roy Chanslor, Lillie Hayward, and Laird Doyle, based on the story *Women Are Bum Newspapermen* by Richard Macaulay. Photographed by Tony Gaudio. Edited by Terry Morse. Opened Strand Theatre, N.Y., July 11, 1935.

(Cast) Bette Davis, George Brent, June Martel, Dorothy Dare, Joseph Crehan, Winifred Shaw, Roscoe Karns, Joseph King, J. Farrell MacDonald, J. Carroll Naish, Walter Walker, DeWitt Jennings, Huntley Gordon, Adrian Rosley, Georges Renevent, Grace Hale, Selmer Jackson, Gordon Westcott.

(27) *SPECIAL AGENT*—a Claridge Picture released by Warner Bros. Produced by Samuel Bischoff in association with Martin Mooney. Directed by William Keighley. Screenplay by Laird Doyle and Abem Finkel, based on an idea by Martin Mooney. Photographed by Sid Hickox. Edited by Clarence Kouster. Remade by Warner Bros. as *Gambling on the High Seas* in 1940 with Jane Wyman in the Davis part. Opened Strand Theatre, N.Y., September 18, 1935.

(Cast) Bette Davis, George Brent, Ricardo Cortez, Jack LaRue, Henry O'Neill, Robert Strange, Joseph Crehan, J. Carroll Naish, Joseph Sawyer, William B. Davidson, Robert Barrat, Paul Guilfoyle, Irving Pichel, Douglas Wood, James Flavin, Lee Phelps, Louis Natheaux, Herbert Skinner, John Alexander.

(28) *DANGEROUS*—a Warner Bros. Vitaphone Picture. Production supervisor, Harry Joe Brown. Directed by Alfred E. Green. Screenplay and original story by Laird Doyle. Photographed by Ernest Haller. Working title: *Hard Luck Dame.* Remade by Warner Bros. in 1941 as *Singapore Woman* with Brenda Marshall. Davis won her first Academy Award as Joyce Heath. Opened Rivoli Theatre, N.Y., December 25, 1935.

(Cast) Bette Davis, Franchot Tone, Margaret Lindsay, Alison Skipworth, John Eldredge, Dick Foran, Walter Walker, Richard Carle, George Irving, Pierre Watkin, Douglas Wood, William B. Davidson, Frank O'Connor, Edward Keane.

(29) *THE PETRIFIED FOREST*—a Warner Bros. Vitaphone Picture. Production supervisor, Henry Blanke. Directed by Archie Mayo. Screenplay by Charles Kenyon and Delmer Daves, based on the play of the same name by Robert E. Sherwood. Photographed by Sol Polito. Edited by Owen Marks. Davis darkened her hair to its natural color for the role of Gabby Maple. An unconvincing remake by Warner Bros. in 1945, *Escape in the Desert,* featured Jean Sullivan in the Davis part and Helmut Dantine in the Bogart role—as an

escaped Nazi! Opened Radio City Music Hall, N.Y., February 6, 1936.

(Cast) Leslie Howard, Bette Davis, Genevieve Tobin, Dick Foran, Humphrey Bogart, Joseph Sawyer, Porter Hall, Charley Grapewin, Paul Harvey, Eddie Acuff, Adrian Morris, Nina Campana, Slim Johnson, John Alexander.

(30) *THE GOLDEN ARROW*—a First National Picture released by Warner Bros. Production supervisor, Samuel Bischoff. Directed by Alfred E. Green. Screenplay by Charles Kenyon, based on the play *Dream Princess* by Michael Arlen. Photographed by Arthur Edeson. Edited by Thomas Pratt. Opened Strand Theatre, N.Y., May 3, 1936.

(Cast) Bette Davis, George Brent, Eugene Pallette, Dick Foran, Carol Hughes, Catherine Doucet, Craig Reynolds, Ivan Lebedeff, G. P. Huntley, Jr., Hobart Cavanaugh, Henry O'Neill, Eddie Acuff, Earl Foxe, E. E. Clive, Rafael Storm, Sara Edwards, Bess Flowers, Mary Treen, Selmer Jackson.

(31) *SATAN MET A LADY*—a Warner Bros. Vitaphone Picture. Production supervisor, Henry Blanke. Directed by William Dieterle. Screenplay by Brown Holmes, based on the novel *The Maltese Falcon* by Dashiell Hammett. Photographed by Arthur Edeson. Edited by Max Parker, reedited by Warren Low. Alternate working titles: *The Man in the Black Hat, Men on Her Mind,* and *Hard Luck Dame.* This poor film provided the impetus for Davis to break her Warner Bros. contract. Opened Strand Theatre, N.Y., July 22, 1936.

(Cast) Bette Davis, Warren William, Alison Skipworth, Arthur Treacher, Winifred Shaw, Marie Wilson, Porter Hall, Maynard Holmes, Olin Howard, Charles Wilson, Joseph King, Barbara Blane, William B. Davidson.

(32) *MARKED WOMAN*—a Warner Bros. First National Picture. Produced by Hal Wallis in association with Lou Edelman. Directed by Lloyd Bacon. Screenplay by Robert Rosson and Abem Finkel, with additional dialogue by Seton I. Miller. Photographed by George Barnes. Music by Leo F. Forbstein. Edited by Jack Killifer. Defeated by Warner Bros. in her court case, Davis gamely returned from England to make this very successful picture. Opened Strand Theatre, N.Y., April 11, 1937.

(Cast) Bette Davis, Humphrey Bogart, Eduardo Ciannelli, Jane Bryan, Lola Lane, Isabel Jewell, Rosalind Marquis, Mayo Methot, Ben Welden, Henry O'Neill, Allen Jenkins, John Litel, Damian O'Flynn, Robert Strange, Raymond Hatton, William B. Davidson, Frank Faylen, Jack Norton, Kenneth Harlan.

(33) *KID GALAHAD*—a Warner Bros. Picture. Executive Producer, Hal B. Wallis, in association with Samuel Bischoff. Directed by Michael Curtiz. Screenplay by Seton I. Miller, based on the novel of the same name by Francis Wallace. Photographed by Tony Gaudio. Edited by George Amu. The song "The Moon Is in Tears Tonight" by M. K. Jerome and Jack Scholl. Davis lip-synced the song as a nightclub singer. Remade by Warner Bros. in 1941 as *The Wagons Roll at Night* and by Paramount in 1962 as an Elvis Presley musical. Opened Strand Theatre, N.Y., May 26, 1937.

(Cast) Edward G. Robinson, Bette Davis, Humphrey Bogart, Wayne Morris,

William Haade, Jane Bryan, Harry Carey, Soledad Jiminez, Veda Ann Borg, Ben Welden, Joseph Crehan, Harlan Tucker, Frank Faylen, Joyce Compton, Horace MacMahon.

(34) *THAT CERTAIN WOMAN*—a Warner Bros. First National Picture. Executive Producer, Hal B. Wallis, in association with Robert Lord. Directed by Edmund Goulding. Screenplay by Edmund Goulding, based on his original screenplay *The Trespasser*. Photographed by Ernest Haller. Music by Max Steiner. Edited by Jack Killifer. Goulding gave Davis the ''star'' treatment. Opened Strand Theatre, N.Y., September 15, 1937.

(Cast) Bette Davis, Henry Fonda, Ian Hunter, Anita Louise, Donald Crisp, Katherine Alexander, Mary Phillips, Minor Watson, Ben Weldon, Sidney Toler, Charles Trowbridge, Norman Willis, Herbert Rawlinson, Rosalind Marquis, Frank Faylen, Willard Parker, Dwane Day, Hugh O'Connell.

(35) *IT'S LOVE I'M AFTER*—a Warner Bros. Picture. Executive Producer, Hal B. Wallis, in association with Harry Joe Brown. Directed by Archie Mayo. Screenplay by Casey Robinson, based on the story *Gentlemen After Midnight* by Maurice Hanline. Photographed by James Van Trees. Edited by Owen Marks. The high-comedy role of actress Joyce Arden was an excellent change of pace for Davis. Opened Strand Theatre, N.Y., November 10, 1937.

(Cast) Leslie Howard, Bette Davis, Olivia De Havilland, Patric Knowles, Eric Blore, George Barbier, Spring Byington, Bonita Granville, E. E. Clive, Veda Ann Borg, Valerie Bergere, Georgia Caine, Sarah Edwards, Lionel Bellmore, Irving Bacon.

(36) *JEZEBEL*—a Warner Bros. Picture. Executive Producer, Hal B. Wallis, in association with Henry Blanke. Directed by William Wyler. Screenplay by Clements Ripley, Abem Finkel, and John Huston, with the help of Robert Buckner, based on the play of the same name by Owen Davis, Sr. Photographed by Ernest Haller. Art direction by Robert Haas. Music by Max Steiner. Edited by Warren Low. Davis's performance was immeasurably helped by Wyler's direction. She won her second Academy Award for the role of Julie Marsden. Opened Radio City Music Hall, N.Y., March 10, 1938.

(Cast) Bette Davis, Henry Fonda, George Brent, Donald Crisp, Fay Bainter, Margaret Lindsay, Henry O'Neill, John Litel, Gordon Oliver, Spring Byington, Margaret Early, Richard Cromwell, Theresa Harris, Janet Shaw, Irving Pichel, Eddie Anderson.

(37) *THE SISTERS*—a Warner Bros. Picture. Produced by Hal B. Wallis, in association with David Lewis, Directed by Anatole Litvak. Screenplay by Milton Krims, based on the novel of the same name by Myron Brinig. Photographed by Tony Gaudio. Music by Max Steiner. Edited by Warren Low. Property was originally purchased for Kay Francis. Opened Strand Theatre, N.Y., October 14, 1938.

(Cast) Errol Flynn, Bette Davis, Anita Louise, Ian Hunter, Donald Crisp, Beulah Bondi, Jane Bryan, Alan Hale, Dick Foran, Henry Travers, Patric Knowles, Lee Patrick, Laura Hope Crewes, Janet Shaw, Harry Davenport, Ruth

Garland, John Warburton, Paul Harvey, Mayo Methot, Irving Bacon, Arthur Hoyt.

(38) *DARK VICTORY*—a Warner Bros. First National Picture. Produced by Hal B. Wallis, in association with David Lewis. Directed by Edmund Goulding. Screenplay by Casey Robinson, based on the play of the same name by George Emerson Brewer, Jr., and Bertram Block. Photographed by Ernest Haller. Song "Oh, Give Me Time for Tenderness" by Edmund Goulding and Elsie Janis. Music by Max Steiner. Edited by William Holmes. One of Davis's favorite roles. She received an Academy Award nomination for Judith Traherne. Remade by United Artists in 1963 as *Stolen Hours* with Susan Hayward. Opened Radio City Music Hall, N.Y., April 20, 1939.

(Cast) Bette Davis, George Brent, Geraldine Fitzgerald, Humphrey Bogart, Ronald Reagan, Henry Travers, Cora Witherspoon, Dorothy Peterson, Virginia Brissac, Charles Richman, Leonard Mudie, Fay Helm, Lottie Williams.

(39) *JUAREZ*—a Warner Bros. Picture. Produced by Hal B. Wallis, in association with Henry Blanke. Directed by William Dieterle. Screenplay by John Huston, Aeneas MacKenzie, and Wolfgang Reinhardt, based on the play *Juarez and Maximilian* by Franz Werfel and the book, *The Phantom Crown* by Bertita Harding. Photographed by Tony Gaudio. Edited by Warren Low. Warner Bros. prestige picture of the year. Opened Hollywood Theatre, N.Y., April 25, 1939.

(Cast) Paul Muni, Bette Davis, Brian Aherne, Claude Rains, John Garfield, Donald Crisp, Joseph Calleia, Gale Sondergaard, Gilbert Roland, Henry O'Neill, Harry Davenport, Louis Calhern, Walter Kingsford, Georgia Caine, Montagu Love, John Miljan, Vladimir Sokoloff, Irving Pichel, Pedro De Cordoba, Gilbert Emory, Monte Blue, Manuel Diaz, Hugh Sothern, Mickey Kuhn.

(40) *THE OLD MAID*—a Warner Bros. First National Picture. Produced by Hal B. Wallis, in association with Henry Blanke. Directed by Edmund Goulding. Screenplay by Casey Robinson, based on the Pulitzer Prize play by Zoe Atkins, adapted from the novel of the same name by Edith Wharton. Photographed by Tony Gaudio. Music by Max Steiner. Edited by George Amy. Opened Strand Theatre, N.Y., August 11, 1939.

(Cast) Bette Davis, Miriam Hopkins, George Brent, Donald Crisp, Jane Bryan, Louise Fazenda, James Stephenson, Jerome Cowan, William Lundigan, Rand Brooks, Cecelia Loftus, Janet Shaw, DeWolf Hopper.

(41) *THE PRIVATE LIVES OF ELIZABETH AND ESSEX*—a Warner Bros. Picture. Produced by Hal B. Wallis, in association with Robert Lord. Directed by Michael Curtiz. Screenplay by Norman Reilly Raine and Aeneas MacKenzie, based on the play *Elizabeth the Queen* by Maxwell Anderson. Photographed in Technicolor by Sol Polito and H. Howard Greene. Music by Erich Wolfgang Korngold. Edited by Owen Marks. Davis shaved her forehead back two inches to give the illusion of baldness under Elizabeth's red wigs. Opened Strand Theatre, N.Y., December 1, 1939.

(Cast) Bette Davis, Errol Flynn, Oliva De Havilland, Donald Crisp, Vincent Price, Alan Hale, Henry Stephenson, Henry Daniell, James Stephenson, Leo G. Carroll, Nanette Fabares (Fabray), Rosella Towne, Maris Wrixon, Ralph Forbes, Robert Warwick, John Sutton, Guy Bellis, Doris Lloyd, Forrester Harvey.

(42) *ALL THIS AND HEAVEN TOO*—a Warner Bros. First National Picture. Produced by Jack L. Warner and Hal B. Wallis, in association with David Lewis. Directed by Anatole Litvak. Screenplay by Casey Robinson, based on the novel of the same name by Rachel Field. Photographed by Ernest Haller. Music by Max Steiner. Edited by Warren Low. Opened Radio City Music Hall, N.Y., July 4, 1940.

(Cast) Bette Davis, Charles Boyer, Jeffrey Lynn, Barbara O'Neil, Virginia Weidler, Helen Westley, Walter Hampden, Henry Daniell, Harry Davenport, George Coulouris, Montagu Love, Janet Beecher, June Lockhart, Ann Todd, Richard Nichols, Fritz Leiber, Ian Keith, Sibyl Harris, Mary Anderson, Edward Fielding, Ann Gillis, Peggy Stewart, Victor Kilian, Mrs. Gardner Crane.

(43) *THE LETTER*—a Warner Bros. First National Picture. Produced by Hal B. Wallis, in association with Robert Lord. Directed by William Wyler. Screenplay by Howard Koch, based on the play of the same name by W. Somerset Maugham. Photographed by Tony Gaudio. Music by Max Steiner. Edited by George Amy. First filmed by Paramount in 1929 with Jeanne Eagels and again by Warner Bros. in 1947 as *The Unfaithful* with Ann Sheridan. Davis received an Academy Award nomination as Leslie Crosbie. Opened Strand Theatre, N.Y., November 22, 1940.

(Cast) Bette Davis, Herbert Marshall, James Stephenson, Frieda Inescort, Gale Sondergaard, Bruce Lester, Elizabeth Earl, Cecil Kellaway, Doris Lloyd, Sen Yung, Willie Fung, Tetsu Komai, Roland Got, Otto Hahn, Pete Kotehernaro, David Newell, Ottola Nesmith, Lillian Kemble-Cooper.

(44) *THE GREAT LIE*—a Warner Bros. Picture. Produced by Hal B. Wallis, in association with Henry Blanke. Directed by Edmund Goulding. Screenplay by Lenore Coffee, based on the novel *January Heights* by Polan Banks. Photographed by Tony Gaudio. Music by Max Steiner. Edited by Ralph Dawson. Working title, *Far Horizon*. World premiere, Premiere Theatre, Littleton, N.H. near Butternut, Davis's Eastern home, April 5, 1941. Opened Strand Theatre, N.Y., April 11, 1941.

(Cast) Bette Davis, George Brent, Mary Astor, Lucile Watson, Hattie McDaniel, Grant Mitchell, Jerome Cowan, Sam McDaniel, Thurston Hall, Russell Hicks, Charles Trowbridge, Virginia Brissac, Olin Howland, J. Farrell MacDonald, Doris Lloyd, Addison Richards, Georgia Caine, Alphonse Martell.

(45) *THE BRIDE CAME C.O.D.*—a Warner Bros. Picture. Produced by Hal B. Wallis, in association with William Cagney. Directed by William Keighley. Screenplay by Julius J. and Philip G. Epstein, based on a story by Kenneth Earl

and M. M. Musselman. Photographed by Ernest Haller. Music by Max Steiner. Edited by Thomas Richards. Location scenes filmed at Death Valley. Opened Strand Theatre, N.Y., July 25, 1941.

(Cast) James Cagney, Bette Davis, Stuart Erwin, Jack Carson, George Tobias, Eugene Pallette, Harry Davenport, William Frawley, Edward Brophy, Harry Holman, Chick Chandler, Keith Douglas, Herbert Anderson, Creighton Hale, Frank Mayo, DeWolf Hopper, Jack Mower, William Newell.

(46) *THE LITTLE FOXES*—a Samuel Goldwyn Production, released by RKO Radio Pictures, Inc. Produced by Samuel Goldwyn. Directed by William Wyler. Screenplay by Lillian Hellman, based on her stage play of the same name, with additional scenes and dialogue by Arthur Kober, Dorothy Parker, and Alan Campbell. Photographed by Gregg Toland. Edited by Daniel Mandell. Davis fought with Wyler over the interpretation of the role of Regina Giddens but received an Academy Award nomination. Opened Radio City Music Hall, N.Y., August 21, 1941.

(Cast) Bette Davis, Herbert Marshall, Teresa Wright, Richard Carlson, Patricia Collinge, Dan Duryea, Charles Dingle, Carl Benton Reid, Jessie Grayson, John Marriott, Russell Hicks, Lucien Littlefield, Virginia Brissac.

(47) *THE MAN WHO CAME TO DINNER*—a Warner Bros. Picture. Produced by Hal B. Wallis, in association with Jerry Wald, Sam Harris, and Jack Saper. Directed by William Keighley. Screenplay by Julius J. and Philip G. Epstein, based on the play of the same name by George S. Kaufman and Moss Hart. Photographed by Tony Gaudio. Edited by Jack Killifer. Davis wanted John Barrymore for the role of Sheridan Whiteside. Opened Strand Theatre, N.Y., January 1, 1942.

(Cast) Bette Davis, Ann Sheridan, Monty Woolley, Richard Travis, Jimmy Durante, Reginald Gardiner, Billie Burke, Elizabeth Fraser, Grant Mitchell, George Barbier, Mary Wickes, Russell Arms, Ruth Vivian, Edwin Stanley, Charles Drake, Nanette Vallon, John Ridgely.

(48) *IN THIS OUR LIFE*—a Warner Bros. Picture. Produced by Hal B. Wallis, in association with David Lewis. Directed by John Huston. Screenplay by Howard Koch, based on the Pulitzer Prize novel of the same name by Ellen Glasgow. Photographed by Ernest Haller. Music by Max Steiner. Edited by William Holmes. Davis felt she was too old for the part of Stanley Timberlake. Opened Strand Theatre, N.Y., May 8, 1942.

(Cast) Bette Davis, Olivia De Havilland, George Brent, Dennis Morgan, Charles Coburn, Frank Craven, Billie Burke, Hattie McDaniel, Lee Patrick, Mary Servoss, Ernest Anderson, William B. Davidson, Edward Fielding, John Hamilton, William Forest, Lee Phelps.

(49) *NOW, VOYAGER*—a Warner Bros. Picture. Produced by Hal B. Wallis. Directed by Irving Rapper. Screenplay by Casey Robinson, based on the novel of the same name by Olive Higgins Prouty. Photographed by Sol Polito. Music by Max Steiner. Edited by Warren Low. Davis received an Academy Award

nomination for the role of Charlotte Vale. Opened Hollywood Theatre, N.Y., October 22, 1942.

(Cast) Bette Davis, Paul Henreid, Claude Rains, Gladys Cooper, Bonita Granville, Ilka Chase, John Loder, Lee Patrick, Franklin Pangborn, Katherine Alexander, James Rennie, Mary Wickes, Janis Wilson, Frank Puglia, Michael Ames, Charles Drake, David Clyde.

(50) *WATCH ON THE RHINE*—a Warner Bros. Picture. Produced by Hal B. Wallis. Directed by Herman Shumlin. Screenplay by Dashiell Hammett, with additional scenes and dialogue by Lillian Hellman, based on her play of the same name. Photographed by Merritt Gerstad and Hal Mohr. Music by Max Steiner. Edited by Rudi Fehr. Lukas won an Academy Award for his role of Kurt Muller. Opened Rialto Theatre, N.Y., August 27, 1943.

(Cast) Bette Davis, Paul Lukas, Geraldine Fitzgerald, Lucile Watson, Beulah Bondi, George Coulouris, Donald Woods, Henry Daniell, Donald Buka, Eric Roberts, Janis Wilson, Mary Young, Kurt Katch, Erwin Kalser, Clyde Fillmore, Robert O. Davis, Frank Wilson, Clarence Muse, Anthony Caruso, Howard Hickman, Elvira Curci, Creighton Hale, Alan Hale, Jr.

(51) *THANK YOUR LUCKY STARS*—a Warner Bros. Picture. J.L. Warner in charge of production. Produced by Mark Hellinger. Directed by David Butler. Screenplay by Norman Panama, Melvin Frank, and James V. Kern, based on a story by Everett Freeman and Arthur Schwartz. Photographed by Arthur Edeson. Music and lyrics by Arthur Schwartz and Frank Loesser. Musical direction by Leo F. Forbstein. Dances created and staged by LeRoy Prinz. Edited by Irene Morra. Davis sang "They're Either Too Young or Too Old" and jitterbugged with Conrad Weidel. Opened Strand Theatre, N.Y., October 1, 1943.

(Cast) Dennis Morgan, Joan Leslie, Edward Everett Horton, S. Z. Sakall, Richard Lane, Ruth Donnelly, Don Wilson, Henry Armetta, Joyce Reynolds—with guest stars Humphrey Bogart, Eddie Cantor, Bette Davis, Olivia De Havilland, Errol Flynn, John Garfield, Ida Lupino, Ann Sheridan, Dinah Shore, Alexis Smith, Jack Carson, Alan Hale, George Tobias, Hattie McDaniel, Willie Best, Spike Jones and His City Slickers.

(52) *OLD ACQUAINTANCE*—a Warner Bros. Picture. J. L. Warner in charge of production. Produced by Henry Blanke. Directed by Vincent Sherman. Screenplay by John Van Druten and Leonore Coffee, based on the play of the same name by John Van Druten. Photographed by Sol Polito. Music by Franz Waxman. Edited by Terry Morse. Filmed before *Thank Your Lucky Stars,* but released afterward. Opened Hollywood Theatre, N.Y., November 2, 1943.

(Cast) Bette Davis, Miriam Hopkins, Gig Young, John Loder, Dolores Moran, Philip Reed, Roscoe Karns, Anne Revere, Esther Dale, Ann Codee, Joseph Crehan, Pierre Watkin, Marjorie Hoshelle, George Lessey, Ann Doran, Leona Maricle, Francine Rufo.

(53) *MR. SKEFFINGTON*—a Warner Bros. Picture. J. L. Warner in charge of

production. Produced by Julius J. and Philip G. Epstein, based on the novel of the same name by "Elizabeth." Photographed by Ernest Haller. Music by Franz Waxman. Edited by Ralph Dawson. Davis was nominated for an Academy Award for her portrayal of Fanny Skeffington. Perc Westmore's makeup was revolutionary. Opened State Theatre, N.Y., May 25, 1944.

(Cast) Bette Davis, Claude Rains, Walter Abel, Richard Waring, George Coulouris, Marjorie Riordan, Robert Shayne, John Alexander, Jerome Cowan, Johnny Mitchell, Dorothy Peterson, Peter Whitney, Bill Kennedy, Tom Stevenson, Halliwell Hobbes, Bunny Sunshine, Gigi Perreau, Dolores Gray, Walter Kingsford, Molly Lamont.

(54) *HOLLYWOOD CANTEEN*—a Warner Bros. Picture. J. L. Warner in charge of production. Produced by Alex Gottlieb. Directed by Delmer Daves. Screenplay and original story by Delmer Daves. Photographed by Bert Glennon. Edited by Christian Nyby. J. L. Warner contributed a large portion of the proceeds to the Canteen. Opened Strand Theatre, N.Y., December 15, 1944.

(Cast) Joan Leslie, Robert Hutton, Janis Paige, Dane Clark, Richard Erdman, James Flavin, Joan Winfield, Jonathan Hale, Rudolph Friml, Jr., Bill Manning, Larry Thompson, Mell Schubert, Walden Boyle, Steve Richards—with guest stars the Andrews Sisters, Jack Benny, Joe E. Brown, Eddie Cantor, Kitty Carlisle, Jack Carson, Joan Crawford, Helmut Dantine, Bette Davis, Faye Emerson, Victor Francen, John Garfield, Sydney Greenstreet, Alan Hale, Paul Henried, Andrea King, Peter Lorre, Ida Lupino, Irene Manning, Nora Martin, Joan McCracken, Dolores Moran, Dennis Morgan, Eleanor Parker, William Prince, Joyce Reynolds, John Ridgely, Roy Rogers and Trigger, S. Z. Sakall, Alexis Smith, Zachary Scott, Barbara Stanwyck, Craig Stevens, Joseph Szigeti, Donald Woods, Jane Wyman, Jimmy Dorsey and His Band, Carmen Cavallaro and His Orchestra, Rosaria and Antonio, Sons of the Pioneers, Virginia Patton, Lynne Baggett, Betty Alexander, Julie Bishop, Robert Shayne, Johnny Mitchell, John Sheridan, Colleen Townsend, Angela Green, Paul Brooke, Marianne O'Brien, Dorothy Malone, Bill Kennedy.

(55) *THE CORN IS GREEN*—a Warner Bros. Picture. J. L. Warner in charge of production. Produced by Jack Chertok. Directed by Irving Rapper. Screenplay by Casey Robinson and Frank Cavett, based on the play of the same name by Emlyn Williams. Photographed by Sol Polito. Music by Max Steiner. Edited by Frederick Richards. The play was the true story of Emlyn Williams and his schoolteacher, Miss Cooke. Opened Hollywood Theatre, N.Y., March 29, 1945.

(Cast) Bette Davis, John Dall, Joan Lorring, Nigel Bruce, Rhys Williams, Rosalind Ivan, Mildred Dunnock, Gwenyth Hughes, Billy Roy, Thomas Louden, Arthur Shields, Leslie Vincent, Robert Regent, Tony Ellis, Elliot Dare, Robert Cherry, Gene Ross.

(56) *A STOLEN LIFE*—a Warner Bros. Picture. A B.D. Production. Directed by Curtis Bernhardt. Screenplay by Catherine Turney, adapted by Margaret

Buell Wilder, based on the novel by Karel J. Benes, *Uloupeny Zivot.* Photographed by Sol Polito and Ernest Haller. Music by Max Steiner. Edited by Rudi Fehr. Davis played twins, Kate and Pat Bosworth. The split screen work was the most expert up to that time. A remake of the 1939 Paramount Elisabeth Bergner picture, *The Stolen Life.* Opened Hollywood Theatre, N.Y., May 1, 1946.

(Cast) Bette Davis, Glenn Ford, Dane Clark, Walter Brennan, Charles Ruggles, Bruce Bennett, Peggy Knudsen, Esther Dale, Clara Blandick, Joan Winfield.

(57) *DECEPTION*—a Warner Bros. Picture. J. L. Warner in charge of production. Produced by Henry Blanke. Directed by Irving Rapper. Screenplay by John Collier and Joseph Than, based on a play variously titled *Monsieur Lambertheir, Satan,* and *Jealousy* by Louis Verneuil. Photographed by Ernest Haller. Musical score and Hollenius's Cello Concerto by Erich Wolfgang Korngold. Edited by Alan Crosland, Jr. Davis discovered she was pregnant during filming and tabbed the picture *Conception!* Opened Hollywood Theatre, N.Y., October 18, 1946.

(Cast) Bette Davis, Paul Henreid, Claude Rains, John Abbott, Benson Fong, Richard Walsh, Suzi Crandall, Richard Erdman, Ross Ford, Russell Arms, Bess Flowers, Gino Cerrado, Clifton Young, Cyril Delevanti, Jane Harker.

(58) *WINTER MEETING*—a Warner Bros. Picture. J. L. Warner in charge of production. Produced by Henry Blanke. Directed by Bretaigne Windust. Screenplay by Catherine Turney, based on the novel of the same name by Ethel Vance. Photographed by Ernest Haller. Music by Max Steiner. Edited by Owen Marks. First Davis film since *Satan Met a Lady* to get a critical lambasting. Opened Warner Theatre, N.Y., April 7, 1948.

(Cast) Bette Davis, Janis Paige, James Davis, John Hoyt, Florence Bates, Walter Baldwin, Ransom Sherman.

(59) *JUNE BRIDE*—a Warner Bros. Picture. J. L. Warner in charge of production. Produced by Henry Blanke. Directed by Bretaigne Windust. Screenplay by Ranald MacDougall, based on the play *Feature for June* by Eileen Tighe and Graeme Lorimer. Photographed by Ted McCord. Music by David Buttolph. Edited by Owen Marks. Davis's first comedy since *The Man Who Came to Dinner.* Edith Head designed the wardrobe. Debbie Reynolds had a bit part. Opened Strand Theatre, N.Y., October 29, 1948.

(Cast) Bette Davis, Robert Montgomery, Fay Bainter, Betty Lynn, Tom Tully, Barbara Bates, Jerome Cowan, Mary Wickes, James Burke, Raymond Roe, Marjorie Bennett, Ray Montgomery, George O'Hanlon, Sandra Gould, Esther Howard, Jessie Adams, Raymond Bond, Alice Kelley, Patricia Northrop.

(60) *BEYOND THE FOREST*—a Warner Bros. Picture. J. L. Warner in charge of production. Produced by Henry Blanke. Directed by King Vidor. Screenplay by Lenore Coffee, based on the novel of the same name by Stuart Engstrand. Photographed by Robert Burks. Music by Max Steiner. Edited by Rudi Fehr.

Film was condemned by the Catholic Church and slightly reedited to conform to "objectionable in part" rating. Reviews were the most scathing of Davis's career. Opened Strand Theatre, N.Y., October 21, 1949.

(Cast) Bette Davis, Joseph Cotten, David Brian, Ruth Roman, Minor Watson, Dona Drake, Regis Toomey, Sarah Selby, Mary Servoss, Frances Charles, Harry Tyler, Ralph Littlefield, Creighton Hale, Joel Allen, Ann Doran.

(61) *ALL ABOUT EVE*—a Twentieth Century-Fox Picture. Produced by Darryl F. Zanuck. Written and directed by Joseph L. Mankiewicz, based on the story *The Wisdom of Eve* by Mary Orr. Photographed by Milton Krasner. Music by Alfred Newman. Edited by Barbara McLean. Davis and Merrill fell in love during shooting and married shortly after picture was completed. Davis received an Academy Award nomination as Margo Channing. Film garnered record number (14) of Academy nominations. Opened Roxy Theatre, N.Y., October 13, 1950. Hollywood premiere, Grauman's Chinese Theatre, November 9, 1950.

(Cast) Bette Davis, Anne Baxter, George Sanders, Celeste Holm, Gary Merrill, Hugh Marlowe, Thelma Ritter, Marilyn Monroe, Gregory Ratoff, Barbara Bates, Walter Hampden, Randy Stuart, Craig Hill, Leland Harris, Claude Stroud, Eugene Borden, Steve Geray, Bess Flowers, Stanley Orr, Eddie Fisher.

(62) *PAYMENT ON DEMAND*—an RKO Radio Picture. Produced by Jack H. Skirball and Bruce Manning, Directed by Curtis Bernhardt. Screenplay *The Story of a Divorce* and original story by Bruce Manning and Curtis Bernhardt. Photographed by Leo Tover. Edited by Harry Marker. Filmed before *All About Eve* but released afterwards. Howard Hughes insisted on a new, happier ending. Jane Cowl died before the picture was released. Opened Radio City Music Hall, N.Y., February 15, 1951.

(Cast) Bette Davis, Barry Sullivan, Jane Cowl, Kent Taylor, Betty Lynn, John Sutton, Frances Dee, Peggie Castle, Otto Kruger, Walter Sande, Brett King, Richard Anderson, Natalie Schafer, Katherine Emery, Lisa Golm, Moroni Olsen.

(63) *ANOTHER MAN'S POISON*—an Eros Production, released by United Artists. Produced by Douglas Fairbanks, Jr., and Daniel M. Angel. Directed by Irving Rapper. Screenplay by Val Guest, based on the play *Deadlock* by Leslie Sands. Photographed by Robert Krasker. Music by Paul Sawtell. Edited by Gordon Hales. Davis's first film produced in England. Opened Metropolitan Theatre, Brooklyn, N.Y., and saturated booking, Loew's Theatres, N.Y., January 6, 1952.

(Cast) Bette Davis, Gary Merrill, Emlyn Williams, Anthony Steel, Barbara Murray, Reginald Beckwith, Edna Morris.

(64) *PHONE CALL FROM A STRANGER*—a Twentieth Century-Fox Picture. Produced by Nunnally Johnson. Directed by Jean Negulesco. Screenplay by Nunnally Johnson, based on a story by Ida Alexa Ross Wylie. Photo-

graphed by Milton Krasner. Music by Franz Waxman. Edited by Hugh Fowler. Davis received special billing for her cameo role, "Bette Davis as Marie Hoke." Opened Roxy Theatre, N.Y., February 1, 1952.

(Cast) Shelley Winters, Gary Merrill, Michael Rennie, Keenan Wynn, Evelyn Varden, Warren Stevens, Beatrice Straight, Ted Donaldson, Craig Stevens, Helen Westcott, Bette Davis.

(65) *THE STAR*—a Bert E. Friedlob Production, released by Twentieth Century-Fox. Produced by Bert E. Friedlob. Directed by Stuart Heisler. Screenplay and original story by Katherine Albert and Dale Eunson. Photographed by Ernest Laszlo. Edited by Otto Ludwig. Davis received an Academy Award nomination as Margaret Elliott. Opened Rivoli Theatre, N.Y., January 28, 1953.

(Cast) Bette Davis, Sterling Hayden, Natalie Wood, Warner Anderson, Minor Watson, June Travis, Katherine Warren, Kay Riehl, Barbara Woodel, Fay Baker, Barbara Lawrence, David Alpert, Paul Frees.

(66) *THE VIRGIN QUEEN*—a Twentieth Century-Fox Picture. Produced by Charles Brackett. Directed by Henry Koster. Screenplay and original story *Sir Walter Raleigh* by Harry Brown and Mildred Lord. Photographed in Cinemascope by Charles G. Clarke. Music by Franz Waxman. Edited by Robert Simpson. Perc Westmore again created the Elizabeth I makeup, shaving Davis's forehead back two inches. Mary Wills created the costumes. World premiere Strand Theatre, Portland, Me., July 22, 1955. Opened Roxy Theatre, N.Y., August 5.

(Cast) Bette Davis, Richard Todd, Joan Collins, Jay Robinson, Herbert Marshall, Dan O'Herlihy, Robert Douglas, Romney Brent, Marjorie Hellen, Lisa Daniels, Lisa Davis, Barry Bernard, Robert Adler, Noel Drayton, Ian Murray, Margery Weston, Rod Taylor, Davis Thursby, Arthur Gould-Porter.

(67) *THE CATERED AFFAIR*—a Metro-Goldwyn-Mayer Picture. Produced by Sam Zimbalist. Directed by Richard Brooks. Screenplay by Gore Vidal, based on the teleplay of the same name by Paddy Chayefsky. Photographed by John Alton. Music by Andre Previn. Edited by Gene Ruggiero and Frank Santillo. Ma Agnes Hurley is Davis's favorite role. Barry Fitzgerald died before the picture was released. Previewed at Fox Beverly Theatre, Beverly Hills, April 20, 1956. Opened Victoria Theatre, N.Y., June 14.

(Cast) Bette Davis, Debbie Reynolds, Ernest Borgnine, Barry Fitzgerald, Rod Taylor, Robert Simon, Madge Kennedy, Dorothy Stickney, Carol Veazie, Joan Camden, Ray Stricklyn, Jay Adler, Dan Tobin, Paul Denton, Augusta Merighi, Sammy Shack, Jack Kenny, Robert Stephenson, Mae Clarke.

(68) *STORM CENTER*—a Phoenix Production, released by Columbia Pictures. Produced by Julian Blaustein. Directed by Daniel Taradash. Screenplay first titled *This Time Tomorrow*, then *The Library* by Daniel Taradash and Elick Moll. Photographed by Burnett Guffey. Music by George Dunning. Edited by William A. Lyon. Exteriors shot in Santa Rosa, Calif. Made before *The Catered Affair* but released afterwards. Previewed at Columbia Studios,

July 11, 1956. World Premiere, Midtown Theatre, Philadelphia, Pa., July 31. Opened at the Normandie Theatre, N.Y., October 20.

(Cast) Bette Davis, Brian Keith, Kim Hunter, Paul Kelly, Kevin Coughlin, Joe Mantell, Sallie Brophy, Howard Wierum, Curtis Cooksey, Michael Raffetto, Edward Platt, Kathryn Grant, Howard Wendell, Burt Mustin, Edith Evanson.

(69) *JOHN PAUL JONES*—a Samuel Bronston Production, distributed by Warner Bros. Produced by Samuel Bronston. Directed by John Farrow. Screenplay by John Farrow and Jesse Lasky, Jr., from the story *Nor'wester* by Clements Ripley. Photographed in Technicolor by Michael Kelber. Music by Max Steiner. Edited by Eda Warren. Produced in Spain. Davis's scene shot at the Royal Palace at Versailles. Previewed at Warner Bros. Studio June 2, 1959. Opened Rivoli Theatre, N.Y., June 16.

(Cast) Robert Stack, Marisa Pavan, Charles Coburn, Erin O'Brien, Tom Brannum, Bruce Cabot, Basil Sydney, Archie Duncan, Thomas Gomez, Judson Laure, Bob Cunningham, John Charles Farrow, Eric Pohlmann, Pepe Nieto, John Crawford, Patrick Villiers, Frank Latimore, Ford Rainey, Bruce Seaton— and MacDonald Carey, Jean Pierre Aumont, David Farrar, Peter Cushing, Susana Canales, Jorge Riviere—and Bette Davis as Catherine the Great.

(70) *THE SCAPEGOAT*—a du Maurier-Guinness Production released by Metro-Goldwyn-Mayer. Produced by Michael Balcon. Directed by Robert Hamer. Screenplay by Gore Vidal and Robert Hamer, based on the novel of the same name by Daphne du Maurier. Photographed by Paul Beeson. Music by Bronislau Caper. Edited by Jack Harris. Produced in England. Davis's scenes were severely edited. Previewed at MGM Studio, July 16, 1959. Opened Guild Theatre, N.Y., August 6.

(Cast) Alec Guinness, Bette Davis, Nicole Maurey, Irene Worth, Pamela Brown, Annabel Bartlett, Geoffrey Keen, Noel Howlett, Peter Bull, Leslie French, Alan Webb, Maria Britneva, Eddie Byrne, Alexander Archdale, Peter Sallis.

(71) *POCKETFUL OF MIRACLES*—a Franton Production, released by United Artists. Produced by Frank Capra in association with Glenn Ford and Joseph Sistrom. Directed by Frank Capra. Screenplay by Hal Kanter and Harry Tugend, based on the screenplay *Lady for a Day* by Robert Riskin and the story *Madame la Gimp* by Damon Runyon. Photographed in Eastman color and Panavision by Robert Bronner. Music by Walter Scharf. Edited by Frank P. Keller. Davis's changing role metamorphosed her from the gin-soaked Apple Annie to the regal Mrs. E. Worthington Manville. Previewed at Grauman's Chinese Theatre, Hollywood, Calif., October 13, 1961. Booked into 650 theaters across the nation, December 18.

(Cast) Glenn Ford, Bette Davis, Hope Lange, Arthur O'Connell, Peter Falk, Thomas Mitchell, Edward Everett Horton, Mickey Shaughnessy, David Brian, Sheldon Leonard, Ann-Margret, Peter Mann, Barton MacLane, John Litel, Jerome Cowan, Jay Novello, Frank Ferguson, Willis Bouchey, Fritz Feld, Ellen

Corby, Gavin Gordon, Benny Rubin, Jack Elam, Mike Mazurki, Hayden Rorke, Doodles Weaver, Paul E. Burns, George E. Stone, Snub Pollard.

(72) *WHAT EVER HAPPENED TO BABY JANE?*—a Seven Arts Associates and Aldrich Production, released by Warner Bros. Executive Producer, Kenneth Hyman. Associate Producer and Director, Robert Aldrich. Screenplay by Lukas Heller, based on the novel of the same name by Henry Farrell. Photographed by Ernest Haller. Music by Frank DeVol. Edited by Michael Luciano. Davis received her ninth Academy Award nomination for her role of Baby Jane Hudson. She sang "I've Written a Letter to Daddy." B.D. Merrill played a small role as a 'remembrance.' Previewed at Pantages Theatre, Hollywood, Calif. October 16, 1962. Opened in 116 theaters in N.Y. and N.J., November 6, 1962. Earned production cost back in eleven days in this booking alone.

(Cast) Bette Davis, Joan Crawford, Victor Buono, Marjorie Bennett, Maidie Norman, Anna Lee, Barbara Merrill, Julie Allred, Gina Gillespie, Dave Willock, Ann Barton.

(73) *DEAD RINGER*—a Warner Bros. Picture. Produced by William H. Wright. Directed by Paul Henreid. Screenplay by Albert Beich and Oscar Millard, based on the story *La Otra* or *Dead Pigeon* by Rian James, Spanish production with Dolores Del Rio released in 1946. Photographed by Ernest Haller. Music by Andre Previn. Edited by Folmar Blangsted. Davis played twins, Margaret de Lorca and Edith Phillips. She was photographed for the last time by Haller, who died shortly after the picture was finished. Makeup by Gene Hibbs. Henreid's daughter, Monika, played the role of Davis's maid. Opened in 90 theaters in N.Y. area February 19, 1964.

(Cast) Bette Davis, Karl Malden, Peter Lawford, Philip Carey, Jean Hagen, George Macready, Estelle Winwood, George Chandler, Mario Alcade, Cyril Delevanti, Monika Henreid, Bert Remsen, Charles Watts, Ken Lynch.

(74) *THE EMPTY CANVAS*—a Joseph E. Levine-Carlo Ponti Production, released by Embassy Pictures. Produced by Carlo Ponti. Directed by Damiano Damiani. Screenplay by Tonino Guerra, Ugo Liberatore, and Damiano Damiani, based on the novel *La Noia (Boredom)* by Alberto Moravia. Photographed by Roberto Gerardi. Edited by Renzo Lucidi. Produced in Italy. Davis used a Texas drawl and a blond Hans Brinker-type wig to add interest to her New Wave mother role. She was billed as "Miss Bette Davis" for the first time. American premiere engagement, El Rey and selected theaters, Los Angeles, Calif., March 10, 1964. Opened N.Y. May 15.

(Cast) Bette Davis, Horst Buchholz, Catherine Spaak, Daniela Rocca, Lea Padovani, Isa Miranda, Leonida Repaci, George Wilson, Marcella Rovena, Daniela Calvino, Renato Moretti, Edorado Nevola, Jole Mauro, Mario Lanfranchi.

(75) *WHERE LOVE HAS GONE*—a Joseph E. Levine Production, released by Paramount. Produced by Joseph E. Levine. Directed by Edward Dmytryk.

Screenplay by John Michael Hayes, based on the novel of the same name by Harold Robbins. Photographed in Technicolor and Techniscope by Joseph MacDonald. Title song by Sammy Cahn and James Van Heusen, sung by Jack Jones. Edited by Frank Bracht. Paramount sued Davis when she refused to film a new ending showing the mother going mad. She won the case. Opened Capitol Theatre, N.Y., and neighborhood theaters November 2, 1964.

(Cast) Susan Hayward, Bette Davis, Michael Connors, Joey Heatherton, Jane Greer, DeForest Kelley, George Macready, Anne Seymour, Willis Bouchey, Walter Reed, Ann Doran, Bartlett Robinson, Whit Bissell, Anthony Caruso, Jack Greening, Olga Sutcliffe, Howard Wendell, Colin Kenny.

(76) *HUSH . . . HUSH, SWEET CHARLOTTE*—an Associates and Aldrich Production, released by Twentieth Century-Fox. Produced and directed by Robert Aldrich. Screenplay by Henry Farrell and Lukas Heller, based on a story by Henry Farrell, *Whatever Happened to Cousin Charlotte?* Photographed by Joseph Biroc. Musical score by Frank DeVol, title song by Mack David, sung by Al Martino. Edited by Michael Luciano. Joan Crawford became ill during shooting and was replaced by Olivia De Havilland. Davis sang title song accompanied by a harpsichord. Opened Village Theatre, Westwood, Calif., December 15, 1964, to qualify for Academy Awards; opened Capitol Theatre, N.Y., March 3, 1965.

(Cast) Bette Davis, Olivia De Havilland, Joseph Cotten, Agnes Moorehead, Cecil Kellaway, Victor Buono, Mary Astor, William Campbell, Wesley Addy, Bruce Dern, George Kennedy, Dave Willock, John Megna, Ellen Corby, Helen Kleeb, Marianne Stewart, Frank Ferguson, Mary Henderson, Lillian Randolph, Geraldine West, William Walker, Idell James, Teddy Buckner and His All-Stars.

(77) *THE NANNY*—a Seven Arts-Hammer Film Production, released by Twentieth Century-Fox. Produced by Jimmy Sangster. Directed by Seth Holt. Screenplay by Jimmy Sangster, based on the novel of the same name by Evelyn Piper. Photographed by Harry Waxman. Edited by James Needs. Produced in England. Opened at the Normandie Theatre, N.Y., and neighborhood theaters, saturation booking, November 3, 1965.

(Cast) Bette Davis, Wendy Craig, Jill Bennett, James Villiers, William Dix, Pamela Franklin, Jack Watling, Maurice Denham, Alfred Burke, Nora Gordon, Sandra Power, Harry Fowler.

(78) *THE ANNIVERSARY*—a Seven Arts-Hammer Production, released by Twentieth Century-Fox. Produced by Jimmy Sangster. Directed by Roy Ward Baker. Screenplay by Jimmy Sangster, based on the play of the same name by Bill MacIlwraith. Photographed in wide screen and Technicolor by Harry Waxman. Edited by Peter Wetherly. Original director Alvin Rakoff was replaced by Baker. Produced in England. Previewed at Rialto Theatre, London, January 11, 1968. Opened neighborhood theaters, saturation booking, N.Y., March 20, 1968.

(Cast) Bette Davis, Sheila Hancock, Jack Hedley, James Cossins, Christian Roberts, Elaine Taylor, Timothy Bateson, Arnold Diamond.

(79) *CONNECTING ROOMS*—an L.S.D. Production, released by Hemdale. Produced by Harry Field and Arthur Cooper. Directed by Franklin Gollings. Screenplay by Franklin Gollings, based on the play of the same name by Marion Hart. Produced in England in 1969 but released at the same time as was *Madame Sin* in May, 1972. To be released in the United States.

(Cast) Bette Davis, Michael Redgrave, Alexis Kanner, Kay Walsh, Gabrielle Drake, Olga Georges-Picot, Leo Genn, Richard Wyler.

(80) *BUNNY O'HARE*—an American International Pictures release. Executive Producers, James H. Nicholson and Samuel Z. Arkoff. Produced and directed by Gerd Oswald. Coproducer, Norman T. Herman. Screenplay by Stanley Z. Cherry and Coslough Johnson, based on the story *Bunny and Billy* by Stanley Z. Cherry. Photographed in wide screen and color by Loyal Griggs and John Stephens; second-unit camera work by Michael Dugan. Edited by Fred Feitshans, Jr. Film was shot on location near Albuquerque, New Mexico. Previewed at Picwood Theatre, Los Angeles, Calif., June 24, 1971. Opened at neighborhood theaters, N.Y., October 18, 1971.

(Cast) Bette Davis, Ernest Borgnine, Jack Cassidy, Joan Delaney, Jay Robinson, John Astin, Reva Rose.

(81) *MADAME SIN*—a 2 X Production. Produced by Julian Wintle and Lou Morheim. Directed by David Greene. Screenplay by Barry Oringer and David Greene, from an original concept by Lou Morheim and Barry Shear. Photographed by Tony Richmond. Robert Wagner and Sir Lew Grade arranged the financing for the pilot film as a proposed television series, but the film was released as a feature in Europe May 12, 1972. Released as an "ABC Movie of the Week," January 15, 1972.

(Cast) Bette Davis, Robert Wagner, Denholm Elliott, Gordon Jackson, Dudley Sutton, Catherine Schell, Paul Maxwell, Piksen Lim.

(82) *THE JUDGE AND JAKE WYLER*— Universal T.V. Produced by Richard Levinson and William Link. Directed by David Lowell Rich. Teleplay by David Shaw, Richard Levinson, and William Link. Photographed by William Margulies. Edited by Budd Small. Shot as a pilot film for a proposed television series, then extra footage added for sufficient television feature length. Originally written for a male lead. Released as an "NBC Movie of the Week," December 2, 1972.

(Cast) Bette Davis, Doug McClure, Eric Braeden, Joan Van Ark, Gary Conway, Lou Jacobi, James McEachin, Lisabeth Hush, Kent Smith, Barbara Rhoades.

(83) *LO SCOPONE SCIENTIFICO*—*(The Scientific Cardplayer* or *The Game)*—C.I.C. Production. Produced by Dino de Laurentis. Directed by Luigi Comencini. Screenplay by Rodolfo Sonego. Photographed in wide screen and color by Guiseppi Ruzzolini. Film made $1 million in Italy, Opened Roma Theatre, Rome, Italy, October 16, 1972. To be released in the United States.

(Cast) Alberto Sordi, Silvana Mangano, Joseph Cotten, Bette Davis, Domenico Modugno, Mario Carotenuto.

(84) *SCREAM, PRETTY PEGGY*—Universal T.V. Produced by Lou Morheim. Directed by Gordon Hessler. Teleplay by Jimmy Sangster and Arthur Hoffe. Photographed by Lennie South. Edited by Larry Strong. Released as an "NBC Movie of the Week," November 22, 1973.

　(Cast) Bette Davis, Ted Bessell, Sian Barbara Allen, Charles Drake.

INDEX

READ THESE BEST SELLERS
FROM BERKLEY